CONSUMING THE PAST

# Consuming the Past

The Medieval Revival in fin-de-siècle France

Elizabeth Emery and Laura Morowitz

ASHGATE

Published by
Ashgate Publishing Limited
Gower House
Croft Road
Aldershot
Hants GU11 3HR
England

Ashgate Publishing Company
Suite 420
101 Cherry Street
Burlington, VT 5401-4405
USA

Ashgate website: http://www.ashgate.com

British Library Cataloguing-in-Publication Data
Emery, Elizabeth (Elizabeth Nicole)
    Consuming the past : the medieval revival in fin de
    siecle France
    1.Art, French - 19th century 2.Medievalism - France -
    History - 19th century 3.Middle Ages in art 4.Middle
    Ages in literature
    I.Title II.Morowitz, Laura
    709.4'4'09034

Library of Congress Cataloguing-in-Publication Data
Morowitz, Laura.
    Consuming the past : the medieval revival in fin-
    de-siècle France / Laura Morowitz and Elizabeth
    Emery.
        p. cm.
    Includes bibliographical references and index.
    ISBN 0-7546-0319-9
    1. France--Civilization--1830-1900. 2. France--
    Civilization--1901-1945. 3. France--Civilization--
    Medieval influences. 4. Medievalism--France--
    History--19th century. 5. Medievalism--France--
    History--20th century. I. Emery, Elizabeth (Elizabeth
    Nicole) II. Title.

DC33.6 .M67 2003
944.081'2--dc21
                                        2002027801

ISBN 0 7546 0319 9

Typeset in Palatino by Manton Typesetters, Louth,
Lincolnshire, UK and printed and bound in Great
Britain by Biddles Ltd, Guildford and King's Lynn.

# Contents

# Figures

# Acknowledgments

Writing *Consuming the Past* has been a true pleasure, not only because of the delight with which we unearthed, collected and studied original documents about fin-de-siècle medievalism, but above all because of the opportunity it afforded me to work with Laura Morowitz, whom I had long admired as a scholar. Listening to her keen insights, discussing our finds, learning from her extensive knowledge of French art and history and developing from colleagues to friends have been among the highlights of this project.

Funding for much of the research I conducted was provided by grants from the National Endowment for the Humanities, Montclair State University and the State of New Jersey (Separately Budgeted Research, Career Development and Global Education awards), by the Northeast Modern Language Association and by New York University's Institute for Advanced European Studies. Such generous support allowed me to work in France at La Bibliothèque Nationale (Bibliothèques de l'Arsenal, de Richelieu, de Tolbiac, de l'Opéra), the Maison Emile Zola, Le Musée de la Publicité, Le Musée des Arts Décoratifs, La Bibliothèque historique de la Mairie de Paris, Le Musée Carnavalet, Le Musée Rodin and Le Musée de Montmartre. I extend warm thanks to the helpful librarians and archivists of these French institutions, as well as to their American counterparts: The New York Public Library, The Library of Congress, Columbia University, Pennsylvania State University, the Spencer Museum at the University of Kansas and the Schimmel Rare Book Library at Rutgers University. Their generous public access policies, extraordinarily resourceful librarians and rich collections of fin-de-siècle documents contributed immeasurably to this project.

A number of colleagues and friends have been extremely generous with their time and I thank them warmly for their collegiality and informal discussions or conference panels about the Middle Ages and its post-medieval reception, issues of nineteenth and twentieth-century politics, religion and art, and for their support, encouragement, and technical advice. Among them are Nancy Regalado, Timmie Vitz, Bill Calin, Gwendolyn Morgan, Kathleen Verduin, Richard Utz, Richard Shryock and Sharon Johnson, Françoise Lucbert, Laurie Postlewate, Mary Shepard, Tina Bizzarro, C. J. Talar, Michael Glencross, Ségolène Le Men, Stephanie Moore, Charles Affron, Claudie Bernard, Carolyn

Snipes-Hoyt, Helen Solterer, Holly Haahr, Pamela Genova, Robert Morrissey, Lois Oppenheim, Stacey Katz, Michel Zink, Mark Cruse, Kate Loysen, B. Christopher Wood, Katherine Emery and Dan Kane. Above all, I extend my gratitude to David Emero, who gracefully sacrificed innumerable weekends, enthusiastically traipsed through cathedrals, museums, libraries and along pilgrimage routes and who has taken up French to read more about them.

Elizabeth Emery


What a singular pleasure it is to befriend someone whose company you cherish and whose scholarship you deeply admire. Such have been the joys of sharing this project with Elizabeth Emery, whose contagious enthusiasm, unflagging dedication and inspiring insights have made co-authoring this book an invaluable and delightful adventure. I hope it is the first of many collaborations.

My contribution to this study has its roots in my Ph.D. thesis, and therefore owes considerable debt to all those who helped it take shape, especially my advisor Robert Lubar. Special thanks go as well to Drs Linda Nochlin and Jonathan J.G. Alexander. My research was made immeasurably easier by the kind assistance of Madame Chantal Bissou at the Musée Départemental Maurice Denis 'Le Prieuré,' and the staff of the Bibliothèque Nationale, Paris. A special note of gratitude goes to the staff of the Herbert D. and Ruth Schimmel Rare Book Library of the Jane Vorhees Zimmerli Art Museum for allowing us access to their wonderful storehouse of primary texts and journals on fin-de-siècle France. Special thanks go to our editors, Pamela Edwardes, Lucinda Lax and Katharine Bushell for their enthusiasm and assistance in this project.

Along the way countless friends and colleagues shared their insights and offered new readings. These include Maura Reilly, Debra Wacks, Ariella Budick and Lisa Rafanelli. I am blessed with three dear friends who have made their life work studying the fin de siècle: to Francoise Lucbert, Barbara Larson and Lori Weintrob, these pages are indelibly marked by your insights and your ideas on the period. Françoise Lucbert and Wolfgang Sabler opened their hearts and shared their thoughts on fin-de-siècle and present-day France, for which I shall always be grateful. I thank Laurie Lico Albanese, who works with words, for understanding without my saying a word.

As with any project of long duration, the daily support of colleagues and the love of family are essential in seeing through to the end. I am grateful to Wagner College for financial assistance and recognition, and for providing me with the best group of colleagues I could ever hope for. Finally, to the people who give everything I do its *raison d'etre*: my Eric, my Isabelle and my Olivia. Thank you for all those nights and evenings you let me go off to the nineteenth century and the Middle Ages and thank you for always making the twenty-first century an irresistible place to return to.

Laura Morowitz

# Introduction

Painters and poets of [the Romantic period], whatever their gifts, saw in the Middle Ages a shop of unworn accessories, they took from it picturesque artistic and dramatic elements, handsome wall hangings and gestures, without restraint, without criticism, and their Middle Ages were not true. We are tired of the picturesque lie. Romanticism died from it. The men of the second half of the last century were overcome by an immense need for truth […] a host of distinguished men […] created the science of our national archeology, revealed it to artists and scholars, introduced it in classical teaching methods, interested high society, familiarized even the masses with our artistic past […][1]

Charles Morice, 'Introduction' to Les Cathédrales de France

In 1914, Charles Morice assessed French attitudes toward the Middle Ages, noting the important shift that had taken place in the last three quarters of the nineteenth century as scholars and archeologists began to share their knowledge of the period with the wider public: with artists, scientists, students, the cultural elite and even the working classes. Indeed, at this time everything associated with the medieval world – from works of art to religious belief – caught the attention of both the intelligentsia and society at large. At the end of the nineteenth century, people from all over the political and social spectrum praised the Middle Ages and avidly consumed 'medieval' products.

They created holidays to honor medieval legends Joan of Arc and Roland, they collected medieval art, they went on pilgrimages, they eagerly read novels set in the Middle Ages, they frequented popular Montmartre cabarets featuring Gothic decorations and they re-enacted medieval celebrations such as the 'Feast of Fools.' If, as recent scholars have asserted, the nineteenth century 'made' and 'invented' the Middle Ages, it was done with particular relish at the turn of the century.[2] It would seem that no arena – whether cultural, political or popular – remained untouched by interest in the Middle Ages. A cursory list of figures who engaged directly with medieval themes or subjects reads like a Who's Who of the fin de siècle: Emile Zola, J.-K. Huysmans, Charles Morice, Paul Claudel, Edouard Drumont, Puvis de Chavannes, Maurice Denis, Claude Monet, Paul Gauguin, Jules Grévy, Maurice Barrès, the Baron de Rothschild, the Duc d'Aumale, Yvette Guilbert and Vincent d'Indy, as well as countless functionaries, administrators and curators who embraced the medieval heritage and put it on display at fairs, exhibits, religious ceremonies and national festivals. Decades dedicated to progress, rationalism and science had not stifled enthusiasm for the medieval past.

Despite the overwhelming popularity of the Middle Ages at the end of the nineteenth century, there is no comprehensive study devoted to the widespread impact of medieval art, religion and history in France at this time. Earlier periods of medievalism in France and England have been extremely well documented; histories of the Romantics, of Victorian architecture or of the Pre-Raphaelites are incomplete without discussion of Sir Walter Scott, Victor Hugo, Gothic revival churches, or the Arts and Crafts movement.[3] It is thus all the more surprising that the medievalism of late nineteenth-century France remains largely unexamined and to a large extent, unknown.[4] Indeed, it is generally accepted that widespread popular interest in the Middle Ages in France did not begin until well into the twentieth century.

In the last few years, an increasing number of articles, journals, book series and essays have begun addressing the importance of the Middle Ages for specific groups of writers and artists in numerous countries and in different periods, from the Renaissance to the twenty-first century. In general, they explore medievalism in its widest sense (Leslie Workman has defined it as 'the continuing process of creating the Middle Ages'). While fascinating and helpful for the definition of medievalism itself, our project focuses more specifically on the multiple medievalisms of a single period (1871–1905) and the ways in which competing claims placed on the past affected subsequent reception of the Middle Ages.[5] Influenced by the theories of collective memory proposed by historians including Maurice Halbwachs, Maurice Agulhon, Pierre Nora and Robert Gildea, we argue that there is no single vision of the past shared by all members of society. Rather, the various stories about the Middle Ages proposed by different groups tend to emerge from their specific needs. As a result, multiple narratives about the Middle Ages often compete and overlap.[6] As we will argue, there were many different kinds of interest in the Middle Ages throughout the nineteenth century, often related to specific experiences, social changes or political objectives. In order to understand the fascination with the Middle Ages at the end of the nineteenth century in France, it is imperative to go beyond the general concept of 'medievalism' in order to examine the particular manifestations of medievalism in this period.[7]

*Consuming the Past* thus seeks to document and to explore the rich and complex discourses about the Middle Ages in France from the end of the Franco-Prussian War to the Separation of Church and State (1871–1905). The book proposes that the fin-de-siècle public's fascination with the Middle Ages was not simply a fad, confined to one segment of the population; it was, in fact, a wide-spread phenomenon that engaged people from all social and economic classes.[8] In their acceptance of old stereotypes about the Middle Ages and their interest in new discoveries made by historians and philologists, those living at the turn of the century conceived the Middle Ages much more richly than their ancestors had done. What separated the medievalism of the fin de siècle from earlier nineteenth-century manifestations was its multivalency. As Morice suggested in 1914, the early decades of the nineteenth century tended to adopt the Middle Ages to provide theatrical 'local color'; indeed, the courtly Middle Ages of the French Restoration, the democratic *Moyen Âge* of Victor Hugo and the seigneurial Middle Ages of Napoléon III follow this paradigm.[9] Those at the end of the century continued to refer to these themes, yet they also refitted and appropriated the Middle Ages along a broad political and artistic spectrum influenced by new developments in technology, transportation, education, mass media and government.

Above all, as Morice suggests, the last quarter of the nineteenth century differed from earlier periods in its focus on the Middle Ages in their own right. A new aesthetic promoted links among arts and science, thus encouraging amateurs to join archeologists in attempting to discover the 'truth' about the Middle Ages as told in medieval documents, monuments and works of art. In the 1880s and 1890s, studies of medieval literature were first introduced in the high school and college curriculum; the Louvre opened a wing of medieval sculpture, and medieval scholars Gaston Paris, Louis Petit de Julleville and Léon Gautier published a number of works (including *La Poésie du moyen âge*, 1885–1895, a history of medieval French theater, 1880–1886, and *La Chevalerie*, 1884, respectively) that are still considered important for the study of the Middle Ages. In addition, new developments in technology made inexpensive reproductions of medieval art widely available for private consideration. By the turn of the century, the Middle Ages had developed from a popular French theme in literature and art (Morice's 'accessory shop') into a serious and popular subject of both 'archeological' and amateur study.

At the end of the nineteenth century, the Middle Ages went on display for the public in ways they never had before: in books, magazines, museums, antique stores, bourgeois salons and spectacles linked to public holidays. Increasingly, the French could examine genuine medieval artifacts in spaces as varied as government buildings, churches, galleries, World's Fair exhibits and magazines. Such public display allowed medieval tapestries, stained glass, armor, paintings, furniture, illuminated manuscripts or liturgical objects to become a ubiquitous part of the modern landscape, leading to even greater popular curiosity about the period. Indeed, the French attempted to 'regain the past' by 'consuming' medieval cultural artifacts, appropriating them and showcasing them in varied and novel ways.

An explosion of accumulated goods and a vast increase in private consumption in the last decades of the nineteenth century caused the medieval world to be perceived as both a lost golden age and as a period newly available to the consumer for 'recreation' through the acquisition of material objects and its active counterpart: spectacle.[10] It is impossible to understand the institutionalization of medievalism during this period – in art history, in the creation of a national heritage, in the opening of specially designated museums and religious sites, in the renewal of pilgrimages – without considering the parallel fascination with collection and display. From the marketing of *Primitif* painters to the development of medieval pilgrimage sites as tourist destinations, the past was quite literally up for sale.

Often, as we will see, the practices of collecting and consuming the Middle Ages occurred in response to contemporary fears about increased individualism and a seemingly fragmented social structure. France was fraught with strife in the last decades of the nineteenth century. The country lost the Franco-Prussian war (1870–1871) only to see more citizens killed in the civil unrest of the Paris Commune (1871). The 1880s were marked by debates about the role Catholicism should play in political spheres; these discussions culminated in the 1905 decision to separate Church and State. Government scandals, the Panama Canal Company bankruptcy (1891–1892), anarchist bomb attacks (1892–1894) and the Dreyfus Affair (begun in 1894) persuaded the French that their society was degenerating. Perhaps most obviously, the fin-de-siècle fascination with the Middle Ages arrived at the threshold of a new century, a moment when relations of class, gender and identity were being debated and reformulated.

Not surprisingly, the medieval world was conceived as the opposite of this fragmented modern era.[11] Seen as a period of unity, even its name, *Le Moyen Age*, is singular in French. This idealized image of a medieval world bound by social cohesiveness surely comforted a period rent by bursts of anarchist violence, worker demonstrations and battles between Church and State. The literature, science, art and religion of the Middle Ages, on the other hand, seemed to weave a durable social fabric based on uncompromising and uncorrupted faith. If these notions of the medieval past (like all historical constructions) were built on a series of falsely ideal concepts, the public's investment in such systems was no less real.[12] Like the delicate stained-glass windows so beloved in the period, the fragmented pieces of the Middle Ages were continually reassembled, fitted into a whole, reconstituted to form an image both enduring and meaningful for individuals. A cathedral, for example, could be considered a house of worship for Catholics, while artists might appreciate it as a temple of art. Tourists, however, would appreciate its music and ceremony, while politicians might appropriate it as the perfect example of democratic building practices. Often, multiple fears and hopes came together in medievalism: anti-Semites, for example, hailed the Middle Ages as a response to their longing for unity, to their anti-capitalist sentiment and to their religious dissatisfaction. Catholics celebrated its religious traditions, while Republicans heralded the development of Gothic art as the first French 'freedom of the press.'[13] Despite the multiple claims made about the Middle Ages at the end of the century, the period began to be consecrated in the public eye, hailed as the origin of the modern French nation and of France's artistic hegemony.

The near-universal enthusiasm for the Middle Ages at the end of the century provides one of the central problems for *Consuming the Past*. Why, after disputing the origin of the French nation and the role of the Middle Ages for nearly a century,[14] was there such passion for them in the years 1871 to 1905? We use a variety of methodologies to explore this question. As a literary historian and an art historian, we approach our material from a variety of angles, always aiming for an interdisciplinary approach to better capture the depth and texture of the period.[15] Throughout the book, we look at the fin-de-siècle interest in the Middle Ages through a number of different theoretical prisms, while never allowing theories to overshadow the voices and opinions of the time that we have tried to document. We attempt to expose attitudes toward fin-de-siècle medievalism while interpreting them against a wider cultural field in order to explore the irresistible attraction the Middle Ages held for the French at the turn of the nineteenth century.

Primary and archival sources examined include the work and correspondence of artists, historians, politicians, scholars, museum curators and religious leaders, popular guide books and travel narratives, political pamphlets, Republican school primers, posters and articles from the illustrated press. In addition to reading political, literary and artistic works in the context of specific political and social events, in the tradition of historians like Eugèn Weber, Charles Rearick, Maurice Agulhon or Pierre Nora, our examination of the renewed passion for religious experience – conversions to Catholicism, visiting cathedrals or following medieval pilgrimage routes – considers concepts such as David Freedberg's 'power of images,' while looking to Michel de Certeau for reflections about the problems of faith in an increasingly secular world. Our discussion of the production and reception of public spectacles often borrows terms from Walter Benjamin, Theodor Adorno, Pierre Bourdieu and Guy Debord, yet we also consider more anthropological analyses such as those of Victor Turner and Mikhail Bakhtin.

In our discussion of the 'consumption' of the medieval past by an affluent bourgeoisie, we draw on the classical sociological theories of Karl Marx, Thorstein Veblen and Max Weber, but temper them with more recent approaches such as that of Lisa Tiersten, which focus less on economics and class struggle than on the historical and cultural factors inherently tied to the rise of consumer culture. The works of T. J. Clark, Rosalind Williams, Thomas Crow, Griselda Pollack and Molly Nesbitt offer rich models for relating the art and aesthetic of the period to the wider arena of economics and class conflict. We are also indebted to the many scholars, including Michael Miller, Whitney Walton and Rémy Saisselin, who have illuminated the developing 'consumer mentality' of this period.

Indeed, although our book is entitled *Consuming the Past*, we do not examine the Middle Ages only as a product. We are certainly interested in the ways in which medieval objects or legends were consumed: displayed and sold, purchased by fin-de-siècle buyers as a result of marketing (the use of medieval references to sell popular goods, for example) or of institutional display (buying a ticket and visiting museum collections). But we are also fascinated by another meaning of the word *consuming*, the destruction or modification of a substance. As medieval works or figures were removed from their original contexts to become a part of private or public collections, their original meaning often vanished. This seeming destruction, however, often led to new and more fertile modern creations or even to renewed conservation of the medieval heritage. As one interpretation of the Middle Ages seemed to be destroyed, new ones were in constant formulation. The very act of appropriating vestiges of the medieval past allowed the French to participate in, indeed to construct or reconstruct the Middle Ages. And in this sense the Middle Ages themselves consumed their buyers: people of the fin de siècle were fascinated by medieval artifacts and engaged themselves with visiting them, studying them, collecting them and preserving them.

The link that held together most of these disparate representations of the Middle Ages – from high culture to low – was, as Morice suggested in 1914, the desire to engage with the medieval past in a serious fashion, to find the 'truth' about the period. In particular, we are interested in those points of intersection where the popular and the scholarly come together. This is true, for example, of the marketing of the *Primitif* painters, of the relation between private interiors and museum displays and of the revival of medieval-style pilgrimages, which preached anti-materialism while seducing the modern pilgrim with 'educational' souvenirs. Rather than oppose the two, we wish to show that popular appreciation of medieval objects and legends developed side by side with direct study and thoughts about medieval cultural productions. Though often contradictory, competing scholarly and popular versions of the Middle Ages actually worked together to increase awareness of the importance of the medieval French past in a period beset by disorienting historical and social events. The variety of different discourses about the Middle Ages laid the foundation for what would subsequently become a rich and often ambiguous narrative about France's relationship to the medieval past, a kind of consecration of the French Middle Ages that persists today.

Although *Consuming the Past* fills in the blanks about the little-known fin-de-siècle French Gothic revival, it would be impossible to provide an exhaustive overview of French medievalism after 1871. Indeed, it would take many books to do justice to the mind-boggling number of references to the Middle Ages at this time; allusions to the period permeated the fabric of daily life. We have thus made difficult choices in limiting the scope of our study, which traces several different cultural realms touched by the phenomenon: public and private venues, political and religious arenas, art-historical and literary publications, high culture exhibits and low culture celebrations. We focus primarily on the period between 1871 and 1905, for example, because the Franco-Prussian war sparked widespread popular interest in the Middle Ages, while the 1905 separation of Church and State changed attitudes toward medieval art. The new laws triggered waves of anti-clerical vandalism, notably against ecclesiastical structures from the Middle Ages. Such destruction mobilized artists, writers and politicians, who came to the defense of the medieval heritage and worked to pass laws to protect it. This highly publicized campaign to preserve the patrimony led to a new wave of public interest in medieval art as a national treasure in the years preceding World War I and the devastation that followed it.[16]

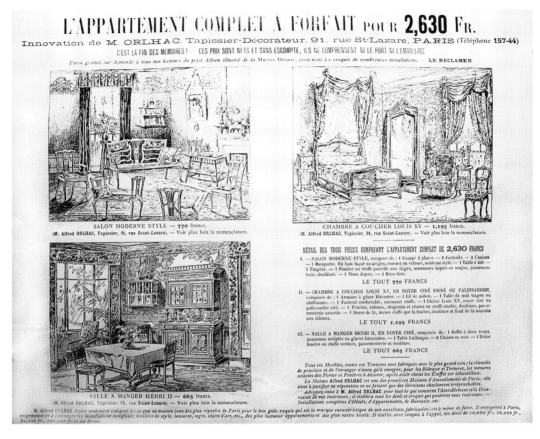

We hope that our introduction to the Gothic revival in fin-de-siècle France will encourage further scholarly exploration of this fascinating movement. Related topics that we will not have the space to discuss thoroughly here include links between medievalism and the development of Art Nouveau art and architecture,[17] the profound impact of Viollet-le-Duc's Gothic-inspired theories on modern architecture,[18] attraction to the Middle Ages as linked to colonialism,[19] fin-de-siècle interest in Oriental and Byzantine influences on medieval French art,[20] the growth of individual and institutional art collections at the time,[21] the links between the illuminated manuscript, its reproduction using modern technology and its impact on fin-de-siècle graphic design,[22] the influence of widely-used medieval poetic forms – notably ballads and rondeaux – on Symbolist poetry or the proliferation of medieval themes in the official Salons. While there are also many interesting points of overlap with British medievalism of the nineteenth century, we have chosen to focus on the French context, which was late in recognizing British achievements.[23]

We also recognize that, during the fin de siècle, the French appreciated, reconstructed and reanimated other eras, notably eighteenth-century France.[24] A 1900 advertisement for the interior decorating firm of M. Alfred Orlhac shows the simultaneity of such trends (Fig. 0.1). Modern, medieval and eighteenth-century periods were available for those willing to pay several thousand francs. 'The end of memoirs,' claims the advertisement; wealthy readers of *Le Figaro illustré*, where the full-page layout was published, could dispense with literary accounts of the period by living in historically-accurate rooms. While these various homages to the past might clash, they could – and often did – harmoniously co-exist.[25] Thus, the medievalism of the fin de siècle is part of a much broader phenomenon of revivalism; it is one manifestation of a desire to escape the present by studying the past (and especially the *French* past).

In *Consuming the Past*, we have chosen to focus specifically on medievalism because it was a rich phenomenon that appealed to a broad spectrum of society. The eighteenth century, as Debora Silverman has shown, came to be associated with nostalgia for the Ancien Régime and as such it appealed primarily to a cultural and scholarly elite interested in rococo style and the Japanese arts.[26] While the eighteenth century came to reflect the Ancien Régime, the Middle Ages evoked a very different set of meanings. As we will see in Chapter 1, some understood the period as a monarchy, while others anachronistically represented it as the first flowering of French democracy. The Middle Ages paradoxically appealed to a wide variety of social groups – Catholics, monarchists, Republicans, cultural elite and working class – in a way that the eighteenth century did not.

While focusing on French medievalism in this period, we have limited ourselves to the Parisian area (except in Chapter 6, where we discuss pilgrimages, which drew the Parisian public to the provinces). Medievalism was widespread throughout France and representations of medieval plays, exhibits dedicated to medieval art and medieval fairs took place throughout the country.[27] Focusing on Paris, the nation's capital, provides us with a homogenous geographical space in which to study the period's fascination with the Middle Ages: many of the leading writers, artists, musicians, politicians and clergymen were based in Paris and the large majority of newspapers and journals reported Parisian events. In addition, many of the important social spectacles – artistic Salons, operas, World's Fairs, cabaret performances and street fairs – took place in the city.

Because *Consuming the Past* seeks to reveal medievalism's hold over late nineteenth-century France, each chapter focuses on a manifestation of interest in the Middle Ages that, while seemingly associated with one social group, also drew in others. We have chosen only one or two examples of medievalism per chapter in order to examine each of them from a variety of perspectives. In contrast to Janine Dakyns's study, *The Middle Ages in French Literature, 1851–1914*, which classifies various types of medievalism in each chapter ('The Romantic Middle Ages', 'The Symbolist Middle Ages'), we examine the complex legacy of medieval characters, historical issues and cultural creations. By focusing on elements from the Middle Ages, including medieval *Primitifs*, Joan of Arc and Roland, the Germanic invasions of the fifth century, the Hundred Years' war, cathedrals, stained glass, tapestry, pilgrimages, church theology and medieval forms of entertainment, we are able to trace the overlapping ideas about the Middle Ages and to explore the ways in which their intersections led to the period's validation in the late nineteenth century.

Chapter 1, 'The Middle Ages belong to France: nationalist paradigms of the medieval,' takes the 1904 Exposition des Primitifs français as a starting point to examine how – by the beginning of the twentieth century – the long-maligned Gothic heritage of France had come to be championed as a reflection of 'French hegemony in art.' From Royalists to Republicans, politicians staked claims to the symbolic interpretation of the Middle Ages and their historical figures, notably Joan of Arc and Roland. This section provides an overview of French attitudes toward the Middle Ages, their history and their art from the Revolutionary period through World War I.

Influenced by exhibitions that put medieval artists on display, nineteenth-century French artists often found themselves emulating their ancestors. Chapter 2, 'Packaging the *Primitifs*: the medieval artist, the *Neo-Primitif* and the art market,' explores the construction of the image of the artist in art history and literature. Many artists regarded their Gothic counterparts as devout *naïfs*, *Primitifs* or monk-artists, while others saw beliefs about the medieval artist as central to the formation of artistic identity. Their nostalgia for a pure past relates to conflicts within the art market and to the growing perception of art as a commodity. Beliefs about the medieval artist are central to the formation of artistic identity among members of the Symbolist avant-garde.[28]

Exhibitions of art continue to play a prominent role in Chapter 3, 'From the living room to the museum and back again: the institutionalization of medieval art.' New museums devoted to medieval art flourished at this time and private collectors, curators and bourgeois consumers all collaborated in the sponsorship, organization and publicizing of exhibitions. The opening of a medieval wing at the Louvre, the purchase of important tapestries such as the *Dame à la Licorne*, as well as the display of Gothic works at the 1889 and 1900 World's Fairs, are contrasted in their systems of display and their manner of exhibit. We then compare these public spaces with the medievalized interiors of several well-known cultural figures and collections. We reveal the links between private collectors, scholars, curators, artists and entrepreneurs in forging a new fascination with medieval objects.

As museum displays, reproductions and new artistic creations increasingly featured moveable works of art, or bibelots, detached from their original context, artists protested. J.-K. Huysmans, Charles Morice and Marcel Proust, among others, argued that medieval art lost its meaning when separated from the Catholic belief that had inspired it. Even non-believers came to champion the Gothic cathedral as an *ur*-museum, a truly 'authentic' place to contemplate and understand medieval art. Chapter 4, 'The Gothic cathedral in fin-de-siècle France: from *Gesamtkunstwerk* to "French genius",' discusses the increasingly popular tendency to treat Gothic churches as museums, ultimate works of art in which the combination of music, incense, liturgy and architecture inspired the visitor to worship both religion and art itself. Such widespread interest in churches also led to increased appreciation of the cathedral's component arts, including stained glass, sculpture and tapestry.

With the development of new technology, museums and churches advertised their acquisitions in illustrated periodicals, while taverns, administrative buildings and bourgeois home owners decorated interior spaces with mass-produced reproductions of medieval artwork. Chapter 5, 'From cathedral to cabaret: the popularity of medieval stained glass and tapestries,' draws attention to the ways in which institutional display and marketing techniques increased public demand for imitations of medieval art, consequently provoking the ire of scholars and specialists. Art historians felt that the very qualities that rendered medieval art valuable – its purity, its communal production and its uniqueness – were compromised by widespread reproduction and distribution, and fought to preserve what they considered the 'authentic' qualities of medieval art.

While French consumers could buy reproductions of medieval art, they also traveled all over France to visit 'authentic' sites dedicated to such works. Growing interest in the French national heritage, the proliferation of tourist guides and books and the influence of Catholic publications such as *La Croix* and *Le Pèlerin* – mouthpieces for a flourishing pilgrimage movement – produced a veritable explosion of travel to both medieval and modern religious sites. Chapter 6, 'Marketing the sacred: medieval pilgrimages and the Catholic revival,' examines the paradox of expanded tourism to medieval holy sites at a time when an increasingly secular government was dissolving religious congregations and tearing down churches. Religious and secular groups alike praised pilgrimage sites, hoping to encounter the medieval world en route to them.

Though many groups protected existing medieval monuments, others worked to recreate those that had been destroyed or forgotten. The final chapter, 'Feasts, fools and festivals: the popular Middle Ages,' focuses primarily on the hugely popular *Paris en 1400* and *Vieux Paris* exhibits at the 1900 World's Fair in Paris, life-size recreations of entire medieval neighborhoods. From soirées in honor of François Villon and Feast of Fools celebrations held in the Latin Quarter to the translation and staging of medieval plays and the publication of modern ballads and rondeaux, the French were fascinated by the spirit of the Middle Ages that scholars had discovered in medieval texts. We explore how this popular vision of the medieval period intersects with larger issues of the commercialization of leisure and the creation of the French past as spectacle, an issue vital to understanding Parisian culture at the dawn of the twentieth century.

Numerous themes appear throughout the chapters, tying the most avant-garde productions to more traditional events and to popular celebration. We hope that by showing the prevalence of medieval themes at all levels of society – from popular cabarets and fairs to museums and universities – the book will shed new light on the ways in which fin-de-siècle France envisioned, appropriated and consecrated the Middle Ages. The period embraced historical figures, religious sites and artwork as *lieux de mémoire*, the term Pierre Nora has coined to refer to treasured aspects of the French patrimony that provide the country with a stable cultural identity.[29]

It is our firm belief that the insights gleaned from the book will illuminate a period very different from our own, but in whose image we recognize many of our own preoccupations and indeed, as Dean MacCannell has suggested, our enduring obsessions:

Modern society, only partly disengaged from industrial structures, is especially vulnerable to overthrow from within through nostalgia, sentimentality and other tendencies to regress to a previous state, a Golden Age which retrospectively always appears to have been more orderly and normal.[30]

Inhabitants of turn-of-the-century Paris, spellbound by dazzling electric lights, their visages reflected in the countless new shop windows, their eyes filled with the gleam of new merchandise, could nevertheless find beautiful a very simple image: a single flickering candle burning steadfast on a Gothic altar, its warmth and incandescence undiminished, even heightened, by the endless glitter of the modern city. It is this paradox that forms the heart of our study and leads us forward in our look at the past.

# 1

# The Middle Ages belong to France: nationalist paradigms of the medieval

The hegemony of France, in the twelfth and thirteenth centuries, in art as in literature, is no longer contested today. Scholars from Germany, England, Scandinavia, Italy are enthusiastic in recognizing our glory.
    – Georges Lafenestre, organizer of the 1904 *Exposition des Primitifs français*[31]

The 1904 Exposition des Primitifs français opened to an enthusiastic French public whose taste for the Middle Ages had been stimulated during the previous decades. The finest examples of French medieval art, including paintings, drawings, manuscripts and tapestries, filled the Pavillon de Marsan at the Louvre and the Bibliothèque Nationale.[32] The exhibit included many of the most lauded masterpieces of the period, such as the *Très Riches Heures du Duc de Berry* and the *Apocalypse Tapestries* from the Cathedral of Angers,[33] as well as hundreds of panels and manuscripts by anonymous masters from Paris, Dijon, Limoges, and other French towns (Fig. 1.1). The organizers of the show, who included the leading lights of French cultural institutions, made no attempt to hide the underlying nationalist agenda of the exhibition: in the catalog, foreign countries are dismissed nation by nation – from Belgium to Germany and Italy – as mere copyists. According to them, the lauded French masters of the Middle Ages had 'nothing to learn from anyone'; the world had finally recognized the excellence of humble French medieval artists.[34]

   The chief organizer of the exhibit, Henri Bouchot, refused to apologize for such blatant flag-waving, though he attempted to defend himself against the charges of nationalism that followed the exhibit's opening:

The exhibition of the French *Primitifs* does not aim to show the superiority of the French over neighboring peoples, but simply to demonstrate their parallel existence among others and, in certain cases, their priority [...] Certain people have spoken with disdain of false patriotism, of the unforeseen nationalism lurking beneath the title of French *Primitifs*. There is nothing to deny, French *Primitifs* are neither Belgian *Primitifs* nor Italian *Primitifs* [...][35]

Moreover, claimed Bouchot, it was perfectly natural and understandable to take pride in the achievements of one's country and to do so while avoiding explicit bias. He constantly contradicted such seemingly modest sentiments, however, with his sustained dismissal of the art of other nations in comparison with French genius.[36]

1.1 *La Résurrection des Martyrs (The Resurrection of the Martyrs)* from the *Apocalypse d'Angers*, 1378

The impressive exhibition was seen as the culmination of efforts in the fin de siècle to champion French medieval heritage and to use it to reflect the healthy state of the nation. As such, it was only one chapter of a far longer story that stressed the continuity between the glorified Middle Ages and the present. Exhibition organizers such as Lafenestre emphasized this tradition: 'From the time that our ancestors the Gauls, so fond of lively colors and sonorous words, were initiated into the seductions of Greco-Roman culture by their conquerors, the practice of the visual or literary arts has scarcely been interrupted in our country.'[37] This noble taste, he maintained, had continued to inspire contemporary French artists and their audiences, who now claimed to dominate the rest of Europe.

The exhibit was indeed a rousing success; audiences flocked to see the works, the art press devoted considerable space to covering the event and art scholars and connoisseurs were convinced that they had established beyond doubt the supremacy and originality of the French *Primitifs*.[38] Popular reaction to this exhibit, like the national reverence given to medieval legends Joan of Arc and Roland, reveals the extent to which, by the early twentieth century, the French celebrated the art and history of the Middle Ages as a reflection of their nation and its excellence. But such near-universal praise of the French Middle Ages and their art was a recent phenomenon. As Janine Dakyns has convincingly argued, the representation of the Middle Ages in the nineteenth century had fluctuated with changing political regimes. As Republicans and Catholics successively held influential government positions, political factions alternatively championed or cursed the Middle Ages.[39] In fact, only thirty years before the *Primitifs* exhibit, the Middle Ages had not enjoyed any kind of uniform national consensus. Medieval historian Fustel de Coulanges decried his contemporaries' partisan understanding of the period in an 1872 *Revue des Deux Mondes* article about justice in the feudal world. In this article, Fustel argues that it is imperative for the French to reconsider their medieval heritage in order to resolve their differences about French identity:

> Each person makes his own, imaginary Middle Ages [...] and each person forms his faith and his political credo according to the error he has chosen or the error to which his education has bound him. There are as many ways of considering the Middle Ages as there are political parties in France: it is our historical theories that divide us the most.[40]

In order to understand the overwhelming patriotic embrace of medieval art that occurred during the 1904 Exposition des Primitifs Français, it is important to examine changing attitudes toward the Middle Ages throughout the nineteenth century in France.

## The Middle Ages of nineteenth-century France

Although it has often been stated that the Middle Ages were 'made,' 'rediscovered' or 'invented' by the nineteenth century, they had never truly been forgotten.[41] The period continued to be discussed in religious, historical and literary texts from the sixteenth to the nineteenth century, often to justify the rights of the monarchy or to bolster theological stances.[42] The Middle Ages came back into vogue, however, in late eighteenth-century France, as writers such as La Curne Sainte-Palaye and the Count of Tressan created interest in what would become known as the 'troubadour genre.'[43] As Lionel Gossman has argued in his seminal work on Enlightenment medievalism, the translation and dissemination of Sainte-Palaye's works widely influenced the medievalism of the European Romantics. Such interest found its equivalent in the 'troubadour style' of early nineteenth-century paintings.[44] As Dakyns and Jean-Yves Guiomar have shown, this 'pre-Romantic' attraction to the Middle Ages was largely inspired by politics: interest in a golden age of chivalry paralleled the return of the monarchy during the Restoration.[45]

The 'Gothic furor' or 'frenzy'[46] that spread from England to France in the early years of the nineteenth century differs from the Enlightenment treatment of the Middle Ages in the enthusiastic emotions of its supporters and the fashionable taste for things Gothic. This fascination with the entertainment value of historical figures, ruins, 'pure' faith, dreams and mystery has been described by authors such as Louis Maigron, Dorothy Doolittle, Patricia Ward and Janine Dakyns.[47] During the French 'Gothic Revival,' literary texts such as Alfred de Musset's *Rolla* and François René de Chateaubriand's *Le Génie du Christianisme* evoked nostalgia for a time of pure faith, while Victor Hugo's *Odes et ballades* and *Notre-Dame de Paris* conjured up visions of knights errant, wandering minstrels, evil priests and gallows. These themes were reflected in the art of the period: the colorful, chivalric paintings of Pierre-Henri Révoil and Fleury-François Richard, the vogue for dressing in 'robes à la châtelaine' and 'manches à gigot' and the penchant for decorating houses with Gothic furniture.[48] Théophile Gautier mocked the excesses of this period's fondness for all things medieval in his 1833 story, 'Elias Wildmanstadius,' in which the protagonist's predilection for the Middle Ages, its decoration and its customs lead him to build and occupy his own, imaginary medieval world. As Maigron argues, the medievalism of this period was largely a fad, a popular – and relatively superficial – craze that would soon be replaced by others. Dakyns, too, ascribes the end of this period to a saturation of the market: as medievalizing activities became increasingly outlandish they became the object of ridicule. She suggests that these excesses, combined with a change of political climate that accompanied the July Monarchy, marked the end of the popular French Gothic Revival of the early nineteenth century.[49]

The Romantic interest in things medieval left two important, though conflicting, imaginary representations of the Middle Ages that corresponded to the competing political ideologies of the time. Both concepts – a Catholic Middle Ages of piety and simplicity and a Republican Middle Ages of oppression, heroic battles and popular revolt – would live on in the national memory to re-emerge at the end of the century. Although the French vogue for the Middle Ages was influenced by the works of Madame de Staël, the Schlegels, and Walter Scott, influential writers such as Chateaubriand and Victor Hugo fixed the symbolic registers that would remain attached to the Middle Ages in France. One has only to glance at the late poems of Paul Verlaine, whose 1880 *Sagesse* expressed nostalgia for the purity and stability of the Middle Ages, to recognize the influence of Chateaubriand: 'It is toward the enormous and delicate Middle Ages/That my wounded heart must navigate/Away from our days of carnal spirit and sorry flesh/[…]/High theology and solid morals/Guided by the unique folly of the Cross/On your wings of stone, oh wild Cathedral!'[50]

Chateaubriand's *Le Génie du Christianisme* (1802) evoked the Middle Ages as a peaceful time in which a naive yet powerful faith controlled the lives of worshipers. One of the chief goals of his book was to prove that the fine arts flourished because of Christianity. According to him, medieval piety had inspired the construction of Gothic cathedrals and monasteries, which were modeled on the forests in which the primitive Christians had worshiped. Gothic arches were intended to reproduce the natural lines of intertwined branches, while music and ornamentation recreated the natural harmonies and murmurs of nature. The cathedral became the symbol of this spiritual Middle Ages: 'the age of magic and enchantments.'[51] The numerous illustrated editions of *Le Génie du Christianisme* published in the nineteenth century spread his nostalgia for the artistic and spiritual purity of this alleged lost Golden Age. Chateaubriand's wishful vision of a simple time of piety was incorporated and echoed in the works of authors and artists including Paul Verlaine, J.-K.

Huysmans, Paul Claudel, Léon Bloy, Marcel Proust, Maurice Denis, Pierre Puvis de Chavannes and Joséphin Péladan, in addition to those art historians who eagerly accepted his theories about the origin of Gothic forms.[52] Catholic figures Louis Veuillot, Léon Gautier, Charles de Montalembert and Victor Laprade fought incessantly to commemorate the 'pure' and 'magical' Middle Ages imagined by Chateaubriand and to rejuvenate the reputation of medieval heroes such as Joan of Arc.[53]

Chateaubriand began the nineteenth-century vogue for the concept of an idyllic Middle Ages through a reassessment of Catholicism, yet much nineteenth-century interest in the Middle Ages stemmed from a much more secular source, Victor Hugo's *Notre-Dame de Paris* (1831). While Chateaubriand focused on 'the genius of Christianity,' Hugo singled out the 'genius of the people.' The novel centers around Notre-Dame de Paris, the cathedral at the heart of both medieval and modern Paris, which he represented as a symbol of the French nation's democratic and artistic heritage. Hugo emphasized the national importance of Notre-Dame de Paris in his novel by linking the development of Gothic architecture to the rise of democracy in France. Paradoxically, he envisioned the cathedral, one of the most sacred of places, as a symbol of freedom from the restraints of religion.[54] For him, the 'somber style' of Romanesque architecture was a direct transcription of the tyrannical priesthood that he envisioned as the power controlling the early Middle Ages. Gothic architecture's form, however, seemed to represent freedom, a reflection of the liberty unleashed by the Crusades:

> The cathedral itself, once such a dogmatic edifice, henceforth invaded by the bourgeoisie, by the commune, by liberty, escapes from the priest and falls under the power of the artist. The artist builds it as he likes. Farewell mystery, myth, law. Here are fancy and capriciousness [ ... the cathedral] belongs to imagination, poetry, people.[55]

Hugo's representation of the cathedral builders as rebellious free spirits, who began 'freedom of the press' by including anti-clerical messages in their sculpture, endeared Gothic architecture to the generation following the French Revolution. His scorn for 'vandalism' – both demolition and callous restoration of old architectural structures – contributed directly to the popular enthusiasm behind Viollet-le-Duc's subsequent restoration of the cathedral. Hugo's concept of a democratic Middle Ages dominated by the power of the people was historically inaccurate, yet it appealed to the imagination of the nineteenth century: for years Republicans, including Viollet-le-Duc, described Gothic architecture as the product of a secular movement and idealized the Middle Ages as a time of popular festivity and revolt against Church authorities.[56]

Viollet-le-Duc, the architect responsible for the renovation of Notre-Dame de Paris as well as those of Saint-Denis and the cathedrals at Amiens and Vézelay, was the nineteenth century's greatest advocate of the Gothic style, which he praised as 'national architecture' and 'the symbol of French nationality.'[57] He and a group of prominent advocates of the Gothic style, including Adolphe-Napoléon Didron (the founder of *Les Annales archéologiques* and secretary of the Commission des Monuments Historiques), Prosper Mérimée (novelist and Inspecteur général des monuments historiques) and Jean-Baptiste Lassus (architect in charge of the Sainte-Chapelle restoration), were seminal in convincing the art history establishment – which tended to prefer classical forms and to dismiss medieval architecture as inferior – of the national importance of the Gothic.[58] Indeed, these scholars were the first to advance many of the theories about medieval art – its innovation, its logic and its unity – that would become mainstream in the last quarter of the century. The theoretical writings of this group (many of whom were devout Catholics), however, were predominately secular, as Viollet's nationalist claims on the Gothic style suggest. Viollet's structural rationalism left little room for faith and although he admitted the critical importance of Catholicism in the construction of Gothic cathedrals, he tended to downplay it.[59]

Religious or rationalist interpretations of the Middle Ages and medieval art established the primary lenses through which nineteenth-century France would continue to regard the Middle Ages. Chateaubriand furthered a Catholic and sacred interpretation, while Hugo and Viollet-le-Duc advanced a democratic and secular view of them. Indeed, foreign contemporaries were quick to remark on this feud as the origin of the mid-nineteenth century French neglect of medieval art and literature, as did T. F. Crane in a February 1879 article for the *North American Review*:

[…] The mediaeval literature of France has been exposed to the extreme criticism of two schools, one cherishing for it a blind worship, not because it is national (its truest title to reverence), but because it is Catholic, the other refusing to see any good in a literature which is the exponent of a spirit they fear and hate.[60]

These two mutually exclusive conceptions of the same period and events reflect the ways in which politicians of the early nineteenth century conceived of the French nation and its goals: they saw it as divided between Catholic royalists and Republican free-thinkers, each with different agendas for the country's future. In an electoral pamphlet of 1820, politician and historian François Guizot described the internecine squabbling of modern France in precisely these terms; he argued that the country's disagreements simply perpetuated the ancient battle between the Franks (the aristocracy) and the Gauls (the people), a feud that had begun with the Germanic invasions of the Middle Ages:

The [French] Revolution was a war, a real war, like those that the world recognizes between foreign peoples. For more than thirteen centuries now France has contained two such peoples, conqueror and conquered. For more than thirteen centuries now the conquered people have struggled to break the yoke of the conquerors. Our history is the history of this battle.[61]

According to this theory, Catholics and Republicans, like Franks and Gauls, were mortal enemies who, after thirteen centuries of fighting, were unlikely to stop doing so. Guizot's comments foreshadow the history of nineteenth-century France, in which regime after regime would dispute the power and symbols of their competitors as they gained control.

In *The Middle Ages in France,* Janine Dakyns traces the ways in which each group of authorities claimed the Middle Ages for different purposes: the Restoration embraced the troubadours; Napoléon III favored a religious and authoritarian Middle Ages to justify his reign; Republicans claimed the 'democratic' Middle Ages of Hugo. In each case, as she shows, those who had previously praised the Middle Ages would then renounce them. The best example of this is reflected in the writings of Jules Michelet, whose Romantic adulation of the Middle Ages as the time of the 'people' quickly shifted to disgust as the period was adopted by Napoléon III and his Church-supported government.[62] It was not until after the Franco-Prussian war that a majority of the French nation no longer contested the importance of the Middle Ages for modern France.

### The Franco-Prussian War and the development of the patriotic Middle Ages

In the years between the 'Gothic furor' of the Romantics and the 'Gothic revival' of the fin de siècle, writers and scholars Paulin Paris, Francisque Michel, Viollet-le-Duc, Adolphe and Edouard Didron, Jules Michelet, Edmond Quicherat and Louis Petit de Julleville – to name only a few – continued to study and debate various aspects of the Middle Ages.[63] Yet as Charles Morice noted in 1914, although their valuable work laid the foundation for this 'national science of archeology' and began attracting the public, it was only in the last quarter of the nineteenth century that their work bore fruit and that the Middle Ages and their artistic achievements were widely recognized at all levels of French society.[64] One of the primary reasons for the public's renewed interest in the Middle Ages after the Franco-Prussian war was that government leaders, intellectuals and journalists of all sides proposed the study of the Middle Ages as a cure for the moral, patriotic and political wounds of the defeated nation.[65]

The humiliating defeat of the Franco-Prussian war, followed by the Paris Commune (which resulted in the deaths of more than 20 000 people), was capped by the Treaty of Frankfurt (10 May 1871), which gave the provinces of Alsace and Lorraine to the German Empire. To add insult to injury, the French had to pay 5 billion gold francs ($1 billion) to the Germans, submitting to occupation until this debt had been repaid. As a result, a crushing sense of defeat and a 'rhetoric of sickness' permeated the political, religious and literary discourse of nineteenth-century Europe.[66] The sense of loss was so bitter that 17 years later politicians and officials still spoke of the war as if their wounds were fresh.[67]

For the *Revanchards*, who vowed to rebuild the defeated French nation, Germany became the national enemy, the invading horde responsible for demolishing modern French civilization. Historians like Fustel de Coulanges proposed that France was reliving a historical precedent: the Germanic invasions of the fifth century. Suddenly, the internal battle among Catholics and Republicans in France became less important than the need to rally against the invading exterior force. The three years following the war thus saw a surge of interest in the fifth-century invasions, which, as François Guizot's 1820 pamphlet had suggested, had long been considered the origin of the modern French nation and its political troubles.[68] In an 1872 article for *La Revue des Deux Mondes* entitled 'L'invasion germanique au cinquième siècle,' Fustel de Coulanges explained that incorrect theories about this invasion were largely responsible for his contemporaries' conception of national identity. This event had taken on 'enormous proportions' in the national imagination because the idea of a brutal invasion caused the French to believe that Gaul was weak. He felt that this single *a priori* assumption about the Middle Ages created a chain reaction of false historical premises that linked the conquering Germans to virile royalty and the Gauls to powerless serfs:

> It seems as though [the invasion] changed the face of the country and gave its destinies a direction they would not have had without it. [The conquest] is, for many historians and for the masses, the source of the entire Ancien Régime. The feudal lords pass for the sons of the Germans and the serfs of the glebe for the sons of the Gauls. A conquest – that is to say a brutal act – is thus posited as the unique origin of ancient French society. All of the great feats of our history are explained and judged in the name of this first iniquity. The feudal system is presented as the reign of the conquerors, the emancipation of towns as the awakening of the defeated and the revolution of 1789 as their revenge.[69]

Fustel's article clearly identifies his contemporaries' reliance on the theory of the German invasion for their conception of the origins of the French nation. He then spends the rest of the essay debunking this notion by revealing the inherent weakness of the Germans, who were conquered in turn by the Romans. His essay is a point-by-point refutation of most of the nineteenth-century beliefs about the importance of Germanic tribes in the development of the French nation; it culminates in proving that medieval France successfully survived the invasions in the Middle Ages as it would in the nineteenth century. 'It is a strange error,' he writes, 'to have thought that Germany was the "fabric of the human race and the womb from which nations emerged".'[70] For Fustel, who continued to publish influential articles in *La Revue des Deux Mondes* in the three years following the war, the true origin of the French nation lay in its medieval ancestors' successful integration of Roman culture and social structures.[71]

Fustel argued that France had been in the throes of an identity crisis since the French Revolution and until his contemporaries re-evaluated their past and came to a consensus about medieval history, the nation would never heal:

> This ancient past [...] still exerts a curious domination over us. There is not one Frenchman, no matter how ignorant, who does not speak of the Middle Ages, who does not think he understands it, who does not pretend to judge it [...] Yet the idea we make of it, true or false, has such a hold on our spirit that the flow of nearly all our thoughts and opinions comes from it. Note why two men think differently about questions of government and politics, it is nearly always because they have two

different ways of judging the Ancien Régime. Two men meet and argue about public affairs; you think they are talking about urgent concerns, – most often they're quarreling about the Ancien Régime, and because they are in disagreement about the way they understand the past, it is impossible for them to agree about the present […] Thus history forms our opinions.[72]

In this article, Fustel proposes an important social role for historical studies: France's current moral weakness stems not from the war, but from its inability to come to an agreement about how to interpret its history. Fustel asked his contemporaries to adopt a common understanding of historical events from the Middle Ages. His articles of this time insisted that creating a single and widely-recognized story about the national past was critical to establishing a united population. Such theories were not new – only a few years earlier, for example, Viollet-le-Duc had proposed that a nation's unity came from its study of a shared past – but they gained credence in the troubled period following the war.[73] By insisting on the social advantages of creating a universally accepted version of French history, Fustel de Coulanges anticipated the works of twentieth-century scholars who study the 'invention of tradition,' the capital role narrative plays in building nationalism.[74]

Other intellectual figures from different political backgrounds followed Fustel in rallying to convince their countrymen of the need for a universally accepted version of French history. In *La Revue des Deux Mondes*, Louis Vitet argued that 'Understanding our history correctly is the key to all our problems, the principle by which to regenerate order and progress.'[75] Many other writers, from Gaston Paris and Paul Meyer to Gabriel Monod, the founder of the *Revue historique* (begun in 1876), agreed that the reconsideration of French history, beginning with the invasions of the fifth century, was of the utmost importance for the health of their country.[76] Instead of fighting about the present situation of France, everyone could embrace the Middle Ages as the birthplace of the nation, a time when France was indisputably great. In this new understanding of French history, based on the Middle Ages, the French accepted a kind of primordial link greater and more powerful than all of the issues that divided them.[77] Medieval France, which survived the Germanic invasions by building a solid society based on successful previous models, served as a positive example for rebuilding the wounded French nation.

## Understanding the Middle Ages: patriotism and national unity

In the direct aftermath of the Franco-Prussian war, many valued the Middle Ages not only for the national unity they inspired, but also for the moral lessons they could impart. In what Christian Amalvi has called 'the fever of analogy,' school officials, politicians and journalists resuscitated events from medieval history – the German invasions of the fifth century, the Hundred Years' War – and rewrote them as ideals to help France cope with the post-war situation.[78] François Coppée and Henri d'Artois drew on these parallels in an 1878 play, *La Guerre de Cent Ans*: 'Indeed, it could be beneficial to evoke on the French stage, alongside the memories of former disasters, the spectacle of heroic efforts made by our ancestors to repair and reconstruct our country.'[79] A children's school primer of 1885 puts this concept into action. It contrasts the nation's devastation after 1870 with French suffering at the hands of the British during the Hundred Years' War: 'France has never known a more tragic epoch. Neither the religious wars of the sixteenth century, nor modern wars such as that of 1870 could give the full idea of the people's suffering during these 116 years.'[80] Past defeat offered proof that France could return victorious, as the historian A. Carel pointed out: 'we recovered in the fourteenth century; we shall not despair; history shows how a wise, vigorous and persevering reform can save and restore everything.'[81]

Early Republican historians constructed a Celtic and medieval past which echoed their own political ideologies.[82] The first president of the League of Patriots, Henri Martin, a noted historian, extolled the Celtic past over the 'Latinate' seventeenth century.[83] In his *Art national* (1883) the critic Henri Raison du Cleuziou also lauded Martin for 'nationalizing' and 'de-Catholicizing' Gothic art.[84] These historians praised the Republic for reawakening the 'true' soul of France, lost and scattered during centuries of monarchist rule. In Emile Chatrousse's sculpture 'Aux martyrs de l'indépendance nationale' (1870), this dual heritage (Gallic and medieval) was given distinct visual form (Fig. 1.2). Vercingétorix is shown shaking hands with Joan of Arc beneath an effigy of the Republic.

As official spheres placed emphasis on the moral value of the Middle Ages, this period experienced what Michel Winock has called 'the apotheosis' of legendary medieval figures such as Joan of Arc and Roland, who became symbols of patriotism and national independence.[85] Their success, even in failure, made them emblems of a French nation under duress. Léon Gautier explained such logic in his 1875 edition of *La Chanson de Roland*: 'Roland, too, was defeated; but such a loss did not have the slightest diminishing effect on his glory and Charlemagne, at any rate, avenged him with a brilliant and decisive victory. While waiting for Charlemagne, we consoled ourselves with Roland.'[86] He extolled Roland as 'France made man' and praised his song as 'the national epic,' a work that rivaled the *Iliad*.[87] Joan of Arc, in turn, became 'the patron saint of an invaded nation' and the 'messiah of nationality.'[88] Innumerable poems, songs, books, plays, school celebrations and artistic commissions sprang up around their names, while scholars celebrated their selfless contributions to the nation.[89] An 1897 newspaper article from *Le Temps*, proposing a school festival in honor of Joan of Arc, summarizes the appeal of these heroes in the two decades following the war: 'Invincible love for the homeland, stronger than death, than discouragement or defeat and all of the quarrels between Armagnacs and Burgundians [a reference to arguments between Catholics and Republicans via the opposing camps of the Hundred Years' War], this is what is taught by the humble countrywoman who preached the union of all Frenchmen and who gave her life for France.'[90]

1.2    Emile
Chatrousse, *Aux
martyrs de
l'indépendance
nationale (To the
martyrs of
national
independence)*,
1870

In the 1870s, reading about or discovering new aspects of medieval art, history and literature became a badge of patriotic honor. Scholars published a host of texts highlighting the role of medieval rulers in unifying the French nation; a number of these appeared not only in scholarly publications, but also in mainstream periodicals such as *La Revue des Deux Mondes* and *Le Temps* and in school primers.[91] Such popular consideration of the past allowed France to obtain the energy to move forward and to rebuild its confidence. It is no coincidence that the decades following the war resulted in the public recognition of the institutions and publications that we consider integral to medieval studies today, a body of scholarly works that insist on the cultural achievements of the medieval French nation. Paul Meyer and Gaston Paris founded *Romania* in 1872 to compete with *Germania* and in 1874 they began publishing medieval texts in the *La Société des Anciens Textes Français* series.[92] These years saw the beginning of a number of other important publications including Godefroy, *Le Dictionnaire de l'ancienne langue française* (1881); Louis Petit de Julleville, *L'Histoire de la langue et de la littérature françaises* (1896) and *L'Histoire du théâtre en France* (1880–1886); and Emile Mâle, *L'Art Religieux du XIIIe siècle en France* (1898). The nation rewarded Gaston Paris, Paul Meyer and Léon Gautier for their contributions to philology by electing them to chairs at the Collège de France or by nominating them to distinctive positions in the academic and literary circles of France.[93]

The nationalism evident in the 1904 Exposition des Primitifs français – whose seeds had been sown by the mid-century – thus had its roots in the post-war attempt to boost French self-confidence. The creation of a vivid medieval past helped rebuild the morale of a dejected, insecure nation. Despite the fact that the Middle Ages could still be claimed for a variety of agendas, the French had responded to Fustel de Coulanges's pleas of 1871: they no longer disputed the medieval period's importance for their shared national identity.

## The rival Middle Ages of fin-de-siècle France

As Rosemonde Sanson argues, the only common religion of fin-de-siècle France was patriotism; it appealed as strongly to those on the left as to the right.[94] Medievalism, which became affiliated with patriotism, thus lured individuals and groups from both sides of the political fence because each found in the past an answer to the malaise of their present. Sadly, however, the unifying spirit of a common medieval ancestry soon showed its limitations, as did other attempts – such as the *Ralliement* – to 'reunite' divisive factions in Republican France.[95] The *Ralliement* began when Leo XIII recognized the stability of the Third Republic, which had gained a majority of voters, and urged Catholics to accept it as a legitimate government. In turn, the *Ralliés* hoped that the Republic would cease its anti-clerical campaigns and that liberal Catholics would be led back to the Church. But like the 'non-partisan' idealism behind the appropriation of figures like Joan of Arc and Roland, the *Ralliement* crumbled when put into practical application.

An 1894 bill proposing a 'festival of patriotism' in honor of Joan of Arc reveals both the precarious nature of the French political embrace of a universal Middle Ages and the weakness of the *Ralliement*. The bill was introduced in 1884 by Joseph Fabre, a Republican who wanted to use 8 May, the anniversary of the day Joan and her troops had liberated Orléans from the English siege in 1429, to celebrate national unification: 'On this day all Frenchmen could unite in a healthy communion of enthusiasm. Joan does not belong to any one party; she belongs to France.'[96] Throughout the century Joan had been claimed by Catholics as a saint and martyr and by Republicans as a figure of military revolt and a victim of Church oppression. 8 May had often been celebrated, but generally as an exclusively Republican or Catholic holiday. The novelty of this bill was to bring the two camps together in a non-partisan embrace of Joan's national symbolism. Despite great popular support, the bill was rejected by the Republican majority for fear that Catholics would use it as a religious holiday to rival the recently instituted (1880) and pro-Republican Bastille Day.[97]

Ten years later, Fabre reintroduced the bill, arguing that the holiday would bring together 'old and new France.'[98] This time popular support was overwhelming, until Republican fears were realized: Catholics began to plan the holiday as a way of stirring up anti-Republican sentiment and to compete with Bastille Day. The vote passed the Senate with the help of Prime Minister Charles Dupuy, who eloquently argued that Joan could not be claimed by either camp because her relevance was so inherently national. A festival of patriotism would: 'commemorate and invigorate national pride in the soul of all Frenchman, everywhere in France.'[99] Despite the approval of the Senate, the bill did not make it to a general vote in time to institute the holiday. The failure of this measure set off anti-clerical demonstrations throughout the country and the festival was not celebrated until 1920, at the instigation of Maurice Barrès.[100] This example helps illuminate the failure of the *Ralliement*: neither the Church nor the Republic could let go of a deep-seated mutual mistrust. Despite good intentions and politicians' agreement on ideological issues such as the importance of Joan of Arc, Catholics and Republicans could not agree about the practical applications of instituting such a festival because their partisan spirit drove them to suspect each other's intentions.[101]

The 1904 exhibition reflected the universal public acclaim accorded to French medieval art, yet within this united discourse raged a fierce battle to see who 'owned' and could 'use' this medieval heritage. The political split between Catholics and Republicans carried over into fin-de-siècle art-historical debates about the Middle Ages. Just as Joan was claimed by both sides during discussions about an 1894 festival in her honor, so the arguments inspired by the Exposition des Primitifs français and other public displays of medieval art illustrate how deeply politicized reference to the medieval heritage had become by the 1890s. The organizers of the exhibition insisted on the 'secular' inspiration of the *Primitifs*, at the expense of the more conservative religious artist: 'The cloisters, traditional and limited in their hieratic conceptions of ideas and forms, were from very early on counterbalanced by lay artists, who issued from the communes. It was they who led art down a freer and more personal path, breaking with tradition … '[102] As in the state museums established under the Third Republic, such scholars divorced medieval art from its religious context.

Critics of every political persuasion promoted Gothic art and the Gothic artist as embodiments of the French national genius, and contemporary artists who made reference to the Gothic tradition were seen as defenders of France, revivers of the national spirit. Yet at the same time, each group claimed the Middle Ages for its own purposes. While liberals celebrated Claude Monet's *Rouen Cathedral* series precisely because it had severed the link between Gothic architecture and Christian faith, conservative critics such as Alphonse Germain praised artists who evoked the spirit of painter-priests and monks. Characteristically, Republican praise focused on the patriotic, national heritage of these artists (in the vein of Hugo), while critics on both sides stressed the religious (and sometimes racial) inspiration that went into the creation of such works. By the end of the century, the Middle Ages – while universally accepted as a time of French superiority – were still contested territory, a grail over which the most democratic Republicans and the most avid of conservatives clashed swords.

## The Republican Middle Ages and fin-de-siècle art

In 1893, the progressive Parisian journal, *La Revue Blanche,* published a satirical fairy tale entitled 'Le Bon Camelot.'[103] The title played on the multiple meanings of the term 'camelot' – an idealized medieval kingdom, an activist, a seller of shoddy merchandise and an advertising tool – in order to satirize the corrupt and materialistic Republic. The most recent Republican scandals included the President of the Republic's resignation because his son-in-law had illegally sold government awards (1887) and the serious financial scandals that implicated leaders of the left after the liquidation of the Panama Canal Company (1891–1893). Set in a forest, the story related a meeting between the characters Camelot and Parlementaire. After hearing of the 'faults and crimes' with which Parlementaire had been charged, Camelot decided to assist him in hopes of gaining a lordship. Through the magical spells of a fairy, 'Bad Faith,' and the help of Camelot, Parlementaire cleared his name and won the next election as 'the choice of all citizens.' Upon taking office, Parlementaire's first priority was to elect Camelot to the post of Inspecteur du service hygiénique des chancelleries et consulats.

Manifesting political mistrust of the Republican government, the fairy tale is also illuminating on another level; the tendency of the Republic to associate itself with lauded medieval heroes and legends in order to cleanse itself of scandal had become so entrenched in the popular imagination that it could be parodied in texts like 'Le Bon Camelot.' After two decades of rule, the Third Republic was no longer the underdog. Rather, it had come to be perceived as a sanctioned, stable – though often corrupt – form of government.[104] The reference to Camelot, legendary medieval court of virtue and justice, parodies the way the Republican government wanted people to perceive it. And, indeed, throughout the 1880s and 1890s, the Republic commissioned works from writers, artists and political figures – such as Claude Monet, Eugène Grasset, and Jean-Paul Laurens – who portrayed the Republic as the legitimate successor to previous French regimes by underlining the direct link between medieval and modern France. Revealing the similarities between the current government and that of the Middle Ages (which Republicans saw as marked by communal order and individual liberty, French superiority and bourgeois emancipation) allowed the Republic to distance itself both from French monarchist rulers and from the radical Revolutionary governments of 1789 and 1848. Medieval history was thus evoked to sanctify the Republican aim of centralizing the state and of expanding and consolidating the French empire. Such parallels between Republican and medieval France, like Fustel de Coulanges's denial of the German influence and his revelation of the direct link between Rome and modern France, served to legitimize the regime and to justify specific Republican policies.

One of the ways of insisting on the superiority of Republican France was to elide the religious conflicts that lay behind historical events and heroic acts. Republicans nationalized the Christian past and wove it into a heroic tale, often by downplaying religious settings and motivations (adopting Joan of Arc, for example, as a secular representative of the martyrdom of the people by the Church). They were thus able to portray the practices and institutions of the Republic as aligned with a long and noble democratic tradition. Germain Bapst analyzed the public spectacles of the Middle Ages for readers of *La Revue Bleue* in 1891. Describing the young girls sent to greet medieval processions, Bapst rhetorically asked: 'What has changed in regard to these old municipal customs? During official travels today, do we not still see young girls, dressed in all three colours [blue, white, and red …] in the name of the people, offering good wishes and bouquets to the head of State?'[105] A poster designed by Eugène Grasset, an artist championed for his Art Nouveau designs in various media, forms the visual equivalent of such rhetoric (Fig. 1.3).[106] Based loosely on the format of a manuscript leaf, Grasset's image evokes courtly announcements of festive events. He integrates text and image with stylized border motifs, while displaying the signature fluid lines of Art Nouveau. At the right, the emblem of the Third Republic (based on the insignia of medieval water carriers) serves to tie together the medieval and contemporary patriotic ceremony.[107]

Another Republican technique used to claim the Middle Ages for its camp was to insist on the inherent patriotism of medieval French art. Louis Gonse, a crucial figure within the Republican arts administration (member of the Conseil Supérieur des Beaux-Arts, Vice-President of the Commission des Monuments Historiques and long-time editor of the *Gazette des Beaux-Arts*), attempted to reaffirm the supremacy of medieval French art: 'And of what more pure artistic glory could the French nation boast? What other people could wear such a rich and splendid crown?'[108] He portrayed medieval works from other nations as inferior borrowings from French masterpieces. He encouraged his readers to take pride in French heritage; history proved that France would once again overcome foreign competition to emerge victorious. Like Bapst and Grasset, Gonse drew specific parallels between

1.3   Eugène Grasset, *Les Fêtes de Paris (The Fêtes of Paris)*, 1885

the moderate Republic and the political climate of the Middle Ages. Writing about the period from Louis le Gros (c. 1080–1137) to Philippe Auguste (1165–1223), Gonse declared that these medieval rulers were responsible for the growth of French patriotism:

These four reigns [sic] established the basis of French unity. The ideas of solidarity, of association, of unity, came to life and along with them, that selfless and superior sentiment called patriotism [...] it is with the communal and parish troops that the king wins his victories; they are the solid bourgeoisie of Dreux, of Soissons, of Beauvais ...[109]

The use of terms such as 'solidarity' and 'association' were hardly coincidental; they intentionally evoked the political parlance of the period, most notably the social policy of *Solidarité* championed by Léon Bourgeois in the 1890s.[110] The present was read into the past, the fin de siècle suited in the protective armor of an idealized and distant era.

Such nationalist agendas relied on the anti-Germanic sentiment that had its roots in the defeat of the Franco-Prussian war and still rankled twenty years later. In 1890, Antonin Proust (a former Minister of the Arts who played a key role in the cultural affairs of the Republic),[111] demanded the removal of a mosaic decorating the Escalier Daru of the Louvre. The mosaic, entitled 'Le Moyen Age,' had been designed by the history painter Jules-Eugène Lenepveu and was one of several representing different schools and periods of art history.[112] In this mosaic Lenepveu had dared to include an allegorical figure of 'Allemagne.' Alfred de Lostalot reviewed the incident for the *Gazette des Beaux-Arts*.[113] It was regrettable, claimed de Lostalot, that Lenepveu had not read Louis Gonse's recently published *L'art gothique* (1890), for if so, ' … the author of the mosaic that now decorates the staircase of the Louvre would have learned that Gothic art is a French art and that, consequently, one could not symbolize it by a figure of Germany without infringing on truth and patriotism.'[114] As Antonin Proust told the Chambre des Députés, such an image could not be tolerated, for even the Germans themselves no longer contested the supremacy of France in the development of Gothic art.[115]

The Republican appropriation of the Middle Ages as a patriotic period is also reflected in the works of extremely successful Academicians such as Jean-Paul Laurens.[116] His *Descente de tournoi au Moyen Age* (Fig. 1.4) won the contest sponsored by the Gobelin Tapestry Works for a large-scale hanging to decorate the Archives Nationales. Set within a plunging architectural vista, Laurens's winning cartoon featured a vast spectacle of gleaming knights and graceful ladies. While his design more closely resembles sixteenth-century tapestries than medieval because of his incorporation of perspectival illusion and his inclusion of old French inscriptions, his emphasis on the courtly setting and his use of stylized floral motifs, heraldic symbols and trumpeting angels all signaled 'medieval' to the nineteenth-century viewer. Like Grasset's poster, Laurens's Art Nouveau flourishes update and simultaneously refer to earlier images; its reference to the Franco-Flemish tapestry tradition and medieval pageantry made Laurens's work well suited for a state building dedicated to historical research. Its insistence on strength, loyalty and longevity, values inscribed on the tapestry's banners (*fortis*, *fidelis*, *semper*) also evoked elements important to the constructed political identity of the Republic. Moreover, it reflects the general Republican embrace of the Middle Ages in art: focus on patriotic, historical or celebratory scenes from the French past; glorification of national defense or democratic traditions; and attempts to anchor the Third Republic solidly as the legitimate heir to the French monarchy.

**1.4** Jean-Paul Laurens, *Descente de tournoi au Moyen Age (Setting out for a tournament in the Middle Ages),* 1890s

### The Catholic Middle Ages and fin-de-siècle art

Republican artists were not alone in claiming the Middle Ages to validate their achievements. In 1927, Maurice Denis, a Symbolist artist, published a eulogy for his friend Henri Cochin, a conservative Catholic deeply admiring of medieval culture. Praising the taste of his late supporter, Denis noted that it was specifically Christian intellectuals who were responsible for the revival of Gothic art under the Third Republic:

> Remember, too, that in this intellectual milieu the taste for the art and letters of the Middle Ages was well developed. Around 1870, it was Catholics who piously kept up the cult of Dante, the Italian *Primitifs* and the Gothic cathedrals, which the last Romantic wave had already abandoned.[117]

While separated by a wide political gulf, ardent Catholics on both right and left were united in their passion for the Christian faith.[118] These groups often shared a distaste for the bourgeois class (a result, as well as a cause, of their profound hatred for the Republic). Many of the social problems that so disturbed enemies of the Republic – rising industrialism, bourgeois power, the collapse of faith – seem to have found their antithesis in the distant Middle Ages. For some, the medieval period provided a true model for a radically restructured society. All too often, however, recourse to the medieval past degenerated into escapism at best and reactionary nationalism at worst.

While the intentional destruction of medieval cathedrals during the Revolution would be redressed by both figurative and literal constructions of the cathedral in the fin de siècle,[119] writers argued that the very existence of Revolutionary secular art had done irreparable harm to the French artistic tradition. According to the staunch anti-Republican critic Alphonse Germain, the aesthetic of Jacques-Louis David 'caused more harm to sacred art than the winds of disbelief and doubt.'[120] Blatant disrespect for this heritage had led to a century of neglect of the finest medieval art, which had only recently begun to be understood and appreciated again. Mourning the deliberate vandalism of Gothic art often went hand in hand with a desire to resurrect the religious and social structure of medieval France.

A corollary to such nostalgia for medieval art and society held that the medieval tradition had never completely died and could thus be rejuvenated. Such was the attitude fostered in the pages of *Le Spectateur catholique*, a Catholic journal that published the work of many Symbolist artists, including Maurice Denis, Félix Vallotton and Emile Bernard.[121] In response to calls for a 'renaissance of medieval art,' the critic William Witter declared that 'one cannot revive what has not died. And the Middle Ages were never killed and their spirit lived more powerfully than ever!'[122] For conservative critics, Gothic art was both a victim of the Revolution and its victor; it refused to be vanquished in a secular world.[123]

Just as Laurens's tapestry for the Archives Nationales embodies ideas at play in the Republican (re)construction of medieval France, numerous artworks in the fin de siècle reflected the Christian Middle Ages embraced by conservatives. Maurice Denis provides us with a particularly good set of examples. His *Saint Hubert* panels, created for the conservative Catholic politician Denys Cochin in 1895, are clearly indebted to Gothic sources. Moreover, the medieval references of these paintings functioned to signal Cochin's allegiance to religious, nationalist and Royalist tenets.

Born in 1851, Denys Cochin entered politics in the 1880s, serving as deputy of the eighth arrondissement from 1883–1918. Although often grouped with the liberal right wing, Cochin was an ardent defender of Church power in France and was a leading opponent of the separation of Church and State in 1905.[124] Cochin shared his fervent Catholicism with his brother Henri (a close friend of Denis)[125] and with his father, Auguste, who often said that 'All that is good is Christian.'[126] Indeed, the social critic Léon Bazalgette accused Cochin of wanting to stifle Republican spirit under the reactionary rule of the Church. Cochin did wish to see the religious devotion of medieval times brought back to life; he admired the 'chivalrous' spirit of that age.

In a speech given at the Collège Saint Vincent at Senlis, Cochin peppered his nationalist rhetoric with references to the Middle Ages:

In addition, there is, or more particularly there was, a public spirit in France; a generous chivalrous spirit, not always very practical, but always worthy of attention […] Whether back in the time of the Crusades, or throughout the long period of national and popular struggles against the English, or, finally, in the glorious wars of the beginning of this century, we always find our ancestors animated by this noble spirit that I describe.[127]

Maurice Denis catered to such respect for the spirit of the Middle Ages in his decoration of the politician's sitting room on the rue de Babylone.

In 1895, Cochin commissioned Denis for the project.[128] The decoration consisted of seven panel paintings, a ceiling painting and one stained-glass window (Fig. 1.5). Cochin decided on the theme of the *Légende de Saint Hubert*, which described the miraculous conversion of Hubert in 663 AD. According to the legend, while hunting a deer Hubert saw – between the antlers of the animal – a vision of the crucified Christ. Not only did the legend focus on Cochin's favorite sport (hunting), the politician explained in a letter to Denis, but its religious message also appealed to his passionate Catholicism:

[…] And so the story of St Hubert comes to mind. Sometimes when we are least expecting it – we read about this in the lives of the saints, but it can happen to any of us any time – in the midst of wars or pleasures, a religious thought suddenly stops us in our tracks; the shining cross appears between a deer's antlers and the hunter falls to his knees. This is why I spoke to you of St Hubert.[129]

Denis painted various stages of the hunt in his seven panels, which include portraits of Cochin, Denis and their intimate friends and family.[130] In addition, he covered the ceiling with images of angels. For the stained-glass window he designed, Denis chose the theme of *The Path of Life*, including portraits of Cochin's two young daughters.

In his painted panels, Denis clearly evoked a specific Gothic reference: Franco-Flemish 'Chasse' tapestries (see Fig. 3.4).[131] Not only was such reference historically appropriate for the 'ancient' legend, but Denis's choice of sources linked Cochin with the devout aristocratic patron of the Gothic period. The tilted ground, flattened forms, strong vertical emphasis of the trees and saturated colors of the panel point to the formal elements of the medieval tapestry, while the leaping dogs, prancing horses and costumed figures recall the frequent subject matter of such scenes. So, too, the series of panels recalled the format of tapestry cycles. Furthermore, Denis's use of sporting, leisurely scenes to refer to underlying Christian themes was a popular practice in medieval tapestry art.[132]

Moreover, the choice of Franco-Flemish tapestries had an obvious nationalist appeal; along with stained glass, Gothic tapestries were widely regarded as supreme examples of French cultural dominance in the Middle Ages.[133] In addition, the culture evoked was an aristocratic, courtly one, a vanished culture of hierarchy and ritual deeply pleasing to the Royalist mentality. The sport of hunting was one practiced by the highest strata of both medieval and nineteenth-century society. Cochin himself often attended hunting parties of the French aristocracy, to which he invited Denis. 'The sport,' he claimed, ' … was the only one worthy of esteem … '[134] The most frequent setting for the medieval 'Chasse' tapestry was the palace or château. By including portraits of Cochin's family and friends in these 'medievalized' hunting

1.5 Maurice Denis, *Le Lâcher des chiens (Unleashing the dogs)*, panel from *The Legend of St Hubert*, 1896–1897

parties, Denis intimated that Cochin's milieu kept alive these chivalric, aristocratic rituals.

Both the choice of subject and the formal reference to specific medieval sources were in tune with Cochin's religious outlook. The theme of Saint Hubert stressed the ubiquity of religion, the triumph of Christian faith in the secular world. Much as Cochin urged that the medieval spirit of chivalry be resurrected in contemporary life, Denis wrapped his Gothic references in a modern aesthetic package. Nothing better illustrates how perfectly Denis's *Saint Hubert* cycle gave form to the Christian Middle Ages than the use to which these panels were put. Following the separation of Church and State in 1905, when the Archdiocese of Paris lost its home, Cochin invited priests to use his sitting room to conduct private masses.[135] Filled with Denis's Gothicized works, Cochin's apartment must have seemed a haven of old-world piety and values in a secular world.

The vision of the Middle Ages reflected in Denis's *Saint Hubert* panels was shared by another close friend, Adrien Mithouard, publisher of the conservative journal *L'Occident*, which began in 1902. In the pages of this periodical, Mithouard presented his nationalist rhetoric, which promoted France as the epicenter of western civilization because of its valuable racial and Christian heritage. Mithouard's ideas often paralleled those of the nascent Action Française party, but differed in at least one crucial regard: while the ideology of l'Action Française embraced the classical roots of French culture, Mithouard upheld Gothic art as the truest embodiment of the French spirit: 'rational,' harmonious and profoundly Christian, all at once. Like Cochin and Charles Morice, Mithouard insisted on the continuing presence of the Gothic spirit in modern life; for him, for example, the essence of Gothic art had been reanimated by the Impressionists, for both groups had nourished their art from the national soul of the Ile de France.[136] For Mithouard, the Gothic age was not a closed chapter of history, but a way of life, a mentality currently under siege in Republican France, yet capable of triumphant rebirth under the right social conditions.[137] It was the constant awareness of the Christian spirituality underlying material life – the very theme of Denis's *Saint Hubert* panels – that constituted the Gothic essence for Mithouard. Inherent in the beliefs of Germain, Cochin, Denis and Mithouard, and in those of other staunchly Catholic writers, was the conviction that France's past and future glory lay in her Christian heritage. Such notions easily blurred into the desire for an exclusively Christian French nation, a goal that intersected with the explosion of xenophobia that wracked fin-de-siècle France.[138]

**'Each person makes his own, imaginary Middle Ages'**

A common nineteenth-century myth perpetuated by Chateaubriand located the origins of Gothic architecture in the medieval forest. If we use this image as an analogy, by the fin de siècle this forest was composed of many different kinds of trees, whose branches splintered off into as many directions as there were political positions. As Fustel de Coulanges had put it in 1871, 'Each person makes his own, imaginary Middle Ages.' The democratic reading of the Middle Ages sprang from the writings of Victor Hugo, while a more conservative reading of the medieval period 're-baptized' the past and upheld it as an ideal for modern Catholic and Royalist values. Yet underlying these partisan appropriations of the Middle Ages was a recognition of Fustel's message about the importance of embracing a common story about the origins of French history. Each group agreed that medieval figures, artwork and religion gave France its first indisputable period of cultural superiority and considered this fact with pride. Raymond Poincaré, in a speech given ten years before he became President of the Republic (1913), expressed this feeling clearly:

[Joan of Arc] sails above political parties, she is the prisoner of no sect, no group, no school [...] Each of us has the same right and the same duty to admire her and to love her, for she embodies and incarnates the elements common to French feelings and to all political parties: the steadfast devotion to our country [*la patrie*] and to our passion for national independence.[139]

Despite the often contradictory nature of the claims made upon characters and art from the Middle Ages, patriotic fervor generally superseded everything else; by the 1880s all agreed that the Middle Ages were the key to French identity.

Indeed, the nationalist rhetoric that animated the 1904 Exposition des Primitifs français was not new but, as we have seen in this chapter, shaped throughout the course of the nineteenth century. The rediscovery of the French *Primitifs* and the elaborate exhibit provided for them by the Third Republic proved without a doubt the government's commitment to French heritage. As the catalog pointed out in less than modest terms, the Middle Ages 'belonged' to France. The Parisians were 'the first builders, the first constructors of Europe, their stained glass and their goldwork owed nothing to anyone [...] And the sculptures of the cathedrals, the stained glass of Chartres, the French manuscripts, existed long before Cimabue [a thirteenth-century Italian *Primitif*] came on the scene.'[140]

Both Republicans and Catholic politicians like Cochin had great stakes in claiming the glories of the Middle Ages, yet they were not alone in championing the French *Primitifs*. Many avant-garde artists had long been fascinated by the *Primitif* artist for entirely different – even contradictory – reasons, many of which were antithetical to the qualities praised by the official artistic establishment. In an attempt to liberate artists from the taint of politics, Symbolist artists from Maurice Denis to Paul Gauguin fixed on the *Primitifs* as pure creators, able to withstand the temptation of worldly concerns. As our next chapter will reveal, the ideal of the French *Primitifs* shaped the artistic identity of late nineteenth-century artists and often merged with it.

# 2

# Packaging the *Primitifs*: the medieval artist, the *Neo-Primitif* and the art market

The painter has the emaciated face of an ascetic. He is an enthusiast, a believer; the faith he carries inside consumes him […] He is no longer a man, he is prayer incarnate, he is faith, he is spirit freed from matter, aspiring to the Infinite … [141]

Georges Olmer, *L'Exposition des Beaux-Arts: Salon de 1886*

At the Salon of 1886, Puvis de Chavannes, one of the most celebrated contemporary French artists, exhibited two pendant works, *Vision Antique* and *Inspiration Chrétienne* (Fig. 2.1).[142] While the former offered a dreamy landscape of reposing nudes, the latter focused on a somber painter-monk, hard at work in a fifteenth-century Italian cloister modeled to look like the Camposanto at Pisa. The critic Georges Olmer, reviewing the Salon, was clearly moved by the mystical nature of Puvis's painting. He was not alone. In contrast to the explicitly nationalist discourse associated with the Exposition des Primitifs français and the Republican arts administration, other critics, artists and scholars of the fin de siècle constructed a different image of the *Primitif*, one that rested on his piety and self-sacrificing purity.[143]

While in the late nineteenth century the medieval artist was seen as a kind of national hero who had captured the glory of France for eternity, this was not his only role. For artists deeply conscious of the demands of the art market, the medieval artist served another important purpose. He stood as a testimony to artistic authenticity and integrity, shielded from materialism. His image rested on a set of shared and oft-repeated qualities: he was naive, devout beyond reproach and humble to the point of self-sacrifice. While twentieth-century historians have sought to recover the social conditions and workshop practices of medieval artists, their nineteenth-century precursors were more often influenced by aesthetic concerns, especially in response to the tensions and paradoxes of the burgeoning art market.

Three specific constructions of the medieval artist occupied nineteenth-century viewers: the *Primitif*, the *imagier* and the painter-monk. As understood by the nineteenth century, the *Primitif* was untrained, arriving at his creation through spiritual revelation (Fig. 2.2).[144] In contrast, the *imagier* was considered an anonymous artist who often produced inexpensive woodcuts, banners or other works with popular appeal. Like both the *Primitif* and the *imagier*, the painter-monk was seen as religiously inspired, but he took his renunciation

2.1   Pierre Puvis de Chavannes, *Inspiration Chrétienne (Christian Inspiration)*, 1886

of the material world to the farthest degree, turning his back on the world in order to work in a secluded cloister.

In the various texts and homages that appeared in the fin de siècle, writers and artists repeatedly highlighted two 'characteristics' of the medieval artist (*Primitif, imagier* or painter-monk): his anonymity and his (supposed) lack of acquired skill. Both of these qualities conflicted with the demands of the contemporary art market. Communally produced works and the absence of a recognizable 'style' went against the prevailing strategies of dealers, who emphasized the unique qualities of the artists they represented.[145] The anonymity of the medieval artist thus rendered his works troubling for the market.[146] Frustrated by the extreme artistic competition and inequality of rank among their peers, contemporary artists idealized the (largely fictional) 'anonymity' of their Gothic forebears, in part because the lack of training that these artists (erroneously) attributed to the *Primitif* would have ensured his failure in the nineteenth-century art market.[147] As we shall see, the anonymity of the medieval artist was also understood to signify an entirely different social practice of art making.

As broadly understood in the fin de siècle, the fifteenth-century painter used a 'medieval' mind-set to work within the framework of medieval

2.2 Jean
Fouquet, *Portrait
de Charles VII,
King of France*

conventions and structures. According to this notion, he was a complete *naïf*,
a child-like soul possessed of spiritual purity and candid spontaneity.[148] The
naiveté ascribed to the medieval artist, however, was inaccurate; awkward
drawing and lack of refinement were not regarded positively by the medieval
or Quattrocento patron. Despite the fact that many of these so-called *Primitifs*
had spent long periods as apprentices or had been educated in renowned
workshops, nineteenth-century viewers preferred to see the Gothic artist as
self-trained.[149] Many late-nineteenth century artists would transform this
lack of academic polish into a positive value beyond critical reproach.
Fascinated by medieval *Primitifs*, contemporary French artists attempted to

follow in their footsteps. By emulating the humble *imagier*, the anonymous craftsman, they hoped to recapture the spiritual inspiration of medieval art. Modeling themselves after artists whose works had been destined for the church and religious communities, fin-de-siècle artists – many of whom found favor within the growing Symbolist movement[150] – attempted to locate a model of artistic practice that was not indebted to the art market. By referring to artists such as Puvis de Chavannes, Maurice Denis or Eugène Grasset as *Primitifs*, one automatically linked them to a higher purpose, thus distinguishing them from the commercially oriented *pompiers* or darlings of the Salon. Critics frequently attributed traits thought to have descended from Gothic ancestors – but in reality formulated in the nineteenth century – to contemporary artists.

The growing art market posed a visible threat to artistic identity in the fin de siècle. This menace contributed to the importance attributed to the medieval artist. While other prototypically French artistic paradigms – the rococo artisan or the classical genius embodied by Poussin – satisfied *nationalist* needs, only the medieval artist was regarded as a completely free producer, indebted neither to market patronage nor to secular demand.[151] The impossibility for nineteenth-century artists to achieve this freedom in their time, despite their earnest engagement with medieval art, fueled their fantasies about the Middle Ages.

This chapter examines prevalent fin-de-siècle attitudes toward the medieval craftsman and the art market during a time when critics and artists alike feared that money was spoiling artistic production and public taste. We explore several tropes surrounding the medieval artist – the *Primitif*, the *imagier* and the painter-monk – as they were expressed in art-historical texts, novels, journals and the writings of practicing artists, who consciously applied these terms to their own work. By discussing groups of artists like those centered around J.-K. Huysmans and his Ligugé monastery or Armand Point and his Haute-Claire community, we will see how medievalism drew avant-garde artists to issues in the Parisian art world, even as it distanced them from the city itself.

## The artistic department store

'The moment the artist thinks of money, he loses his sense of Beauty.'[152]
Maurice Denis, 5 September 1885

'I need a lot of money. You understand that I will not spend my savings in Florence. Speaking of which, if you know of a way to sell paintings for very high prices, please tell me. I do not know which Saint to pray to.'[153]
Maurice Denis, December 1892

As Denis's quotes reveal, the Symbolist artist was caught in a double-bind. While they longed to free themselves from what they perceived as a corrupt state-controlled system of art making and distribution, what real alternatives existed for them? In many cases, the success of these artists was less a conscious attempt to court the market than an unintended consequence of their discourse, which drew a strict dividing line between themselves and their Academic peers.

Of all the great vices attributed to successful Academic artists in the fin de siècle, the worst was their insatiable greed. In the eyes of the more idealist-minded Symbolist painters, the Academic artists incarnated materialism; their love of the sensuous and their lust for money defiled even their religious works. In countless reviews and articles, Symbolist writers heaped scorn on the Salons.[154] Albert Aurier, the impassioned art critic, repeatedly condemned 'the great national bazaars that we call Salons … ,' while Octave Mirbeau viciously characterized the art scene as scrambling to make way for knick-knacks.[155] Despite the fact that certain artists appreciated by the Symbolists – notably Puvis de Chavannes – commanded extraordinarily high prices for their works, it was those working in an Academic style that drew their fire. According to critics such as Aurier, Joséphin Péladan and J.-K. Huysmans, the bankrupt values and 'decadence' of the Academic artists were most glaringly revealed in their religious works, which contrasted sharply with the 'Christian Inspiration' lovingly depicted by Puvis.[156] The documentary style of the Naturalist painters was thought to be particularly inappropriate for subjects of a sacred nature.[157] The painter Emile Bernard referred to such artists as 'false priests who intercept the light,' while Huysmans condemned the award-winning Jean Béraud for having 'painted Jesus in the dining room surrounded by Jewish bankers.'[158] For these writers, the worldly success of Academic painters spoiled whatever spiritual value their subject matter might possess.

Professed scorn for profit, however, contrasted sharply with the realities of the fin-de-siècle art market. The fierce rejection of consumerism was conditioned by specific developments within the artistic sphere and in the culture at large. During the last decades of the nineteenth century, which saw the proliferation of independent dealers and galleries, art acquired an increased commodity value.[159] Yet ironically the commercial value and allure of art depended heavily on its function as a symbol of 'pure' creativity, on its illusory divorce from the values and structures of capitalism.[160] For art to maintain its market appeal, its actual ('real') relation to the market had to be continually obscured. With the ever-expanding art trade (led by dealers such as Ambroise Vollard), the rise of advertising and the blurring of the boundaries between the two, the work of all artists – whether Academic or avant-garde – could come surprisingly close to the flood of consumer products on sale in Paris.[161] Even artists who did not participate in the officially sponsored exhibitions had to answer to their independent dealers and to the dictates of the market.

In fact, although it was to markets and bazaars that the Salon was often derogatorily compared, the galleries (as well as the new Salon du Champs-de-Mars) aspired to imitate the fashionable new department stores of Paris. Exhibits of fine arts emulated the display, decoration and comfortable upscale décor of shops like the Bon Marché and they appealed to the same clientele:

the bourgeois public.[162] In turn, shops appealed to the taste and refinement of their customers, displaying merchandise in vitrines that clearly recalled museums and palaces of Fine Arts. One of the best examples of this tendency can be seen in Emile Zola's *Au Bonheur des Dames*, a fictional portrayal of Le Bon Marché and its elaborate 'exhibits' that so astonish the store's patrons.[163] Department store owners sponsored concerts, fairs and educational exhibits to draw in customers.[164]

Fully aware of these developments, critics and artists within the Symbolist milieu praised those creators, past and present, who chose to pursue a more 'noble' path of art. The critic Gaston Lesaulx predicted that the new 'ideal' painters would follow in the footsteps of 'Jesus chasing the sellers from the Temple, they will chase from art the brazen merchants who turn crimson with shame.'[165] Writing in his journal, Maurice Denis entreated his friends to 'have the courage to resist: 1) our overexcited sensibility; 2) our public that wants artistic impressions in five minutes!; 3) and our dealers.'[166]

Many of Denis's fellow Nabis – the group of self-declared artistic 'prophets' whose radical artistic innovations were in no small part influenced by their love of medieval art – also insisted on a distinction between their 'little bourgeois canvases' (works that they grudgingly made for the sole purpose of earning money) and their true art, their 'icons.'[167] The choice of the term 'icon', most often used in the late nineteenth century to describe the sacred Christian images of Byzantium, not only underlined the quasi-Eastern influences of the Nabis, but also highlighted their exalted spiritual intent, which was at odds with the materiality of 'bourgeois' objectives. According to Thadée Natanson, Paul Ranson believed that there were only two classes, 'artist and bourgeois,' while Joséphin Péladan, the leader of the Rose+Croix circle, also denounced the 'bourgeois genre': 'To my painter, two words: The incontestable – undeniably I contest you – worse still – I negate you, you and yours.'[168] If artists and bourgeois consumers were ever more firmly bound together in this period, the Symbolist drive to sever this link accelerated full force into the twentieth century.

Indeed, many Symbolist strategies may be understood as an attempt to resist the 'pagan' decadence of art, to renounce the material world, in a manner somewhat akin to the ascetic artist of the Middle Ages. Artists struggled to free themselves from the 'body' of painting and the materiality of the text. Their embrace of the symbol, whether platonic essence or visual abstraction, aligned them with the medieval creator who read the world as a symbol for the beyond.[169] 'The artist becomes the disciple of the ancient masters by abdicating his modernity,' claimed Emile Bernard.[170] Renunciation and sacrifice were the *modus operandi* of Symbolist artists who attempted to reach beyond the givens of the empirical world. This disavowal of modernity often reached its most vivid extreme in emulation of the medieval painter-monk.

## The medieval artist: drawing on faith

In his novel *La Femme Pauvre* (1897), the Catholic writer Léon Bloy created a character, Léopold, who is presented as the 'renewer of manuscript illumination.'[171] He is a contemporary artist so talented that he has discovered and recreated the lost techniques of medieval illuminators by studying books of hours in libraries and private collections: he has seen those of René d'Anjou, Anne de Bretagne, and Hans Memling. His skill had also gained him access to *Les Très Riches Heures du Duc de Berry*, whose scenes he had copied at Chantilly.[172] The public, however, scorns his accomplishments because they appreciate art only as an investment. It takes a Symbolist critic, Marchenoir (himself 'a kind of medieval man'), to recognize his value, which is evaluated in a satire of bourgeois tastes:

[...] The formidable critic demanded, in the name of the bourgeoisie, the harshest tortures for that Léopold, who was threatening to resuscitate a dead art of which businessmen had never heard. Was this art, seemingly wrapped in the crypts of the Middle Ages, really going to come back to life again, all because of the insolent will of a man unfamiliar with modern acquisitions?[173]

The martyred Léopold, a devout and destitute genius, dies sacrificing himself for others just after he has completed the book that might have made his fortune. He served as a surrogate for all fin-de-siècle artists who proudly turned their back on the marketplace.

According to Bloy, medieval artists had not produced art in order to earn money, but as an expression of their deep piety (see, for example, Fig. 6.3). Working in small communities, these artists had given little thought to their artistic reputation and even less to material reward. This notion of the self-sacrificing medieval artist was widespread at the time. Emile Bernard, too, described indifference to material comfort as an inherent characteristic of the medieval period: 'Nothing hobbled the spirit of men; doubt was not yet born and millions of beings participated in freeing the tomb of Christ [in the Crusades] without thinking for an instant about what they would eat en route or what clothes they would wear.'[174] Huysmans, too, praised the humility, the lack of ego that had enabled medieval artists to subsume their work into a greater whole. He interpreted the building of the cathedrals as a 'great Crusade' and wondered how the workers came together: 'Were they a company of *imagiers*, a brotherhood of holy workers who traveled from place to place, assistants to masons, to the laborers of God, to monks? [...] No one knows. Humbly, anonymously, they worked [...] and they did not work unless they were in a state of grace.'[175] Moreover, according to Huysmans, mysticism and faith were responsible for the greatest works that ever existed: *Primitif* paintings, Gregorian chant, Romanesque and Gothic architecture.[176] The Nabi artist Jan Verkade, who joined the Beuron monastery in 1894, was no less convinced that medieval art was the embodiment of deep faith: 'The Middle Ages believed in God, put their trust in the merits of Christ and the intercession of the Blessed Virgin and Saints and found joy in the festivals. Of this the cathedrals, the paintings of the Madonna, the figures of the Saints and the mystery plays all tell us.'[177]

Contemporary journals popularized these notions about *Primitifs* and *imagiers*. In 1894, Remy de Gourmont, novelist, literary critic, man of letters and a conservator at the Bibliothèque de l'Arsenal, and Alfred Jarry, the artist and playwright, began co-production of *L'Ymagier*, a journal dedicated to introducing readers to the anonymous works of humble medieval image makers and their modern counterparts (including the editors, who contributed their own designs).[178] An introduction to the first issue made the editors' goals explicit:

Religious or legendary images and nothing more, with just enough words to persuade, with an idea or two, those who have not been attentive to them. Images carved above all in wood […] Here, then, we preach the lesson of the old *imagier* and we tell, with our sketches, the joy of those who, for a single penny, decorated their walls with the secrets of archangels – the joy of a Breton peasant who finds in the peddler's basket rough faces carved by Georgin, symbolic and poignant hearts, Christs whose pain soothes our pains, miraculous virgins and mysterious knights, messengers of the king, who bring news of joy – and legendary Genevièves and powerful mitered saints, taller than belfries.[179]

The first frontispiece of the journal featured a woodcut tentatively attributed to Emile Bernard (Fig. 2.3). In an imitation of the scenes often found at the beginning of medieval manuscripts, a working scribe is visited by an angel. The crude hatchings and lack of detail align this image with medieval prints, while the scribe himself spells out the title of the journal, thus linking artists past and present. Importantly, the image is not signed, its anonymity a further connection between contemporary artist (Bernard) and Gothic scribe. Inside the journal's covers, readers could find anonymous graphics and *images d'Epinal*, medieval documents, Latin verse, folktales, songs and religious poems, all reproducing the folk images for which *imagiers* were renowned.[180] In addition to medieval woodcuts, which were mixed with modern imitations, some issues published excerpts from medieval French literature (in old French and modern translation), including Arnoul Gréban's *Le Mystère de la Passion*, *Le Miracle de Théophile* and *Aucassin et Nicolette*.[181] It is interesting that although Jarry would go on to be one of the biggest provocateurs of the period by standing tradition on its head in the pseudo-medieval *Ubu Roi*, he began with serious recognition and study of medieval art.

Medieval prints had clearly caught the attention of avant-garde writers and artists. Even before the publication of this journal dedicated entirely to folk images, Léon Bloy had published similar works – based on medieval models – in the more literary *Le Mercure de France* (Fig. 2.4).[182] Assuming that medieval *imagiers* were unschooled, writers Gourmont, Jarry, and Bloy created their own works, confident that their dedication to the ideal of medieval art would make up for any lack of formal artistic training.[183] *Le Mercure de France* also published stories and texts that furthered the notion of the innocent, success-scorning medieval artist, while Albert Robida portrayed

L'ymagier

Tome Premier

PARIS
9, Rue de Varenne

2.3   Emile
Bernard, Cover
page of
*L'Ymagier* 1
(October 1894)

*imagiers* in a variety of texts (see Fig. 7.8).[184] In 1892, 'Le Livret de l'Imagier,' a column written by Gourmont and Yvanhoé Rambosson, vividly portrayed the 'naive and glorious *imagier*,' who, though living in the Renaissance, has yet managed to 'conserve in his heart the principle of the Middle Ages, the ardent spiritualism of Gothic art, the hatred of materialism and of the new school's pastichicized classicism!'[185] If artists had salvaged their faith and purity in the midst of the pagan Renaissance, so too, the authors implied, could the contemporary artist living in the materialist and positivist fin de siècle.

According to these *topoi*, the medieval *imagier* and the *Primitif* had rescued art from materialism. All of this had begun to change, however, with the dawn of the Renaissance. A severe blow was dealt to the spiritual role of the artist and art began its inevitable decline. As Bloy's character Marchenoir put it, perhaps one day it would be possible to admit that 'the so-called religious painting of the Renaissance' was as calamitous for Christianity as

Luther himself.[186] In a letter to the Nabi Jan Verkade, Denis vowed that if he had been born in Florence at the time of Savonarola (1452–1498), he would certainly have defended the medieval aesthetic against 'the invasion of pagan classicism': 'I would have been one of those pious latecomers, faithful to the sacred traditions of the past, for whom the new ideas signaled an imminent decadence.'[187]

According to the popular myth, the painter-monk, like the *imagier* and the *Primitif*, saw his art as an extension of his spiritual activity. Throughout most of the nineteenth century, the Italian *Primitif* Fra Angelico had been upheld as the paradigmatic artist-monk.[188] Denis, Huysmans and Péladan celebrated Fra Angelico as an innocent, a 'painter-priest' whose frescoes embodied the naive faith of the Middle Ages.[189] Among the hundreds of works on display at the Salon of 1882, viewers encountered Albert Maignan's *Le sommeil de Fra-Angelico*. The artist having fallen asleep, his work is completed by two angels, who add the finishing touches to his canvas. In this painting, as in Puvis's *Inspiration Chrétienne*, Fra Angelico – the epitome of the *Primitif* painter-monk – receives his artistic revelations directly from God's messengers.

In December 1905, Denis wrote an article for the reactionary journal *L'Occident*; it discussed the late Charles-Marie Dulac (1865–1898), commonly regarded as a latter-day Fra Angelico. Dulac, who had converted to Catholicism and lived in monasteries, had exhibited regularly at the Salon du Champs-de-Mars and the Salon des Indépendants.[190] This artist, claimed his admirer Huysmans, 'cherished poverty, scorned fame, ate like a hermit, slept when he could find a monastic bed and painted barely for himself and all for God.'[191] Dulac stood in sharp contrast to the economically motivated modern artist; Huysmans described him as a direct descendent of the medieval creator.[192] In beginning plans to assemble an artistic community attached to his monastery at Ligugé, Huysmans had considered Dulac as a founding member.[193] The young artist's sudden death in 1898 hampered these plans, though they further solidified his angelic reputation.

For nineteenth-century artists, the medieval painter-monk lived under seemingly ideal creative conditions: convinced of his faith, free from economic worries, detached from the public by the walls of the cloister and dedicated to a community that sustained him and from which he drew sustenance, the medieval painter-monk, they felt, had only to please God. While Maignan may have depicted Fra Angelico in peaceful slumber, artists of the fin de siècle awakened him, claiming him as a model for their own activities.

### The avant-garde artist as painter-monk

Artists of the Symbolist movement often admired the formal style of the medieval artist; they also passionately envied his social position as part of a collective artistic brotherhood formed by monastery, guild or workshop. In their understanding, the artistic brotherhood fostered anonymity by dis- couraging the success of individual members. Indeed, artists' groups such as the Nazarenes had their mythic origins in the Middle Ages. They kept alive the early nineteenth-century dream of the artistic brotherhood, to which they gave new importance in the fin de siècle.[194] The Symbolist journal *La Plume*, for example, advertised the founding of an artists' colony in 1897, declaring that all artists must come together in a spirit of cooperation and unite against materialism in favor of a simple way of life.[195] Huysmans's

1903 novel *L'Oblat* also read like an advertisement for artistic confraternities, extolling the virtues of monastic brotherhoods.

In addition to these movements and those of the Nabis and the Rose+Croix, both Van Gogh and Bernard dreamed of founding artistic communities, the latter suggesting that Gauguin would have to serve as the 'Abbot.'[196] Bernard wrote several letters describing his plans for 'Les Anonymes,' an artistic society dedicated to joint production, 'not glory, not commerce, not reputation.'[197] In an 1899 letter to Huysmans, Bernard named several artists devoted to this project, including Denis, Roussel, Bonnard, Vuillard and Sérusier.[198]

Huysmans went beyond envisioning such an artistic brotherhood; he established one. In January of 1899 he wrote to Bernard of his frustrated desire to 'begin a colony of Christian artists, Benedictine oblates, in the shadow of the old cloister that remains there [Ligugé].'[199] Attracting oblates, secular Catholics who lived or worked near a monastery without taking the vows that would bind them to the time-consuming and physically demanding obligations of prayer and fasting required of monks, seemed more feasible to Huysmans than convincing artists to become monks.[200] He had been dreaming of living in 'an easy-going order […] a world of scholars and writers' since his conversion to Catholicism in 1892. In fact, he and his friend Gustave Boucher had taken a number of active steps toward establishing a committed group of Catholic writers and artists and talented priests who would live together in conjunction with a medieval abbey or monastery. To this end, he visited Saint-Wandrille, Fiancey, Saint-Maur, Dourgne, Solesmes and Ligugé.[201]

After much planning, Huysmans hit on the idea of assembling a community of oblates, who would have more time than monks to dedicate to art. In 1898, he purchased a plot of land at Ligugé, near Dijon, and with an architect he planned a house – La Maison Notre-Dame – that would function as a communal home with a first floor for Huysmans and a second floor of guest rooms for other oblates.[202] Huysmans invited many of his writer friends to reside there, among them Paul Morice, Louis Le Cardonnel, Paul Claudel, Louis Massignon and the painter Georges Rouault. Rouault, who remained there for two years, described the spirit of the community:

> We were a few friends who formed a little group around Huysmans, and we tried to lay the foundation for artistic and intellectual work that would be dedicated and selfless. Huysmans wanted to bring together men who, having abandoned the farce of Paris, would count neither on money nor on influence […] It was a rule of the group to shun publicity, as well as everything that would ordinarily flatter one's vanity.[203]

Huysmans remembered his days at Ligugé, surrounded by like-minded artists and in constant contact with the monks and oblates who lived there, as the 'happiest of his life.'[204]

The monastery or artistic religious community exerted an enormous attraction on a generation discouraged by the individualism and materialism of modern life. Several of the Nabi artists shared this intense identification with the painter-monk. Like their medieval predecessors, they decorated churches and were attracted to monastic life. As a teenager, Denis believed that he had been called by God to repair and adorn Christian churches:

And then – oh it would be so beautiful – I would erect in the middle of profane Paris a sumptuous chapel, which my brothers and I would dedicate ourselves to decorating with paintings, frescoes, panels, predellas, lunettes [...] And each year our artistic-religious society would come to hear mass with a canvas in hand [...] the exhibition would end with a second mass in our church![205]

In 1900, Denis began his first commission for the Jesuit church of Sainte Marguerite in Vésinet, drawing heavily on the influence of Fra Angelico.[206] The sweet, graceful figures, pastel palette and cool landscapes of Denis's work recall Angelico's San Marco frescoes.

Beginning in 1904 – after the Nabis had ceased to function as an artistic unit – Paul Sérusier also undertook a series of decorations for the church baptistry in Châteauneuf du Faou.[207] In these works, he employed the Beuron method, a system of mathematical laws and artistic canons developed by Father Didier Lenz, a former student of the German Nazarenes. Lenz, founder of a monastery at Beuron, Germany, believed that a set of universal laws formed the foundation of all great artistic works.[208] In September 1892, two other Nabi artists, Jan Verkade and Mogens Ballin, embarked on a trip to Italy, where they spent long periods in Catholic monasteries.[209] When they reached Fiesole, Ballin (born of an Orthodox Jewish family) decided to convert. At a Franciscan monastery in that city he received religious instruction from monks and was baptized. In November of the following year, Verkade made his pilgrimage to the monastery of Beuron, becoming a novice in June 1894; he spent the reminder of his life there. On several occasions, Sérusier was tempted to join him at the monastery.[210]

While not all artists took their emulation of the painter-monk to the extreme of pronouncing monastical vows, the ideal of the medieval artistic community often lay behind plans for communal production. Collaborative projects such as the work created by the Nabis for the Symbolist theater (including productions of plays by Maurice Maeterlinck, Remy de Gourmont, Henrik Ibsen and Paul Laforgue) encouraged comparison between the Nabi artists and their humble predecessors.[211] In a letter written to Sérusier, Verkade alluded to the desire for communal production envisioned by the Nabis. He blamed the inability to achieve this goal on journalists, who singled out artists in accordance with the strategy of dealers: 'That would have been the goal of those whom I call Nabis. But the search for personality, the invention of journalism, dispersed all this beautiful power.'[212] As Verkade noted, the art trade depended in part on the production of unique, recognizable artists. Coverage of exhibits in the art press, too, tended to focus on individuals. Jointly authored creations conflicted with the 'star' system at work in both the art market and art criticism. By this period, however, the painter-monk, the emblem of communal production, had nevertheless come to have a distinct allure, to which few artists, dealers or buyers were immune.

## The fin-de-siècle artist as *Primitif*

Many artists – and the critics who lauded them – used a variety of strategies and approaches to align themselves with their medieval predecessors. References to modern artists often made use of loaded terms, descriptions, titles and techniques associated with the Middle Ages. As we have seen, some artists attempted to create alternative living conditions, forming 'brotherhoods' that would bring them closer to the medieval ideal. It is important to acknowledge, however, that in their emulation of the medieval artist, they privileged a very select set of characteristics associated with the 'medieval.' Like all appropriations of the past, theirs was a creative reinterpretation. In addition to social factors, they highlighted the formal and social attributes that best paralleled those of the *modern* artist, including naiveté, humility, flattened form, non-naturalistic color, etc. They 'rewrote' the image of Gothic art, eliminating from their story those aspects in conflict with their own ideals.

There had always been a taste for medieval subjects at the Salons, such as those produced year after year by Academicians like Laurens or Maignan.[213] By the fin de siècle, lugubrious historical subjects had given way to mystical Christian themes or to paintings showing devotees in churches.[214] The trend was for a more subjective and less 'documentary' interpretation of the Middle Ages (Fig. 2.5). Moreover, in the fin de siècle, artists intentionally set out to create medievalizing techniques or forms. Works such as Jacques Aymer de la Chevalerie's *Sainte Radegonde* (Salon of 1899), with its frontal symmetry and miniaturist townscape, was clearly intended to mimic the 'hieratic' and 'naive' aspects of the newly popular *Primitif* painters.[215] At the Salon du Champs-de-Mars in 1896, Armand Point exhibited his *Avril*, a 'fresco painting made according to the tradition of the *Primitifs*.'

By adopting pre-industrial techniques and by upholding and referencing a system of artistic production that was decidedly anti-modern, artists hoped to endow their work with a kind of 'purity.' In both their choice of 'medieval' sources, as well as the very formal elements that they borrowed, such artists were particularly discriminating. They emphasized those qualities that accorded with and justified their own pictorial style, while they largely discarded others (such as the hyper-real detail of many medieval manuscripts) that found no echo in Symbolist aesthetics. In this sense, they contrasted with Academic artists working with medievalizing subjects or props, such as Jean-Paul Laurens or Charles Dondelet. They consistently highlighted those traits of Symbolist works – naiveté, crudeness, flatness, non-naturalistic color – that matched their own vision of the medieval artists as humble, anonymous, devout seers. The actual historical functioning of medieval works, their reception and visual effect on the medieval viewer, were not of primary concern to the Symbolist painters.

In their translation of medieval images, Symbolist painters often emptied their works of detail. While in the medieval work lack of detail was often the product of material or financial limitations (the crude techniques of the

2.5   Ruck,
'Mélissinde – *Le
vitrail est fermé, te
dis-je, plus
d'effrois!*' From *La
Princesse
lointaine*, 1910

woodcut or pilgrim badges intended for a popular audience, for example), it became a conscious choice in the work of certain Symbolists. Eradication of minutiae signaled the artist's renunciation of the sensual, the temporal.[216] By forcing the medieval image through an ever more purifying sieve, the Symbolists hoped to produce works even less worldly than those of their medieval forerunners. At the same time, the elimination of detail confused the boundary between medieval style and modern; it evoked at once the aesthetic of medieval art and the new art form of the poster. While such simplifications were in part employed to 'cleanse' Symbolist art of its material associations, they also served to tie Symbolist aesthetics to the flattened designs of posters, a largely commercial medium. By drawing on medieval precedent in their simplifications, the Symbolists could distance themselves from the commercial associations of their own poster-derived style (see Fig. 1.3).[217]

For examples of pictorial 'sacrifice' and renunciation we can look at paintings such as Denis's *Ascent to Calvary* (1889) (Fig. 2.6) or *Procession under the Trees* (1892). Details of figures and clothing have been pared away, leaving simplified shapes dispersed throughout the canvas. Texture and surface detail (two pictorial elements fundamental to a sense of *trompe-l'oeil* realism) have been severely curtailed. Denis believed such works to be the visual equivalent of ascetic Catholicism: 'An art that is made up of sacrifices, from which sensuality is excluded, that prefers expression through form to expression through color, such an art holds in Aesthetics the place of Cartesianism in philosophy [...] and matches the magnificence and severe ordinances of Catholic dogma.'[218] Bernard also aimed to purge his work of materialism, employing the pictorial 'sacrifice' associated with the medieval artist. In a letter to his fellow artist Emile Schuffenecker he criticized Gauguin for failing to do the same: 'Where is the grandeur of sacrifice? What is color? A seduction of the senses; can you build an art with that?'[219]

The work of many Symbolists took on medieval flavor by borrowing formal themes and styles – a preference for flatness and simplification over *trompe l'oeil*, the adoption of tempera painting, references to Gothic statuary or stained glass – as in the *cloisonniste* works of Bernard.[220] A recent study by Vojtech Jirat-Wasiutynski and H. Travers Newton, Jr. argues that Gauguin, too, consciously modeled his working methods on those of pre-Renaissance artists: his use of flat, chalky surfaces was done in emulation of *Primitif* murals. Gauguin's techniques and materials, including the addition of glue to his paint and even the use of pounced transfer drawings, all served to give his paintings the appearance of frescoes, distinguishing them from the slick, skilled paintings of his Academic contemporaries. In drawing on these media and methods, Gauguin aligned himself with the naive masters of the past, while adding a distinctly 'barbaric' and 'primitive' note to his paintings.[221]

Formally, certain Symbolists often made reference to the manuscripts and illustrated books created by the medieval illuminator (and paid homage to them in journals like *L'Ymagier*). These artists were well aware that many of

2.6  Maurice Denis, *Montée au Calvaire (Ascent to Calvary)*, 1889

the finest illustrated works had been made within monasteries. Interest in medieval manuscripts, both their imagery and their style, had been fostered by the works of William Morris and his circle at the Kelmscott Press.[222] By the 1890s, artists like Grasset and Carlos Schwabe had adopted many of Morris's techniques, producing their own version of illuminated books. In his 'Définition du néo-traditionnisme,' Denis described his love for medieval manuscripts: 'I dream of ancient missals with rhythmic borders, of sumptuous initials ornamenting Church song books, of the first wood engravings – that correspond in their preciousness and delicacy to our literary complexity.'[223] While drawing on the format of the manuscript, artists like Denis eliminated the awkward perspectival schemes found within them. More importantly, they negated a crucial characteristic of the medieval manuscript – its exclusivity and uniqueness.[224] They borrowed formal elements from this most private of media for their prints produced in multiples. They succeeded in tempering a machine-made art (the poster) through allusion to the handmade medieval work.[225]

In 1889 Denis began his illustrations for the poet Paul Verlaine's *Sagesse*, a lyrical poem about the poet's conversion to Catholicism.[226] In a later article, Denis stated that he had created his *Sagesse* illustrations in 'the style of *ancien bois*.'[227] Images like *Shining Hope* (1888–1911) and *O Vous, comme un qui boite* (1889), with their simplified, 'naive' drawing, their religious imagery and their grainy, unrefined surface, seem to capture the awkward urgency of early medieval woodcuts (Fig. 2.7).[228] Denis was clearly influenced by the crude hatching and compressed spaces of Gothic woodcuts. It was precisely for their medieval flavor that the poet Adolphe Retté praised these drawings: 'From the point of view of technique, many [*Sagesse* illustrations] are excellent; in contemplating such border-designs, such *culs-de-lampe*, one thinks automatically of certain missals of the Middle Ages, masterpieces by anonymous *imagiers*.'[229] In Denis's work, artistic conventions of the woodcut are highlighted, exaggerated, but not directly imitated. The language of medieval prints seems to have been updated, translated into a modern idiom, a new aesthetic.

To borrow a phrase from Norman Cantor's best-selling book on twentieth-century medievalists, many Symbolist painters paid homage to medieval artists while simultaneously *inventing* them. The artists they admired were as much a product of their imagination as of historical reality. To answer the harsh critical judgements leveled against their style, they 'remade' medieval art to validate late nineteenth-century values. Their preferred stylistic conventions of flatness, simplification and pure colors were singled out in medieval works.[230] Consciously renouncing the techniques of *trompe-l'oeil*, chiaroscuro and perspective, they regarded the medieval artist's ignorance of these methods, too, as a deliberate choice. They did not acknowledge that the medieval artist's 'errors' in perspective or realism were at times the result of inability rather than intentional distortion. As a result, their works resemble those of the medieval era not only because artists actually drew on these sources, but because they 'found' their own style ready-made in works created centuries earlier, resulting in a creative reworking of traditional sources. Such selective appropriations of the medieval are hardly new, nor should they be seen in a negative light: the interpretation of the past by the present is an inherent component of medievalism, as it is of most new cultural production.[231]

What distinguishes the medievalism of the Symbolists is their far greater receptivity to the aesthetics of artists working prior to the Renaissance.

2.7   Maurice Denis, illustration for *Sagesse* by Paul Verlaine, 1889

These aesthetics were often crude, unclassical and based on an artistic sensibility at odds with Academic principles. In contrast to earlier groups equally committed to 'reviving' medieval art – the Nazarenes for example or the Pre-Raphaelites – artists of the fin de siècle were far more radical in abandoning post-Renaissance rules of space, color, proportion and illusionism. The heightened expressivity of medieval art surely gave fin-de-siècle artists license to emphasize such elements in their own work, combining a variety of sources (medieval, non-Western, popular) into something new and powerful.

    If their engagement with medieval art did not release artists like Denis from the economic realities of their time, it did serve a liberating function.

They came to medieval art not as scholars, or not only as scholars, but as impassioned viewers. They rediscovered aesthetic pleasures, such as the smoldering color fields of stained glass, that had been closed off by the prevailing discourse of the French Academy.[232] If the emulation of medieval art and medieval artistic production could not completely transform the practice of the Symbolists, it kept alive the notion of a structure and aesthetics alternate to prevailing trends. Their goal of reviving the social value and connection of the medieval artist may have been impossible to realize, but it was no less sincere. Artists such as Denis, Gauguin and Bernard used the model of medieval art to help them achieve goals that are truly modern. These include the creation of a language directly in communication with viewers, without need for the intermediary of accumulated knowledge, exploration of the materiality of the work of art and the expression of the artist's direct response to subjects without a premeditated list of forms in which to couch their vision.

It was thus to their great delight that critics began mentioning the term *Primitif* in discussing the work of numerous Symbolist artists. Armand Point made the comparison explicit in his article on 'Les Primitifs et les Symbolistes.'[233] Since the 1870s, Puvis de Chavannes had been repeatedly hailed as a new 'Giotto,' a modern day *Primitif*.[234] Few who spoke at the banquet held in his honor at the Hôtel Continental on 16 January 1895 neglected to compare him to the Italian master. Péladan even went so far as to claim that Puvis was more *Primitif* than the *Primitifs*:

> If one hangs a Puvis next to the *Grape Harvest* of Gozzoli, one would discover not only their relationship, but also that it is Puvis who, of the two, seems to be the *Primitif*. What he paints has neither place nor date; it is of everywhere and for always, a *Primitif* abstraction, a poetic spiritual dream, an ode to eternal humanity.[235]

Despite Puvis's own denial of a mystical bent in his art, critics continued to see his work in such spiritual terms, aligning him with the pious masters of the past.[236] Critics likewise praised the 'naive robustness' of Sérusier's work and the 'primitive beauty' of Denis's art.[237] In turn, Denis compared Sérusier's Châteauneuf murals to the work of the French *Primitifs*, inserting him into an established French lineage.[238] Two contemporary artists in particular, Eugène Grasset and André (or Andhré) des Gachons, were especially favored by Symbolist critics, who depicted them as revivers of the French spirit and the Christian Age of Innocence because of their vaguely chivalrous subject matter, replete with galloping horses, languid princesses and young knights.[239] *La Plume* devoted an entire issue to Grasset, who was celebrated for 'making the chivalrous past live again.'[240] Grasset and his artistic collaborator, Pierre-Victor Galland, 'had begun to resuscitate the traditions of the great masters of medieval works.'[241] Camille Lemonnier characterized Grasset as an 'artist from the epochs of prayer and faith, illuminating through terrestrial images the coming of Paradise, expressing the appeals to God at the heart of all human actions.'[242] Repeatedly compared to a medieval monk and cleric, des Gachons was lauded for bringing together: 'a curious group of artists and

2.8  Andhré des Gachons, Cover page of *L'Album des Légendes*, 1894

poets who are dedicated to the delicious art of making our past come alive again, of making the legends flourish once more, of carrying on the traditions of the *neo-Primitifs*.'[243] In his cover for the July 1884 issue of *L'Album des légendes* (Fig. 2.8), des Gachons gives visual form to such concepts of revivalism. The modern young woman, wearing a dress of Belle Epoque design, imaginatively enters the Middle Ages through her reading: journals like *L'Album des légendes*, historical novels or modern reprints of medieval texts.

While critics were eager to portray these artists as *neo-Primitifs*, their 'resuscitation' of medieval art was derived from serious study of extant medieval works that had become newly accessible, as we shall see in the following chapter, through public exhibits and displays. The journals of these artists testify to their frequent visits to collections and museums and their firsthand examination of paintings, prints, and decorative arts.[244] The prominence of such displays made the *Primitifs* accessible not only to the Symbolists, but to a far larger audience, which eagerly consumed them.

## Packaging the *Primitifs*

By the 1890s, the mythic figure of the *Primitif* had caught the imagination of the bourgeois audience as well as that of members of the official arts network. Emulation of the medieval artist gave rise to a paradox: while the adoption of 'medieval' paradigms aided artists' retreat from the marketplace, it increased demand for their works. The retreat into the past – perhaps to the chagrin of the artists themselves – was also a successful marketing strategy.[245]

Critics such as Armand Dayot had predicted that such *Primitif* fever would expand beyond avant-garde circles and enter the official Salons. As early as 1884, he took to task the artist Ernest Ange Duez for wanting to be the new Fra Angelico. Commenting on *Saint François d'Assise: Miracle des Roses*, Dayot warned:

> Duez will never be a mystic, and it is in vain that he tries to become the Fra Angelico of his time [...] With your solid and far-reaching talent, be the painter of lucid and powerful things from our period. Give up this peculiar idea of wanting to revive these sick and hallucinatory scenes of hysteria and catalepsy for our modern eyes so filled with light and so fond of subjects borrowed from human history or natural life.[246]

Yet by 1890, dealers gladly lavished the term *Primitif* on painters like Charles-Marie Dulac, who was dubbed the modern-day 'Angelico' after a successful one-man show at Vollard's Gallery: 'Following the example of Fra Angelico, before taking up his brushes he would kneel in prayer awaiting inspiration.'[247] Even dealers, whose earnings depended on maximizing profit, began to echo the awed and reverential tone of Huysmans and Bloy. Huysmans himself revealed a canny understanding of just how marketable the *Primitifs* had become. In contrast to outrageously priced paintings in Paris, the liquidated treasures of old convents seemed like bargains:

> I see that in Hamburg one can still find *Primitifs* at far less costly prices! Here the prices are crazy, absolutely prohibitive. It is true that there are quite a few fakes – it is Zola who buys those – and at top prices. In contrast, bibelots from churches are still affordable. I bought heaps, old St Sacrement, censers, chappes – I carried off what I could from the liquidation of a convent—And relics!![248]

No one was more aware of the 'craze' for the medieval artist than Henri Bouchot, chief organizer of the 1904 Exposition des Primitifs français. Conscious of the market's thirst for the *Primitifs*, Bouchot declared that a loftier goal than commerce had inspired the organizers of the exhibit: 'The Exposition of the French *Primitifs* has not been conceived only to make certain antique dealers wealthy: its goal serves a higher and nobler purpose.'[249] As we have noted, the show celebrated these 'naive' artists for their contribution to the artistic heritage of France, yet by vaunting these artists – among them Jean Bourdichon, Jean Fouquet, Nicolas Froment and Jean Clouet – it created a new set of artistic 'stars' whose works would henceforth command far greater prices. By 1904, the term *Primitif* had become serious business, as had Gothic manuscripts, tapestries, stained glass, paintings and missals in the earlier part of the century. They were avidly acquired, often by aristocratic patrons.[250]

*Primitif* 'fever' also helped lead to the establishment of centers like Haute-Claire, an artists' colony whose main objective was to boost the sagging decorative arts industry. Crafts produced at Haute-Claire, made by hand, were imbued with the allure of 'authenticity.' Their commercial status was obscured; those at the colony 'lived freely and each in his own way.'[251] Indeed, the place served as a virtual retreat for members of the Symbolist movement, drawing painters and poets such as Louis Anquetin, André-Ferdinand Hérold, Jean Moréas, Odilon Redon, Jean Delville, Camille Mauclair and Joséphin Péladan. Located in a former cloister in the Loire valley, Haute-Claire had been founded in 1896 by the Rose+Croix artist Armand Point.[252] Deriving inspiration from William Morris, the craftspeople at Haute-Claire produced paintings, sculpture, tapestries, furniture, stained glass, enamels and a wide array of other items. Point, for example, was listed in the exhibition catalog as a 'painter, enameler, engraver, etc.' The works produced at Haute-Claire were medieval in style; one such is *Le Portique de la Musique*, a triptych co-created by several Haute-Claire students.

In 1899 the Symbolist poet Stuart Merrill wrote the catalog essay for an exhibition of Haute-Claire works. Throughout the catalog, Merrill compared Haute-Claire artisans to medieval craftsmen. He also declared the colony part of a larger national effort to 'reclaim the artistic traditions of the race': 'It is the French Middle Ages that Armand Point attempts to link with the tradition of the art industry, without, however, neglecting the grace, finesse and elegance offered by the Italian Renaissance.'[253] The tradition of the humble medieval artist was not only praised for its anonymity and beauty, but increasingly as a patriotic contribution to national industry.

In 1899, a large Haute-Claire exhibition took place at the Galerie Georges Petit, which catered especially to the nouveau riche.[254] The same locale had served to introduce the work of the painter-priest Charles-Marie Dulac. Hardly a religious setting – neither cloister nor church – the gallery resembled nothing so much as the Bon Marché, the luxurious department store of the bourgeoisie.[255] The opulent draperies and graceful staircases served to obscure the commerical nature of the department store product and they served a similar function at the Galerie Georges Petit. The works of the modern day *Primitif*, viewed in this elegant setting, could disavow their status as commercial products while appealing to a wealthy clientele. Astute critics did not ignore this phenomenon, in art as in literature, as Léon Blum sharply pointed out in a critique of Huysmans's *L'Oblat*:

It is in the alliance of art and monastical life that [Huysmans] seeks the rich future of the Church […] He would like to found an artistic convent, a luxurious house for God […] But in the history of the Middle Ages we see nothing of the kind […] While Durtal signs his books and sees in art a luxurious present, he promises his Benedictine abbey a prodigious success. A serious contradiction whose mark will be carried by the book and that will spoil its action and its unity.[256]

The artists may have felt as though they had escaped the material world by withdrawing to monasteries, but their products were enormously successful and brought them fame in the world outside.

If these artists were caught in the conundrum of helping to popularize the very sources that they valued for their seemingly 'unmarketable' qualities, it is symptomatic of the period. For these members of an emerging or proto-consumer culture, the dead-end cynicism and mentality of 'selling-out,' so prevalent in our own day, was not yet commonplace.[257] Surely there were many who still believed an alternative structure of art-making did, or could, exist, and chose medieval models as a way to make it so. We should remember that when artists like Manet or Huysmans or critics like Blum turned their sharp eyes and bitter wit on the 'double-bind' of the artist, they were prescient, even shockingly prophetic. Yet such observations were in no way typical of their time. While, as we have shown, a language for articulating these concerns had emerged, it was by no means widely spoken. The attraction that artists felt for medieval art was complex, not only a response to growing trends in the art market, but also a genuine desire to learn from the visual and social practice of these earlier creators.

This desire reached not only artists and collectors, but the wider public. While collectors could hunt down extant works in dilapidated cathedrals and monasteries, the bourgeois consumer could follow the new-found celebrity of these figures through journals like the *Gazette des Beaux-Arts*, *L'Illustration* and *Le Figaro illustré*, which featured reproductions of their works. As these paintings entered museums, they simultaneously entered the middle-class living room, in the form of photographs, drawings and tear-out reproductions of new acquisitions. While the Symbolists had fought hard to protect their beloved *Primitifs* from the grip of consumerism, the walls they erected were not as solid as they had hoped. In truth, the spaces of *Primitif* fever – the museums, the national exhibits, the cloister, the parlor and the Symbolist soirée – had begun to intersect and to overlap. We explore this mingling of the private and the public appropriation of medieval art, its collection and consumption, in our next chapter.

**3**

# From the living room to the museum and back again:
# the institutionalization of medieval art

It is a consequence of this fatal spirit of imitation that our interiors, where we need light in order to work, are obscured by the immoderate use of colored stained glass; that our small hearths are cluttered by great andirons in forged metal, made for the vast mantels of feudal fireplaces; that the contours of our seats, rather than accommodating the supple graces of contemporary women, with their lightly pleated garments, take on the rigid form of the high cathedrals of the Middle Ages and transform the fin-de-siècle *Parisienne* into a Blanche of Castille in spite of herself, making her into a penitent château-dweller.[258]

'La Maison moderne – Etudes de décoration et d'ameublement' (1886)

Writing in the pages of *La Revue Illustrée*, this observer noted that the fascination with medieval objects had permeated both the private dwellings and the public spaces of fin-de-siècle France. Indeed, as our last two chapters have shown, by the turn of the century bourgeois Parisians were well acquainted with medieval art. While newly-opened medieval museums abounded with works from every epoch of the Middle Ages, well-to-do property owners often transformed their homes into medieval castles, complete with works of stained glass, tapestry and suits of armor (Fig. 3.1). Novelist Emile Zola provides an excellent example of this trend, all the more surprising given his well-publicized dedication to modern art and his avowed anti-clericalism.[259] This chapter raises several important questions related to the intersection of private and public appropriation of medieval objects in this period. What was the relationship between the antiquary of old and the modern collector who filled apartments with medieval treasures and modern replicas of Gothic masterpieces? How did such private consumption reflect and influence larger public displays of medieval objects in the period? And at what level did popular consumption of medieval objects connect with scholarly research and the didactic goals of the national museum? In exploring these questions, this chapter traces the journey of medieval works of art at the end of the nineteenth century, from living rooms to major public displays (museums and World's Fairs) and back to the 'sanctuary' of the private interior.

In late nineteenth-century France, presentations of public medieval collections ranged from the 'objective' and scientific (the Musée de Sculpture

3.1  *Zola dans son cabinet à Médan*, 1887

Comparée at the Trocadéro) to the poetically evocative (the Musée de Cluny). No longer the sole province of the cultivated private collector, medieval works could be seen and enjoyed by a large public. At the same time, acquaintance with medieval works no longer required leaving one's home: developments in printing, including the ability to print lithographs inexpensively and side-by-side with text, produced new high-quality reproductions that were featured in illustrated periodicals, books and catalogs, thus introducing thousands of new viewers to the medieval heritage.[260] The exhibitions, publications, auctions, art-historical discourse and private consumption of medieval works were inherently bound to each other and to the larger bourgeois audience.

Thanks to the growth of the illustrated press and its fascination with celebrities at the end of the nineteenth century, we know a great deal about the private spaces of well-known writers including J.-K. Huysmans, Pierre Loti, Jean Moréas, Anatole France and Emile Zola, all of whom – despite their decidedly different literary affiliations – avidly collected medieval art.[261] The birth of 'at home' photography, in which photographers traveled to artists' homes to capture them in their 'natural' surroundings, allowed the public to see these famous people in their living rooms or studies.[262] Such images were published widely in European and American journals such as *Nos Contemporains*, *L'Illustration* and *Harper's Weekly*. Journalists also interviewed artists at their residences, leading to a vogue for books such as Maurice Guillemot's 1887 *Villégiatures d'artistes* and Jules Huret's

1891 *L'Enquête sur l'évolution littéraire*, which framed their interviews with descriptions of the artists' interior decorations. We thus learn that Huysmans lined his study with medieval wood sculptures, old bronzes, fragments of biblical bas-reliefs, angel statues and engravings by Dürer and Rembrandt,[263] while Pierre Loti threw wild 'fifteenth-century' parties in his Gothic dining room, in which 'there was no stone, no piece of paneling, no detail of architecture, furnishing or ornament that was not of purely fifteenth-century origin' (Fig. 3.2).[264] Jean Moréas, the author of the 1886 'Symbolist manifesto,' lived in the Latin Quarter in a 'house with stained glass and exposed beams, with scarlet ceilings and an oak staircase,' while Anatole France worked at a Gothic table from 'the Faubourg Saint-Antoine or the chapel of Dreux,' while seated on a 'Gothic throne covered with a maze of heraldic devices.'[265] Perhaps most surprising, however, was the public's discovery that Zola, a devout positivist, 'cloistered' himself for most of the year in a 'castle' in Médan, which he crammed with stained-glass windows, suits of armor from various centuries, reliquaries, paintings of saints and medieval tapestries.[266] Like Anatole France, he sat on a 'Gothic throne,' emblazoned with the device *Si Dieu veut, je veulx* (which he adopted as the medieval motto of the Hautecoeur family in his novel *Le Rêve*).

The interior decoration of these bourgeois artists and intellectuals and public reactions to it offer an excellent example of the shifting status of artifacts and display in the late nineteenth century: media coverage of the bourgeois fascination with bibelots was combined with reports about new institutional exhibits, thus blurring the distinction between private and public display and amateur and professional discourse about collecting. The museum collection and exhibition of medieval objects found a counterpart in private homes, where the pleasure and status of aesthetic display (rather than the desire to instruct or educate) motivated the purchaser. The two forms of display – bourgeois interior and museum, private and public – fed each other, increasing attendance at public museums and the production of scholarly tomes, while driving up prices for extant medieval collectibles as well as faux-medieval furniture and *objets d'art*. The scholarly value and cachet of medieval works in turn inspired a renewed interest on the part of collectors and a fashionable craze for medieval decor. Serious scholarship and private collecting began to overlap.

If a large gap seemed to separate the private display of the neo-medieval living room and the public exhibits of the medieval museum, in reality the two spaces were often intertwined. Several of the medieval museums – among them the Musée de Cluny – borrowed their style of display from residences, transforming the public space of the museum into a kind of private living room. In turn, the hodge-podge display of randomly juxtaposed objects, stripped of their original function, was familiar to viewers of both domestic interiors and the well-attended World's Fairs. Much as in today's antiques market, amateur collectors of authentic medieval works (among them writers Anatole France and J.-K. Huysmans) were not always dilettantes, but often seasoned connoisseurs of medieval works and of medieval scholarship.

If this somehow seemed a less 'noble' engagement with the Middle Ages, these decorator-collectors were in good company; the earliest public collections of medieval art in France owed their origins to men of similarly unfailing 'good taste.' Both the medievalesque décor of wealthy apartment dwellers and the medieval museums under the aegis of the Third Republic had their historical roots in the private collections of such impassioned medievalists as Alexandre Lenoir and Alexandre du Sommerard. What began as a private passion – the collection and consumption of medieval works of art – was transformed by the late nineteenth century into an edifying and ennobling search for the origins of French heritage, a journey made accessible to the larger viewing public.

To understand the complex relationship between the production of medieval scholarship and the consumption of medieval works requires familiarity with the bibelot, a nineteenth-century object of predilection. Janell Watson, Rosalind Williams and Rémy Saisselin have studied the extent to which the bibelot (knick-knack, curio, or other collectible) fascinated the bourgeoisie. While each category of object had unique characteristics and value, all of them were united in their logic of display, which was dependent on the capitalist market. Indeed, as Watson has pointed out in a brilliant study of material culture in nineteenth-century

France, bibelots could be distinguished from earlier 'collectibles' by their central qualities of gratuitousness and mobility.[267] Freely exchangeable on the marketplace, bibelots had migrated from their original setting (often churches, palaces or monasteries) to another – the antique store, museum or living room – shedding their original use and intention along the way. To some extent, the logic of the bibelot operated in all of the spaces devoted to medieval works, whether private interior (its most common locale) or public museum. While the art-historical discourse and scholarly discussion surrounding these objects focused, in turn, on their religious, spiritual or communal use value, the pieces themselves were inevitably detached from their origins, available primarily for aesthetic contemplation by artist, connoisseur or bourgeois viewer.

Whether in the living room of Emile Zola or in the halls of the Louvre, the medieval works found there had been removed from their original context. As a result, they should be studied along with the acquisition and display of other kinds of displaced objects. Their de-contextualization was perhaps most evident at the retrospectives of the Expositions Universelles, where the works were divorced from their function and jumbled within the 'fine-arts' section of the Petit Palais. As this chapter will argue, the more historically important the piece, the more it was directly implicated in the market, drawing additional viewers to museums, spawning the purchase of reproductions or inspiring the products of contemporary artists and artisans. An acknowledgment of the ubiquitousness of the bibelot in fin-de-siècle culture underlies much of the discussion in this chapter.

## The museum as collection: the Musée des Monuments français and the Musée de Cluny

From its origins, the collecting of Gothic works in Europe was associated with private consumption. Like the collector of classical antiquities, who blended erudition with an eclectic fascination with *curiosities*, the earliest collectors of medieval works displayed their art for a small circle of intimates.[268] The beginnings of the Gothic Revival in Europe can be traced to the whimsical palace of Strawberry Hill, west of London, built by novelist Horace Walpole in 1749.[269] In contrast to the later 'structural rationalism' of Viollet-le-Duc, Strawberry Hill was medieval neither in its methods of construction nor in its design. Instead, the castle was a kind of theatrical set, with freely assembled pointed arches, pseudo-Gothic chambers and liberally scattered medievalesque furnishings and *objets d'art*. By 1784, the private home had become an attraction; visitors were required to purchase tickets and received a printed guidebook. A similar whimsy characterized James Wyatt's Fonthill Abbey, purchased by novelist William Beckford and sold in 1822.[270] A product of the interest in the 'picturesque' and 'romantic' and in the literary works of the Gothic Revival, Strawberry Hill was related to the tradition of the collector's cabinet, an accumulation of curious objects displayed for private pleasure and amusement. Later, Fonthill Abbey, too, became a tourist attraction.

As Romanticism washed over Europe in the early nineteenth century, many private collectors in France, who shared the picturesque sensibility of Beckford and Walpole, became attracted to the troubadour style. While the troubadour style signified an allegiance to the Restoration and a rejection of the Revolution, it remained largely a phenomenon of private collecting, accompanied by a renewed taste for Gothic costumes, furnishings and objects.[271] At the beginning of the nineteenth century, France offered a particularly hospitable climate for such activities, largely because so many works were on the market or in private hands, snatched up from the widespread destruction of Gothic churches during the anti-clerical rages of the 1790s.[272] In fact, during the formation of the Commission des Monuments Français in the 1790s, thousands of medieval works were confiscated from nobles and churches (including Notre-Dame de Paris, Saint-Germain-des-Près and the Sainte-Chapelle) and deposited in the collections of the Bibliothèque Nationale. In this decade, the library's holdings of French manuscripts increased by over 15 000 works.[273]

The extensive looting and destruction of religious edifices during the Revolution was, ironically, also responsible for the very first public museum with a substantial collection of medieval art, the Musée des Monuments Français.[274] It, too, was linked to the sensibilities and collecting – or rather salvaging – activities of an individual, the artist Alexandre Lenoir. In 1791 Lenoir was appointed guardian of the Petits-Augustins, a former convent used for the storage of religious and aristocratic objects confiscated during the iconoclastic excesses of the Revolution. The museum opened to the public in 1795 as a 'historical and chronological museum' and would remain in operation until 1816, when many of the works were returned to their former owners at the Restoration.[275] Each room or suite of the museum was devoted to a separate century of French sculpture: as the viewer passed from the earlier medieval objects to those of more recent origin, the rooms became successively brighter, symbolizing the passage from the Dark Ages to the Enlightenment. The majority of medieval works – including many tombs and monuments taken from Saint Denis – were assembled in the Salle du 13ième. With its blue-starred vaults and stained-glass windows from Saint Germain-des-Près, the room was described as 'damp' and 'gloomy.' In addition, the museum served as a place for commissioning and displaying new art inspired by the Middle Ages: exhibits of troubadour-genre paintings took place in the courtyard.[276]

The Musée des Monuments Français served a very important function: it protected medieval works even after they had been removed from their original religious context. What had begun as Christian symbols and monuments to God's glory now became national treasures. The works thus underwent a double transformation: stripped of their original intention and function they became exemplary works of art, prized for their beauty and for their contribution to the national heritage. In this manner, such tokens of 'superstition' and 'blind Christian worship,' so abhorrent to the Revolutionary thinkers of Lenoir's generation, were reappropriated. Placing these works in the context of public display not only allowed them to serve a political function, but opened the door to considering them as purely aesthetic objects. They would later come to be seen as such in the museums and in the living rooms of the fin de siècle and even, as we shall see in Chapter 5, within their original church setting. As Susan Pearce notes, such de-contextualization and reassembly is one of the defining characteristics of both public and private collections:

> This is the central paradox of all collected pieces. They are wrenched out of their contexts and become dead to living time and space in order that they may be given an immortality within the collection. They cease to be living goods in the world and become reified thoughts and feelings carefully kept by preservation. They are made to withdraw from daily life in order to enable another order of life to come about.[277]

With its dimly lit, tomb-scattered rooms, the Musée des Monuments Français also partook of a Romantic spirit akin to the private collections and Strawberry Hills of the day.[278] As Francis Haskell has noted, Lenoir's museum revealed a growing fascination with history, with the mores and period details of each epoch. While the museum housed objects from antiquity to the nineteenth century, it was the medieval rooms that had the most profound effect on both casual visitors and later historians, including Jules Michelet, who felt that Lenoir had helped them truly understand the past.[279]

The most important French medieval museum of the nineteenth century, the Musée de Cluny, was the direct heir of the Musée des Monuments Français in many ways. The museum was originally established by the collector Alexandre du Sommerard in July 1834, but after his death in 1842 the collections of Lenoir and du Sommerard were combined according to a proposal by Lenoir's son Albert and turned into a national museum under the direction of du Sommerard's son Edmond. He remained curator from the museum's opening in 1844 until his death in 1885.[280] Set in a former *hôtel de ville* used by the Abbots of Cluny, the museum was very much the product of the Sommerards' Romantic sensibility. Alexandre's goal, expressed in his motto, *More majorum*, was to make the past live again, to keep the ways of his ancestors.[281] He wanted to create a space that would make medieval history seem real and tangible. He and his son, who followed in his father's footsteps, inaugurated a new concept of the museum, which rested on ensemble display. A wide variety of objects from the Middle Ages, both utilitarian and artistic, were displayed throughout the halls of the museum, itself a Gothic mansion. Different media from the same period, including furniture, sculpture, tapestries, suits of armor, paintings, ivories and enamels, were often placed in a single room, creating a kind of total environment in which the visitor could imaginatively occupy the role of lord or knight (Fig. 3.3).[282] Indeed, visitors like Jules Janin felt as if they had 'stepped into the Middle Ages.'[283] We might apply a term like 'fetishistic collecting'[284] to Cluny, whose aim was to make the medieval past live again rather than to serve either as a display of national pride or as a kind of object library for scholars.

*3.3  Chambre dite de François 1er à l'Hôtel de Cluny*

The interest in evoking local color – begun with Lenoir and taken much further with du Sommerard – might be seen to have its apogee and true successor in the 'living museum,' displays like the *Paris en 1400* and *Vieux Paris* exhibits at the 1900 World's Fair, which featured costumed minstrels and artisans.[285]

Growing steadily, the Musée de Cluny obtained its most famous possession in 1882: the *Dame à la Licorne* tapestries (Fig. 3.4).[286] In fact, a number of its most renowned works entered the collection in the last quarter of the nineteenth century.[287] Du Sommerard's son Edmond died in 1885, whereupon the museum was placed under the charge of Alfred Darcel and the Commission des Monuments Historiques, thus securing its place as a national treasure (a recent name change – 'Le Musée du Moyen Age' – has further elevated the du Sommerards' project). By the 1880s, visitors to the museum included a 'large majority of artisans and workers.' As it was open every day but Monday, the working class could visit on Sundays.[288] For its many visitors, Cluny undoubtedly served as a peaceful refuge from the modern city. Surrounded by hand-crafted works, viewers lost themselves in the hushed sanctity of the rooms. This display functioned as a transitional

3.4   *La Dame à la Licorne*: *A mon seul désir*, 1484–1500

space between the private collector's 'castle' and the medieval museums established under the Third Republic.

If aesthetes like du Sommerard turned their living rooms into museums, the Musée de Cluny turned the museum into a living room. While the mixed media display of the Cluny rooms had as its aim the revival of the past, its logic nevertheless had much in common with the eclectic display of the collector's parlor (see Fig. 3.3). The rooms of Cluny serve to remind us that interest in the medieval past was just as 'authentically' inspired by a craze for decorating as by a study of extant medieval artifacts. As both the Musée des Monuments Français and the Musée de Cluny reveal, the history of public and private collections of medieval works were deeply interwoven. While public sites for the display of medieval art had been established by the late eighteenth century, private collectors of medieval works continued to expand their holdings. Museums benefitted from private collectors and borrowed ideas from their methods of display, while collectors profited from the legitimizing discourse of scholars and museums to authenticate their medieval pieces.

The *Gazette des Beaux-Arts*, founded in 1859 by Charles Blanc with the explicit aim of 'enlightening amateurs and keeping them informed about developments throughout the world,' often included lengthy articles about private collectors and their holdings.[289] This was not, of course, the first periodical to deal with art, art history, or art collection, but it was one of the first to target a mainstream audience. Where earlier periodicals such as *Les Annales archéologiques* (founded in 1844) or *Le Bulletin archéologique* (the official publication of the Comité Historique des Arts et Monuments) were written largely by and for a sophisticated and scholarly audience or were associated with official organizations, *La Gazette des Beaux-Arts* was conceived specifically for the amateur.[290]

In March 1891, for example, readers could learn about the Strauss collection recently donated to the Musée de Cluny by the Baron Nathaniel de Rothschild.[291] Begun by the conductor Isaac Strauss, the collection consisted of a great deal of medieval Judaica, including furniture, tapestries, jewelry, manuscripts and drawings, undoubtedly functioning in part to 'prove' the positive Jewish contribution to France's medieval heritage (a contribution disputed by many historians, writers and political figures).[292] While museums clearly gained precious holdings in this manner, the collectors also benefitted by joining the artistic pantheon of men like Lenoir and du Sommerard. Those who amassed coherent groups of objects – collections instead of a random assortment of objects – were praised for their taste and their erudition.

One of the most important private collections of medieval art, the Spitzer collection, was well publicized, especially in the *Gazette des Beaux-Arts*, which published a full-scale catalog devoted to it. In 1878 Frederic Spitzer had opened the Musée des Arts Industriels in his private Paris hôtel. The March 1890 issue detailed the extensive holdings of ivories, goldwork, religious objects and tapestries featured in the collection.[293] The catalog was compiled by important scholars of the period, including the deeply respected Emile Molinier (who had played a large role in the medieval retrospective of the 1889 World's Fair). A work of notable erudition, the catalog aimed for the kind of 'objective' and 'genealogical' approach that had come to characterize Republican museums. The full catalog retailed for 250 francs, but the truly discriminating consumer could purchase a deluxe version for 3000 francs. Thanks in part to the splendor of the catalog, the sale of Spitzer's collection (in 1893) brought in over 9 million francs.[294] The publication of such catalogs benefitted both parties. Collectors gained an aura of respect for their taste and the prices of their works increased as a result of professional appraisal. Scholars, too, because of their attention to collectors, could be more certain of gaining access to important groups of works for their own research, publication and eventual exhibits. Museums displayed these works, private collectors footed the bills and journals published the scholarly articles that brought them wide public notice.

**The museum as classroom: The Musée de Sculpture Comparée au Palais du Trocadéro**

In addition to the Musée de Cluny, by the turn of the century several more permanent sites for the exhibition of medieval art had been established in Paris. The burgeoning displays and art-historical discussion of medieval art are part of the larger nineteenth-century phenomenon of 'museumification,' which was inseparable from the increased commodification of art.[295] The didacticism of the museum was part of a larger context of using history to educate the masses for nationalist purposes.[296] Though a number of earlier sovereigns had opened museums to put the history of France on display or to assert power, under the Republic the function of the museum was clearly outlined and quite specific.[297] As Tony Bennett has argued, the museum served to educate, in the broadest sense, both the French public and the artists and artisans who would regularly visit:

> However imperfectly it may have been realized in practice, the conception of the museum as an institution in which the working classes – provided they dressed nicely and curbed any tendency toward unseemly conduct – might be exposed to the improving influences of the Middle Classes was crucial to its construction as a new kind of social space.[298]

The methods of display, therefore, were designed primarily to fulfill this function. In contrast to the 'fetishistic' display of Cluny, both the Musée de Sculpture Comparée and the medieval department of the Louvre aimed for an aura of scholarly objectivity, what we could term 'systematic collecting.'[299] The curators of the scientific and natural history museums that originated in the period also practiced such systematic collecting and classification. In contrast to the unique objects of the *Wunderkammer* or cabinet of curiosities, the museum strove for objects representative of types that would lead to a fuller understanding of the evolution of art. At the same time, they provided numerous models and examples for contemporary artists, whose innovative art, many critics argued, should take account of the French tradition.

The Musée de Sculpture Comparée au Palais du Trocadéro was the work of Viollet-le-Duc, who proposed the idea of the museum to the Minister of Culture, to Jules Ferry and to Antonin Proust in November 1879, though the idea had originally been proposed by artists employed in the molding industry in 1848 as a way of 'studying and researching' sculptures inaccessible to Parisians.[300] Under the Commission des Monuments Historiques, the museum was opened to the public on 28 May 1882, with the explicit goal of displaying reproductions of the most important examples of monumental sculpture, both French and foreign. The museum also met Viollet-le-Duc's other well-known agenda, showing antique and medieval works side by side 'in order to dispose of the notion of a so-called inferiority of the latter.'[301] Works from the twelfth through the nineteenth century were reproduced and displayed: while foreign sculpture occupied the Paris wing, the Passy wing held antique, Greek, Roman, Christian, Merovingian, Carolingian and Gothic works, including full-scale models of the doorways of many celebrated French cathedrals.

The display at this museum corresponded to an older logic of cataloguing, a kind of 'systematic collecting' paralleled by the interest in periodization on the part of medievalists. In contrast to the more 'amorphous' Middle Ages embraced by early nineteenth-century collectors, the positivist nineteenth-century scholars set out to chronicle and distinguish among the various eras of the Middle Ages, to understand, for example, the sequential development from Romanesque to Gothic.[302] The works shown at the Musée de Sculpture Comparée were not chosen for their Benjaminian 'aura,' their ability to resurrect the past, but rather as key specimens in the developmental history of style, as fossils, each of which helped fill in missing pieces. As such, the works in the museum were not, in fact, 'authentic' examples at all, but rather plaster copies of entire facades or of architectural fragments. Such works served foremost to instruct, to provide easily accessible study material for scholars, restorers and artists.

In 1883, the first catalog of the museum's holdings was published, written by Paul Frantz Marcou in a descriptive and scientific tone, with clear reference to important documents of the period. The museum library opened to the public in 1889 and from 1885–1914, Anatole de Baudot, Vice-President of the Commission des Monuments Historiques, conducted courses on French architecture there. These classes, which insisted on the 'genius' and 'innovations' of medieval French architecture, were seen as a complement to Viollet-le-Duc's *Dictionnaire raisonné* and were influential in forming new generations of artists and architects.[303] The Musée de Sculpture Comparée was thus less a place to leave one's own world behind in order to immerse oneself in the Romantic Middle Ages than a site of study, a giant text with three-dimensional illustrations, in which to gain inspiration for future projects. Such scholarly rigor and erudition also characterized the other important Republican site for the permanent display of medieval works, the Département de la Sculpture du moyen âge et de la Renaissance of the Musée du Louvre.

## The Louvre: Département de la Sculpture du moyen âge et de la Renaissance

In 1893, the Louvre inaugurated a new wing devoted to sculptures and *objets d'art* of the medieval and Renaissance periods. The existence of this new wing can be attributed primarily to the efforts of one man, the pioneering medievalist Louis Courajod (1841–1896). Courajod's ideas are now largely forgotten, but at the end of the century he rivaled Emile Mâle as the period's foremost medieval art historian.[304] Writing in a style at once lucid and polemical, Courajod took it upon himself to re-interpret the history of Gothic art. Believing that the Academy and 'aristocratic' forces had conspired to rid Gothic art of its 'savage' and 'authentic' elements, Courajod was determined to bring them back to light. He argued tirelessly for an understanding of medieval works as the product of a popular, communal art that arose directly from the masses, an interpretation that dovetailed nicely with his own leftist, socialist agenda.[305]

Courajod pursued several theses throughout his writings and in the series of lectures that he delivered at the Ecole du Louvre in the early 1890s.[306] He most often repeated that Gothic art was essentially barbaric, deeply influenced by Eastern culture rather than organically developed from late Roman elements. For Courajod, the French needed to look for the roots of their 'true' culture not in the Mediterranean, but in the Christian East. Accordingly, for him the Celtic populations of Gaul maintained their culture *in spite of* the Roman invasions; they were a people with ties to both East and West.[307]

Within these contentions lay Courajod's second important thesis, his assertion that 'classical' or Roman culture had been dangerous and stultifying for French art. In his diatribe against Roman art, Courajod portrayed it as an invader on French soil that had never succeeded in winning over the masses.[308] For him, it functioned instead as a bureaucratic imported art. Courajod went even further, giving his argument contemporary relevance by casting the modern Academy as the modern-day successor to Rome, a body producing art by and for an 'elite' establishment: 'Roman art remained profoundly foreign to the popular masses, as distant, surely, as are today some of our arts cultivated in the hothouses of certain worldly or Academic milieus.'[309]

At 34 Courajod was named assistant to the Department of Conservation of Sculpture and *objets d'art* of the medieval and Renaissance periods at the Louvre. Promoted to curator five years later, he was the driving force behind the opening of the Medieval and Renaissance Sculpture Department in 1893. On the occasion of the opening, Courajod published his *Histoire du département de la sculpture moderne au Musée du Louvre*, in which he chronicled the pre-history of the new sculpture wing.[310] He traced its formation to the 1850s, citing the correspondence between the sculpture department, the Minister of Culture and the head of the Louvre's sculpture wing, Léon de Laborde. On 29 October 1850 de Laborde called for perseverance in the creation of a special Musée de Sculpture du moyen âge et de la Renaissance, despite previous lack of popular enthusiasm for it.[311] As Courajod noted, the public had been slow to recognize the national treasures of the medieval age: 'The taste and fashion of the day would still seem to allow the medieval and Renaissance periods to be appreciated only for their bibelots. We cannot refrain from mentioning the sudden decline in public sentiment.'[312] To counter this phenomenon, the director had requested 'the complete and chronological organization of art history from the medieval and Renaissance periods […] the most interesting period for French art.'[313] With this call, the collection began in earnest, characterized by a 'judicious spirit of scientific classification.'[314] In a spirit of scholarly rigor, Courajod and his colleagues expanded and attempted to 'complete' the existing monuments in the Louvre (derived mostly from the royal collections, the Ecole des Beaux-Arts and certain pieces from Lenoir's Musée des Monuments Français).[315] In his zeal, Courajod collected well over one thousand pieces, from thirteenth-century standing Madonnas to fragments of architectural capitals and large-scale tombs.[316] The motivation behind the collection was no longer pleasure or an attempt to escape into the Romantic past, but didacticism: the desire to teach the public to appreciate medieval and Renaissance art as more than mere bibelots.

Despite Courajod's unexpected death in 1896, by the first decade of the twentieth century the collection had blossomed into a real department, arranged in a roughly 'chronological' and 'scientific' (if hardly 'complete') manner.[317] Critics widely praised the results of Courajod's 'dream' of completing Lenoir's Musée des Monuments Français.[318] The ground floor along the Court of the Old Louvre was now given over to sculpture, with the medieval and Renaissance pieces located in five rooms along the Seine, near the Pont des Arts.[319] The focus of the collection was on royal portraiture and tombs. In Room 55 the visitor encountered works from the twelfth through the fourteenth century, including architectural fragments, a *Christ Crucified* and a *Seated Virgin*. This led into Room 56, which held numerous Virgins of the sixteenth century as well as the greatly treasured portraits of Charles V and his wife Jeanne de Bourbon. A fifteenth-century doorway led to Room 57, containing Gothic fragments, including ruins of sculpture from Notre-Dame de Paris. Statues and *gisant* tombs (such as the one of King Philip VI of Valois by André Beauneveu, and the tomb of Philippe Pot [1494]) were displayed in Room 58. The final room, 59, displayed 'Gothic' statuary by Michel Colombe along with Renaissance marbles.

The strict isolation of sculptured works from medieval pieces in other media contrasted sharply with the more cluttered *tableau vivant* display at Cluny. To glimpse French *Primitif* painting, for example, the visitor to the Louvre would have had to cross over to Room 'L' of the Grand Gallery of paintings, leaving behind the sculpture wing. Despite Courajod's rage against the dry bureaucratic model of the Academy and the Republican art establishment, the Louvre collection that he helped to found participated very much in the positivist and 'objective' mode of the late nineteenth century. Ironically, however, while Courajod championed a 'popular and communal' art of the Middle Ages, the setting of his scholarship was perhaps the most erudite and least 'popular' of all the displays of medieval art in the fin de siècle. This irony was not lost on visitors, who, like Durtal, the protagonist of several J.-K. Huysmans novels, found the *Primitifs* of the Louvre 'lonely.' Within the sterile walls of the museum, divorced from the furniture, tapestries, and other works of art that originally surrounded them, the *Primitif* paintings become mere objects, no longer capable of resurrecting a period atmosphere.[320]

## Medieval art at the World's Fairs

While didacticism held sway at museums like the Louvre and the Musée de Sculpture Comparée, the Expositions Universelles of the late nineteenth century combined these instructional goals with a more accessible and popular appropriation of the Middle Ages. As part of a wide effort to celebrate 'French genius,' both the 1889 and 1900 fairs included large retrospectives of medieval art (this aside from the roundly celebrated *Paris en 1400* and *Vieux Paris* exhibits that enthralled visitors in 1900).[321] These shows performed the important function of reconciling consumer products with medieval works: displays of Gothic art were incorporated into the larger setting of the fair, much of which was devoted to the promotion of commercial objects.[322] Moreover, the larger function of the exhibition (dating back to the displays at the Crystal Palace in 1851) also served to reconcile a still flourishing tradition of luxury hand-production with new machine-based works.[323] The Expositions also harmonized other modes and methods of display in the late nineteenth century, mingling the didactic goal of the museum and its aim of democratizing taste, with works culled from established private collections.

At the 1884 World's Fair, under the impetus of Antonin Proust, who then held the title of President of the Union Centrale des Arts Décoratifs, many French church treasures were gathered into a large retrospective of medieval art.[324] They included works in various media and from a wide range of medieval periods, from a Carolingian ivory triptych to a seated wooden Virgin of the thirteenth century and to the famed tapestries from the Cathedral of Angers (see Fig. 1.1). A large share came from private collectors (many from the Spitzer collection), shown side-by-side with those lent from large provincial museums.[325]

Curators arranged the works chronologically in two large rooms of the Palais du Trocadéro. Writing in the catalog accompanying the show, the critic Edmond Bonnafée noted that the first masterpieces of French art were created within religious institutions during the Middle Ages. The instructive value of the retrospective was clear: 'At the entrance, here are the most ancient treasures of our churches and our abbeys. The monastery is our first *atelier*.'[326] For Molinier, the retrospective served as 'one of the greatest educational projects accomplished during the last ten years.'[327] The Trocadéro exhibit was unparalleled in its scope and in its ambitious attempt to juxtapose works normally found in very different display conditions:

For those of us who live among dead things, working without cease to reconstitute their chronology, their nationality, their family, the Trocadéro will be an abundant mine of revelations. Never have the treasures of our churches been presented in such an ensemble; never have we reunited them neither side by side, nor with these similar specimens from our Parisian *cabinets*. Among the monuments borrowed from private collections and from provincial museums, a large number are exhibited here for the very first time and have never before been seen at any Exhibition.[328]

Despite its instructional function and its implicit nationalist agenda, the retrospective also harked back to the tradition of private collecting, as Edmond Bonnafée astutely noted: 'It is still, if you like, an incomparable *cabinet d'amateur*; because the amateur is named France and all or nearly all that he displays is his work and carries his signature. In this high society salon, all of us speak the same language and understand one another implicitly.'[329] According to Bonnafée, France itself had become a collector; his rhetoric removes the elitism from private collecting and unites all in the glory of their shared patrimony. As in the rhetoric surrounding medieval legends in Chapter 1, appreciation for the medieval legacy often transcended divisive political issues.

Such heritage was patently harmonious with recent Republican achievements. Hailing the medieval tradition, the retrospective clearly served to counterbalance the Exposition's emphatic celebration of technology. Modern France, symbolized by the shining new Eiffel Tower, had not forgotten its past. To this end, the vestibule of the Galerie des Machines was lined with six stained-glass windows designed by Charles Champigneulle. The six windows, *La Céramique*, *L'Orfèvrerie*, *Le Verre*, *La Tapisserie*, *La Pierre* and *Le Bois* drew more on Renaissance than Gothic prototypes in their use of perspective and their inclusion of classical architecture and *putti*. Yet the underlying theme of the series – the division of art into material or media – clearly referred to the practices of medieval artisanal guilds, further suggesting a continuity rather than a break between medieval and Republican France. In contrast to many private collectors, the Republican organizers clearly aimed to show that the distant past and the industrial present were not antithetical, but shared in the same spirit. This was a strategy often adopted by Republican politicians. In this, the designs of Viollet-le-Duc served as a precedent – his constructions of glass and steel created a kind of modern medieval art infused with Gothic design principles, but incorporating the materials of the new age. Such examples were hugely influential and contributed to the development of new nineteenth-century architectural styles, notably evident in the Art Nouveau constructions of Hector Guimard and Victor Horta, among others.[330]

The 1900 World's Fair encouraged the use of medieval art to inspire and educate contemporary artists, all in the context of promoting Republican notions of progress. Among the hundreds of exhibitions was an impressive retrospective of stained glass, situated in a pavilion on the Esplanade des Invalides. Arranged around a central court in the Petit Palais were French works from 'the beginning to the end of the nineteenth century.'[331] Organized by Emile Molinier, Roger Marx and Paul Frantz Marcou, the exhibits included goldwork, bronzes, enamels, furniture, wood, tapestries, glasswork, ivories, lead pieces, antique ceramics, faience and porcelain. A central ring of furniture surrounded this display, beginning with medieval furniture on the left and proceeding through furniture from the age of Louis XVI. As Debora Silverman has noted, rococo furniture design was widely acclaimed at the exhibit. However, the show also included many notable examples of thirteenth-century champlevé enamel work, medieval tapestries and fifteenth-century *Primitif* paintings.[332]

In contrast to the system employed at the Musée de Cluny, the works of the 1900 retrospective were not organically united in a thematic presentation, a kind of medieval chamber come to life with authentic objects. Nor did they follow the 'systematic' and 'chronological' display seen at museums such as the Louvre or the Musée de Sculpture Comparée. Instead, the works were presented in a disjunctive manner, each offered as a kind of singular masterpiece, all under the roof of a proper art museum, the Petit Palais. Without doubt, displaying the pieces in this context and in this manner assured that the viewer would recognize them first as aesthetic or artistic achievements, rather than as relics of the past or as objects of historical study. As works of art, they could be more easily transformed back into commodities, valued above all for their artistic aura.[333] They had once belonged to noble families and wealthy collectors, yet the Exposition offered them to the contemplation of all its visitors, who could take pride in these objects as 'theirs.' In this manner, the World's Fairs and the numerous publications that accompanied them – from guidebooks to weekly articles in notable academic journals – bridged the gap between the erudite scholar, the bourgeois consumer and the private collector.

## Medieval art for all: publications and advertisements

If the World's Fairs succeeded in bringing medieval art to the masses, publications (and the advertisements that sustained them) furthered this phenomenon. The six volumes of Viollet-le-Duc's hugely popular *Dictionnaire raisonné du mobilier français de l'époque carolingienne à la Renaissance* were published from 1858–1875 and, as scholars complained, Viollet's elaborate and detailed drawings made it all too easy to reproduce medieval furniture.[334] Such works, in addition to new illustrated periodicals including *La Revue des arts décoratifs* (1880–1902), *Art et décoration* (1897–1914) and *Art décoratif* (1898–1914), also presented the public with readily accessible models to copy. The advent of chromolithography had made possible the production of luxury color facsimiles of medieval manuscripts, while companies such as Firmin-Didot and Hetzel sought to produce less expensive versions for a wider audience.[335] Such a variety of publications made it possible to access medieval art without ever leaving one's home. Bourgeois and working-class consumers could consult high quality reproductions and scholarly texts from their armchairs, while turning their homes into castles by purchasing inexpensive reproductions of authentic works.

Numerous catalogs of private and public collections were also available for purchase in the fin de siècle. The Spitzer collection existed in regular and luxury versions, while, as Michael Camille noted, by 1904 readers could purchase their own abbreviated 'simulacra' of the *Très Riches Heures du Duc de Berry*: Paul Durrieu published the first monograph of the manuscript (in an edition that contained 65 black and white heliogravure reproductions) to coincide with the Exposition des Primitifs Français.[336] In addition to the more deluxe publication, readers could garner the latest scholarly and popular discourse on medieval art through numerous journals such as the *Gazette des Beaux-Arts* and the more popular *L'Illustration* and *Le Figaro illustré*, which reported regularly on recent exhibitions, books and museum acquisitions, often publishing lithographs or photographs of the

3.5   Copper and
enamel book
plaque (Limoges,
13th century), in
the Collection
Spitzer

works of art. Even readers of the daily newspaper *Le Temps* followed the
new works entering public museums such as the Musée de Cluny or the
Louvre.[337] Such publications offered lengthy academic articles on medieval
artists and works of art, presented side-by-side with advertisements for
the sale of medieval works, of products to 'medievalize' one's own dwelling,
of reproductions of medieval 'masterpieces' and of pictures of celebrity
living rooms. They even made the works in private collections, such as the
numerous pieces assembled by Ernest Odiot – from eleventh-century ivories
to a fourteenth-century statue of Saint John the Baptist – or by Spitzer
known to a wide public (Fig. 3.5).[338]

If the bourgeois and working-class audience learned about medieval art through these publications, they also became better consumers because of them. In fact, the high regard in which society held good collectors derived in part from familiarity with the activities of medieval patrons. The Duc de Berry, for example, became a widely revered figure at the end of the nineteenth century; art critics and scholars viewed him as a man of wealth and taste who singlehandedly brought some of the greatest Gothic works into existence.[339] Thanks to an inventory published by Jules Guiffrey in 1894 and to luxurious books like *Les Travaux d'art exécutés pour Jean de France, duc de Berry, avec une étude biographique sur les artistes employés par ce Prince*, published the same year, readers knew about more than the *Très Riches Heures* manuscript. They could read about his entire collection and his relationship with the artists of his day.[340] By acquiring objects belonging to the Duc de Berry, or by finding unusual pieces of medieval art, modern *bibeloteurs* could distinguish themselves from their peers; they took pride in their collections, knowing that they were following in the footsteps of the Duc de Berry, the Duc d'Aumale (his descendant and future owner of *Les Très Riches Heures*), the Medici princes, Lenoir or du Sommerard.

Scholars and art historians also raised the status of the collector by promoting interior design as a national contribution that rivaled research. Even a scholar as demanding and nationalistic as Alphonse Germain (who championed many of the 'idealist' artists in the Rose+Croix circle) insisted that the French medieval tradition resided in the art of interior design, of decorating the 'home.'[341] In his text on *Notre Art de France* (1894),[342] Germain noted that the destiny of French greatness now lay in the decorating of châteaux, of public buildings and above all of ordinary houses:

To all those artists who are left indifferent by the vain successes of exhibitions, – there are some left, thank God! – and who endeavor to make their work say something and dream of a real direction for it, those artists should meditate about this theme: the intimate art of decoration and putting it into practice. And if they are determined to stamp this art with an indigenous originality, to base it on the principles appropriate to it, oh! they should draw inspiration from our thirteenth-century ancestors.[343]

For Germain, the art of decorating was inherently French, thus not a lesser art.[344] Designers and artisans of medieval churches, buildings and houses had inevitably stamped the period with its unique character. By decorating and furnishing private dwellings, these artists had brought glory to France. Consequently, a nineteenth-century Duc de Berry had only to provide new opportunities for French artists. Collectors and interior decorators could contribute to the greatness of the nation by sharing their acquisitions with a larger public.

The democratization of medieval art unleashed by such mainstream discussion of collecting and decorating reached its zenith with do-it-yourself medievalizing products for the home. While the wealthy had real stained glass, the less affluent also had access to medieval-style products (albeit in inexpensive and far less labor-intensive materials). Companies such as Les

3.6   Poster for
the Vitraux
'Glacier,' 1890s

3.6   Poster for the Vitraux 'Glacier,' 1890s

Vitraux Français sold translucent sheets with stained-glass patterns –
advertised as 'imitating old stained-glass windows' – that could be stuck on
windows to provide a vaguely château-like flavor. Prices started at only 12
francs 50! Another poster, for the Vitraux Glacier, shows a cozy interior
where two bourgeois women and a girl busy themselves masking the
industrial view outside with cut-out paste-on panels that reconfigure the
room as a medieval chapel, complete with a figure representing Saint
George (Fig. 3.6). Likewise, two journals – *L'Enlumineur* (1889–1900) and *Le
Coloriste-Enlumineur* (1894–1895) – began to publish do-it-yourself manuscript

illumination by providing outline drawings, letters and ornaments that could be copied.[345] Like the advertisements for the Vitraux Glacier, these journals targeted a predominantly female audience.

Other companies promised to do the decorating for the consumer: for several thousand francs one could hire a decorator to come and set up a Louis XI living room or kitchen (see Fig. 0.1), while department stores such as Le Bon Marché displayed and sold inexpensive reproductions of medieval furniture.[346] Advertisers widely used medieval references and figures such as Joan of Arc and Saint George to sell an assortment of products for the bourgeois consumer; from beer and cheese to magazines, chocolate and photography supplies, this strategy proved enormously successful.[347]

Like the paste-on sheets of neo-medieval design, the appeal of such products was largely transparent: with a bit of money and some ingenuity, consumers could become king or queen of their own castle (while imitating literary and artistic celebrities of the day). Such emulation of the taste, style and attitudes of famous people was a staple strategy to acquire status in the nineteenth century (and well into the twenty-first). Like the 'palaces of Fine Arts' and exclusive spaces like the Jockey Club, the acquisition of 'medieval' style offered the bourgeoisie and even the lower classes a taste of the noble life while enabling them to demonstrate their understanding of French heritage.[348] As Whitney Walton notes in her discussion of the displays of the Crystal Palace: 'as with the popularity of old styles, then, the taste for ornamentation linked bourgeois consumers with their aristocratic prede-cessors as members of the consuming, discriminating, and therefore ruling class.'[349] Advertisements and publications had indeed created a new breed of interior decorators, often less concerned with the values of the Middle Ages than with its noble accouterments.

### Back to the living room: medieval art and the bourgeois interior

With the proliferation of display sites and the growing consumer market for reproductions and simulations of celebrated medieval masterpieces and their style, the boundaries between the display practices of department store, museum, *cabinet* and bourgeois interior had blurred if not altogether disappeared. Huysmans, ever an astute critic of the cultural tastes of the middle class, bemoaned this phenomenon in an article criticizing the Musée des Arts Décoratifs: 'Isn't it enough that anyone can copy the furniture of the Musée de Cluny by the gross! I understand that we're not obligated to buy, but we can't avoid seeing them because they fill entire boulevards and streets!'[350] Huysmans's complaint against 'fakes' is a thinly disguised polemic against the mass production of once 'authentic' objects. He deplores just the kind of mingling – between museum and showroom, between consumer and collector, between scholar and *bibeloteur* – that operated in the display spaces of the fin de siècle. In the observations of critics and scholars such as Huysmans, we find an acknowledgment that the 'culture of the bibelot' had taken over even museums like Cluny. Medieval displays had gone from the museum to the living room and even onto the streets.

Huysmans laments the proliferation of cheap imitations, but his concern stems less from seeing these objects on the boulevards and in boutiques than from his worry about what imitations will do to the value of the originals and to the reputation of those who, like him, collect them.[351] The ability to recognize and to acquire a particularly rare or unique object conferred a certain prestige that set one apart from others, yet this system no longer functioned once the same object could be reproduced and purchased by anyone. At that point, only a specialist would be able to distinguish it from the thousands of poorly rendered copies.[352] And this increasingly seemed to be the case: medieval furnishings and bibelots filled the houses of Parisians to such an extent that those who considered themselves 'true' or 'discerning' collectors had to create new means of distinguishing themselves from the masses.

The criticism of Zola published by a number of his contemporaries centers on concern about distinguishing 'real' collectors from 'bricabracomaniacs.' Goncourt categorized Zola's office as '[…] quite ruined by an infectious *bibeloterie*,' while Maurice Guillemot was 'disoriented' by 'all of this astonishing bricabracomania':

[…] triptychs of *Primitif* paintings, displays of suits of armor, old fabrics, stained-glass windows […] and it is not that Emile Zola is an amateur; when one questions him about it, he does not dwell on the objects, one does not feel that he is like Goncourt or Anatole France, who take pleasure from the rare bibelot that one caresses with one's fingers, that one turns over and over, that one fondles, no, he has accumulated all of this to create a decor that suits him, his instinctive Romanticism sharpened by medieval church things.[353]

Zola's fondness for religious artifacts from the Middle Ages seemed highly suspect to these visitors, especially since he generally condemned the Catholic Church in his novels and publicized himself as a man of science with an appreciation of modern art and photography. Pictures revealed the truth of the journalists' impressions: if anything, they had downplayed the overall effect of what Maupassant had called 'the most romantic of residences'! (see Fig. 3.1). Both narrative accounts and photographs point out the inconsistencies between Zola's milieu and his underlying moral and intellectual make-up: he was not really the scientist he claimed to be, but an eccentric 'bricabracomaniac' who loved medieval art.[354] The novel *L'Oeuvre*, in which Zola's character Sandoz describes his 'buying frenzies' at second-hand shops, did nothing to contradict such impressions.[355]

Guillemot had insisted that Zola was not like Anatole France and Goncourt, who knew the history and origin of each of their objects; Huysmans mocked Zola for spending outrageous sums on acquiring 'fake' *Primitif* paintings.[356] Maupassant perhaps most clearly pointed out the differences: '[…] Zola is not a collector. He seems to buy haphazardly, randomly following his over-stimulated desires, according to the whims of his eye, the seduction of form and color, without bothering about authentic origins or indisputable value as would Goncourt.'[357] By contrasting their collecting acumen to that of Zola – he accumulates objects whether they are authentic or not because he enjoys the effect they produce; he does not caress them or explain their history – these writers maintain their own superiority by proposing new definitions of the good and bad collector.[358]

Justifying their own collections, 'connoisseurs' based their standards on museum models that valued authenticity, coherency and social utility. The rhetoric used by 'good' collectors (Anatole France, Edmond de Goncourt, J.-K. Huysmans) imitated the legitimizing discourse of the scholars who conferred a seal of approval on collectors like Rothschild and Odiot, thus turning their private acquisitions into museum exhibits dedicated to edifying the public.[359] Such discourse, based on that found in the periodicals of the time, distinguishes them from mere 'accumulators' like Zola, who enjoyed his ensemble without paying great attention to the individual elements within it and to their relationship to the whole. By the end of the nineteenth century, to be considered a good collector one could no longer simply amass eclectic and rare objects. Increasingly, one needed to combine passion, taste and intelligence, keeping in mind display models and scholarly discourse that justified one's choice of objects.

One of the most idiosyncratic fictional collectors of the time put this new rhetoric of collecting to good use to legitimate his collecting habits. Des Esseintes, the hero of Huysmans's 1884 novel *A Rebours*, cloistered himself in his house as did Zola, but unlike Zola he carefully amassed medieval objects to create a harmonious and coherent ensemble. Des Esseintes more closely resembles du Sommerard, who created special rooms to showcase each of his collections. He carefully arranges a pulpit and an altar, for example, to recreate the holy atmosphere of a medieval chapel, while he collects other objects to fashion a somber monk's cell. Like Lenoir and du Sommerard, des Esseintes feels as though he is preserving history by saving it from vandalism – a direct result of the Revolution and the bourgeois power it unleashed – and by reassembling it in the light of its original medieval context:

[…] most of the precious objects catalogued in the Musée de Cluny, having miraculously escaped the vile brutality of the sans-culottes, are from the old abbeys of France. Just as the Church preserved philosophy, history and literature from barbarism in the Middle Ages, so it has saved the plastic arts, protected until now those wonderful models of fabric and jewelry that manufacturers of holy objects spoil as much as they can even though they are unable to alter their initial, exquisite form. It was thus not surprising that he had sought out these antique bibelots, that he had, like many other collectors, taken these relics away from the Paris antique stores and the country secondhand shops.[360]

But while des Esseintes imitates the rhetoric of collecting by discussing origin, authenticity and value, he also perverts the system. Instead of maintaining the cultural heritage he seems to admire by preserving it for future generations (as did Lenoir and du Sommerard), des Esseintes consumes it; he removes medieval art and manuscripts from their religious and communal context by putting them on exclusively private display. What is more, he parodies and perverts the religious spaces he has recreated by secularizing them: he preaches sermons on dandyism from the pulpit, while using the altar to display special editions of Baudelaire's poetry. He subverts religious artifacts by appropriating them for private use, while replacing religious values with commercial.

This behavior reflects what Janell Watson has called 'the movement of the museum into the salon [...] the museum as interior becomes a private shrine of the cult of Art.'[361] While this chapter has examined the intersection of private collection and public display, the next will explore the problems created by collectors such as des Esseintes, who disassembled the communal collections of cathedrals and monasteries in order to transform them into private shrines of medieval art: they amassed religious objects for purely private consumption without regard for their original context or their value for the French patrimony. In doing so, they aestheticized such works to an extreme degree, returning them to the category of bibelot. As many argued, it was only by situating medieval works in context – in the cathedral surrounded by Christian ritual – that their importance would be revealed.

# 4

# The Gothic cathedral in fin-de-siècle France: from *Gesamtkunstwerk* to 'French genius'

When one sees the number of deputies who, when they have finished voting for anti-clerical laws, leave to tour the cathedrals of England, France and Italy, bring back for their wife an old chasuble to make a coat or door covering, concoct plans for secularization in their studies in front of the photographic reproduction of a *mise au tombeau*, haggle with a secondhand dealer over the leaf of a retable, travel as far as the countryside to find fragments of choir stalls that will serve as umbrella stands for their antechamber, and go on Good Friday to the 'Schola Cantorum' if not to l'église Saint-Gervais, to listen 'religiously', as one says, to the mass of Pope Marcellus, one imagines that when all discerning people are persuaded that the government has an obligation to subsidize religious ceremonies, we will have confirmed many anti-clerical deputies as allies and stirred them up against the Briand project.[362]

Marcel Proust, 'La Mort des cathédrales' (1904)

The increased public demand for medieval décor created a system of supply and demand based heavily on the purchase or theft of bibelots from museums, churches and other monuments. Proust's criticism of his contemporaries suggests that the dispersion of medieval art was particularly rampant in the years just before and after the 9 December 1905 law that officially separated Church and State in France, thus ending the state's fiscal support of religious ceremonies while calling for an inventory of the goods contained in formerly state-supported edifices. The law attributed ownership of houses of worship to the commune, the department or the state, depending on a number of criteria, including the provenance of funds used to build the structure and the date of its construction.[363]

As anti-clerical legislation began to proliferate in the 1890s, a number of writers and artists began warning of its dangers. J.-K. Huysmans's 1903 novel *L'Oblat* describes the reaction of Benedictine monks to laws forbidding unauthorized associations. Fearful that their order will be dissolved by the state, the monks pack their belongings and abandon their abbey for the more hospitable political climate of Belgium. A year later, Proust published the provocatively entitled 'La Mort des cathédrales' in *Le Figaro* (16 August 1904), arguing that without state subsidy of church services, cathedrals would become 'empty shells,' archeological wonders whose original purpose would remain a mystery for future generations. Although their response seemed exaggerated,

Huysmans and Proust actually *underestimated* the extent of the damage caused by the separation of Church and State. Religious edifices were hit particularly hard. As Louis Réau has demonstrated dramatically in *L'Histoire du vandalisme*, religious orders ejected from buildings now considered 'state property' often liquidated their assets to finance their exodus; empty churches and abbeys remained largely unguarded, thus falling prey to antique dealers and collectors; religious structures were turned into town halls or museums.[364]

In contrast to those motivated sheerly by profit, writers and artists including J.-K. Huysmans, Marcel Proust, Maurice Barrès, Emile Mâle, Charles Morice and Auguste Rodin represented medieval edifices as works of art in which the harmonious ensemble of individual parts and different media working together created a unique experience. This concept resembles what Wagner called a *Gesamtkunstwerk* or a total work of art. Thanks largely to the efforts of artists, writers, scholars and museums, many early twentieth-century viewers, originally interested in acquiring bibelots, developed a more refined appreciation of their original context and its importance for the French patrimony. As this chapter will show, they began to acknowledge the Gothic cathedral as the ultimate example of this ideal; it served as a kind of *ur-*museum in which different media, presented in the context for which they were originally designed, fused into a unique experience.

## The specter of the separation of Church and State

In 'La Mort des cathédrales' Proust harshly criticizes the hypocrisy of his contemporaries. Anti-clerical deputies visit cathedrals in England, France and Italy, collect fragments of medieval religious art to use as scarves, curtains or umbrella stands, line their studies with reproductions of medieval religious paintings and go to concerts of medieval religious music on Good Friday. Proust contrasts their near-obsessive appreciation of medieval religious art to their enthusiasm for the anti-clerical laws that will destroy the very heritage they so enjoy.[365] It is no coincidence that Proust focuses, in the opening quote of this chapter, on purely secular activities: travel and tourism to cathedrals, the buying and selling of religious art, the transformation of the accessories of religious ceremony into utilitarian objects and the appreciation of church music in a concert setting. Proust emphasizes what many of his contemporaries chose not to see: medieval religious art was part of a larger system dedicated to the celebration of the Catholic liturgy. His contemporaries' paradoxical appreciation for all things medieval save Catholicism corresponds to what Françoise Choay has termed a 'museum mentality,' a tendency to value or preserve individual artworks while disregarding the larger context in which they originally functioned.[366]

Indeed, Proust's argument seeks to transform contemporary attitudes toward the cathedral by emphasizing its function: it is, above all, a house of worship. Although his contemporaries increasingly visited cathedrals as they would museums, he reminds them of the religious foundation responsible for their construction and survival. Proust's goal here is not to bolster Catholicism by arguing that beautiful art stemmed from Christianity (as had others, like Chateaubriand or Denis), but rather to argue for the aesthetic value of the cathedral itself. Proust would preserve Catholicism to protect Gothic art. He portrays cathedrals as 'the highest and most original expression of France's genius' because of the links between their form and function. By insisting on the artistic importance of the liturgy – 'It can be said that a performance of Wagner at Bayreuth is not much compared to high mass in the cathedral of Chartres' – Proust makes a valuable and persuasive argument for government support of religious services as performing arts. His reference to Wagner portrays the cathedral as a *Gesamtkunstwerk*, a total work of art, in which each detail has its place as an inseparable part of a whole. 'The Catholic liturgy is one with the architecture and the sculpture of our cathedrals; the former, like the latter, derive from the same symbolism [...] there are hardly any sculptures in cathedrals, as secondary as they may seem, that do not have symbolic value. Well, it is the same for religious ceremonies.' He argues that cathedrals will die – they will become nothing more than casinos, concert halls, or museums – if the celebration of the religious services for which they were originally constructed is halted.[367]

Proust appeals to his contemporaries on several levels: he draws an analogy with Wagner (hugely popular at the end of the nineteenth century), he fuels their patriotism (the high mass in French cathedrals is even better entertainment than Wagner's German operas) and he targets their growing interest in museums and archeology. He points out that each piece of a cathedral's art is symbolic; it occupies a place within the Catholic liturgy: 'The same symbolism extends even to music, which can be heard in the immense nave and whose seven Gregorian tones represent the seven theological virtues and the seven ages of the world. They find a counterpart in each work of art.' Accordingly, stained glass, sculpture, architectural design and religious music provide valuable information about the cultural practices of the past and especially about the importance the cathedral builders attached to form, function and symbolism. If the government subsidizes research and theatrical productions at Roman arenas in the south of France, Proust argues, why should it not subsidize religious 'performances' in the cathedral of Chartres?

Proust was prescient in directing his argument about conservation to the cathedral's function, which he portrayed as an integral part of the aesthetic experience it constituted. In fact, Proust sounds more like an anthropologist than a budding novelist. His essay also echoes the writings of a contemporary Austrian art historian and museum conservator, Aloïs Riegl, who, in 1903, developed a theory to assist art historians with the conservation of monuments. In his 1903 *Der moderne Denkmalkultus* (*The Modern Cult of Monuments*), Riegl divided predominant nineteenth-century attitudes toward art into two major and conflicting categories: 'recollection' and 'contemporaneity.' Values of 'recollection,' which are based on aesthetic, historical and conservatory goals, tend to conflict with values that praise a monument's role in contemporary life, its current 'use value.' Riegl labels this latter category, 'of contemporaneity,' as particularly important for religious architecture, whose status as a functioning house of worship tends to overwhelm its identity as an object of antiquity.[368]

Like Riegl, Proust argues that 'use value' is a unique and distinguishing feature of religious architecture. Contemporaries are unanimous in recognizing the architectural significance of the cathedral – its 'value of recollection' – yet they are blind to its 'use value'; they consider it as they would a prized Roman ruin, an object valuable only as a marker from the past. Accordingly, they do not recognize that its values 'of contemporaneity' – the church services – might be valuable and see no need to subsidize them. The art-loving anti-clerical deputies appreciate the cathedral not as a functioning building, but as a relic of a previous time. Proust's analogies – Wagner's operas performed at Bayreuth, re-enactment of Roman spectacles in the south of France – thus attempt to reclassify the cathedral according to the values 'of contemporaneity' that his contemporaries *do* recognize. By asking his readers to imagine a future in which the Catholic services performed in the cathedral are only a recreated spectacle from the past, he links the liturgy to the 'value of recollection' his contemporaries already acknowledge.[369]

The effectiveness of Proust's essay can be gauged by the reaction of the deputies he criticized. Paul Grunebaum-Ballin, the adjunct director under Aristide Briand during the promulgation of the law separating Church from State, cited Proust's defense of churches in a legal document commenting on each aspect of the Briand Law, while novelist and politician Maurice Barrès congratulated Proust for coming to the defense of the cathedral.[370] The title of Proust's essay became common currency and echoes can be detected in the titles of many subsequent books and articles in defense of religious architecture: Barrès, *La Grande pitié des églises de France* (1914), Morice, 'Mort et résurrection de la cathédrale' (1914); Rodin, 'Le Dernier Testament' (1914); and Proust's republication of essays about churches, 'Les églises assassinées' (1918).

## Gothic architecture in the nineteenth century: from grotesque to sublime

But why was Proust's provocative title – 'The Death of Cathedrals' – so effective and so accepted by Republican deputies, especially when the subsidy of church services was one of the primary targets of the separation of Church and State? If Proust's essay so impressed and mobilized people in 1904, it was largely because the Gothic cathedral's position in the public eye had changed during the nineteenth century. It had developed from a neglected structure into a beloved national figure that was championed as 'the French Parthenon,' 'the genius of the French nation,' and the 'synthesis of our country.'[371]

Considered 'grotesque,' 'misshapen' or 'crude' in the seventeenth and eighteenth centuries, the term 'Gothic' was synonymous with the Dark Ages as much for the seeming excesses of its style as for its purported architects: the Barbarians.[372] In fact, nearly all architecture from the sixth to the fifteenth centuries was dismissed as 'Gothic,' though subsequent writers distinguished between 'old' and 'modern' Gothic (today's distinction between Romanesque and Gothic).[373] Medieval architecture had fallen into such disfavor that guidebooks of Paris from the seventeenth and eighteenth centuries devoted little space to it, while the architects of Louis XIV and XV gave *carte blanche* to the destruction of medieval buildings in order to 'beautify the city' with modern structures.[374] The lack of consideration given to Gothic architecture at the beginning of the nineteenth century can be gauged by Victor Hugo's writing, notably the inflammatory poems and essays he published between 1824 and 1832 ('The Black Band,' 'On Destruction of Monuments in France' and 'War on Demolition Gangs') in which he protested against contemporary 'vandalism' – demolition and restoration – and argued that it must be stopped.[375] A prime example of such polemics arises in the third book of *Notre-Dame de Paris* (1831); the author describes the cathedral while inveighing heavily against the 'stupidity' of those who hammered off statues, replaced stained glass with normal glass and 'amputated' a steeple in order to replace it with a mound of lead resembling a 'pot cover.' The book itself was influenced by the conservation movement: in his enigmatic preface, Hugo suggests that the entire novel was written as a meditation on the engraving 'ΑΝΑΓΚΗ' (fatality) carved into the cathedral and its subsequent erasure. Without active attention to documenting and conserving works of the Middle Ages, Hugo insisted that France would see its past crumble away.

Hugo's influence on his contemporaries should not be underestimated. The book spawned popular debates on the unscrupulous projects of the 'bande noire,' a group that bought valuable old properties in order to tear them down and sell the materials for scrap, thus bringing attention to the status of medieval monuments.[376] Such vocal defense of churches gave support to the administrative projects of François Guizot, then Minister of the Interior, and enabled him to win funding for committees that would create an 'Inspecteur général des monuments historiques.' From 1830 to 1837 these new organizations grew to encompass a Commission des Monuments Historiques (devoted to physical restorations) and a Comité des Arts et Monuments, to which Hugo was named. Hugo served this group – responsible for publicity and ideology regarding the protection of monuments – for thirteen years (1835–1848). Even after he left it, he continued to correspond with architect and conservator colleagues – Didron, Mérimée, Lassus, Viollet-le-Duc and others – until his death in 1885. He assisted in the conservation of monuments throughout Europe and truly achieved the goal enunciated in the 1832 author's preface to *Notre-Dame de Paris*: 'Let us inspire the nation, if possible, to love national architecture. This is, the author declares, one of the principal goals of this book; this is one of the principal goals of his life.'[377]

The committee's secretary, Adolphe-Napoléon Didron or 'Didron aîné' (after his death in 1867 his adopted son Edouard would carry on his father's work), was heavily influenced by Hugo and worked tirelessly to make the Middle Ages better known. In the inaugural issue of *Les Annales archéologiques*, he argued that one of the periodical's goals would be to make the Middle

Ages a topic 'of predilection.'[378] His work was successful and the periodical is one of the best nineteenth-century repositories of information about medieval architecture, stained glass, music, symbolism and theology. Indeed, although unacknowledged by Emile Mâle, who is credited for first equating the Gothic cathedral to the *Speculum Majus* of Vincent de Beauvais, it was Didron who first made the parallel in the pages of *Les Annales archéologiques*.[379] He was also one of the first and most staunch supporters of labeling Gothic art a truly French art, a 'national' art.[380]

The group that comprised the Comité des Arts et Monuments, many of whom contributed articles to *Les Annales archéologiques*, was also responsible for many of the most important cathedral restorations of the nineteenth century: Notre-Dame de Paris (Lassus and Viollet-le-Duc), Chartres (Lassus) and Amiens (Viollet-le-Duc) among others. The activities of these figures and their students led to one of the most interesting and long-lasting manifestations of medievalism in the nineteenth century: the thousands of projects to restore and conserve medieval French religious architecture all over France. We will not discuss this phenomenon at length, as art historians have adequately discussed it elsewhere. Jean-Michel Leniaud's encyclopedic *Les Cathédrales au XIXe siècle*, for example, provides an excellent overview of the architects, politicians, organizations, budgets and initiatives involved in the century-long project to restore cathedrals.[381] The movement exerted a profound influence on the public, which, through such projects, saw their medieval heritage valorized by specialists.

The Comité des Arts et Monuments was also at the front lines of what would become a veritable battle to prove that Gothic art was a national style. Throughout the middle of the century, its members argued with the French Academy and its Ecole des Beaux-Arts about the importance of Gothic style, bickering about obtaining commissions for restoration and new construction and about how young architects should be educated. As Barry Bergdoll has shown, vicious disputes about the solidity of the Gothic style, the intention of its architects and its importance as a national style characterized their numerous exchanges about cathedrals.[382] Although such battles took place primarily in the pages of publications such as *Les Annales archéologiques* or *Le Moniteur des architectes*, others spilled out into the mainstream press, appearing in *L'Univers* or *La Revue des Deux Mondes*. A case in point was Viollet-le-Duc's disputes with l'Académie Française and l'Ecole des Beaux-Arts. Viollet was a largely self-educated architect, who held in contempt the Academy's rules, classical preferences and censure of artistic freedom. Nonetheless, when his connections with the imperial family led to his appointment as Professor of Art History and Aesthetics at l'Ecole des Beaux-Arts in 1863 (without the support of the Academy itself), he accepted it. His lectures and other writings, in which he proposed radical ideas for reforming the education system in France (including replacing l'Ecole des Beaux-Arts with a system based on that of medieval guilds), caused a highly public controversy carried on in the pages of *La Revue des Deux Mondes*. The exchange provoked his resignation.[383]

Such disputes brought Viollet great notoriety, especially as he continued to feud with the Academy. He proposed *Le Dictionnaire raisonné de l'architecture française du XIe au XVIe siècle* (published from 1854 to 1868) in part to supplant the 1832 *Dictionnaire méthodique d'architecture* of Quatremère de Quincey (secrétaire-perpétuelle of the Academy), which had harshly criticized the 'decadence' of the Gothic style.[384] The combative rhetoric exchanged by both sides drew attention to Viollet's new theories, which gained more and more credence throughout the century as he published them in *Le Dictionnaire raisonné*, *Le Dictionnaire du mobilier français* (1858–1875) and *Entretiens sur l'architecture* (1863 and 1872). In these works, as well as in his lectures on architecture, he argued (as had Didron) for Gothic art as inherently 'national' and 'rational,' the first truly French style. His enthusiasm for the excellence and logic of medieval principles of construction would culminate in his theory of 'structural rationalism.' From Gothic buildings, Viollet posited, architects could learn to design buildings true to the conditions imposed by need as well as by the specific properties of the materials employed, while still leaving room for invention. This theory, combined with his call for a return to national building styles, would influence a host of young architects who read these works and attempted to put them into practice.

A great number of late nineteenth-century churches reveal the impact of Viollet-le-Duc's theories; architects took up his challenge to use new materials while paying homage to the logic and symmetry of Gothic forms. A few examples include Adrien Lusson and Louis-Auguste Boileau's Eglise Saint-Eugène on the Rue Sainte-Cécile in Paris, Léon Vaudoyer's Sainte-Marie-Majeure in Marseille and Alexandre Astruc's Notre-Dame du Travail on the Rue Vercingétorix in Paris.[385] Indeed, as Bertrand Lemoine has pointed out, there were nearly two hundred Gothic-inspired churches being constructed in France in the mid-nineteenth century, not to mention castles and private residences. Many of these were based on authentic Gothic models, while others were inspired by the theories and drawings of Lassus and Viollet-le-Duc.[386] The effect of Viollet-le-Duc's theories on Art Nouveau architects has been discussed by scholars at length: these architects include Hector Guimard, Victor Horta and Antonio Gaudí, who applied the forms to secular and religious architecture alike.[387] Viollet's influences on modern architecture are too numerous to discuss here, but thanks to his writings a new generation of architects from all over the world studied Gothic architecture and took inspiration from it in developing new styles.[388]

By the 1870s, Viollet-le-Duc was so well known a public figure that he was approached by P. J. Hetzel, the editor responsible for marketing novelists Victor Hugo and Jules Verne. Hetzel asked Viollet to write a series of popular works that would present his theories in simple terms for the public. The subsequent volumes, *Histoire d'une maison* (1873), *Histoire d'une forteresse* (1874), *Histoire de l'habitation humaine* (1875), *Histoire d'un hôtel de ville et d'une cathédrale* (1878) and *Histoire d'un dessinateur* (1879), were published for children under the rubric of La Bibliothèque d'Éducation et de Récréation. They brought his theories to the mainstream and consecrated medieval architecture – in the new generation's eyes – as a national art and as the origin of modern French architecture.[389]

Hugo, Didron, Viollet and their followers created and popularized a national myth that struck a chord with many contemporaries.[390] If anti-clerical deputies championed the cathedral in 1904, it was, as Proust suggests, less from faith than from the cathedrals' association with widespread beliefs about aesthetics, religion and patriotism. Many contemporaries had come to understand the Gothic cathedral as the 'French Parthenon,' a tourist destination of national significance. By the turn of the century, nearly all French people agreed that Gothic churches – superior artistic structures built for worship – constituted the 'genius of the French nation' and the 'synthesis of our country.' The cathedral – literally the seat of a bishop – had come to be synonymous with Catholic churches built in the Gothic style, a rich example of the glorious scientific, religious and artistic achievements of medieval France. It is no wonder that Proust's intimation that the cathedrals were being 'assassinated' provoked strong reactions in their defense.

## The aesthetic of the *Gesamtkunstwerk*

While most people in late nineteenth-century France had come to understand the cathedral as a significant national structure or as a valuable vestige of the French past, increased secularization meant that they did not always believe in the importance of the cathedral's religious function. As Huysmans would point out in the 1890s, his contemporaries tended to practice 'monumental materialism'; they worshiped churches as monuments or museums, not as complex works of art with specific religious and symbolic meaning. They thus respected cathedrals as tourist destinations while overlooking the importance of music, stained glass, sculpture, illuminated breviaries, altars, paintings and religious ceremonies, whose union produced an atmosphere conducive to worship.[391]

Proust's emphasis on Wagner and the widespread French appreciation of his operas, in which painstaking attention to lyrics, music, costume, lighting, repeated motifs and voices combine to provide a multi-faceted experience, reveals the increased aesthetic sensibility of the cultural elite in 1904. By this time le *wagnérisme* had become mainstream, despite the battles waged about Wagner, his music and his anti-Frenchness since the 1850s.[392] As Proust suggests, many Frenchmen had come to understand Wagner's operas as works dependent on symbolism. From his first performances in Paris in the 1850s, Wagner tended to be admired by artists such as Gérard de Nerval, Charles Baudelaire, Théophile Gautier and Franz Liszt. He was, however, ridiculed by mainstream music critics, who belittled him as 'the Courbet of music' and rejected his theories – especially that of the *Gesamtkunstwerk* – as pretentious posturing.[393] His term gained credence, however, as aristocrats, as well as the Emperor, accepted him in their salons and as young writers, led by Catulle Mendès and the Parnassians, and painters (Renoir, Bazille,

Manet and Cézanne) performed his music, attended concerts or created paintings based on his themes.[394] Wagner's anti-French attitudes during the Franco-Prussian war led to protests over attempts to stage his operas in France; he was not widely accepted again until the 1890s. Yet in spite of the overt political condemnation of Wagner and his works, underground Wagnerism continued to flourish. This was especially true in the salons of his disciples, the Paris community known as 'Petit Bayreuth,' made up of friends and supporters who assembled an amateur orchestra dedicated to performing his works.[395]

Bayreuth, which had opened in 1876, became a nearly holy site of 'pilgrimage' for those of Wagner's fans who could not see his operas performed in France.[396] Visitors were inspired by the radical difference between Wagnerian productions and French theatrical practices. The dark theater – a stark change from the brightly lit French auditoriums – in which spectators focused on an illuminated stage, evoked religious responses from visitors, who described the 'epiphanies' they experienced during the concerts. Joséphin Péladan, for one, spent the summer of 1888 in Bayreuth. Watching *Parsifal* inspired him in a 'flash' to envision the entire structure of the Rose+Croix brotherhood and to become a 'disciple of Wagner.' In 1894, he published *Le Théâtre complet de Wagner*.[397] The originality of Wagner's subject matter, elaborate sets and costumes, often inspired by medieval art and legends, created a lasting impression on French audiences. Figure 4.1, Philippe Chaperon's sketch of the set for the 1861 Paris premier of *Tannhaüser*, gives an example of the magnificence of such spectacles. His drawing represents the hall of the singers of Wartburg (Act Two of the opera) in all of its Gothic splendor, including thirteenth-century sculptures, pointed arches and pennants. Wagner was so pleased with this set that he ordered a reconstruction of it for subsequent performances.[398]

Proust's equation of the opera to high mass at Chartres was in the air of the time; the numerous medieval-themed European operas and elaborate sets of the period led one to draw this parallel.[399] But the extravagance of Wagner placed him above the others and devotees increasingly linked the musical experience to religion and their attendance at concerts to pilgrimages. Lavignac's 1897 *Le Voyage Artistique à Bayreuth*, in which he insists that the 'true pilgrim must go there [Bayreuth] on his knees,' gives an idea of the reverence attached to Bayreuth, but a number of other publications of the time also paid homage to Wagner, the most respectful of which was *La Revue wagnérienne*.[400] Begun after Wagner's death by Edouard Dujardin and Houston Stuart Chamberlain, the publication sought to translate and disseminate Wagner's theoretical writings, which were not well known in France. Each issue (the first was published on 8 February 1885) is brimming with information about upcoming Wagner events in Europe, translated Wagner essays, poems or tributes to his genius, or reviews of current productions of his work. Many of the contributors – including Paul Verlaine, Stéphane Mallarmé, Odilon Redon and Teodor de Wyzewa – were affiliated with what would come to be known as the Symbolist movement. After the demise of

the magazine in 1888, other journals took up the slack and periodicals such as *La Plume*, *La Revue Blanche* and *La Vogue* dedicated numerous articles to Wagner and his work.[401]

What most attracted the group of young poets loosely classified today as Symbolists to Wagner was, as Richard Sieburth has pointed out, less his music than the ideas it inspired. Fin-de-siècle writers and artists worked in a rarefied atmosphere – Elaine Brody has called it a 'kaleidoscope,' but one could just as easily label it 'life considered through a stained-glass window,' as did Paul Valéry – in which artists, musicians and writers collaborated and inspired one another, working side by side to create interdisciplinary works of art that appealed to the spectator on many different levels.[402] Because of their interest in what a modern audience would call 'multimedia,' they were particularly influenced by Wagner's conception of the *Gesamtkunstwerk der Zukunft*, a total art of the future, which had been filtered, in France, through Baudelaire's 1861 essay 'Richard Wagner et Tannhäuser à Paris.'[403] Baudelaire interpreted Wagner's theory that different arts working in combination could achieve more than the individual arts working alone in light of his own belief in synesthesia. For Baudelaire, synesthesia involved the ability of the arts to convey the same ideas through different media that appealed to all the senses: 'Since the Day God articulated the world as a complex and indivisible whole, things have always expressed themselves by reciprocal analogy.' In this section of his essay about Wagner, Baudelaire cites his own poem 'Correspondances' as an example of this 'reciprocal analogy,' in which 'perfumes, colors and sounds' respond to one another in 'a shadowy and profound unity.'[404] For Baudelaire (unlike Wagner), different media – music, literature, painting, stained glass – do not simply work together; they also translate one another as part of a mystical, God-granted system of essences.[405]

'Correspondances,' which begins with the lines, 'Nature is a temple where living pillars/Let loose, at times, obscure words,' harks back to the Romantic tradition of Goethe and Chateaubriand, who posited the origin of Gothic architecture in early Christian worship in nature. In fact, Baudelaire couches his representation of synesthesia in religious vocabulary. Baudelaire found the same effects of spiritual elevation – common to his belief in the product of synesthesia – in three prose pieces by artists who attempted to translate Wagner's music into words: 'the sensation of *spiritual and physical beatitude*; of *solitude*; of the contemplation of *something infinitely large and infinitely beautiful*; of *an intense light* that delights *the eyes and the soul to rapture*; and finally the sensation of *space spread out to the farthest limits imaginable.*' 'No other musician,' he writes, 'excels like Wagner at *painting* space and depth, both material and spiritual.'[406]

Baudelaire's reverent writings about synesthesia would prove of capital importance for the Symbolist movement and would introduce French Symbolist writers and painters to Wagner. They claimed him as one of their own, probably because of Baudelaire's misrepresentation of the theory of the *Gesamtkunstwerk* (which was far from identical to Baudelaire's *correspondances*).[407] For Symbolists, both Baudelaire and Wagner, like the cathedral builders before them, attempted to reach 'spiritual and physical beatitude' and 'rapture' by creating hybrid works of art that depended on a variety of appeals to the senses. J.-K. Huysmans would further link this aesthetic to the Middle Ages in his 1898 novel *La Cathédrale*, where he labels symbolism 'the psychology of cathedrals' and the 'essence of the Middle Ages,' the theory that made Gothic architecture effective as a total work of art: '[…] the Middle Ages […] knew that everything on earth is a sign, a figure, that the visible is only worth what it exacts from the invisible.' He even went so far as to equate the theoreticians of medieval symbolism to nineteenth-century Symbolists, notably Stéphane Mallarmé.[408]

The concept of the cathedral as a total work of art was not new and Huysmans was certainly familiar with the concept from reading *Les Annales archéologiques*, in which Didron discussed the function of arts within the cathedral. But, as we saw in Chapter 2, authors and artists of the fin de siècle were often frustrated by the prevailing materialist methods and subjects. They discovered in the cathedral a model for what they were trying to do in art, a way of transcending materialism by establishing a system of correspondence with a higher plane of thought. Writers including Léon Bloy and Jean Moréas (author of the 'Symbolist manifesto') further underlined the link between the Middle Ages and the nineteenth century and came to be considered practitioners of medieval traditions in art.[409]

Many late nineteenth-century readers thus mistakenly came to consider Baudelaire, Wagner, the Symbolists and the cathedral builders as kindred spirits, devoted to a belief in the total work of art. Maurice Denis, for example, claimed that Symbolist aesthetics could be found *avant la lettre* in Gregorian chants and Gothic cathedrals; he believed that Symbolists sought to express themselves:

> [...] through the harmony of forms and colors, through the material employed [...] They believed that for every emotion, every human thought there existed a plastic or decorative equivalent, a corresponding beauty. And it is probably to ideas like these that we owe, among other things, *Primitifs*, Gregorian chant, and Gothic cathedrals.[410]

While considering the cathedral as an impressive work of art drew attention to the important feats of France's medieval forebears, it also detached Gothic architecture from its religious function, thus placing it on a par – as Proust had noted – with Wagner's secular operas.

## The cult of the total work of art

One of the best examples of the tendency to conflate medieval works with a quasi-religious cult of the total work of art can be seen in Huysmans's seminal work *A Rebours* (1884). This novel, labeled the 'breviary of the decadence' by Arthur Symons and 'bedside table reading' by Paul Valéry, shook up the literary world and brought mainstream attention to little-known writers and artists such as Paul Verlaine, the Goncourt brothers, Gustave Moreau and Félicien Rops.[411] Des Esseintes, the solitary hero, withdraws from the modern world and into his own 'refined Thebaïd,' a kind of private museum that caters to his eccentric tastes. In each part of his house, he mixes medieval religious objects such as altars with his new objects of veneration: contemporary art and literature. Accordingly, he commissions special manuscript illuminations of three of Baudelaire's poems, which he sets in an ecclesiastical frame on his dalmatic-covered mantel between two monstrances. Similarly, he orders a unique copy of *Les Fleurs du Mal* in the form of a missal, which he reads with devotion. He admires Gustave Moreau's *Salomé* for the opulence of its setting – 'the throne like the high altar of a cathedral' – and for the contrast between this seemingly religious setting and the sacrilegious nature of the scene portrayed.

In each chapter of the novel, des Esseintes seeks pleasure – *jouissance* – through the combined effect of the objects he assembles in his private chambers: color, texture, scent, sound and flavor work in tandem to create an effect impossible to achieve by the simple juxtaposition of individual objects. In the creation of his monk's cell bedroom, for example, he took special pains to mix the colors of the paints, to reproduce a floor worn by monks' sandals, to find a bed that would evoke that of a spartan cell, to add a prie-dieu and real candles used for mass. The total effect of the room infuses him with a sense of well being, Baudelaire's 'spiritual and physical beatitude.' It is the relationship among all of the objects and their appeal to his imagination that makes the space pleasurable for him.

The idea of the total work of art is a fundamental aspect of des Esseintes's aesthetic sensibility. In fact, when he mentions Wagner, it is in these terms. He refuses to attend concerts in Paris because of the rowdy public, but also because the French are not faithful to Wagner: they will not stage his operas in their entirety. Des Esseintes's appreciation of Wagner's work corresponds to his own preference for unity and interrelation among works of art:

[…] He knew very well that there was not a scene, not even a phrase of one of the prodigious Wagner's operas that could be detached from its ensemble with impunity. The pieces, cut out and served on the platter of a concert, lost all signification, remained bereft of meaning, considering that, like chapters that complete one another, all working toward the same conclusion, the same goal, his melodies allowed him to draw the personality of his characters, to incarnate their thoughts, to express their motives, visible or secret and that their ingenious and persistent recurrences were only understandable for listeners who followed the subject from its introductory scene and saw the characters take shape and grow little by little in a milieu from whence one could not remove them without seeing them wither, like branches severed from a tree.[412]

Des Esseintes's insistence on the organicism of Wagner's opera – a living being whose component parts function together to produce its originality – corresponds to his own practice of creating rooms in which each aspect is inseparable from the total effect created by the elements working together. All of his pleasurable experiences result from attempts to reach a higher plane of aesthetic fulfillment through the 'reciprocal analogies' among different media and their appeal to his senses. In fact, for Symbolist writers influenced by Wagner, the pleasure gained from such encounters with art constituted a kind of religious experience; it was proof of the sacred nature of good art. Teodor de Wyzéwa, for example, praised Wagner's belief in 'art as salvation' in an 1885 article for the *Revue wagnérienne*: 'salvation will come to man through Art, which will explain truth, will expel disastrous blindness from souls […] Art is bad if it remains only an Art; Art is sacred if it is a way of making us seek for happiness.'[413]

Des Esseintes's reverence for composite works of art – and especially his admiration for religious settings – was shared by contemporaries and notably by young artists, especially Symbolists, who read *A Rebours* and took it as a bible. They, too, admired religious art in terms of its aesthetic power. Max Elskamp proclaimed the décor of Catholicism 'the most marvelous in the world,' while Georges Rodenbach called the trappings of Catholicism inventions of genius: 'All of Catholic liturgy, with its décors and its accessories, of which each is an invention of genius, satisfies those who are obscurely tormented by a conflict of the ideal and of sensuality.'[414]

Rodenbach puts his finger on the attraction of medieval Church settings for artists like des Esseintes: perceived similarities between Symbolist theory and medieval art created an aesthetic experience that could substitute for religion. The Catholic liturgy, as Rodenbach points out, is a total work of art in which one can find the *jouissance* that des Esseintes sought in his creation of various rooms of his house. A system that values individual 'happiness' or 'rapture' as a sign of the sacred justifies removing the liturgy from its Catholic context and using it as an example of the exalted nature of good art.

As we have seen, consumers of the fin de siècle increasingly searched for or built private spaces in which they could satisfy their taste for both pleasure and the ideal. Such desires resulted in the establishment of numerous 'private museums' and also in a predilection for visiting 'authentic' spaces – monasteries and churches – associated with the medieval past.[415] Gothic cathedrals were particularly popular because of the 'genuine' religious role they had fulfilled since their inception. Religious art seen in a church – in the context for which it was created – seemed much more 'authentic' than the same work seen in a museum. Durtal, the hero of Huysmans's post-conversion novels (*Là-Bas*, *En Route*, *La Cathédrale* and *L'Oblat*), firmly believes in this theory. Through this character, an older Huysmans corrected the 'dilettante' attitudes of des Esseintes by showing the superiority of art still displayed in its original context. Accordingly, Durtal is amazed by the harmony of medieval art in Gothic chapels; they appeal to him in terms that evoke Baudelaire's synesthesia: 'The ideal of all of these works is the same, achieved by different means.'[416]

> Ah! the true proof of Catholicism was this art that it had founded, this art that no one had yet surpassed! In painting and sculpture it was the *Primitifs*; the mystics in poetry and prose; in music, plain chant; in architecture, Romanesque and Gothic. And all of this held together, blazed in a single bouquet, on the same altar; all of this culminated in a crest of unique thoughts: revere, adore, serve the Provider, by showing him, reflected in the soul of his creature as in a faithful mirror, the still immaculate loan of his gifts.[417]

Again and again Durtal returns to the importance of the *whole* and argues against removing works of art from the context to which they belong. Gothic churches, whose 'use value' had kept ornate altars, choir stalls, chasubles, chalices, monstrances, sculptures, paintings, stained glass, music and ceremony together from the Middle Ages to the nineteenth century, provided a clear working example of the objectives of Baudelaire's *correspondances*.

### Dilettante medievalists and the cathedral experience

Such fascination with medieval art and architecture as 'proof' of nineteenth-century Symbolist theories explains, in part, the cathedral's growing popularity in the art and literature of the fin de siècle. Decadent and Symbolist poets idolized the cathedral for its hushed interior, its beautiful art, its music and the feeling of reverence it inspired. Huysmans, who converted to Catholicism in 1892, would later complain about the excesses of medieval 'tourism,' 'museum building,' and 'cult of art' practiced by those of his contemporaries who 'appropriated liturgical forms to apply them to human passions.'[418] His own character, des Esseintes, who inspired the trend, is the perfect target of his criticism: his elaborate project to create total works of art that lift him to a superior emotional plane (a substitute for established religion) leads him to recreate religious spaces – altars, pulpits, chapels – for his own pleasure. This is clear in his monk's cell bedroom as well as in his admiration for medieval music. He likes only Gregorian chant – 'the soul of the Middle Ages,' 'the eternally chanted prayer, modulated to the élans of the soul [...] toward le Très-Haut' – because of its ability to lift his soul and transport him from his *spleen*:

How often had des Esseintes been seized and bent down by an irresistible inspiration as the 'Christus factus est' of the Gregorian chant rose through the nave whose pillars trembled in the shifting clouds of the censers, or as the 'De profundis' harmony moaned, lugubrious as a repressed sob, poignant as a despairing cry of humanity weeping for its mortal destiny, imploring tender mercy from its Savior![419]

Like Baudelaire's *correspondances* and his account of Wagner's *Tannhaüser*, in which the epiphany of the listener comes from the fusion of architectural space, song, touch and scent, des Esseintes is inexplicably moved by performances of Gregorian chant. He is attracted to religion, but rationalizes this fascination by attributing it to the aesthetic sensations – the human passions – it produces in him. While fascinated by the trappings of Catholicism, especially medieval Catholicism, he refuses to recognize his appreciation as other than a private emotional response to the beauty of archaic art.

As Proust remarked in the quote that opens this chapter, many of his contemporaries similarly enjoyed Gregorian chant, 'listening religiously' to 'la messe du pape Marcel', a sixteenth-century composition by Palestrina that builds on a famous medieval song and was thought to have 'saved' polyphonic liturgical music during the Reform. Medieval and Renaissance music – especially plain chant – enjoyed an enormous revival at this time, largely through the efforts of priests Dom Pothier and Dom Guéranger and musicians Charles Bordes, Alexandre Guilmant and Vincent d'Indy, who established 'Les Chanteurs de Saint-Gervais' (1892) and the Schola Cantorum of Paris (1894) in order to explore French national music, especially plain chant.[420] They set up the school in a former Benedictine monastery on the rue Saint-Jacques in Paris and soon had branches in a number of major French cities.

This revival of plain chant, in which a secular school allied itself with the monks of Solesmes to restore the medieval rules governing the performance of Gregorian chant, proved so popular that bi-monthly concerts were sold out and a number of newspapers including *Le Temps* dedicated lengthy articles to the phenomenon.[421] Describing the music as 'pure, limpid, serene, luminescent,' 'accessible to all, made for all,' music critic Pierre Lalo applauded the Schola Cantorum's goal of 'restoring in its primitive purity' this medieval music.[422] Even modern composers sought inspiration in medieval music. Erik Satie's *Quatre Ogives* experiment with the conventions of plain chant, while his *Sonneries de la Rose-Croix* were used by Péladan's group to accompany quasi-medieval ceremonies.[423]

The overwhelming public interest in medieval music as an exotic vestige from the past is like des Esseintes's fondness for his monk's cell. Spectators admired art and music as individual pieces – bibelots to be collected and enjoyed for personal pleasure – without considering their original context or communal value. In the last decades of the nineteenth century, the religious vocabulary used by artists and writers to praise art brought the vocabulary of the 'cult of art' very close to that used for traditional forms of religion. Yet as A. G. Lehmann has pointed out, Symbolists talked a great deal about making art a religion, while not going much further than turning it into a 'private cult.'[424]

### The cathedral as literary *topos*

Even the cathedral was detached from its context; at the end of the century it had become a prized literary theme. Although the Gothic cathedral had been a popular and contested symbol since the publication of Victor Hugo's *Notre-Dame de Paris* (1831) and throughout the century with Viollet-le-Duc's publications about medieval architecture, the subject exploded in the illustrated press of the 1880s and 1890s. Periodicals of this time, like *Le Chat Noir*, *Le Courrier Français*, *La Plume*, *L'Image* and *Le Mercure de France* abound with cathedral-inspired poems ('La Voix des cathédrales,' 'Vitrail,' 'Cantique,' or 'Chapelle'). The names of new periodicals – *Le Clocher* (1881) and *Le Beffroi* (1900) – also reflect this predilection.

The fascination with the cathedral became crystallized in the person of Mérovak, a mysterious self-created performance artist who was dubbed 'l'homme des cathédrales' by *La Plume*, which ran long feature articles about his life and works. Mérovak's drawings of cathedrals were in great demand, often commissioned by leading public figures whose names were inscribed within the artwork. Figure 4.2 provides a characteristic example of Mérovak's style. He frames his view of the cathedral in delicate painted arches while paying special attention to the cityscape in which the church is situated. The smaller-scale depiction of the medieval city at bottom left evokes early Renaissance predellas, while his carefully crafted border designs and complementary text intentionally reference medieval manuscript design. Mérovak's artwork, bell-ringing, organ playing and illustrated conferences about cathedrals proved so popular that in 1898 and 1899 he embarked on travels throughout France to publicize French cathedrals and was included as a featured performer in the *Vieux Paris* exhibit at the 1900 World's Fair.[425]

The journals that sprang up in the years following the freedom of the press laws of 1881 (like those that highlighted Mérovak's art) fostered the multimedia esthetic so appreciated in the cathedral: they combined poems and essays with illustrations, reproductions of paintings and musical scores. Paul Valéry called these journals 'little churches where spirits get worked up' and defended the need for them in order to continue innovation in French literature.[426] As a result of this vogue, artists of different religious, aesthetic and political affiliations might publish next to one another, thus mixing 'dilettante' attraction to medieval art with the religious appreciation

4.2   Mérovak, *Drawing of La Rue St. Romain*, c. 1890

of Catholics. Republican Emile Zola's popular novel *Le Rêve* (1888), set in the shadow of a cathedral, spawned a successful lyrical drama of the same name and prompted self-proclaimed 'mystic' Jean Lorrain to identify the novel as crucial for the 'mystical' revival of the 1890s. He attributed the profusion of sketches and homages in periodicals to Zola's enthusiastic portrayal of l'église Sainte-Marie.[427] Other writers, such as Laurent Tailhade, created poem collections dedicated to various parts of the cathedral. *Vitraux* (1885) mixes a paean of praise to the cathedral and the 'golden twilight' that 'bathes its sanctuary' with the 'incandescent flowers' spreading from the stained glass throughout the church. Yet he also incorporates cynical juxtapositions between this beautiful holy setting and the debauched women who sully it.[428] Germain Nouveau, Léon Bloy, Jules Laforgue, Adolphe Retté, Anatole France, Huysmans and Proust also present evocative descriptive passages of the cathedral's atmosphere, reverent feelings of mysticism, legendary dreams of escape to a medieval past or childhood memories of religious experiences. Looking back at this period, poet José-Maria Heredia described the entire Symbolist movement as a 'return to the Middle Ages.'[429]

Yet just as some Symbolists adopted the ideas of Wagner without hearing his music, some fin-de-siècle writers appreciated cathedrals without visiting them. Huysmans said as much in his preface to Remy de Gourmont's *Le Latin mystique*, as he accused the young generation of being dilettantes and slaves to fashion.[430] Such authors praised 'the cathedral' as an idea instead of focusing on specific cathedrals. While there is nothing wrong with taking literary inspiration where one wishes, medieval 'purists' like Bloy and Huysmans seemed to think there was. They took great offense at the seeming betrayal of the cathedral, which they treated with a veneration bordering on that accorded a relic. For them, the only way to approach the cathedral was as a pilgrim from the Middle Ages would have approached a shrine.

In the literature of the fin de siècle, however, Gothic architecture is most often described as a dreamy private space of meditation and inspiration. In fact, literary representations of the cathedral were often so similar that it is difficult to distinguish the poems of secular poets from those of their Catholic friends. Germain Nouveau provides an excellent example of this. He wrote *La Doctrine de l'Amour* (which provides a Chateaubriand-like encomium of Catholic art) from 1879–1881, nearly ten years before he truly converted to Catholicism. Yet because of his exuberant praise of religion critics are often tempted to accept this work as one inspired by his conversion.[431] 'Les Cathédrales,' one of the best-known poems of this collection, reveals, however, the materiality of his aesthetic and imaginary attraction to an ideal cathedral. The first stanza of the poem summarizes many Decadent and Symbolist tributes to Gothic architecture as a mysterious vessel that preserves a medieval world of legends within it:

But glory to cathedrals!
Full of shadow and fire, silence and moans
With their forest of immense pillars
And their population of saints, monks and knights,
They are walled cities above towns,
That keep only the irregular sounds
Of alms, at the bottom of bowls,
Under their hospitable porch.[432]

Richard Griffiths has pointed out that despite the seeming 'religion' of *La Doctrine de l'Amour*, there is a marked difference between Nouveau's aesthetic attraction to Catholic art – 'that of a man impressed by Christianity yet living a life basically unaffected by any beliefs this feeling may have brought to him' – and real belief, 'that of a man of absolute faith, who lives according to the strongest demands of a fanatical humility.'[433]

Paul Verlaine, on the other hand, wrote spiritually honest poems about the cathedral that nevertheless encouraged dilettante admiration of it. His mystical *Sagesse* (1881), a collection of poems tracing the torments of a tortured soul and its embrace of religion, was published just as young poets were reacting against Naturalism and excessive materialism in art, seeking idealism and returning to the Church. The book became a literary staple for believers and non-believers alike; they saw his fervent religious belief and nostalgia for the Middle Ages as a model for their own art. Huysmans portrayed Verlaine as a medieval mystic in *A Rebours* (1884), the book that gave him wide public acclaim, while others labeled him the 'nineteenth-century Villon.'[434] Charles Morice went so far as to call *Sagesse* 'a thirteenth-century

Gothic cathedral' because of the depth of its lyricism and the brilliance of its versification. Maurice Denis linked him to the medieval tradition by creating Gothic-style woodcut illustrations for the book (see Fig. 2.7), while Charles Péguy and Paul Claudel praised Verlaine and took him as a literary mentor.[435] The most often quoted lines of *Sagesse* – 'It is toward the enormous and delicate Middle Ages/That my wounded heart must navigate [...] On your wings of stone, oh wild Cathedral!' – became a kind of battle cry for world-weary Catholics and Symbolists alike.[436]

Huysmans's work, too, alternates between secular and religious themes and further enhanced the cathedral *topos*. After writing *A Rebours* and the Satanic *Là-Bas*, both of which reflect what Griffiths calls a '"dilettante" fascination with medieval religion,' Huysmans converted to Catholicism. He devoted the rest of his life to scholarly studies of the Catholic Middle Ages, yet many critics do not recognize his conversion as legitimate.[437] In fact, not only did Huysmans dedicate himself to the Church, he spent the last years of his life disseminating information about the belief system and aesthetic preferences of what he considered the *real* Middle Ages, the period evoked in medieval manuscripts and art.[438] In reaction to the dabbling interest of his contemporaries, Huysmans hoped to bring attention to authentic medieval sources that explained the original meaning and function of medieval art. To this end, he published a thirty-page index of medieval sources with his novel *La Cathédrale* (1898), an appendix rarely included in modern editions of the book.

Given the enthusiasm of Husymans's and Verlaine's praise of medieval religious ceremony, it should come as no surprise that many artists' conversions took place during religious services in churches and monasteries, as the converts – drawn to churches by friends, families, or aesthetic curiosity – succumbed to the power of the liturgy.[439] Huysmans's theory of the importance of medieval religious art and the aesthetic experience it constituted for his contemporaries should not be underestimated. Frédéric Gugelot has pointed out that 150 intellectuals – mainly authors and artists – converted to Catholicism between 1885 and 1935.[440] Although a few were drawn from other religions, the large majority (75%) fit Verlaine's and Huysmans's mold: they were raised in somewhat pious Catholic homes; they lost their faith as adolescents, generally as a result of secular education; and they returned to the Church at the age (on average) of thirty or forty.[441] Perhaps the best-known of such experiences is that of poet Paul Claudel, who recounted his Christmas 1886 conversion in Notre-Dame de Paris in 'Le 25 décembre 1886' and 'Ma conversion.' Like many of his contemporaries, he had 'forgotten' the Catholicism of his childhood and, as a budding writer, he was drawn to church services as a literary theme that might inspire him to write:

At that time I had just begun writing and it seemed to me that in Catholic ceremonies, considered with a superior dilettantism, I would find an appropriate stimulant and the material for a few Decadent exercises. [...] The choirboys in white robes and the students of the little seminary of Saint-Nicolas-du-Chardonnet who helped them were in the middle of singing what I would later know to be the

*Magnificat*. […] And it was then that the event that has dominated my entire life took place. In an instant my heart was touched and *I believed*.[442]

The Catholic liturgy – where form and content work together – exerted a powerful force on artists steeped in the theories of Baudelaire and Wagner; like Claudel, many came to cathedrals seeking literary inspiration only to find faith and to recognize the spiritual underpinnings of the art they had previously admired from a purely aesthetic standpoint. Many former 'dilettantes' thus converted to Catholicism and began to praise the cathedral for its 'use value,' its ability to fuse art with religious belief.

As a result of this newfound understanding of cathedrals, their original context and their function, even museums came under fire for the artificiality of their display. In his introduction to Rodin's *Les Cathédrales de France*, Charles Morice fiercely criticizes them as wastelands of skeletal bibelots plucked from their original context. He lambasts the 'museum mentality' of his contemporaries and calls for reuniting works of art in settings that bring their meaning back to life:

Museums are more or less luxurious cemeteries, where works, diverted from their initial destination, lose the best of their sense and their splendor. They were composed to embellish and to announce a public place, a church, a courthouse, a reception hall, or a place of meditation: at the cost of what efforts, in the cold commotion of a museum, do we manage to attain the real thought of the artist! The masses never go to museums. The marvels that they see piled up there are, for them, inert, cold, mute, incomprehensible objects. […] The cause of this misfortune is in this fanatical individualism that disperses the elements of the modern world and that we saw dawning in the Renaissance […] hence this desire, more or less reasoned, but universal, for collection, for unity, that we noted earlier […][443]

Morice's harsh criticism of morgue-like museums, like that of Huysmans and Proust (who criticizes the museum and its untouchable display cases as a 'sepulcher'),[444] centers on issues of authenticity, 'use value,' and individualization. For Morice, the modern practice of removing works of art from their original context – a church, for example – causes the work to lose its authenticity (a concept based, as Benjamin has suggested, in its 'use value') and to become a simple bibelot, appreciated for its historical or aesthetic value. A museum, therefore, is an assembly of dead objects, with no meaning but those that the spectator ascribes to them. In a museum, bibelots can only gain meaning through artificial arrangement.[445] The same objects left in their original context, on the other hand, are still alive because of their function; they act within a system of reference that continues to reflect the 'real meaning of the artist that created them.' For Morice, it is imperative to retain as many of these 'living' spaces as possible; without doing this, artists will lose the sense of the collective and the importance of the sense of community involved in creating art.

## 'All of our cathedrals are in our France': the nationalist cathedral

A number of writers worked actively to reshape 'dilettante' attitudes toward cathedrals and to bring attention to the real structures so desperately in need of support. Among these, J.-K. Huysmans was perhaps the most influential. While writing *La Cathédrale*, a tribute to Notre-Dame de Chartres published in 1898, Huysmans realized that cathedrals – because of what Aloïs Riegl calls 'use value' – provide an important bridge between present and past. Huysmans incorporated this belief in his novel. For Durtal, his hero, it is the 'soul' – the communal worship – of a cathedral that differentiates it from a museum:

> I am not speaking of the soul of the monument from the moment when man, with divine help, created it; we are unaware of that soul though precious documents do tell us about Chartres; but of the soul that other churches have saved, the soul they have now and that we help keep alive with our more or less constant presence, with our more or less frequent communions, with our more or less fervent prayers.[446]

Huysmans's description of this 'soul' echoes the medieval understanding of the cathedral as a representation of the Christian community where every member of the church – past, present and future – must participate in maintaining the cathedral, through physical work and through prayer. Without this force, cathedrals will die and will become nothing more than 'inert corpses of stone' filled with 'indecent tourists.' He is disturbed that *real* cathedrals, the center of French communal life since the Middle Ages, are losing influence because of dwindling congregations and apathetic parishioners.[447]

Huysmans's worry about the cathedral stemmed not only from his Catholicism, but also from concerns about how their demise would impact on France. He felt that the 'soul' of these churches constituted the spiritual history of the French nation and transcended the petty social, political and economic worries of his contemporaries. This is evident in his idealized conception of how churches were built: '[Workers] belonged to every class of society […] divine love was so strong that it obliterated distinctions and abolished castes […] We build temples very differently today. When I think of the Sacré-Coeur of Paris, that gloomy, ponderous construction built by men who have inscribed their names in red on every stone!'[448] While his nostalgia for the Middle Ages is palpable in this passage, Huysmans's point has validity: without fostering a sense of community, modern France would continue to disintegrate, torn apart by increased individualism.

Accordingly, Huysmans devotes his novel to 'reanimating' and 'rebuilding' the cathedral, to bringing it back to life through his prose.[449] He knew his works could reach a wide audience and he hoped that they might attract more people to existing cathedrals where contemporaries would learn about the Catholic faith and its communal nature: 'Perhaps this volume will make Notre-Dame de Chartres and her house in Chartres better loved,' he wrote in a letter to the abbess of Solesmes, while telling his confessor that he hoped to reach non-Catholics, 'those for whom conversions are possible.'[450] In fact, his efforts bore fruit: the book was his greatest success yet, selling 20 000 copies in less than a month, and bringing droves of visitors to Chartres; by 1912 the French had even founded a Société des Amis des Cathédrales.[451]

In the midst of this vogue for Notre-Dame de Chartres, another book prompted enormous interest in the cathedral. Emile Mâle's doctoral thesis, the most significant art-historical study on French Gothic art of the time, also appeared in 1898, to great public acclaim. In *L'art religieux du XIIIe siècle en France*, Mâle, too, set out to 'rebaptize' Gothic churches, illuminating their complex symbolism and insisting on their Christian origins. This book differed from the work of his predecessors in its profound iconographical emphasis. Like Huysmans, Mâle believed that the Gothic cathedral functioned as an encyclopedia of the medieval mind. Just as medieval man saw the world as symbolic, cathedrals portrayed the universe as a 'mirror' of nature, learning, morals and history. Mâle drew heavily from the *Speculum Majus* of Vincent of Beauvais, to structure the work and to interpret Gothic architecture as inseparable from the Catholic liturgy. Through the 're-baptism' of medieval art in his book, Mâle re-established the Christian roots of *all* Gothic works, but especially of French ones: '[...] we are also certain that nowhere was Christian thought expressed with such breadth and richness as in France [...] It was in France that medieval doctrine found its most perfect form. Thirteenth century France was Christianity's consciousness.'[452]

The urgency of both Huysmans's and Mâle's projects emerges with even greater clarity when viewed against the secular readings of the cathedral promoted not only by their predecessors (especially Hugo and Viollet-le-Duc), whom they criticize, but also by their contemporaries who worked toward the separation of Church and State. Linked to Mâle's glorification of France's Christian past was his deep reverence for the regimes under which Christianity flourished in the Middle Ages. For Mâle, the monarchy was the best political format for the ideals of Christianity. Speaking of the kings represented in the clerestory windows of the nave in Reims, Mâle wrote:

They are there to remind people that royalty is a divine right, and that a King anointed with holy oil is more than an ordinary man. The strange statues carved on the exterior of the church around the great rose window of the façade, complete this instruction [...] The following scenes were intended to recall that God, in raising kings above all other men, exacts greater virtue from them.[453]

For both Mâle and Huysmans, medieval art evoked a period when order, community and faith still existed, before commercialism had destroyed civil society. Indeed, a sub-theme of *L'art religieux* is the conviction that democracy, encouraged by the invention of the printing press and realized with the French Revolution, had sounded the death knell for Gothic art.[454]

Mâle's approach, his erudite and heartfelt analysis of the interwoven symbolism of each Gothic cathedral, found favor with many Symbolists, including Huysmans, who reviewed the book positively, and Maurice Denis, who quoted and borrowed liberally from Mâle in his own essays.[455] Although he did not draw directly on Wagner, or on theories of his

*Gesamtkunstwerk*, Mâle, like Huysmans, viewed the cathedral as a cohesive whole. Rather than separate his study of the cathedral by media or material, Mâle took iconography and symbolism – the 'mirrors' of medieval theologian Vincent de Beauvais – as the organizing principle of the book. He promoted the cathedral as the product of a synthesizing vision, a harmonious ensemble that resulted from the shared piety of all those who labored on it: 'For them [the men of the Middle Ages], the cathedral was a total revelation. Speech, music, the living drama of the mystery plays, the immobile drama of the statues, all of the arts were combined there. It was something more than art [...].'[456]

*L'Art religieux du XIIIe siècle en France* praised the cathedral as 'the genius of Christianity' and the 'genius of France.' It added significantly to public appreciation of the cathedral and emphasized the sophistication of France's medieval forebears and their concept of symbolism. Mâle's work, which closed with the phrase 'When shall we understand that in the domain of art France has accomplished nothing greater?', only further consecrated the cathedral as a national monument.

Proust relied heavily on Huysmans's and Mâle's concept of the 'soul' of cathedrals in composing 'La Mort des cathédrales.'[457] Although glossing over the religious importance of churches, he would borrow liberally from Mâle's argument and would cite verbatim the three pages of *L'Art religieux du XIIIe siècle* dedicated to the symbolism underlying the Catholic mass. Each of the priests' actions, the lights, costumes, music or timing have meaning, he insists, as do the sculptures, stained glass and architecture of the Gothic cathedral.[458] Proust's essay, written six years after Huysmans's and Mâle's works, shows the extent to which, by 1904, contemporaries better understood and valued both the theories of Baudelaire and Wagner and the medieval aesthetic underlying the cathedral. By the early twentieth century, people lined up to watch high mass in Chartres as they had formerly flocked to Bayreuth.

Theories comparing the cathedral to a work of art had existed throughout the nineteenth century, notably in the publications of Didron and Viollet-le-Duc. As Mâle pointed out in 'La Peinture sur verre en France,' one of Viollet's first memories consisted of a visit to Notre-Dame de Paris in which he heard organ music at the moment he looked at the stained glass, thus imagining that the windows were singing to him.[459] Yet such theories did not become popular with a mass audience until long after Viollet's death. Proust's 1904 argument about the 'death of cathedrals' would prove effective precisely because of the early twentieth-century public's increasingly sophisticated appreciation of synthesis among the arts. His appeal to aesthetics and to nationalism reached even those politicians who refused to consider the 'use value,' the 'soul' of Gothic cathedrals. By evoking Wagner, Proust carefully insisted on the inseparability of liturgical ceremonies and architecture, while arguing about the importance of conserving an inherently *French* tradition that pre-dated the theory of the *Gesamtkunstwerk* by hundreds of years.

In the wake of the separation of Church and State, a number of artists, journalists and politicians from different backgrounds and political stripes would join ranks with Huysmans, Mâle and Proust to protest the lack of effective conservation laws in France and to change attitudes about medieval structures. Although they all valued the cathedral for different (and often conflicting) reasons, they also recognized the importance of establishing laws to protect it. Maurice Barrès, the nationalistic writer and deputy who valued the cathedral less for its religion than for its 'Frenchness,' proposed a number of conservation laws. For him, cathedrals were not just houses of worship, but also an integral part of French heritage, the heart of the 'family' that constituted the French nation and 'a house of the collective.'[460] As Georges Grosjean pointed out in his 1904 booklet entitled *Pour l'art contre les vandales*, it was not just Catholics, social elites, aestheticians, or free-thinking intellectuals who supported laws to preserve France's national heritage: 'it is the heart of all France that beats with [Barrès's ... ].'[461]

Artists, too, increasingly hailed the nationalist spirit of the cathedral, rather than focusing solely on religious or aesthetic appeal. The sculptor Auguste Rodin discovered the beauty of cathedrals late in life and published – with the help of Charles Morice – a book of meditations and sketches entitled *Les Cathédrales de France* (1914). In this illustrated book, he compared cathedrals to 'a fastener that reunites everything: it is the knot, the pact of civilization.'[462] His appreciation of the cathedral knew no bounds and he described it as 'the synthesis of the country. I repeat: rocks, forests, gardens, northern sun [...] all of our France is in our cathedrals [...].' Later in this work he would describe this national treasure as integral to the nation's survival: 'The country cannot perish as long as Cathedrals are here. They are our Muses. They are our Mothers.'[463] By appealing to the sense of the collective, by convincing contemporaries that taking pieces of the cathedral was like pillaging their own family, Barrès, Rodin and intellectuals of all political and religious affiliations helped persuade contemporaries of the importance of preserving cathedrals, interesting and unique testaments to the genius of their French ancestors. Each of these passages uses terms – synthesis, fastener, knot, pact – that insist on a link between French art, spirit and cultural identity, past and present.

Indeed, such appreciation of the cathedral as a sublime figure of French achievement, a collection of many different arts functioning together to create an even greater effect, inspired anger toward those who divested it of even its smallest pieces. As Georges Grosjean suggests in *Pour l'art contre les vandales*, antique dealers and amateurs who broke up total works of art to appropriate bibelots for living rooms and museums were the enemy of the French collective – 'les vandales' – the heartless individualists working against the common good. He proposed fighting against them as a 'crusade.'

## The cathedral and the museum: the work of art in the age of mechanical reproduction

Churches were one of the last remaining places in modern France where one could find medieval art still functioning in the context for which it had been designed. It is no wonder – given artists' concerns about individualism, social fragmentation, industrialization and loss of meaning – that they began to realize not only that cathedrals served as the perfect model of the 'total work of art' they valued, but also that their continued use made them unique. Unlike other arts, many of which could be reproduced by modern techniques, it would be impossible to recreate a functioning medieval cathedral in the modern world. While museums provided artificial reconstructions of the past, cathedrals were authentic: they continued to function in accordance with their original meaning. The combination of the various arts used in the celebration of the Catholic liturgy was even more sublime than Wagner's operas because the 'sets' could not be reproduced; they played an integral role in the performance. As Thorstein Veblen suggested in 1899, it is the scarcity, the rarity of such experiences that would make the leisure class most treasure a product such as a cathedral.[464]

Although conspicuous consumption threatened to separate medieval objects from their religious context at the turn of the century and to transform them into bibelots, the intellectual elite began to change its attitude thanks to the efforts of writers and artists like Huysmans, Mâle, Barrès, Proust, Morice and Rodin. They began to balk at breaking up 'total works of art' and instead lovingly cherished them as 'fasteners,' 'syntheses' and 'collectives' of French spirit. The cathedral (and by extension the Middle Ages) came to incarnate an ideal of the lost French community, the shared national space of an increasingly disparate and self-centered people. Worries about individualism, authenticity and meaning converged in a fascination with the cathedral, the link to a mythical France where everyone worked together for the common good. A cathedral, as Proust would suggest in 'Combray,' is a four-dimensional space ('the fourth being Time'), that 'unfurl[s] its nave across the centuries.'[465] Visiting the cathedral was like finding one's roots and reaffirming one's commitment to working as part of a religious or secular collective.

Yet while the intellectual elite had come to venerate the cathedral and its component arts – stained glass, tapestry, silverwork, and the like – such ideals of community and national patrimony had not yet been completely accepted by the bourgeoisie and the lower classes. Like des Esseintes, many still longed to build their own cathedral-like dream worlds. As a result, the wide variety of extant medieval objects collected and displayed in the fin de siècle at art museums, at exhibitions and in private realms received a mixed reception. Perhaps no objects garnered more attention – or caused fiercer debates – than authentic examples of medieval stained glass and tapestries removed from their religious context. Regarded as prime symbols of both the Christian heritage and French artistic supremacy, such works were highly coveted and came, in this period, to be far more widely displayed and collected. It was precisely their migration from the sacred realm of cathedrals and monasteries to the spaces of leisure and fashion that caused dismay among critics and champions of the Middle Ages. As we shall see in the next chapter, medieval stained glass and tapestries represented values under siege in turn-of-the-century France.

# 5

# From cathedral to cabaret: the popularity of medieval stained glass and tapestries

If stained glass has retained its place of honor in our churches, if it employs a considerable number of artists and artisans, its use in the window decoration of some public government buildings, in the most comfortable homes and in certain meeting places such as restaurants and brasseries, has provided much more work, in the last few years, for our specialized workshops. The *bon marché*, child of fashion, has vulgarized the stained glass we now see everywhere. At this end of the nineteenth century, bastardized Gothic and mutant Renaissance howl at being mated with the old-fashioned windows of cabarets and a few boutiques.[466]

Edouard Didron, Speech to L'Union centrale des arts décoratifs (1898)

In the protest of Edouard Didron, echoed by countless fin-de-siècle critics, we encounter the central issues surrounding the popularization of Gothic art in this period. As the previous chapters have shown, the French public had easy access to authentic examples of medieval stained glass and tapestries through newly established museums and exhibits, through the hugely attended World's Fairs, through cathedrals and through numerous publications and journals. Indeed, the late nineteenth century witnessed an unprecedented revival of these media, fueled by their religious and nationalist associations. With this new vogue came the production of works by contemporary artists, including the leading avant-garde, who were deeply influenced by Gothic windows and tapestries.

It was not only in churches, museums and other spaces associated with the fine arts, however, that medieval works could be seen. They had also invaded the haunts of the bourgeoisie; increasingly, they could be found in spaces dedicated to leisure, capital and fashion. The double-natured revival of these media gave rise to what many at the time perceived as a paradox: demand for them hinged on what was labeled their 'purity' and 'pre-industrial' authenticity (characteristics endlessly praised by art historians), yet these qualities were compromised by such popularity. To satisfy the bourgeois audience, companies mass produced and heavily marketed faux-medieval or medieval-inspired stained glass and tapestries. Perhaps the most powerful example of this phenomenon was the stained glass decorating the new 'cathedrals of modern commerce,' the department stores like Les Grands Magasins du Printemps and the Bon Marché, immortalized in Emile Zola's fictional *Au Bonheur des Dames*.[467] By referring to the Middle Ages, these works simultaneously evoked and exorcized the specter of the commodity: while they summoned up a past that predated the alienation of labor and the demise of the craft system, they were very much a part of the broader commodification of culture in late nineteenth-century France.[468]

On many levels, Gothic stained-glass windows and tapestry cycles underwent a 'revival' in the fin de siècle. Art-historical texts repeatedly discussed and reproduced them, thus making up for years of neglect. Critics established a specific discourse surrounding these works, emphasizing aspects such as naiveté, relationship to architecture and contrast with easel painting; they created associations that were repeated throughout the period and led, in turn, to a modern revival of these media. In fact, many of the new rules considered essential for modern stained-glass windows and tapestry were based on and derived from Gothic examples. Inevitable clashes arose when modern artists, both decorative artisans and avant-garde painters, attempted to invoke or rework these models, to make, as one critic put it, works 'both old and new.'[469] The fin-de-siècle artists' embrace of these media was a function of the works' wider popularity and a response to the underlying issues that rendered medieval stained glass and tapestries so attractive to late nineteenth-century viewers. Like so much else associated with the glorified Middle Ages, the popularity of medieval tapestries and stained glass resulted from growing nationalism, neo-Catholicism and fear of modernity.

The idealized view of these works made its way into artistic theory and production, transforming the style of many Symbolist painters, who wished to endow their works with equal spiritual and aesthetic value. Yet a renewed popularity of these media also occurred in an arena far removed from the esoteric milieu of the Symbolists: the cafés, taverns and nightclubs of popular Paris. While drawing on popular interest for these medieval media, bourgeois establishments mixed medieval stained glass and tapestries with less expensive modern imitations, thus turning all of them into bibelots. Such combinations formed what critics considered an unholy alliance of modern and medieval that would lead to the demise of both. What these critics failed to realize, however, was that the factors leading to the mass reproduction – the 'bastardization' – of stained glass were simultaneously responsible for their critical re-evaluation and embrace.

This chapter begins by examining the popular use of medieval art and its modern imitations in bourgeois residences, taverns and cafés, a practice that art historians rejected, condemning the use of sacred media in secular locations. Next we question such stereotypes about medieval stained glass and tapestry as they appear in the literature and critical discourse of the fin-de-siècle period. Scholarly texts, journal articles and reviews of both temporary exhibits and permanent collections abound with distinct narratives about the importance of site-specific integrity for these media and the dangers of fragmentation. To what extent was the avant-garde interest in stained glass and tapestries and artists' emulation of medieval art a response to such discourse? Exploring the work of several artists, including Edouard Vuillard, Paul Sérusier and Maurice Denis, reveals the ways in which accepted ideas about stained glass and tapestry influenced late nineteenth-century art.

## From cathedral to cabaret

Didron's outcry against the 'bastardization' of medieval art was not completely unwarranted. As Marcel Proust pointed out, the politicians who wrote the anti-clerical laws leading to the separation of Church and State had ransacked cathedrals, country churches and old monasteries to collect sacred works of medieval art that they could use to decorate their houses; they mixed ancient and modern objects to create a décor that struck their fancy. The vogue for medieval art and for creating medievalesque living rooms separated formerly religious artifacts from their sacred context, turning choir stalls into umbrella stands and placing them next to modern carpets, paintings or bric-à-brac.[470] In bourgeois homes and in the numerous 'Gothic' taverns and cafés that cropped up in the 1880s and 1890s, medieval tapestries and stained glass served purely as decoration, indistinguishable from modern reproductions. Emile Zola, for example, collected twelfth- and thirteenth-century stained-glass fragments formerly belonging to churches. Yet he did not feature them in a private chapel; instead, he displayed them in his study or on doors leading to his kitchen and staircases. In order to add to the 'medieval' effect of his décor, he designed and ordered modern stained-glass windows featuring themes from his novels. They stood side-by-side with stained glass and tapestry from the Middle Ages (see Fig. 3.1).[471]

The bourgeois taste for stained glass was echoed in the cabarets of Montmartre; such predilections were so pronounced that Paul Valéry described 1880s Paris as 'life considered through a stained-glass window.'[472] Taverns, cabarets and cafés sprang up in Montmartre in the years following the Franco-Prussian war; one of the first and most popular of these was 'La Grand'Pinte,' founded at the top of the rue des Martyrs in 1878 by an art dealer (Fig. 5.1). Labeled a 'Henri II tavern,' it featured decorations and furniture design of decidedly medieval flavor.[473] Intrigued by the medieval decor, which seemed to bring patrons back to the 'good old days,' imitators soon followed.

The most notable example, itself the model for many subsequent establishments, was Le Chat Noir, the cabaret founded by Rodolphe Salis in 1881. According to his collaborator, Emile Goudeau, Salis dreamed of capitalizing on the new trend for 'theme' cabarets by making medieval and Renaissance décor part of the entertainment, thus creating a total work of art in which songs, painting, theatrical presentations, and décor all complemented one another.[474] He went on to create a 'Louis XIII-style cabaret, founded by a *fumiste*' and publicized it as a 'neo-medieval café' (Figs 5.2 and 5.3).[475] The *Chat Noir-Guide* published by Salis parodies a museum catalog by describing

5.1   *Interior of La*
*Grande Pinte,*
*1886*

the provenance of various articles on display in the cabaret, yet it also provides
valuable details about the kinds of decorations found in this allegedly medieval
café. In the Salle François Villon, for example, one finds a *Tapisserie d'Aubusson*
formerly belonging to novelist George Sand, a Delft vase, a Louis XVI mirror
belonging to Marie-Antoinette, a portrait of Villon by Oswald Heidbrinck,
medieval armor and chandeliers, a painting by Calbet of Le Chat Noir in the

CHARACTERISTIC PARISIAN CAFÉS.                          695

happy and contented with the success of their harmless escapade. The population of the Boulevard St.-Michel is accustomed to these noisy ways, but over the water such manners are not appreciated, and the jokes of the medical students have generally led to disturbances when they have ventured to practise them elsewhere than in their own Latin Quarter. Therefore the medical student will tell you that he does not care to cross the river, and that the grand boulevard has no charms for him. His boulevard is that named after St.-Michel, a fine modern thoroughfare, shaded with splendid trees, and lined with shops, restaurants, and innumerable cafés and brasseries, where the students take their "demi-tasse,"their"bock," their vermouth, or their absinthe, and watch the characteristic movement of their " Boul' Mich'," as they call their favorite promenade. A characteristic corner is the Café Vachette, which is patronized by students of all categories — by the "swells," by the sporting and betting men, by the Bohemian student, by the southerner of the type of Alphonse Dau-

det, with long black hair, curly mustache, and forked beard, who wears a flat-brimmed hat tilted on the back of his head, and has a gay word to say to all the impertinent *étudiantes*, who are not all rigorously inscribed on the books of the University. Even the French school-boy goes to the café, and on Saturday especially you see the pupils of the state lycées, the *potaches* as they are called, airing themselves along the "Boul' Mich'," with their hands in their pockets, and their "semi-rigide" képi pulled well down over their ears, smoking gi-

Middle Ages and the skull and right femur of Villon (literary 'relics'), among other assorted objects.[476] Other rooms featured modern stained-glass windows by Adolphe Willette, including *Le Veau d'or*, described as 'worthy of the great stained-glass artisans of the Middle Ages,' and *La Vierge au chat*, 'created for the boudoir of Princess Mathilda and refused for unknown reasons.' A modern mantelpiece and chandelier were commissioned from Eugène Grasset.[477] Even if the Chat Noir was above all characterized by bric-à-brac from various ages, newspaper articles, advertisements and catalogs repeatedly described it as

5.3   *Le Chat Noir: A cozy corner*, 1901

'medieval,' thus firmly anchoring it in the public's mind as a medieval tavern.[478] So many establishments followed suit that Jules Claretie, writing in *Le Temps* in 1884, noted that Gothic cafés were springing up all over Montmartre.[479] Side by side with the new breed of medieval scholarship that sought to document the precise history of medieval French art, there flourished an eclectic, laissez-faire medieval décor.

The idea of a bar as a popular meeting place outfitted in imitation half-timbering with its walls ornamented with bric-à-brac began to be understood as characteristically 'medieval' (Fig. 5.4). John Grand-Carteret discussed the medieval origin of such colorful taverns in an 1886 book, *Raphaël et Gambrinus ou l'art dans la brasserie*:

> We know that the Middle Ages possessed an exceptional sense of interior decoration; it is thus not extraordinary that cabaret walls were not entirely bare. We would, however, err seriously if we attributed today's sense of decoration to them; instead of paintings or frescoes, they had painted walls and ceilings with various ornaments [...] above all, their ornamentation owed its character to leaded windows, to iron fittings, to high chimneys, to wood paneling, to tables and seats.[480]

Grand-Carteret's book describes the excesses of these 'neo-medieval' taverns in great detail. In cafés such as La Grand'Pinte, La Brasserie Flamande and the Taverne Montmartre, the décor, furniture decoration and interior ambience all adopted modern conceptions of a medieval tavern. Grand-Carteret noted that the Taverne Montmartre was the 'most artistic of the brasseries.' Sporting a Louis XIII lantern and stained-glass windows representing the medieval descent from Montmartre, its woodwork was decorated with Gothic and

5.4   Henri Pille,
*Cabaret au Moyen
Age*, 1886

IN THE CAFÉ DU CONSERVATOIRE

gilded letters 'as in a missal,' its walls were hung with 'beautiful and old Flemish tapestries.'[481]

Medieval décor was taken to an even greater extreme at the Café du Conservatoire, where visitors dined, drank and socialized in a space designed to mimic the Gothic cathedral (Fig. 5.5). As in the Limelight, the church turned disco to which New Yorkers flocked in the 1980s, a special *frisson* was added to the cabaret experience by holding secular entertainment in a space evoking purity and religious ambience. The authors of a 1900 guide to 'Bohemian Paris,' for example, described the café as reminding them of Notre-Dame de Paris:

[...] the interior of the place certainly looked like a church – it was fitted to have that significance. The cold, gray stone walls rose to a vaulted Gothic ceiling; Gothic pillars and arches and carved wood completed the architectural effect; statues of saints appeared in niches, some surmounted by halos of lighted candles; and there were banners, bearing scriptural mottoes. The heavy oaken tables on the floor were provided with stiff, high-backed pulpit chairs, beautiful in color and carving and of a Gothic type [...][482]

The bar functioned as the altar, above which hung a large Crucifixion painting. For two francs, customers bought tickets to the 'salle des Poetes,' where up-and-coming poets and songwriters read or sang their works, hoping to have them published in *Le Gil Blas* or other journals.[483] One can clearly gauge growing secular sentiment in Paris by such examples. Other establishments left historical and religious models behind to create picturesque or macabre theme cabarets that took visitors to the farthest reaches of the Earth (the Orient, the Middle East) and beyond (Heaven, Hell, 'Nothingness').[484] As Grand-Carteret observed, artistic arrangements of taverns reflected a troubled time's embrace of 'the god Bibelot' and his thirst for exotic color, style and trinkets.[485] Visiting such taverns was a way of escaping banal reality while parodying high-brow, exclusive references to the past.

It is as a response to the phenomenon of decorating cafés, taverns, and bourgeois homes with both medieval and mock-medieval works that we should situate Edouard Didron's outcry against the 'bastardization' of Gothic art. He was not alone; numerous critics and scholars shared his views. An article appearing in the *Revue Illustrée* in 1886 noted the widespread consumption of stained glass, complaining that ' ... our interiors, where we need light in order to work, are obscured by the abuse of colored stained glass ... '[486] In 1896, Léon Ottin decried the *vitromania* that gripped Paris in *Le Vitrail: son histoire, ses manifestations diverses à travers les âges et les peuples*, a history of stained glass.[487]

It was not the general medieval outfitting of taverns that drew the critics' ire. In fact, as we will see in Chapter 7, such medievalized settings were thought to be perfect backdrops for the spirited high jinks of the proprietors and visitors. Rather, it was the grafting of arts associated with the cathedral, specifically stained glass, onto realms of public consumption and pleasure that seemed to them an act of desecration. Indeed, this was Ottin's major complaint. The sacred medium had been degraded, he claimed, by its frequent use in decorating the new leisure spaces of the middle class: brasseries, casinos, theaters and even the Moulin Rouge.[488] It struck Ottin as a bitter irony that the art form most frequently associated with the sacred medieval cathedral was now the chosen medium for the 'corrupted haunts' of the bourgeoisie. Emile Delalande, reviewing the stained glass appearing at the Salon of 1894, sounded the same note of alarm:

For several years, the public has shown a lively interest in the phenomenon of art applied to decoration and today in particular the art of stained glass seems to be held in special regard. In the past it was reserved almost exclusively for religious buildings, today it enters not only princely mansions, but also our modest dwellings and it even invades, sometimes to our great regret, public establishments.[489]

Ottin's and Delalande's scorn for the use of stained glass in bars, casinos and cafés matched that of Edouard Didron.

For Didron the 'democratization' of culture, the public's taste for cheap luxury, had sullied stained glass: 'M. de Tocqueville said that "in democracies, the industrial arts have a tendency to create imperfect products, in great number and at a low price and to give to these products brilliant appearances, the hypocrisy of luxury being one of the characteristics of democratic mores."'[490] Products of 'great number', 'low price' and false luxury were, of course, mass-produced commodities. While de Tocqueville criticized the 'imperfect' market good, Didron attacked the liberal Republic that had given rise to such culture. Democracy had led to shoddiness and hypocrisy in many realms of life; art, too, had become tainted by the principle of equality and the need to ensure everyone equal access to culture. The spoiled products made for mass consumption, Didron implied, could never compete with 'authentic' stained glass. An anonymous reviewer of the 1900 World's Fair agreed, chiding artists for giving in to the public's craving for 'cheap and imperfect' reproductions of old stained glass.[491]

Both official art-historical texts and the writings and productions of the Symbolists fought to salvage medieval media from corruption, protesting against the ever-spreading bibelot. Writers and artists represented stained glass as a timeless art form resistant to economic compromise. The rules and qualities valued by art critics in medieval stained glass and tapestries – their 'naiveté,' their relationship to architecture and their repudiation of the laws of easel painting – conflicted with mass production. These qualities thus stood in direct opposition to nineteenth-century painting, whose mobility and lack of use value had a great deal in common with the much-maligned bibelot.[492] As both modern works and bibelots were divorced from specific architectural and historical contexts, they became objects of exchange on the market; their value came to rest on aesthetic and monetary considerations. It is hardly an accident that the two most significant characteristics of the bibelot – its uselessness (having no functional purpose) and its mobility (allowing it to change hands repeatedly for profit) – are exactly reversed in the nineteenth-century understanding of Gothic stained glass and tapestries as functional and immoveable.[493] The value of medieval stained glass and tapestries was derived largely in opposition to the modern work and to the bibelot, even while it came to occupy a place beside them – even to replace them – in the new spaces of the bourgeoisie.

But in the cafés and cabarets of fin-de-siècle Paris, the two kinds of production were conflated and collapsed, each shoring up the other's popularity. The discourse of critics such as Ottin and Didron was not only about medieval heritage, the way in which the 'official' story of its noble example conflicted with current usage, but about the underlying fear of seeing medieval works now popularized via museums and reproductions. A rich irony accompanied such statements: the medieval works were praised for their *décoratif* qualities, and harked back to exclusive noble traditions, yet such exclusivity disappeared as the works reached a wide public.[494]

**The stained glass revival: medieval and modern**

Critics like Didron, Delalande and Ottin balked at the coupling of 'bastardized Gothic' and contemporary artistic production in the late nineteenth century. But for many others, the 'mating' of the two would yield not only new appreciation of medieval works, but also new inspiration and instruction for contemporary artists and artisans. It would return medieval stained glass, a 'fallen' medium, to its previously noble heights. Léon Daumont-Tournel spoke for many when he claimed that the study of old stained glass was the best discipline: 'not that we think that the *peintres-verriers* must set about to copy them, reproducing their narrow formulas; but we can, from this study, grasp essential principles that still hold true.'[495] By the end of the century, such study could easily take place at a number of museums.

While numerous cathedrals offered Gothic stained-glass windows *in situ*, the viewer could also see them in spaces specially designed for artistic contemplation, far removed, in fact, from their religious context. Stained glass had been displayed at earlier Parisian fairs, including those of 1855, 1867, 1878 and 1889,[496] but the Exposition Universelle of 1900 featured a retrospective, laid out on the Esplanade des Invalides. It purported to 'begin at the "origins" of stained glass while presenting examples from all ages.'[497] Similarly, viewers of the 1880s and 1890s could visit the Musée de Cluny to see illuminated examples such as the thirteenth-century fragments from the Sainte-Chapelle (Fig. 5.6). For those who did not get their fill there, a special museum devoted to stained glass opened its doors in Paris in 1885. The Eighth Exhibition of the Union Centrale des Arts Décoratifs, held in 1884, was greeted with great fanfare and anticipation.[498] For the first time, a special room had been reserved for the display of medieval stained glass. At the close of the exhibit, Antonin Proust, President of the Union, was entrusted temporarily with the glass fragments belonging to the State; in 1885, he moved these pieces to the Palais de l'Industrie and a new Musée du Vitrail was inaugurated. All of the important art administrators were in attendance.[499]

The glass was arranged chronologically and by region, highlighting 'local' traditions, in a 'systematic collection' somewhat similar to that of the Musée de la Sculpture Comparée au Trocadéro.[500] The display of these fragments allowed the viewer to compare both regional and chronological variations. Interestingly, these works were even more 'de-contextualized' than those in the Musée de Cluny; not only were the windows removed from the church, but the pieces or fragments themselves were separated from the entire window to which they once belonged. They thus no longer formed part of the religious ceremony of a cathedral; they existed only as 'details,' ready-made for analysis. While these works had been produced in a decentralized, pre-industrial France, they were, importantly, displayed in the Palais de l'Industrie, thus reconciling medieval works directly with manufacture under the Third Republic.

A significant aim of the Musée du Vitrail was to inspire the contemporary artist (while surely hoping to enhance pride in the French national heritage). The opening of the museum was therefore widely publicized in the pages of the *Gazette des Beaux-Arts*. Lucien Magne, a leading scholar of stained glass, explained the purpose of the museum to readers: 'From now on, the oldest periods of art will be represented by works of the first order, which will provide a permanent teaching workshop for modern art.'[501] The Gothic works on display were intended to nourish modern artists, who would turn out original pieces infused with tradition, rather than cold imitations. Their

works would incorporate Gothic 'principles' without directly imitating these models. If such Republican institutions 'edited out' the religious significance of these pieces, this was not the case in the art-historical literature devoted to medieval stained glass, which repeatedly emphasized the origin and function of such works.[502]

As exhibitions of Gothic stained glass multiplied, so did the discourse on the works, as had been the case with the French *Primitif* painters.[503] Whether Royalist or Republican, art historians unfailingly emphasized specific elements of Gothic stained-glass windows, most notably their didactic purpose and their decorative qualities. They frequently urged modern artists to incorporate these elements, while cautioning them to avoid mere pastiche.

Critics of all persuasions argued that Gothic stained glass had been created with a noble and pure purpose. They repeatedly stressed its didactic and religious functions. In his book *L'Oeuvre des peintres-verriers français*, Magne noted that stained glass contained 'all of medieval painting' and 'perpetuated traditions and examples for the religious and moral education of the people.'[504] Even secular Republicans like Emile Bertaux, writing in *La Revue des Deux Mondes*, conceded that medieval stained glass had drawn inspiration from the religious teachings of the Middle Ages.[505] Noël Lavergne, a critic and scholar, claimed that the decline of stained glass owed as much to the erosion of religious faith as to political vandalism. Lavergne complained of seventeenth-century stained glass artisans who had abandoned their religious mission in the face of the Reformation:

They preoccupied themselves with showing off their science and their skill, much more than with pursuing the edification of the faithful and praising the glory of God. [...] But other factors must have even further ruined the art of stained glass; among them the so-called Reformation, which destroyed twenty thousand churches in France![506]

For such scholars, stained glass lost its original value with the destruction of the church whose context had given it meaning.

If the Middle Ages had been France's golden age of stained glass, art historians argued, its decadence (like that of painting) could be traced to the start of the Renaissance. In fact, as Anne Harris has argued, its fall from grace can be traced to the French Academy, whose rules about art excluded stained glass (though this went unremarked in critical discourse).[507] Not only had the Renaissance artist abandoned the singular religious impetus behind stained glass, but he had also forsaken the decorative rules unique to the medium. The critic Léon Daumont-Tournel made this point clear, stating that: '[T]he decadence of stained glass dates from the introduction into this art of methods applicable to easel painting, which are in absolute conflict with the decoration of a surface. [...] One could say that from the end of the sixteenth century, the art of stained glass ceased to exist.'[508] By taking on the qualities of easel painting, such narrative alleged, stained glass had approached the artistic form of the commodity. Modeling itself on the mobile narrative oil painting – an art form associated with the rise of private collecting, art dealing and trading – stained glass had lost both its character and its *raison d'être*.

According to this argument, the style of medieval stained glass, with its simple forms, crude figures and flattened perspective, had developed organically from its religious function and goal of reaching a wide, uneducated audience. As other ideals came to be upheld in the Renaissance and reflected in its art – scientific analysis, human achievement and rationalism, a secular notion of the passage of time – the decorative, architecturally-subservient style of Gothic stained glass gave way to imitations of the new Renaissance style. Stained-glass windows came to look and to function far more like independent easel paintings, which could be easily exchanged on the market and reflected a new worldly outlook on life. As this argument insisted, transposing the style of painting to the medium of stained glass had irreversibly soiled it.

Thus, as critics such as Lavergne and Magne argued, two internal problems had endangered stained glass (and by extension the cultural heritage of France itself): increased secularism and a growing art market. These problems began in the early nineteenth century, which saw both the destruction of medieval works in the wake of the Revolution and an abandonment of their aim and style as a result of widespread industrialization. In his book on medieval tapestries, Louis de Farcy bewailed the intentional eradication of Gothic art in the aftermath of the Revolution:

> Blinded by the declamations against the Gothic that were in fashion at the end of the eighteenth century, the chapters of our beautiful cathedrals energetically rivaled each other in destroying stained-glass windows, ornamental brasswork, rood screens, altars and all the rest.[509]

Lavergne proposed that the Revolutionary regime's only interest in stained glass was the malicious pleasure it took from shattering it.[510] 'The majority of tapestries donated to parish churches of Paris in days of old by pious women,' Jules Guiffrey lamented, 'disappeared during the Revolution.'[511]

Dismay at the commercialization of stained glass drove the discourse during the 1890s, manifesting itself in two primary arguments: complaints against bourgeois consumption and debates over the 'painterly' versus 'decorative' nature of stained glass. While such debates might seem purely stylistic, they were in fact far more serious, reflecting the larger debate about individual and collective works of art. Enthusiasm for 'painterly' stained glass implied an embrace of secular art, of the independent artwork and of the skilled individual artist. On the other hand, those, like Magne, who praised its 'decorative' nature, extolled anonymous artisans, working as a collective. They felt that only the revival of a communal spirit of work could ensure the success of contemporary stained glass.[512]

Debates over the value of painterly versus decorative stained glass took place at both the 1894 Salon du Champ de Mars and the Salon des Champs-Elysées. For the first time, special sections of the official salons were devoted to the display of contemporary stained glass.[513] Reviewers divided the works into two categories: 'tableaux en transparence' (essentially paintings translated into glass) and those that exploited the special material properties and unique stylistic characteristics of stained glass (the decorative). Albert Maignan was widely hailed as the greatest practitioner of the first category, while Eugène Grasset was seen as the leader of the second, and widely preferred, group.[514]

Critics like Edouard Didron repeatedly insisted that the modern stained-glass window, like its Gothic ancestor, should emphasize its relationship to the building for which it was designed; they justified their demands with medieval examples.[515] Didron was, in fact, following the traditions established by his father, Adolphe-Napoléon (Didron aîné), who, by 1844, had pioneered the use of 'vitraux archéologiques' and the replacement of damaged glass by works made according to medieval principles.[516] During the 'Gothic' era, claimed Lavergne, 'Stained-glass windows were decorative, above all decorative, while also being symbolic. Those that Abbot Suger had made for Saint Denis, those from this period that still exist in the cathedrals of Chartres, of Bourges, etc. testify to this. The goal is decoration, the beautification of the church.'[517] He thus claimed that the individual style of the medieval artist(s) was subservient to the (religious) needs of the cathedral. By declaring the Gothic windows 'decorative,' Lavergne signified that they aimed to reach the faithful attenders and belonged within the larger context of the church. Furthermore, he argued, they hailed from a time before the artificial separation of fine arts and the 'lower' crafts, which had led to both the alienation of the craftsman and the corruption of art.

Magne likewise insisted on the distance separating the imagery of stained glass from that of easel painting:

The decoration of surfaces by painting, mosaics, stained glass or tapestries, was of necessity governed by similar laws. People at that time would not have understood the notion of an isolated painting aiming to produce the illusion of a figure, a landscape, or a scene. For artists of the thirteenth century, this would have been a secondary application, inferior to monumental decoration, whose grandeur they understood [...][518]

Such examples were intended to reveal that the Gothic artist did not distinguish (as did his modern counterpart) between craft and 'high art.' Nor did he conceive of a work 'isolated' from the totality of cathedral or palace. His greatest goal was to contribute to the overall beauty of these realms, to create something lasting and monumental in its ability to communicate immediately and powerfully. Just as critics had called for a new Fra Angelico to create decorative mural painting (a call to which Puvis de Chavannes as well as many other artists responded),[519] they now insisted that stained glass designs be monumental in nature, emphasizing, above all, their decorative qualities. The decorative work was best appreciated from the vantage point of a viewer taking in the ensemble, located within the specific architectural site for which these works were created and uniquely destined.[520] Such theories tied into and complemented growing artistic preference for the total work of art and admiration for Wagner's theory of the *Gesamtkunstwerk*.

These ideas were put into practice at the *Vieux Paris* exhibit of the 1900 World's Fair, where exhibit organizer Albert Robida commissioned stained-glass windows that not only reflected the subject matter and style of medieval stained glass, but also conformed to their decorative function; he placed them in a recreated medieval chapel that welcomed visitors for concerts of medieval religious music during the fair. The chapel thus appealed more strongly to the aesthetic tastes of visitors than to their religious needs (Fig. 5.7).[521]

While critics reminded artists that they could spoil their stained glass by ignoring the medieval decorative tradition, they also condemned those who went too far in unabashedly imitating medieval examples. Though they paid homage to the Gothic tradition, artists were warned to avoid relying on mere pastiche, ridiculed for the 'nonsense of composing in 1884 a new

5.7  *Intérieur de*
*Saint-Julien-des-*
*Ménétriers*, 1900

stained-glass window in the form and imitation of a thirteenth-century window.'[522] What critics desired was a new approach to the medium, one that was 'both old and new.'[523] Issues concerning 'old' and 'new,' 'decorative' and 'painterly' also confronted the artists who entered an 1892 contest sponsored by the Cathédrale de Sainte-Croix in Orléans. The initiative for this project dated from 1878, when the Archbishop of Lyon invited artists to submit designs for a cycle of ten stained-glass windows depicting scenes from the life of Joan of Arc.[524] Each artist or team of artisans was required to

5.8   Eugène Grasset and Félix Gaudin, Fragment of 'Sacre de Charles VII,' 1893

present ten painted sketches as well as one finished cartoon, from which a detailed section was to be executed and completed. Twelve teams entered the contest. Contestants included Eugène Grasset, collaborating with the stained glass restorer Félix Gaudin, and Albert Maignan, who participated with his partner Charles Champigneulle (Fig. 5.8).[525] In October 1893 the finished sketches were exhibited at l'Ecole des Beaux-Arts in Paris, where they were judged by members of the Academy including William-Adolphe Bouguereau, Léon Bonnat and Pierre Puvis de Chavannes.

To the disappointment of many participants, critics insisted that the artists had failed to navigate between tradition and innovation, resulting in either 'archeological studies' or, conversely, the 'absolute negation of sacred traditions.'[526] The case of Grasset is telling. To the outrage of his defenders, Grasset finished an appalling eleventh place in the contest. While his partner Gaudin claimed that their work gave 'full expression' to French stained glass of the fifteenth century, Didron characterized it as 'purely archeological.'[527] For the judges, Grasset had gone too far. He had lost the delicate balance between Gothic and modern in his image: the latter had simply been omitted, while his detailed physiognomies and precise rendering of the texture and surface of depicted objects placed him in the camp of 'painterly' or *trompe-l'oeil* stained glass. In contrast to his 'secular' stained glass pieces, Grasset omitted any reference to familiar 'commercial' media such as posters, advertising and the extraordinarily popular American stained glass style of the Louis Tiffany workshops.[528] His design declined to link up with the new and marketable forms of stained glass shown at the Salons, which had more direct appeal for the consumer.

Nineteenth-century stained glass artists faced the difficult task of creating a work both traditional and modern, one that avoided explicit reference to the art market while functioning within its system. Even when their works were truly innovative and of unique quality, they inevitably fell short of the medieval ideal. Their assemblage in workshops producing windows for sale on the market automatically condemned them in the eyes of certain critics. The very divisions required in the production of nineteenth-century stained glass – at minimum the separate contributions of designer and craftsman – aligned them on the side of the mass-produced product. Contemporary stained-glass works – despite a high level of aesthetic daring – became the substitute target for far deeper concerns over the division of labor.

Moreover, despite the seeming high-mindedness of the critics' goals of uniting past and present, of bridging old and new through the creation of stained-glass windows, these aims were already familiar to viewers because of their existence in another realm, the blatantly commercial bric-à-brac market. What defined bric-à-brac was precisely its deceptive mingling of old style with modern manufacture; objects of little value, bibelots, were intentionally constructed to make the new look old. While 'bric-à-brac' had originally been defined as second-hand goods salvaged from the palaces and churches of the Ancien Régime, by 1883, as Janell Watson has noted, a French art dictionary indicated its shifting signification:

BRIC-A-BRAC – In its generic sense, this term designates all kinds of old objects such as chests, armor, bronzes, paintings, etc. The public's marked taste for these kinds of objects has led to the development of a new industry, *la fabrication du vieux neuf* […] Often, one must have an extremely well-trained eye to distinguish an authentic and interesting old object from a fake. In general, the word bric-à-brac is used with contempt; in common speech it refers to objects of little value.[529]

Calling for 'both old and new' stained-glass pieces could be perceived as a variation of *la fabrication du vieux neuf* common to bric-à-brac. Critics who called for a renewal of stained glass thus often unwittingly linked medieval stained glass to its 'fake' counterparts when they wished to sever the two. The modern artist needed to strike a delicate balance between evoking old examples and merely imitating them; if he failed to do so, he pleased neither critics nor market, thereby falling into the domain of bric-à-brac. Art-historical writers understood that the stained-glass revival could 'save' the medium, or alternatively lead to its ruin.

## The tapestry revival

Modern critics and consumers, enthralled by medieval craftsmanship and faith, launched the revival of tapestry in the fin de siècle, as they had *Primitif* paintings and stained glass. A revival of interest in Gothic tapestries would help fuel the production of and market for contemporary tapestries, which were also praised in relation to how closely they followed the rules of their medieval counterparts. As we shall see, the stylistic elements critics praised in the medieval tapestry became signifiers for a broad set of values and functions that many thought had disappeared, but still hoped to revive.

Ironically, it was an infusion from the past, specifically the medieval past, that would give tapestries new life in the fin de siècle. For many, a revitalization of the medium was long overdue. With the World's Fair of 1889 on the horizon, critics such as Roger Marx began to call for the reform of traditional French arts. It was time, Marx declared, to rejuvenate the art of tapestry making, to 'remove nineteenth-century tapestry from the clear and unacknowledged domination of the past in order to assign it a character, a date, in order to force it to reflect the resemblance of our time, to enclose the modern ideal within it.'[530]

To accomplish these goals, Marx called on Symbolist painters like Pierre Puvis de Chavannes and Albert Besnard to design cartoons for tapestry manufacture. The formal innovations that he suggested – reduction of tones, simplification of shapes, emphasis on surface – were reminiscent of many Symbolists' painting styles, making them the obvious choice as leaders for design in the field. Moreover, these innovations derived in large part from study of the Gothic Franco-Flemish tapestry tradition. It was, paradoxically, by reference to the past that modern tapestry would emerge.

The tapestry revival of the 1890s went hand-in-hand with the 'rediscovery' and re-evaluation of medieval tapestries. As with stained glass, nineteenth-century 'neglect' of the medieval tapestry heritage was redressed in the closing decades. Old French tapestries could increasingly be seen at a number of museums, salons and exhibitions, most notably beginning in 1882 with the permanent display of the *Dame à la Licorne* at the Musée de Cluny (see Fig. 3.4). Important critics and art historians, among them Jules Guiffrey, who would direct the Gobelins factory from 1893 to 1905, authored a number of books extolling Gothic tapestries.[531] Guiffrey's *La Tapisserie, son histoire depuis le Moyen Age jusqu'à nos jours* (1885) was favorably reviewed by Louis

Gonse in the pages of the *Gazette des Beaux-Arts*:[532] 'Not long ago, ancient tapestries were in the most complete discredit [...] if the superiority of French tapestries since the creation of the Gobelins is a universally recognized fact, the role of artisans stretching back to the most distant periods of our past had not been presented until now in this light.'[533] Other scholars, administrators and critics, such as Phillipe Burty (a noted collector, critic and print maker) and Charles Blanc (the first Fine Arts Director of the Third Republic) lamented past indifference as well as outright hostility to this heritage.[534] Writing about the Angers tapestries found in the city's cathedral (see Fig. 1.1), Louis de Farcy decried the pejorative sense attached to the word 'Gothic' in the eighteenth century.[535]

By the final decade of the nineteenth century, old French tapestries held even greater appeal. The renewed enthusiasm for the Franco-Flemish tapestry tradition was in part a response to English innovation in the field. Works produced at William Morris's Merton Abbey factories were exhibited and highly praised in France, especially following his death in 1896, thus upping the stakes and threatening the French in a field they had long thought of as their own.[536] The great praise lavished on Edward Burne-Jones's *Holy Grail* tapestries (1896), exhibited at the 1900 World's Fair, sent a powerful message about the viability of using the medieval tradition for national inspiration. Just as important as beating the English at their own game, however, was the fact that the medieval tapestry, like the medieval stained-glass window, was endowed with ideological associations that made it especially valuable in the fin de siècle. In direct contrast to the eighteenth-century factory-produced work, Gothic tapestry was seen as part of an organic craft tradition. Important pieces were attributed to amateurs (especially noble women such as Queen Mathilda, wife of William the Conqueror) rather than to professionals.[537] Such ideas made their way into popular publications, including Albert Robida's *Vieille France* series, where he equates the name Bayeux to the 'naiveté' of the embroidered album created by the talented Mathilda and the picturesque battle scenes commemorated by her work.[538]

Scholars understood medieval tapestries as intrinsically tied to the life of the community or the court, an essential part of the architectural setting. Charles Loriquet underlined this point in his 1876 *Les Tapisseries de Notre-Dame de Reims*: 'Both murals and stained glass lost their character when they separated from architecture to take on a life of their own. Textile painting, brought to perfection, arrived in time to take over from painting on glass and from sculpture the lofty position they had abandoned.'[539] While sculpture and even stained glass had been lured into following the 'isolated' production of easel painting during the Renaissance, only tapestry had remained true to its 'decorative' function. Many medieval tapestry cycles, like those of Notre-Dame de Reims or the cathedral of Angers, had been specifically created to decorate cathedrals. Even the more secular works were often invested with a rich religious symbolism as well. The Gothic tapestry could thus serve as a splendid reminder of French Christian culture, at a time when both the national and the religious heritage of France were under fierce debate.

The art-historical discourse about medieval tapestries closely echoed that about stained glass. Both were praised for playing decorative roles within specific architectural contexts, most often religious edifices, which in turn influenced their simplified and monumental style. As with stained-glass windows, the decadence of tapestries was repeatedly blamed on the Renaissance; according to these theories, the Reformation and the increasingly secular direction of art had destroyed the purity of the medium. Above all, the downfall of this art form was seen to be a consequence of a fundamental error: tapestries had abandoned their own rules to mimic those of painting. By borrowing elements from mobile easel painting, tapestries had entered the distasteful domain of the commodity.

For all of the above-stated reasons, the medieval tapestry became the model for the tapestry reforms initiated under the Third Republic. As Pierre Vaisse indicates, critics, administrators and scholars of the period agreed on a crucial point: modern tapestry had to cease imitating oil painting and renounce the *trompe-l'oeil* illusionism foreign to the medium.[540] Tapestry should remain essentially flat. Jules Guiffrey insisted on the importance of simplifying models, diffusing light, emphasizing vigor, defining contours and of reducing colors to the smallest number of elements.[541] Rather than painting on textile, he argued, tapestry should seek its own properties, simplifying, monumentalizing and creating an immediately striking image that did not violate the flatness of the wall to which it adhered.

At this time, the fin-de-siècle artist could turn to numerous medieval tapestries on display as examples of works that had successfully avoided painterly illusionism. Gothic tapestries were often proposed as ideal prototypes for new works in the medium. As Louis de Farcy noted, 'The further one gets from the Middle Ages, the more one loses the traditions of the true art of tapestry, in sacrificing the general effect to details, principal subjects to accessories.'[542] As with stained glass, the tapestry designer had to focus above all on the immediate ensemble effects and to remain aware that his works would be viewed at a distance rather than examined in detail.

A specific discourse was woven around medieval tapestries in the nineteenth century, one that focused on its architectural permanence, its spiritual purity and its decorative qualities. All of these aspects sharply distinguished tapestries from the easel paintings that dominated the Salons and drawing rooms of the period. Ironically, these 'pure' aspects whetted the public appetite for medieval works and resulted in their commercial success: as we have seen, both tapestries and stained glass strayed far from cathedral and museum in the fin de siècle. But this art-historical discourse also encouraged the production and embrace of medieval tapestries and stained glass among artists dismayed by both the public and the art market: the Symbolist avant-garde.

## Stained glass, tapestries and the art of the Symbolists

The burgeoning display and discourse surrounding medieval stained glass and tapestries had profound implications for the broader art world of late nineteenth-century France. Critics had established a noble, pre-industrial and deeply valued model for the avant-garde artist to follow. The Symbolists' adoption and emulation of these media was complex in its motives. They responded both to the particular references and associations of medieval stained glass and tapestries *and* to the new popularity of these media that resulted from their lofty status. For many Symbolists, who sought to 'escape' the taint of commodification in their art, medieval tapestries and stained glass served as the perfect artistic paradigm. These medieval works were closely linked with sacred rather than 'commercial' art forms. While traditional, such pieces pre-dated (and for them entirely surpassed) the cold, skilled productions of the modern age in their 'authenticity' and communicative power.

Fin-de-siècle debates on Gothic *vitraux* and tapestries colored the reception of both medieval and contemporary work. Moreover, the question of influence goes in both directions, for many of the formal qualities praised in stained glass and tapestries – including the decorative – emerged from debates on modern painting.[543] As we saw in Chapter 2, with regard to medieval prints and paintings, the late nineteenth-century critic or artist 'viewed' these medieval works through a lens already adjusted for contemporary art. Thus while the modern artist was encouraged to 'medievalize' his works along the lines of Gothic stained glass and tapestries, these medieval pieces were at the same time designated as modern *avant la lettre*.

This process of reading (and appreciating) the modern in the medieval becomes clearer in the discourse surrounding medieval stained glass and tapestries, such as the following quotation from the critic Daumont-Tournel. Admiring the retrospective of medieval stained glass at the 1900 World's Fair, he praised the early examples as the most aesthetically pleasing and coherent:

The most logical, most rational conception of stained glass was that of the earliest eras, when a stained-glass window was considered a mosaic or a luminous tapestry, the decoration of a flat surface. Until the middle of the sixteenth century, this principle was applied in legendary stained glass and in the ornamental compositions of trees of Jesse. We can retain it by putting aside characteristics of style and attempting to unite it with the tendencies of the art of our time.[544]

Daumont-Tournel rehearses a discourse with which we are now familiar, acknowledging medieval stained glass as inherently flat and decorative and conflating it with other decorative media such as mosaics and tapestries. Such rules allegedly reigned supreme until the sixteenth century, the period of the medium's demise. But Daumont-Tournel openly acknowledges that such reading dovetails with 'tendencies of the art of our time.' The discourse about flatness and decorative qualities is very much at play in the avant-garde painting of the late nineteenth century. The reduction of *trompe-l'oeil* and the embrace of 'flatness' were key elements in the style of artists as varied as Puvis de Chavannes, Paul Gauguin or the Nabis. Moreover, the language used by Daumont-Tournel to describe medieval stained glass finds a curious echo in the writings of Maurice Denis, who describes the new painting style used by his contemporaries. The use of a phrase such as 'the decoration of a flat surface' implies the critic's awareness of Denis's 1890 article 'Définition du néo-traditionnisme,' which began with the famous statement that a painting was, above all, 'a flat surface covered with colors in a certain order.'[545] While compared favorably to modern works, medieval tapestries were thus also considered in relation to the demands and styles of the most recent productions. In turn, modern art absorbed, echoed and exaggerated certain stylistic characteristics found in medieval media and endowed them with the meanings attributed to them in the art-historical literature.

While Roger Marx encouraged the use of medieval models to effect modern tapestry reforms, he was well aware that the popularity of these works had influenced modern painting. 'Gothic stained glass,' claimed Marx, with its 'naiveté and archaism,' deeply appealed to modern taste. Paintings by Symbolist artists Denis, Anquetin or Gauguin would translate beautifully into stained glass, Marx noted, since they were based on a similar aesthetic.[546] The artists themselves made frequent reference to Gothic media in their writings. Commenting on Gauguin, Denis observed that 'in order to find a work in which the presence of sunlight is as real as it is in those of Gauguin, it would be necessary to go all the way back to the art of stained glass, back to oriental carpets.'[547] Both nineteenth- and twentieth-century critics have often compared the painting of many Symbolist and Post-Impressionist artists of the 1890s to medieval stained glass and tapestries.[548] Such comparisons were often made about the works of other artists in addition to Gauguin and Denis, particularly within the Nabi group (including Edouard Vuillard, Paul Sérusier, Pierre Bonnard and Paul Ranson), as well as Georges Rouault, Puvis de Chavannes, Emile Bernard, Gustave Moreau, Georges Seurat and Aristide Maillol.[549] Several of these artists produced their own tapestries with styles deeply reminiscent of Gothic models.[550] The style and value of these medieval media had clearly begun to influence the reception and critical interpretation of the modern artist. A closer look at three of them – Emile Bernard, Edouard Vuillard and Paul Sérusier – teaches us a great deal about the ways in which the Symbolist painters of the 1890s interpreted, emulated and appropriated Gothic stained glass and tapestries.

Emile Bernard was smitten with the art of the *Primitifs* and the stained glass and tapestries of the medieval craftsman.[551] During his stay at the inn of Madame Le Masson in Saint-Briac, Brittany, Bernard painted the glass doors of the dining room and his bedroom windows to simulate stained glass.[552] He later decorated the living room of Theo Van Gogh in a similar fashion: 'Bernard has also painted the glass doors of our drawing room as if they were a medieval church window.'[553] So, too, Bernard and his Pont-Aven friends painted the windows of the inn at Le Pouldu in imitation of stained glass during their stay. On occasion, Bernard tried his hand at the making of

5.9   Emile
Bernard, *Les
Musiciens*, 1892

stained glass and tapestries, in a style clearly influenced by what he had seen at museums such as the Musée de Cluny, and created paintings highly indebted to them (Fig. 5.9). *Les Musiciens*, with its troubadours and ladies-in-waiting arrayed in a forest, condenses space and employs the flattened ground familiar to viewers of Chasse tapestries (Fig. 3.4). The ambiguous spatial relation of the figures seems simultaneously to reference the awkward figure-ground of medieval tapestries and to anticipate the distortions of cubism. The medieval world of courtly love and aristocratic manners is rendered in a distinctly naive and anti-illusionistic manner.

Bernard's painting was equally affected by his interest in these media. He traced the existence of 'purely decorative' color to the tapestries and stained glass of the *Primitifs*.[554] The synthetist style 'invented' by Bernard and Louis Anquetin, labeled 'cloisonnisme' by the critic Edouard Dujardin, immediately recalled medieval cloisonné enamel work and stained-glass windows (Fig. 5.10).[555] The heavy black lines and flat colored surfaces brought to mind the lead tracery surrounding pieces of colored glass (Fig. 5.6), while the distortion of scale evokes the 'primitive' art of Brittany and the illogical world of imagination (more precisely, what they saw as the vivid, pre-modern mind-set of the Breton peasantry).[556] In the months preceding their experiments

5.10   Emile Bernard, *Bretonnes au mur (Breton Women at the Wall)*

with 'cloisonnisme,' Bernard and Anquetin often discussed the merits of medieval stained glass, to which they had easy access in Paris.[557]

Bernard's interest in stained glass, like that of his Symbolist friends, did not casually coincide with the much broader revival of the medium, but was deeply affected by it. The associations of medieval stained glass led these artists to assimilate this art form into their painting style. In this fashion, their painted works were invested with the nationalist and Christian significations associated with Gothic stained-glass windows. The viewer could 'read' these loaded references through the cloisonné-style works. As an artist thoroughly dismissive of the Academic tradition and the demands of the art market, Bernard found in medieval stained glass an example of an incorruptible, naive and deeply spiritual model.

Bernard's vision of stained glass as mesmerizing, simple and full of religious power was echoed in the works of countless writers of the time, including Gustave Flaubert, Stéphane Mallarmé, Laurent Tailhade, Emile Zola, and Gaston Paris. Many used the image of a stained-glass window as a way of referring to the pure figures of medieval religious legends, as did Zola and Paris, while others took stained-glass itself as a literary trope, attempting to capture the jewel-like, luminescent and religious qualities of the medium in their works.[558] Flaubert, inspired by the stained-glass windows of Notre-Dame de Rouen, was one of the first to do this, in *Les Trois contes*; he wanted to publish Hyacinthe Langlois's drawings of the windows alongside his stories, which were meant to 'color them in.' Influenced by Flaubert's stylistic innovation in these tales (published in 1870), many writers – including Tailhade, Catulle Mendès, Germain Nouveau and Paul Claudel – composed poems that attempted to capture the synesthesia of stained glass and its relationship to the sacred space of the cathedral.[559] Fascination with medieval stained glass permeated popular, bourgeois and avant-garde milieus in the 1880s and 1890s.

It was tapestries, however, and particularly the ones on display at the Musée de Cluny, that helped forge the rich and daring style of Edouard Vuillard's paintings. On 16 July 1894, he recorded in his journal some thoughts inspired by a trip to the Musée de Cluny:

Visited Cluny yesterday. Tapestries and illuminated missals. Calendars. In the tapestries I think only of a pure and simple enlargement. My little panel will be made the subject of a decoration. Expression of an intimate sentiment on a large surface, that's all! The same thing as a Chardin, for example. Different from the Italians. Here are tapestries as incredibly learned as a Veronese. Why are they so unknown? Small fragment, very ancient, in large flat tints of such charming color, very powerful segmented color on a clear background. It makes me think of certain of my 'machines'.[560]

In this passage, Vuillard rehearses many of the fin-de-siècle tropes about medieval tapestries. He laments the lack of attention they receive, he praises their purity, and he implies the special 'French' quality that sets them apart from the Italians and links them instead to Chardin, an acknowledged master of the French school.

In his four panel paintings, *Figures and Interiors* (Fig. 5.11), for Doctor Louis Henri Vaquez, Vuillard drew formal lessons from the *Dame à la Licorne* (see Fig. 3.4). Splendid fabrics, floral patterns and all-over composition characterize both series, as does the slightly melancholy, languid mood. In fact, Vaquez owned a fifteenth-century tapestry, which he displayed in the same room as the panels by Vuillard.[561] With these panels, Vuillard managed to turn the apartment of this middle-class bachelor into a château-like haven, not unlike that of Emile Zola. The bourgeois Third Republic and the medieval past could exist in perfect harmony, as the writers of history books and organizers of exhibition displays took pains to show.

If Vuillard drew on one of the most beloved medieval French tapestry cycles, his fellow Nabi artist Paul Sérusier drew on another: the *Apocalypse* cycle from the cathedral of Angers (see Fig. 1.1). These fourteenth-century works, associated with *Primitif* fervor and naiveté rather than with aristocratic and courtly culture, were widely celebrated in the closing decades of the nineteenth century. Jules Guiffrey discovered archival records proving their French origin, while they went on display at the World's Fair.[562] Having faded with time, the simplified physiognomies, limited 'pure' colors and repetitive forms of the tapestries easily attracted comparisons with avant-garde works of the 1890s. Sérusier's images of anachronistic peasants moving slowly through textured green landscapes (Fig. 5.12) recalled the Angers tapestries to several viewers, notably Denis:

5.11   Edouard Vuillard, *Figures et Intérieurs: Le Piano*, 1896

He thought of the profane subjects of the Musée d'Angers or the 'Unicorn' at Cluny when he evoked legendary princesses, at once monastic and rustic, with secret faces, portrayed as in the songs of the Symbolist poets of our youth. He grouped them in compositions without defined subjects, but not without mystery. He gave them the costumes of the period of Queen Anne [of Brittany … ] Images of a fabled past, figures of hieratic grace who make us think of Gregorian chants, of melancholy popular ballads, or of the tunes that one still hears in the most remote corners of Brittany.[563]

5.12   Paul
Sérusier, *Le
Pardon de Notre-
Dame-des-Portes à
Châteauneuf du
Faou*, 1894

Works such as Sérusier's *Le Pardon de Notre-Dame-des-Portes* seemed to echo
the muted charm and stylized poses of the celebrated Angers scenes.
Sérusier's twentieth-century viewers remarked similar influences:

Sérusier believed that the tapestry represents the national art of France [...] His taste
for tapestry came to him no doubt from the profound sense that he had for mural
decoration [...] Perhaps his nostalgia for the Middle Ages came to him in part from
the longing for an epoch when the idea of colored decoration was so easily
associated with the space of mural painting.[564]

Through subtle reference to the awkward forms and faded harmonies of the
Angers tapestries, Sérusier's paintings harked back to the medieval past and
to debates on the *décoratif*. The tapestries' associations – the pre-industrial,
the faith-inspired and the rural – complemented and augmented popular

associations joined to mythical Brittany.[565] While Sérusier clearly responded to the visual qualities of such works, it was the art-historical and critical discourse that had placed such works in the foreground and had established these associations. But while Sérusier used such sources in part to evade the market, he drew on the medieval tapestry at its historical moment of greatest critical and economic saturation.

While the Symbolist avant-garde came to absorb and echo stylistic traits of medieval arts, the medieval works themselves were 'modernized' through an emphasis on qualities familiar from avant-garde painting. Yet it was not visual qualities alone that recommended these works to fin-de-siècle viewers. Now readily available and on display at museums and exhibitions, Gothic *vitraux* and tapestries stood as witnesses to the heights achieved by French artists and artisans prior to the industrial age. At the same time, these pieces were believed to be the product of an age in which the artists themselves – much like the *Primitifs* and painter-monks – were inspired by religious sentiment and impervious to material considerations. Even those who outwardly contested the 'commodification' and popularization of these arts often appropriated and basked in their reflected glory as critics drew analogies between their art and that of the past. Republican critics and administrators eagerly embraced these media, in part to counter the image of a brashly commercial State that had forgotten the true roots of France. At this historical moment, the artworks Republicans used to express their needs happened to coincide with those favored by a disenfranchised avant-garde.

The clash between official discourse, the avant-garde interest in stained glass and the explicit commodification of such works is revealed by an important exhibit at the Galerie Art Nouveau, the gallery/decorative arts shop headed by the dealer Samuel Bing.[566] In 1895, Bing made a trip to the United States to study modern stained-glass production and came away deeply excited by the production techniques and methods of the Louis Tiffany glass workshops. He was curious to see what the workshops could do with designs by young French artists. He chose 11 artists, eight of whom were members of the Nabi group, to undertake the design of stained-glass cartoons.[567] With the exception of Paul Sérusier, three of whose sketches were made into windows, each Nabi had one of his cartoons realized in stained glass. All of the subjects were secular, many of them abstracted landscapes, street scenes, or views of Parisian strollers.[568] Many of the windows violated the prohibition against incorporating perspective in stained-glass windows and bore mottled surfaces more appropriate to painting than to the traditional look of stained glass. The tilted-up planes, flattened forms and sharp angles are borrowed from Japanese prints and from contemporary poster design, relating to other objects produced by Tiffany, such as glass lamps or vases. Vallotton's design, *Parisiennes*, was perhaps most offensive to advocates of old rules of the medium; with his emphasis on large-scale and fashionably-dressed women, his sketch brought to mind fashion plates (and the realm of the department store) rather than the sacred narratives of Chartres.[569]

The windows were exhibited in April of 1895 at the Salon de la Société Nationale des Beaux-Arts and the following December at the Salon de l'Art Nouveau (along with eight additional designs by Sérusier and one by Eugéne Grasset). The criticism that greeted the Nabis' stained glass was closely linked to the discourse emerging from contemporary debates and discussions of medieval works. While certain progressive journals such as *La Revue Franco-Américaine* and *La Revue Blanche* applauded the Nabis' innovations and decorative talents, most of the reviews were negative.[570]

The problem with these windows, which were deemed 'primitive' and 'bizarre' by many critics, was succinctly outlined in the *Revue des arts décoratifs*. According to Victor Champier, these designs were not only 'unattractive,' but possessed a 'dangerous character' because they set a poor standard for other artists and because they played too loosely with accepted traditions.[571] Champier traced their faults back to the intentions outlined by the Tiffany company, whose aesthetic guidelines were paraphrased in his review:

The starting point of American stained-glass windows, it is said, is a return to the mosaic of colored glass displayed in the beautiful Gothic windows of the thirteenth century, without the application of vitrifiable colors which, from the fourteenth century on, tarnished the natural shine of the glass. The reason for this was that, in the churches, too much attention was given to the subject, so that the issue of color came to play a secondary role. The Americans, on the contrary, value color above all.[572]

It was the desire to elevate color above subject matter that had doomed the American stained-glass window, Champier argued, for the didactic and sacred goals of medieval stained glass had been abandoned in favor of aesthetic play. Furthermore, the Americans and their admirer, Bing, lacked a true understanding of the tradition on which they claimed to draw:

I may be excused from going over in detail the mediocre archaeological science to which these solemn debuts bear witness. The period when medieval stained glass most succinctly achieved the goal of a large translucent mosaic is the twelfth century. Yet, the importance given to the subject matter in no way detracted from the splendor of the coloration.[573]

According to Champier, Americans were ignorant of the very traditions they claimed to defend. Bing's misunderstanding of the French tradition, many critics openly argued or implied, was a result of his 'foreignness.' As scholars such as Debora Silverman and Nancy Troy have shown, Bing's German-Jewish heritage prevented him from truly grasping this tradition.[574] No doubt Champier too conflated the brash commercialism of the Americans with Bing's keen – perhaps *too* keen – market acumen.

Such critics implied that the Nabis, like Grasset in his earlier project for the Cathédrale d'Orléans, had lost the delicate balance required to create the Gothic anew. They forced the issue of commodifying the medium by making reference not only to the poster and the print, but to the very act of 'Americanizing' them ('American' being synonymous with ostentatious display and crass merchandising). In the destination for which they were intended (the bourgeois interior or the leisure space), in their style and in their primary place of exhibition, these windows had more in common with mass-produced objects than with medieval artworks. The associations that drew both the Nabis and a large share of the fin-de-siècle audience to medieval art were seemingly contradicted by Bing's commission and this no doubt compromised its chances of success in the marketplace. All attempts to create a new paradigm for stained glass were judged according to Gothic standards, which made new works seem vulgar and parvenu.

The underlying tension between the desire to resurrect the medieval work (here in the form of stained glass and tapestries) and the results of such popularization by both the French and foreigners is further revealed by an explicitly discriminatory quote. Farther along in his text on stained glass, Ottin described the difference between the 'amateur, drawn instinctively to the glass' and 'the Jew, focusing only on the lead tracery, that is to say money – because he hastens to transmute the metal [into cash] before the day is done.'[575] For Ottin, the Jew (like the American) can only 'see' in stained glass the potential for transforming it into money, can only appreciate such works as pure commodity. Such quotes evince the extreme anti-Semitism of the period, the belief that the Jew was incapable of understanding, let alone contributing to the French heritage.[576] At the same time, however, the Jew becomes a stand-in for all those in the Third Republic and abroad who cannot appreciate medieval art except in a sullied and commodified form. Returning to Didron's lament over the 'mating' of 'bastardized Gothic' and 'mutant Renaissance,' we note that his text is rife with the fear of mingling – of Jew and Christian, of bourgeois and working class, of French native and foreigner – of those elements of the fin de siècle in perpetual conflict and potential contamination. Small wonder that critics like Ottin and Didron insisted that medieval stained glass and tapestries remain cloistered in the cathedral, protected, as they no longer could be, from the messy and sordid nature of modern French life.

It was hardly coincidental that the two media that came to experience such a broad revival were those most closely connected with the image of the Gothic cathedral. Such works were inseparable from the structure of the cathedral, tied to its history and distinguished from the widely circulated commodity. The consumption and commercialization that lay behind the popularity of stained glass and tapestries enraged critics like Didron and Ottin, who contrasted the secular appropriation of them in the modern age to their earlier religious function. This search for the 'authentic' religious spirit of the medieval world also contributed to the explosion of religious pilgrimages in the fin de siècle, travels that allowed participants to imagine tracing the footsteps of their medieval forebears. As we shall see, however, such seemingly 'pure' pilgrimage sites were no more immune to 'foreign' influence and to commercialism than the religious art of the cathedrals.

# Marketing the sacred: medieval pilgrimage and the Catholic revival

There is only one way to escape the morass in which we struggle: to return to the old spirit of old ways; to be, as in the past, people who believe in something, who include God in their celebrations as in their national sorrows, and whose belief in eternity, whose preoccupation with accomplishing their mission here on earth, will transform us and enable us to give to History centuries like those of Charlemagne and Saint Louis.

'Le Clerc,' in a front page article for *La Croix*, 3 May 1889.[577]

In the closing decades of the nineteenth century, calls for reviving religious traditions associated with the past – especially the medieval past – flourished and led to widespread organization by the Catholic Church of public prayer, religious celebrations and pilgrimages.[578] As Didron's and Ottin's xenophobic writings about stained glass suggest, one of the many catalysts for this sudden embrace of the 'old spirit of old ways' was the increased 'foreignness' of modern French society, in which conflicting religious beliefs and values created concerns about the social stability of the French nation.[579] Another was the Franco-Prussian war, which exacerbated fears of invasion from without. As we have seen, the defeat constituted a turning point for patriotic appropriations of the Middle Ages; it was also crucial for the Church's embrace of initiatives based on those of the medieval Church. Seen as a national humiliation for Republicans, the war was interpreted as divine justice by many Catholics. In particular, they viewed Napoléon III's withdrawal of the troops supporting the Pope as a cardinal sin for which reparation would need to be made. According to this logic, it had been France's duty since the Middle Ages to battle for the Church and to defend it; by forgetting this divine mission, modern France had betrayed its *raison d'être*. As a result, bishops, priests, mayors and military leaders from all over France implored the French to pray for their sins.[580]

One of the most effective tools for healing a wounded and divided France, they argued, was to renew the medieval tradition of the pilgrimage, defined by an 1899 manual devoted to religious travel as '[...] a pious process performed through a public procession to a privileged sanctuary in order to enter into more intimate communication with God [...] we go on pilgrimages to do as did our fathers *sicut fecerunt patres nostri*; because pilgrimages have always been in the customs of humanity as well as in Church tradition.'[581] Should enough pilgrims pray for the redemption of the country, they argued, they could show God that the 'new France' was 'the France that remembers its traditions, […] the France of Charlemagne and Saint Louis that takes up the cross, walking toward God in whom salvation lies.'[582] They suggested that in recognition of such pilgrims, God would take pity on France, thus wiping out skepticism, agnosticism and greed, restoring the supreme authority of the Pope in Rome and re-establishing a good moral order.

This chapter focuses on the importance of the Catholic Church – particularly the Assumptionist order – in popularizing the religious traditions of the Middle Ages, notably through the pilgrimage movement. The pilgrimage, which blended consumerism, art, tourism and religion, proved a popular vehicle for publicizing the medieval Church and its artistic and spiritual achievements, for winning converts to Catholicism, for fighting foreign influences and for promoting travel to important historical, religious and artistic sites linked to the French nation and its celebrated medieval past.

## *Le Pèlerin* and Le Conseil Général des Pèlerinages

Although pilgrimages have taken place in France throughout history, there was a marked interest in them in the last half of the nineteenth century following the declaration of the Immaculate Conception (1854) and a proliferation of Marial sightings in French towns such as La Salette (1846), Lourdes (1858) and Pontmain (1871).[583] In the aftermath of the Franco-Prussian war, priests from all over France encouraged their parishioners to organize pilgrimages of repentance and atonement for the sins of France and her abandonment of God.[584] As a result, thousands of people began to travel to cathedrals and shrines, following in the footsteps of their ancestors.[585]

A group of priests leading the Notre-Dame de la Salette pilgrimage in 1872 capitalized on the phenomenon by creating a Conseil Général des Pèlerinages, an association that would be dedicated to organizing and directing not only French pilgrimages, but also those to Rome and the Holy Land.[586] Where earlier pilgrimages had often been local affairs, the new group planned to direct and market them on the national level.[587] In fact, it was the Conseil Général des Pèlerinages that organized the first national pilgrimage to Lourdes (1873) and began annual pilgrimages to Rome (1873) and Jerusalem (1882). Their leader, Father François Picard, belonged to the Assumptionist order, founded by Father Emmanuel d'Alzon in 1845 to continue the evangelizing work of Christ and to serve the Church wherever it most needed help.[588] In the aftermath of the war and the rise of the Third Republic, the growing Assumptionist order found its true mission: they would dedicate themselves to 'contributing to the moral and spiritual rebuilding of the miserable homeland,' and to creating a Catholic league that would defend the Church and would 'battle to conquer the freedom of higher education.'[589] They thus took education as their first major initiative, before branching out into other projects designed to win converts to Catholicism: pilgrimages and the popular press.

In 1872, the newly formed Conseil Général des Pèlerinages, led by the Assumptionist Picard, realized that pilgrimages would provide an excellent way of mobilizing Catholics and of gaining new converts. But how could they reach the people to spread their message? A simple project showed Father Picard the way: he had written a sheet of prayers for an upcoming session of l'Assemblée Nationale, then advertised it in a few newspapers and Catholic publications. The response was so great that he received over a million requests![590] The popularity of such brief writings gave him the idea for a weekly bulletin that would list religious events and would serve as the official mouthpiece of Le Conseil Général des Pèlerinages. The first edition of this paper, *Le Pèlerin* (*The Pilgrim*), was published in 1873. Initially, the paper was intended for a few hundred, then a few thousand subscribers, generally priests and Church officials. Accordingly, one finds self-congratulatory announcements about the success of the pilgrimage movement in France, represented as a movement that 'rivals the faith of the Middle Ages that gave birth to the Crusades':

For the last year, France has witnessed one of the most heartening spectacles for Christian souls. After the greatest disasters our country has ever experienced, we are finding that a single thought has suddenly emerged from the nation's heart. Catholic France, brought back to penitence by unhappiness, has spontaneously turned toward She whom Christians call by the name of Mother of Misery and Refuge of Sinners […] Never, since the time of the Crusades and Joan of Arc, have we seen such a movement and a movement so brilliant, so courageous and so Christian. […][591]

In addition to the editorial board's 'patriotic' enthusiasm for pilgrimages and for the modern world's return to the 'faith of the Middle Ages,' one finds a wealth of practical information about upcoming events, including calendars and itineraries, train schedules and rates, advertisements for room and board, glowing descriptions of the pilgrimage sites and their history as well as a surprising number of advertisements.

An 1873 issue, for example, contains advertisements for a variety of products including a number of books (pilgrimage manuals, illustrated histories of the Lourdes pilgrimage, a photo album about Notre-Dame de Lourdes, collected stories of pilgrimage experiences), banners, calendars and offers of food and lodging for various pilgrimage sites. A copy from 1877 prints several pages of advertisements for products and entertainments including plays (*Le Grand mystère de Bethléem*), pilgrimages to La Salette, Pennès vinegar, books and imagery (stories of Marguerite-Marie, religious imagery, a newspaper called *La Défense*), religious jewelry and medals (from several different companies), 'objets de pèlerinage' (made by a number of groups), hotel and mule rentals for La Salette, Sirop Laroze ('works against gastritis'), church organs, 'hygienic cushions' and kitchen stoves.[592] Interspersed with current events, pilgrimage notices and publicity are lengthy 'travelogues,' personal accounts of religious travel and reports from bishops all over France. The weekly newspaper reads very much like a travel magazine; although it was not yet illustrated, the abundance of different sites, cultural and religious activities and information about the history and attractions of each region provided a wealth of information for the reader, who could vicariously explore the history and beauty of the most remote areas of France without leaving home.

By the end of 1876, however, the editorial board had decided to direct the publication to a wider audience and to give it a more didactic slant: the paper would henceforth appear less as a repository for information about pilgrimages than as an illustrated weekly, written in a simple entertaining style for the common people, especially factory workers and countryfolk.[593] The new paper would be directed by Father Vincent de Paul Bailly, whose style appealed to the working class.

The concept of directing *Le Pèlerin* to the people was brilliant. There had been a number of Catholic papers published in the earlier part of the nineteenth century, including *L'Univers* and *Le Magasin catholique illustré*, as well as a number of presses specializing in Catholic subjects, like those run by the prolific Father Jean-Paul Migne. Yet most of these productions were fairly academic, directed at a highly literate public of royalists and clergy; they were, in general, too expensive for the average reader.[594] Léon Curmer's mid-century color publications of *L'Imitation de Jésus Christ*, the *Grandes heures de la reine Anne de Bretagne*, *Les Evangiles des Dimanches et fêtes de l'année* and the *Jehan Foucquet, Heures de Maistre Etienne Chevalier* offered reproductions of medieval devotional manuscripts on the installment plan, but at three to six francs per fascicule (of which there were 50 per volume), they were still far beyond the reach of most people.[595]

Moreover, by the end of the nineteenth century, most of the French population could read and thus constituted the perfect market for the Church's popularly slanted publication.[596] Because of new technology – notably heliogravure, which allowed for less expensive mass reproduction of both text and image – and because of relaxed freedom of the press laws, this was an excellent time to break into the publishing of illustrated periodicals, especially those for the masses.[597] Only La Société pour la Propagande des Bonnes Gravures Religieuses, which produced the sentimental 'images sulpiciennes' much maligned by priests and writers (including Bloy and Huysmans), offered inexpensive religious material in great quantity. But even these, at 25 centimes a picture or 100 francs for a book of hours, constituted luxuries for the working class.[598]

*Le Pèlerin* thus found a niche for itself, setting up as the direct competitor of *L'Illustration* and *Le Monde illustré*, popular secular periodicals to which the Assumptionist Fathers attempted to provide an alternative. In contrast to what they considered the immoral, commercial, pornographic fare of the regular press, they would eagerly embrace its opposite: highly moral stories about famous figures from history and idealized images of a simple, pious, charitable Middle Ages.[599] *Le Pèlerin* was founded above all to foster a love of pilgrimages and Catholic virtues – 'it knows only one political aim: to know, to love, to serve God and by this means to obtain eternal life' – and was sold very inexpensively (only six francs a year).[600]

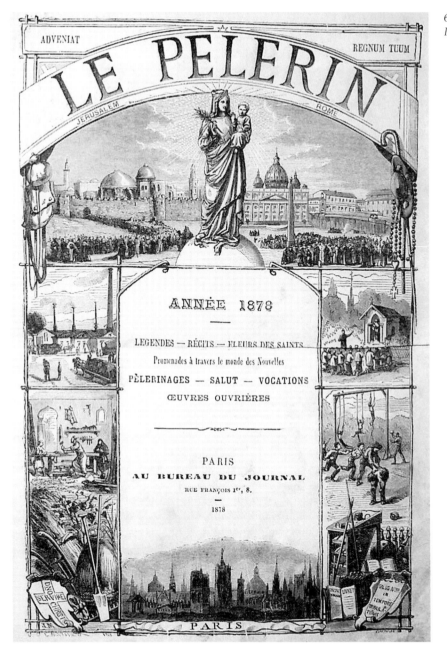

6.1    Cover of *Le Pèlerin*, 1878

Its medieval-inspired cover – 'the new portal to *Le Pèlerin*' – reflected these goals allegorically (Fig. 6.1). The editors clearly explained its significance in the first issue in which it appeared (3 March 1877). At the top of the page, we find an engraving of Notre-Dame de Salut, the medieval statue commissioned by Saint Louis for the main entrance to the Sainte-Chapelle.[601] At her feet are the two cities most admired by *Le Pèlerin*: Jerusalem and Rome. Beneath the text, the hundreds of pilgrims traveling to these cities represent the periodical's goal of mobilizing Catholics. The prison of Pope Pius also figures prominently in the hopes that it will soon be demolished by the works of these travelers. At the bottom of the cover is a darkened image of Paris, 'the infernal city, the impure cesspool, the crater that vomits its revolutionary lava on the countryside.' Yet there is hope for Paris: 'We have placed it like those poor sick souls at Lourdes, at the foot of Mary, she who brings salvation to France contemplates the city with compassion.' Within what they call the 'illuminated page' of the cover, the editors note, one 'travels' from Paris to Jerusalem and Rome via a 'ladder' composed of works of 'social reconciliation': on one side we see work (the factory and farmwork united by the workshop of Saint Joseph) and on the other, the works of laborers in prayer and recreation. These workers are represented as children to underline the importance of Christian children for rebuilding French society.[602] This illustration thus encapsulates the preoccupations of the Assumptionist order at the time: adopting the medieval practice of pilgrimage as atonement for sins in order to rebuild society through work and prayer; fighting to bring back the Pope and with him a reign of goodness and virtue.[603] Church leaders hoped that renewing the spiritual traditions and miracles of the Middle Ages – represented by Notre-Dame de Salut – could restore solid moral ground and positive values in a time they viewed as overrun by mass production, greed and interest in all things material.

In fact, through *Le Pèlerin*, the Church hoped to fight against some of the ravages it saw spreading through France (the 'revolutionary lava' spewed by the city of Paris is a particularly representative image of this sentiment). The Assumptionist reaction to increased secularization was virulent, yet logical. One can only image their shock as a country they had considered 'the eldest daughter of the Church' rapidly embarked on a path of what Republican leaders called 'de-Christianization.' In a matter of just a few years, the country shifted from a leader dedicated to defending the pope (Napoléon III's military support of the pontiff until 1870) to a Republic largely hostile to Catholicism. The violence of the transformation is perhaps best summarized by Léon Gambetta's incendiary 1877 proclamation to the Chambre des Députés: 'Le cléricalisme, voilà l'ennemi.' Many Republican leaders, though not all of them anti-clerical, expressed their relationship to the Church as a battle: 'a duel started between democracy and clericalism.'[604] Similarly, Church leaders began to echo this military rhetoric, representing themselves as 'persecuted' and 'on the verge of battle.'[605] The figure of Notre-Dame de Salut that dominates the cover of *Le Pèlerin* thus represents the power of Mary not only as intercessor, but also as a figure of goodness and light, defended by the pilgrims at her feet against the encroaching powers of darkness that emanate from the satanic Paris that lies beneath her. The Catholic Church, far from fading into the background, took up the gauntlet proffered by Republicans. Priests mightily resisted Republican attempts to oust them from public life by making their own appeals to the general public. They embraced modern marketing techniques, new developments in the illustrated press and organized travel to draw parishioners back to the fold. The new *Pèlerin* was conceived as a weapon

– 'a newspaper of precious propaganda' – to be wielded in the fight against anti-clericalism.[606]

## *Le Pèlerin* and its 'precious propaganda'

One of the primary goals of the new publication was to use images, as had the Church in the Middle Ages, as *exempla* that could attract the masses, teach them about Church history and foster in them a love for good values and Church traditions. According to Father Bailly, *Le Pèlerin* revived, for the first time since the Middle Ages, the Catholic tradition of 'speaking to the eyes through images':

In the Middle Ages there was no section of church walls that was not used for this particularly eloquent language [of images] and besides, the cult itself is a magnificent painting that, in striking the eye, illustrates the great words it offers. Saintly books, missals and hours were resplendent with illuminations, whose richness and pious naiveté daunts imitators. Each page was adorned by a frame, each letter practically a vignette [...] A bit later, our old saints' lives, those from which we often borrow in *Le Pèlerin*, were decorated by engravings in *taille-douce* that, at that time, demanded intense labor; nonetheless, our fathers did not haggle over expenditures for these difficult illustrations. One ancient Bible contains hundreds of these engravings and no editor of our century of photographers has produced an illustrated edition that compares to them. So widespread in the past, imagery was destroyed by Jansenist austerity, it was completely banished from the sanctuary; no respectable priest would have wanted to take care of it; they abandoned images with disgust to merchants alone, and, lacking support, imagery has fallen into ridicule. [...] But the *Pèlerin*, an old traveler who has seen many sanctuaries, who has often scratched off whitewash to find naive and pious frescoes of the past; he who has visited the rich churches of Spain and especially Italy, who, on the banks of the Rhine and in deepest Germany, has admired the stone poems of cathedrals, he demands true images. He attaches images to his coat because looking at the figure of a saint is a prayer, he is pleased by the spectacle of beautiful deeds as by the beauties of nature.[607]

This paean of praise to the historical, aesthetic and didactic virtues of images justifies *Le Pèlerin*'s use of them while attaching the newspaper's agenda to that of the medieval Church and its appreciation of art.

Father Bailly's insistence on the importance of renewing the medieval tradition of teaching and praying through the use of images responds to recent debates about the role the Church should play in society. By recommending a return to the practices of the medieval church, he acknowledges working-class criticism of the Catholic Church's elitism. In a highly publicized 1875 speech to Bishop Dupanloup, Claude-Anthime Corbon, a senator from the working class, had proposed that the Church return to the 'egalitarian' practices of the medieval church.[608] By describing *Le Pèlerin* as reaching out to the masses by sharing the wealth of its art with all, and as communicating the traditions and message of the Church on a level simple enough to include the greatest number of people possible, Bailly responds directly to such concerns.

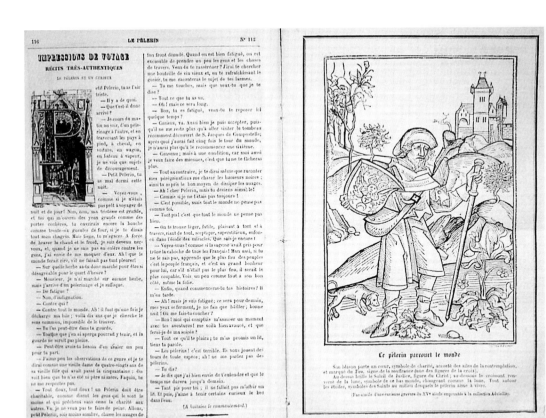

Bailly also proclaims the superiority of medieval manuscript illumination, thus subtly discrediting modern book illustration and diminishing the value of popular reproductions of illuminated Bibles, missals and books of hours.[609] But his praise of medieval imagery serves above all to condemn the Jansenist attitude to iconography and to validate the medieval understanding that splendid images foster prayer and strengthen religious belief. He remarks, in championing this technique, that *Le Pèlerin* is the first modern publication to return to the medieval model of illustrating Biblical stories. His insistence on the modern Church's ability to 'speak to the eyes through images' anticipates what David Freedberg has called 'the power of images,' the 'supernatural effectiveness' of images invested with the divine.[610]

The serious interest of Father Bailly in medieval manuscript illumination, tapestries, statuary and woodcuts from the Middle Ages was manifest in his new publication. It is full of images ranging from reproductions of medieval art, especially that of the *Primitifs*, to modern interpretations of medieval scenes and illustrations of contemporary pilgrimages.[611] Images are nearly always woven into the narrative: they either accompany a story or serve as a point of departure for the text, which explains the image's relevance to the Church and its history.[612] One such example, from 1879, juxtaposes a dialogue about contemporary pilgrimages – 'Travel impressions, very authentic narratives' – with a fifteenth-century woodcut of a pilgrim (Fig. 6.2). The effect is as if the text on the left, introduced by an illuminated letter 'P,' were engaging in a dialogue with the pilgrim figured on the right: 'Little pilgrim, you seem sad.' The interlocutor asks him to tell his story. Under the pilgrim, one finds the following commentary:

His coat of arms bears a heart, symbol of charity, marked by the *Tau*, a sign of suffering (one of the figures of the cross), and flanked by the wings of contemplation. Above, there shines the Sun of Justice, a figure of Christ; below, the upside-down crescent moon, a symbol of this lowly world, as changeable as the moon. All around it are stars, symbols of the Saints among whom pilgrims love to live.[613]

The mixture of medieval and modern images, commentary and fiction creates an interesting blend of entertainment and edification: interpretations of medieval history and art are blended with documents and images from the Middle Ages. Moreover, such juxtapositions in visual style and content implied a continuing tradition that linked medieval and contemporary pilgrims.

Indeed, the new format of the periodical offered something for everyone and had a decidedly medieval flavor, especially given its reproduction of medieval art, its simplified stories of medieval saints, kings and queens from the Middle Ages and their encounters with pilgrimages. Among the heroes of such stories were Charlemagne, Saint Louis, Saint Augustin, Saint Michel, Saint Denis, Saint Hubert, Joan of Arc, Saint Martin of Tours and Saint Genevieve, whose lives and deeds were recounted in detail and accompanied by artwork from various centuries.[614] Figure 6.3, for example, features a portrait of Saint Luke modeled after medieval and Renaissance prototypes such as the portrait of Saint Luke by Jan van Eyck, which depicts the artist seated before his lectern as he paints the Virgin. Here, reference is made to medieval manuscript illumination through the use of Gothic framing and lettering and background motifs. The accompanying article, however, questions the commonly held conceit that the saint painted the first portrait of the Virgin Mary; its authors reappraise his biography. Such stories of medieval saints in the publication were juxtaposed with 'modern saints': clergymen, Catholic leaders, pilgrims, good donors to the church, or the few who had seen the Virgin Mary (the sightings of Bernadette at Lourdes and of Maxime and Mélanie at La Salette were favored subjects). Such stories were also interspersed with images and brief articles about the history of religious holidays and French traditions.[615] The result of this fusion of medieval and modern was to reinforce readers' familiarity with the Christian origin of the French nation (stories abounded about kings and queens, their contact with saints or God, their anointment or their adventures with pilgrims), to show them the 'pure morals' of worshipers in the Middle Ages and to demonstrate how the Catholic Church had succeeded in renewing its links to its 'true' (albeit highly idealized) origins. Such uplifting stories, examples and messages, it was hoped, would help readers to renew their commitment to the Christian values of their French ancestors and to fight for an increased presence of the Church in the corrupted modern time.[616] In its

6.3 'S. Luc, patron des peintres,' *Le Pèlerin*, 22 Nov 1879

new format and with its simple writing and topics, *Le Pèlerin* targeted the working class and rural communities with great results: 'The success of *Le Pèlerin* is due to the form it has adopted [...] it spreads many accurate ideas and breaks into milieus where religious journals are not allowed.'[617] *Le Pèlerin* was enormously successful in its attempts to reach readers; in the early 1880s, its editors published 100 000 copies a year, increasing to 196 300 by 1900 and to 459 000 by 1912, according to *l'Annuaire de la presse*. The newspaper truly succeeded in widely popularizing medieval history and art and had an estimated two million readers.[618]

*Le Pèlerin*'s great success was a result of its willingness to cater to the demands of a new group of readers and to adopt creative marketing campaigns. Intent upon competing with the secular press, the *Maison de la Bonne Presse* actively targeted rural communities that would not ordinarily come into contact with papers. The Assumptionist Fathers were aggressive in creating what they called 'methods of propaganda' for *La Maison de la Bonne Presse* and its Assumptionist publications, which, by 1898, numbered forty-four![619] One of the most effective techniques was to appeal to the clergy, who would read the paper and then distribute copies to parishioners. Other variants of this method involved creating 'committees' willing to distribute the periodical for a small profit or finding people to stand outside the church after services distributing free copies. Any additional copies were left in the church.[620] They mailed free copies to affluent Catholics and developed secondary publications that would be inserted in the paper, including a series of almanacs that was highly successful at increasing circulation.[621]

One of the most popular of these was a saints' lives series that could be detached from the paper or ordered separately as booklets. The sheets were often given to children as prizes or distributed as gifts. The issues were collected, organized by the days of the saints in question and bound in single volumes, which could be consulted throughout the year.[622] Where only aristocrats and affluent bourgeois patrons had been able to purchase reproductions of illuminated books of hours earlier in the century, by the 1880s even the poorest member of society could compile an illustrated personal book of devotion.[623]

A particularly innovative ploy that further underlined the Assumptionists' link to the Middle Ages involved creating a chivalric order, 'Les Chevaliers de la Croix,' dedicated to selling the newspaper:

In the past, defending the weak was the primary objective of knights. The weak of our time are the unhappy people who are tricked, seduced, corrupted by the wicked press. It is up to you to defend them in bringing them the right newspaper. This is the major task at which you must work tirelessly, without ever faltering.[624]

Although today we might laugh at a chivalric order being created simply to sell newspapers, the priests were quite serious about the 'nobility' of their pursuit. They unironically embraced such medieval models as part of their higher apostolic cause, which they labeled a 'crusade': to attract more

Catholics to the Church, thus creating legions of good Christians willing to fight to turn the tide against an increasingly secular society and its evil ways.[625]

Within *Le Pèlerin*, such efforts to increase distribution were applauded by the editors and shared with other readers who were encouraged to emulate such virtuous behavior. Particularly startling in this regard is a December 1896 issue that applauded the 'methods of propaganda' of a parishioner who had distributed 14 000 copies of *La Vie des saints* in three years by giving the booklets as prizes for catechism, by distributing them on Sundays, for holidays and during funerals and by having children recite them.[626] Through such aggressive word-of-mouth marketing (what today we might call 'viral marketing'), the paper did live up to its objectives of spreading the word about the Church, of attempting to combat evil by disseminating information about good morals, and of increasing pilgrimages. Because of its wide distribution, the influence of *Le Pèlerin* extended beyond Catholic circles; its attempts to avoid explicit political orientation (even if political neutrality was nearly impossible for those affiliated with Catholicism at this time), its use of medieval woodcuts and art and its acceptance of poems about pilgrims and religious subjects by a variety of authors and illustrators made it accessible to a wide readership. In *Le Pèlerin*, one finds contributions by authors as varied as Maurice Barrès, Léon Bloy, François Coppée, Léon Daudet, Henri Lasserre and Frédéric Mistral and by illustrators who worked for other publications including *Le Courrier Français* and *Le Chat Noir*: Henriot, Damblans and Uzès.[627] Aside from the religious theme of its articles, its format and use of text and image is not markedly different from other illustrated periodicals of the time, as one can see by comparing an issue of *Le Chat Noir* to an issue of *Le Pèlerin* (Figs 6.4 and 6.5). Indeed, Uzès, who would become the primary illustrator for *Le Pèlerin*, was also a major contributor to *Le Chat Noir*, and he spent much of his time in the 'neo-medieval' cabaret.[628]

By the 1890s, the pilgrimage became an extremely popular literary and artistic motif, even in non-religious circles. It became a powerful symbol of a crusade against the forces of modernity. We can see the popularity of the theme in the titles and content of books published at the time, including Jean Moréas's *Le Pèlerin passionné* (1891), Remy de Gourmont's *Pèlerin du silence* (1896), Marcel Schwob's 'La Croisade des Enfants' (1896), Léon Bloy's *La Femme pauvre* (1897) and Louis le Cardonnel's *Carmina Sacra* (1912), and also in the abundance of poems or stories dedicated to pilgrims and published with woodcuts in publications such as *Le Courrier Français*, *Le Chat Noir*, *La Plume*, *Le Mercure de France* and *L'Ymagier*.[629] Emile Verhaeren's 'Le Pèlerin,' published in *Le Mercure de France* in 1899 and accompanied by a modern imitation of a medieval woodcut of Christ as pilgrim, is typical of this trend.[630] In addition, figures of pilgrims were prominent in the art of the official Salons among both realist and Academic painters, such as Jules Breton, Léon Lhermite and Pascal-Adolphe-Jean Dagnan-Bouveret (Fig. 6.6).[631] While the photographic detail and 'objective' flavor of Dagnan-Bouveret's images

6.4   'Où il est parlé du seul vray miracle idoine à guarir le mauldict mal de Stérilité et du bon Sainct Greluchon qui l'inventa.' *Le Chat Noir*, 26 Sep 1885

sharply contrast with the more simplified and intentionally naive mood of Sérusier's work (see Fig. 5.12), nearly all of these images – of both medieval and modern pilgrimages – represent files of neatly dressed silent or praying figures carrying banners and candles in orderly procession. They are generally depicted inside a church or just outside a church, a critical element in the composition of these scenes.

*Le Pèlerin* was thus extremely powerful and significantly influenced its readers' impressions of the Middle Ages. First, the Assumptionist Fathers made medieval French history well known to large numbers of people through their summaries of the adventures of saints, kings and queens and

6.5 'La Légende de Saint Julien le Pauvre,' *Le Pèlerin*, 10 Oct 1881

the origins of various holidays.[632] Second, their willingness to reproduce authentic medieval and Renaissance prints and *images d'Epinal* familiarized a great number of readers with the techniques, themes, symbolism and styles of the past.[633] These 'crude' and 'popular' woodcuts were intentionally very different from the illuminated manuscripts favored by aristocratic patrons. Third, by including their discussion of new French pilgrimage sites

6.6  Dagnan-Bouveret, *The Pardon in Brittany*, 1886

such as Lourdes, La Salette and Montmartre within a publication brimming with stories about medieval saints and legends, they linked modern religious experiences to those of the past (Fig. 6.7). The parallels they established with the times of Joan of Arc, Charlemagne and Saint Louis were made even more explicit by juxtaposing modern accounts of pilgrimages from contemporaries with stories about medieval pilgrims and their adventures (based on both historical and fictional accounts). Figure 6.7 incarnates this tendency, as a variety of pilgrims from various periods (including St. Louis, Godefroy de Bouillon, Pierre l'Hermite and St. Michel) appear together, dedicated to the French nation and its traditional Catholic values. The link between pilgrim

6.7   Ciapori Puche, *La France de nos pères, Le Pèlerin*, 17 Feb 1883

and Middle Ages was further intensified by the huge popular success of authors such as Henri Lasserre, whose *Notre-Dame de Lourdes* (1869) was heavily promoted by *Le Pèlerin*, which reproduced numerous passages and illustrations from the book. In his work, Lasserre portrayed the village of Lourdes as unchanged since the Middle Ages and featured illustrations that – like an illuminated manuscript – surrounded the story of Bernadette's life.[634]

Following the Assumptionists' lead, thousands of towns all over France retraced their links to the Middle Ages and produced articles for *Le Pèlerin* in which they explained their town's pilgrimage pedigree, summarized the founding story of their shrine and told stories about famous medieval pilgrims who had traveled there.[635] In addition to these historical narratives, they advertised the modern conveniences of their town and described its traditions, its natural beauty and the welcoming committees organized to greet pilgrims. The blend of medieval and modern, coupled with the appeal of 'following in the steps of one's ancestors' and returning to a time before the Church was considered an enemy of the French state, attracted many people, who eagerly traveled from one pilgrimage spot to another.

### Pilgrimage as crusade: the image of the religious journey

Much as *Le Pèlerin* had worked hard to present images of pilgrims as following in the footsteps of their medieval ancestors, the Assumptionist Fathers established rituals calculated to put pilgrims in a 'medieval' state of mind and to use their 'piety' to cleanse the 'rapid routes of pleasure and commerce.'[636]

Accordingly, church organizers worked behind the scenes to organize group travel, obtaining discounts of 20 to 30 per cent, distributing manuals filled with prayers and information about the history of each pilgrimage site and surrounding towns, creating itineraries for the trip and providing housing options for their participants.[637] The experience itself was orchestrated to evoke the traditions of the past; one of the first acts of Le Conseil Général des Pèlerinages was to apply to the Pope for prayers to protect the pilgrims and to ask for a symbol that would distinguish them from mere travelers. Subsequent requests included fixing indulgences for various trips. They published the details of their letters and the pontiff's responses in *Le Pèlerin*. Pope Pius IX chose the red cross to identify pilgrims, as had the Church Fathers in the First Crusade. Such insignia thus distinguished pilgrims while insisting that their holy mission linked them to their religious ancestors and their defense of the French nation.[638] The red cross emblazoned on chests or on banners is ubiquitous in nineteenth-century paintings depicting the Crusades as well as in the images favored by *Le Pèlerin*.[639] The sight of pilgrims wearing the red cross, brandishing banners and pushing or carrying the sick surely called to mind this artistic *topos*, while reinforcing the pilgrims' vision of their holy mission.[640]

The ceremonies surrounding the blessing of the pilgrims were elaborate. Before their departure, they would gather in their churches to receive their fabric crosses, which would be blessed by the presiding priest or bishop. Early issues of *Le Pèlerin*, destined for clergymen, describe the ceremony at length: after the pilgrimage hymn, one learned about the importance of the cross, the emblem of penitence and prayer for their 'peaceful crusade for the deliverance of the Holy Father and for the salvation of France.'[641] Pilgrims then knelt at the foot of the altar and accepted the cross while the priest blessed them and entrusted them (in Latin) with their badge. They would finish the ceremony by reading the pilgrimage prayers printed in the *Manuel des pèlerins*. The religious material contained in these booklets prepared pilgrims for entering into a mystical state in which they would forget the material world and their senses: above all, they were directed to cultivate 'the spirit of piety, charity and penitence.'[642] Personal accounts of pilgrimages published in *Le Pèlerin* dwell upon the effectiveness of such ceremonies for putting one in the proper spirit, and recount the emotion with which groups took up their crosses.[643] Such accessories, hymns and prayers framed the modern journey within a highly aestheticized system of references to the traditions of French forebears culled from art, history and legend. Church organizers thus prepared pilgrims for arrival in a mysterious, immaterial, neo-medieval world of prayer and canticle.[644] Images such as Figure 6.8, in which medieval pilgrims' objectives and traditions mirrored those of their modern counterparts, reinforced this link between past and present.

Travelers may have come close to experiencing such a mystical journey in villages like Conques or Rouen, which retained their medieval character, but one can only imagine the shock of those pilgrims who arrived in Lourdes, which, by the mid-1870s, had become France's premier pilgrimage

Fac-simile, du Manuel du pèlerin à Compostelle.

SUR UN GENTILHOMME QUI A FAIT LE VOYAGE DE SAINT JACQUES, ET S'EST RENDU CAPUCIN

Air du Cantique des Pèlerins

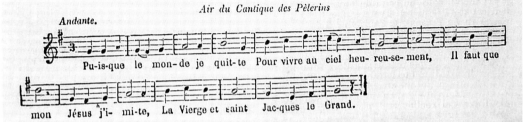

6.8   *Les pèlerins de S. Jacques de Compostelle, Le Pèlerin*, 26 July 1879

destination.[645] Joseph Demarteau, a Belgian pilgrim who wrote letters home during the 1906 pilgrimage, was taken aback by the crush of the crowds, his first impression of the city.[646] Another 1906 visitor, J.-K. Huysmans, was also stunned by the seething masses – to such an extent that he changed the title of his book about the pilgrimage from *The Two Faces of Lourdes* to *The Crowds of Lourdes*. He was disgusted by the abundance of vendors, the tawdry religious trinkets and the difficulty of getting through them to arrive at the Grotto: 'it is unbridled competition, boutiques throughout the city waylaying you at every step; you come, go and swerve, in the midst of all of this hubbub, but you always end up, one way or another, at the grotto.'[647] Pilgrims were amazed by the urbanization of Lourdes, which offered creature comforts for the traveler. Although they had expected to endure the trials of medieval pilgrims like Saint Martin or Saint Genevieve, they found that they could stay in luxurious hotels, eat in fine restaurants, enjoy twenty-four hour electricity and shop for souvenirs, postcards and religious ex-votos. Even the miraculous spring had been modernized for consumer convenience; the Fathers of the Grotto had rerouted it into taps so that visitors could use faucets to pour their fill.

## The pilgrimage as commodity

Emile Zola, who accompanied his wife on a pilgrimage in 1891, provides one of the clearest examples of the clash between the medieval expectations created by the publicity of the Assumptionist Fathers and the banal reality of the city itself. In the novel *Lourdes* (1894), his protagonist, Pierre Froment, is a priest who has lost his faith. He accompanies a sick friend to Lourdes in the hope that she will be healed and that he will regain his belief. Zola devotes the first part of the book to evoking the mystical atmosphere that reigns in the invalids' train on the way to Lourdes as the pilgrims sing hymns and tell the story of Bernadette's vision of the Virgin Mary (the stories and activities often printed in *Le Pèlerin*). Despite this preparation, however, the town's commercialism destroys Pierre's idealized image of the pilgrimage experience:

> [Pierre] recalled old cathedrals shivering with the belief of the masses; he saw once again the antique liturgical objects; imagery, silver and gold plate, saints of stone and wood, whose force and beauty of expression was admirable. It was because, in those far off times, workers believed, gave their flesh, gave their soul, in the overwhelming naiveté of their emotion [...] and today, architects built churches with the tranquil science they put into building five-story houses, just as religious objects, rosaries, medals, statuettes, were mass-produced in the populous part of Paris, by fast-living workers [... .] *All of this clashed brutally with the attempted resurrection, with the legends, ceremonies and processions of dead ages.*[648]

Pierre's indignation results not only from recognizing the falsity of his dream, but also from the disparity between the attempted resurrection of medieval traditions of which he had read and the artificiality and shabbiness of the effects achieved. Above all, he feels tricked by the false marketing that brought him to Lourdes.

Pierre's experience was not unusual. In fact, by the end of the nineteenth century, the pilgrimages themselves had become a victim of the Assumptionist Fathers' success with publicity and many pilgrims complained about their rampant commercialism. Like Zola and Huysmans, they accused the Church of going too far with their publicity in *Le Pèlerin* and in Lourdes and of cheapening the religious experience for 'real' pilgrims by 'selling' the sacred.[649] While the Assumptionists used medieval spirituality and art as a framework of reference to bestow authenticity upon the endeavor, publicity seemed to have turned the pilgrimage experience into a consumer product. Thanks to the inexpensively organized pilgrimages and their souvenirs, anyone could go to Lourdes and anyone could buy one of the many souvenir photo albums or postcards advertised in *Le Pèlerin*.

Pilgrims were, in fact, easily distracted by the commercial offerings of the city. While essays and articles in *Le Pèlerin* focus exclusively on the spirituality of the pilgrimage experience, letters and journals about Lourdes single out material concerns – pilgrims' activities, the sites they visit and the miraculous healings they witness – and describe Lourdes as a marketplace. Demarteau focuses on the layout of the city and its new technology, while Huysmans describes in detail the dizzying number of objects for sale:

Morning to night, no matter where one goes, one revolves around the same track, seeing, in addition to tired faces, nothing but statues of virgins in plaster, their eyes directed to heaven, clothed in white and belted in blue; not one shop without medals, votive candles, rosaries, scapulars, brochures describing miracles; old and new Lourdes choke with them; even hotels sell them; and this continues for streets on streets, for kilometers […] lithographs of Bernadette in a red skirt and blue apron, kneeling, a votive candle in hand, before the Virgin, with Lilliputian statuettes and medals that make one think of play money, coined wholesale in scraps of copper; and all of these objects improve, swell, multiply as one nears the new city; while remaining equally ugly, the statues grow, ending up enormous. The lithographs get larger, disguising the Soubirous girl as a housemaid; the form of the medals grows and their metal changes; gold and silver begin to appear and when one reaches the Avenue de la Grotte, it is the explosion of luxurious bibelots.[650]

Much as the readers of *Le Pèlerin* sent money to *La Maison de la Bonne Presse* in order to receive books of saints' lives, detachable sheets of religious imagery and pictures based on the saints they most admired, pilgrims to Lourdes focused increasingly on the objects – the relics – associated with the trip and less on the experience itself. In this they truly did resemble medieval pilgrims, even if the late nineteenth century saw these distractions as particularly modern.[651]

Many writers saw such blatant commercialism as alien to the true Catholic spirit, yet they often did not blame the Church, which profited handsomely from Lourdes; instead, they criticized the modern cosmopolitan Jew, who had no link to small town life or Christianity. He was held responsible for the blatant commercialism of the pilgrimage site. As some (like Huysmans) saw it, the Jew derived unconscious pleasure from financially exploiting the crowd assembled for worship; he thus undermined the spiritual nexus of the voyage:

Priests should consider how strongly the Jewish element now dominates among the licensed vendors of religious objects. Converted or not, and above and beyond their passion for profit, it seems as though these dealers feel the involuntary need to betray the Messiah once again, by selling him according to techniques whispered by the Devil.[652]

Just as anti-Semitic art historians had claimed that the Jew could only appreciate medieval art as an 'investment,' Huysmans claimed that Jewish shopkeepers – even those who had converted to Christianity – were immune to the spiritually uplifting and morally beneficial elements of the pilgrimage. For such Catholics, the very presence of the Jew in modern France conflicted with the idealized image of a unified Catholic community that the Assumptionist Fathers had worked so hard to build. Moreover, the commercialism associated with the Jew in the nineteenth century was seen as luring the faithful from their spiritual quest.

Indeed, as pilgrimages grew ever more popular, manuals devoted more and more space to instructing pilgrims to avoid concupiscence, curiosity and greed and to reminding them that pilgrimages were not a form of tourism: 'Pilgrimages to the Grotto of Lourdes would deviate from their goal, they would lose all merit if, by our fault, they were to be transformed into simple tourist excursions [...] A pilgrimage is an act of expiation, not a pleasure trip.'[653] Yet while they admonished pilgrims about their behavior, the publications of *La Maison de la Bonne Presse* devoted even more space to advertisements for local attractions.[654] The Church's embrace of modern marketing techniques exacerbated the material temptations to which it was trying to provide an alternative. As pilgrimages flourished, the original purpose of the pilgrimage movement seemed to have been betrayed: travels to pray for the salvation of the country developed into increasingly secular, Church-sanctioned entertainment for Catholics.

Thanks to expanded railway networks, shorter working hours and an increase in disposable income, tourism also developed at this time. As an increasingly secular public no longer participated actively in Catholic rituals, pilgrimages themselves became captivating spectacles.[655] Travelers flocked to cities and towns to watch the pilgrims as they would real-life representations of the paintings they had seen in the Salons, in the pages of *Le Pèlerin*, or on the Parisian stages. Zola provides the perfect example. The resolutely anti-clerical author certainly did not come to Lourdes on a pilgrimage; he agreed to accompany his wife, out of curiosity about the site and its miracles.[656] The Lourdes pilgrimages had become a highly-acclaimed and picturesque tourist attraction, commemorated by hundreds of postcards and souvenir books, by paintings displayed in the annual Salons and by newspapers that regularly reported on them.

Zola the tourist, like his protagonist Pierre, came to Lourdes to find a confirmation of the medieval and modern pilgrimages he had seen in pictures: silent and chaste heads bowed in prayer, figures carrying candles and banners and ostensoirs through a medieval village. Instead, one experienced only the crowd: 'the thousands of pilgrims from the national pilgrimage in a crush [...] streamed through the streets, besieging shops. One would have taken this for the cries, the elbowing, the unruly jolts of a closing fair.'[657] Zola's comparison of Lourdes to a fair provides a particularly interesting indication of the extent to which his preconceived notion of Lourdes is drawn from pictures. Although a pilgrimage is like a fair in the hustle and bustle of the many people present, Zola describes Pierre's imagination of it only in terms of visual input: he returns over and over to the 'sight' of pilgrims and to the objects that surround them (liturgical objects, imagery, silver and gold). He does not have his character dream of the sounds, the movement, or the elbowing of the crowd.[658] Nor does he have him take an active role in the dream pilgrimage, praying with the medieval worshipers; Pierre's lack of faith excludes him from the crowd, which he studies with decidedly Naturalist fervor. Like Pierre, other visitors must have experienced profound disappointment and shock when they did not find the two-dimensional artwork they had imagined in Lourdes; many rejected the pilgrimage (as did Zola) as 'inauthentic' or as a false 'attempted resurrection' of the Middle Ages.[659]

Ironically, the 'authenticity' Pierre Froment sought was itself 'inauthentic,' a product of marketing campaigns like those of *Le Pèlerin*. Pilgrims in the

Middle Ages were no more pious or less greedy than those of the nineteenth century, despite the idealized images of them that were spread through works like Chateaubriand's *Le Génie du Christianisme* and the paintings of artists like Jean-Paul Laurens or Henri Martin. The prime example of Pierre Froment's acceptance of the marketed image is his delight with the 'Panorama' in Lourdes, an exhibit set up for tourists to experience the 'old Lourdes.'[660] Dioramas and panoramas were extremely popular at the end of the century as ways of recreating historical scenes; they consisted of circular rooms in which long painted canvases would rotate around the viewer, creating the effect of attending a historical event.[661] In Lourdes, the dioramas and panoramas were billed as an 'authentic' way of experiencing the city of the past and they could be enjoyed for admission fees of 50 centimes to one franc. As Suzanne Kaufman has pointed out, the Church Fathers in Lourdes once again copied the successful works of Paris entrepreneurs to 'sell' the pilgrimage experience.[662] These paintings are themselves 'inauthentic,' artists' representations of scenes that corresponded closely to the depictions of pilgrimages favored by *Le Pèlerin*. Pierre, however, buys fully into the panorama technique as he discovers in it the ideal pilgrimage he did not find in the 'real' Lourdes.

Pierre's experience is important because it reveals the extent to which, for tourists, Lourdes had become a spectacle for consumption.[663] To a large extent, the town itself had developed into a giant scene for the tourist gaze; the train travel to the site constituted the admission fee and tourists came to Lourdes to watch 'les foules' as they would a theatrical performance or a recreated 'panorama' from the past. Tourists sought, in the pilgrimage spectacle, to confirm what they had seen in pictures; they hoped to be transported back to the Middle Ages to attend an 'authentic' pilgrimage.[664] Their disappointment came from realizing that Lourdes was not medieval after all; it was no different from any other tourist attraction.

### The problem of authenticity

But what constituted an 'authentic' experience of the Middle Ages and for whom? As Fustel de Coulanges had put it in 1871, 'Each person makes his own, imaginary Middle Ages.' The tourist's disappointment when modern places did not in fact seem 'medieval' is only one side of a conceptual battle that took place repeatedly during the fin de siècle. How could one continue to view something – a stained-glass window, a tapestry, a cathedral, a pilgrimage – as sacred when confronted by the conflicting aesthetic or commercial use to which others put it? How could a pilgrimage – traditionally the most holy of quests – retain its religious 'authenticity' when marketed as a tourist attraction? Concerns about mass production and commercialism influenced perceptions of the Middle Ages as they did religion itself. Would a unique liturgical object from the Middle Ages lose its value if it were reproduced industrially and sold for nearly nothing (as were objects at

Lourdes)? Would the uniqueness of religious experience be diluted as pilgrimages became mainstream?

The Assumptionists, who saw the religious function of a pilgrimage as its mark of authenticity, answered these questions with a resounding 'no.' Although they had begun to worry about the commercialism they had introduced in Lourdes, they still understood their activities as 'apostolic,' as a mission to spread the word of God and to bring more people to the Church.[665] As David Freedberg has pointed out, pilgrimages often create a self-perpetuating cycle in which profits are directed back to the cult itself, thus prolonging its existence:

Crowds flock to them; as a result of the ensuing popularity, substantial incomes are generated. Whether manipulated or not, these devotions and these public occasions arise from the attraction, the supernatural charisma one might rightly say, of these simple images. And so the incomes they engender are channeled back to the images themselves, and honor is paid to them in the form of appropriately sumptuous forms of enshrinement.[666]

When criticized for their excess publicity, the Assumptionist leaders argued that there could not be too much of a good thing and that Catholicism and the French nation needed ever more converts and ever more prayers.[667] For them, the 'use value' of the pilgrimages – bringing together a community of believers who would pray for the restoration of the Pope and for the salvation of France – outweighed all other concerns.[668] This focus is clear in *Le Pèlerin*, which did not market the *town* of Lourdes as medieval (as would a tourist magazine); it presented the *spirituality* of the pilgrimage experience as medieval, as a link to the belief and practices of the past (see Fig. 6.7). By focusing on the parallels between modern and medieval pilgrimages, they appealed to Catholics' desire to renew the French *spirit* of the past and to follow in the footsteps of their ancestors. They did not consciously attempt to recreate the Middle Ages through their ceremonies.[669]

In this focus on the spirit rather than the letter of the Middle Ages, the Assumptionists found their counterpart in the Republican critic Louis de Fourcaud, who championed the resuscitation of the Gothic spirit in Republican works of art:

People tell us that we are no longer in the fourteenth or the fifteenth century and that customs have changed. I know it, but I beg you to consider this point: it is not at all a question of retracing our footsteps! It is a matter of reclaiming, above and beyond the superficial approach of previous centuries, the ardent sincerity of the venerable, glorious, anonymous individuals in whose hearts beat our national spirit […] as for us, we will do what our Gothic ancestors did.[670]

The Assumptionists and de Fourcaud insisted that it was the soul, not the outward shell of the Middle Ages, that could be resurrected in the present day.

*Le Pèlerin*'s use of rhetoric linking modern pilgrimages to those of the Middle Ages was, however, interpreted differently by other readers. As de Certeau has suggested, religious discourse, imagery and ceremony become mere 'theater' for those who no longer understand the Church's use of elaborate allegorical systems.[671] Zola's Pierre Froment thus sees in the pilgrimage its purely literal incarnation: an 'attempted resurrection' of the Middle Ages and its trappings, 'the legends, ceremonies and processions of dead ages.' While the Church focused on the pilgrimage's spiritual function ('use value'), Zola represented it in his novel as a mere vestige of the past (its 'value of recollection'). In this, he reveals his own Naturalist *a priori*, transforming his priest character into a scientific observer. Had Zola come to Lourdes with a mission prompted by faith (an act of personal penitence, for example), he might have been able to participate in the pilgrimage and to feel the 'authenticity' conferred by worship. But instead, he sought to remain on the outside, to confirm his ideal of picturesque medieval pilgrimage. The shock he expressed in his notes came from the disparity between his expectations and reality: the Church used modern marketing techniques to lure people to a sacred space where they were inundated with commercial products.[672] Because his expectations relied on his own idealized concept of authenticity (the importance of the scene of prayer over the marketplace), he had difficulty understanding how Lourdes could constitute an 'authentic' pilgrimage experience for someone else.[673]

Like the tourists who sought escape in the 'Middle Ages' through pilgrimages, late nineteenth-century cathedral visitors often focused more on the drama of the Catholic ritual than on its spirit. While believers understood Gothic churches as houses of worship, in which the 'use value' of the Catholic liturgy was integral to understanding the relationships among the component parts of a cathedral, tourists admired only the spectacle of the Eucharist as they would an opera. Because they did not belong to the religious community that gave the cathedral its religious meaning, they could not see the whole picture, nor could they understand the symbolic importance of the ceremony taking place in front of them. Similarly, the tourist at Lourdes could appreciate the aesthetics of the spectacle – the chanting masses with their banners and their crosses, their candlelight processions and their group prayers – yet they might not understand the significance of the event, the spiritual dimension that made this more than a spectacle. Nor could they understand why the Church might have advertised the experience as medieval. Such spectators, who sought a medieval ideal in modern pilgrimages, were sorely disappointed because they had objectified the Middle Ages, turned it into an image, woodcut or painting they might have seen in a periodical or in the official Salons. If Pierre Froment's dream of the Middle Ages insists so heavily upon 'seeing', it is because Zola gives him a spectator's role in the ceremony. Without a full commitment to the modern pilgrimage, the real and imagined scenes will always clash.

Each group thus possessed its own notions of an 'authentic' pilgrimage and an 'authentic' Middle Ages, yet neither group was less a pilgrim. Victor Turner has proposed that 'a tourist is half a pilgrim, if a pilgrim is half a tourist.' Both leave their homes to embark on a quest of personal significance, only to return again.[674] Each of them may have a different motivation or goal, but this goal is important to the individual concerned. As Ian Reader has suggested, pilgrimage has come to mean much more than its original religious connotation suggested, and 'pilgrimage need not, at least in popular perspective, be limited solely to explicitly religious traditions.'[675] As 'tourists' or 'pilgrims' sought different experiences, 'pilgrimage' began to be used more and more frequently as a term that could be applied to serious travel involving respect, reflection or contemplation.[676] In the last half of the century, we thus encounter pious 'pilgrimages' to Bayreuth in honor of Wagner, 'artistic pilgrimages' to visit the treasures of the Duc d'Aumale at the newly created Musée Condé in Chantilly, 'literary pilgrimages' to the homes of famous writers, 'positivist pilgrimages' to the grave of Auguste Compte, or 'Ruskinian pilgrimages' to the sites described by John Ruskin.[677] Even if Lourdes, the allegedly 'authentic' pilgrimage, disappoints, the piousness and respect accorded to secular pilgrimages often did live up to the hushed, silent, reverent pilgrimages idealized in art and literature. Stained-glass windows, tapestries and statues were removed from churches to become objects of art, and similarly the medieval pilgrimage came to be detached from its religious quest, often changed into a new kind of sublime and transforming secular experience.

## Private pilgrimages

As in the case of Zola and his character, who sought a pictorial ideal of the Middle Ages in the pilgrimages of Lourdes, many Frenchmen of the late nineteenth century similarly traveled to confirm their private image of the Middle Ages as escape from and antidote to the modern world. When foiled by what they felt was the 'inauthenticity' of huge popular sites like Lourdes, they either continued their quest for a model that did conform to their idea of an 'authentic' medieval site or they created their own private Middle Ages. Huysmans, for example, was disgusted by what he felt was the 'demonic' nature of commercialism in Lourdes.[678] In search of more solitary experiences related to the Middle Ages, he explored France in order to '[reunite] in a kind of bouquet' different aspects of the time, 'scattered for so many centuries.'[679] As he converted to Catholicism, he constantly sought spaces in which he could feel what he considered the 'real' Middle Ages, dark, silent spaces of prayer surrounded by medieval art. His novels resound with delight when his protagonist, Durtal, who wanders through modern France, is able to find confirmation of what he feels is the 'real' Middle Ages, the isolated medieval churches, monasteries, or church services in which 'l'âme du Moyen Age' manifests itself to him.[680]

Others, less interested in the religious aspects of the Middle Ages, created their own pilgrimages to cathedrals, medieval ruins and monuments to experience what they considered the 'real,' the 'lost' or the 'disappearing' Middle Ages. A profusion of travel guides advertising visits to historic sites – often cathedrals – also cropped up at this time to assist in such 'artistic pilgrimages': the Touring Club of France published monthly issues, beginning in 1891, the Guide Bleu and Baedeker printed new editions of their recommendations for France, while John Ruskin's books about Chartres and Amiens were translated by Marcel Proust, who advocated 'Ruskinian pilgrimages.' One of the most idiosyncratic of these pilgrims was Albert Robida, a novelist, caricaturist and architect, who created an extraordinarily personalized guidebook to 'old France' in his four-volume series, *La Vieille France*. This book followed the tradition of Charles Nodier and Isidore Taylor, the editors of *Voyages pittoresques et romantiques dans l'ancienne France*, whose publication spanned the century (1820–1878) and assembled texts, drawings and watercolors of monuments by a number of writers and artists. Robida, however, was responsible for all of the research, writing and images (about 200 drawings and 40 lithographs per book) in his four volumes: *Bretagne*, *Normandie*, *Provence* and *Touraine*. His goal was not to document various monuments or to reproduce them as accurately or as luxuriously as possible (as had Nodier and Taylor). Rather, he chose those that struck his fancy; contemporaries enjoyed his sketches for their lack of conventionality (see Fig. 7.6).[681] The result is a very intimate travel guide that tells one how to see the best parts of a city – street by street, house by house – and how to appreciate its history. Enthusiasts of medieval architecture could easily walk through town with Robida's book, imagining the medieval city as they consulted his vivid commentary about the streets and their inhabitants.

Yet other pilgrims in search of the Middle Ages were unable to find real examples that corresponded to their imagination. They felt compelled to recreate this world according to their personal vision by collecting medieval art and arranging their own Middle Ages in private displays.[682] Still others, notably writers and artists, 'made' the Middle Ages in their books, paintings, or theatrical sets.[683] Like Zola, whose novel *Le Rêve* (1888) recreates a world founded on medieval values as a kind of fairy tale, they were saturated with the stories and images previously idealized by Romantic writers and artists.[684] Less interested in paying homage to the vestiges of the medieval world still visible in modern France than in creating their own Middle Ages based on an ideal that may never have existed, they often borrowed their imagery from Chateaubriand – preferring to see it as a pure time where pilgrims worshiped in the shadow of the cathedral – or from Victor Hugo – representing the medieval world as a reflection of the bustling *Notre-Dame de Paris*, a thriving medieval city composed largely of vagabonds and unruly students. Pilgrimages to such 'imaginary' Middle Ages flourished at the end of the nineteenth century through incredibly popular plays or operas such as Edmond Rostand's *La Princesse lointaine* (see Fig. 2.8), Maurice Maeterlinck's and then Claude Debussy's *Pelléas et Mélisande*, or Edouard Lalo's *Le Château d'Ys*, all of whose sets represented a dream Middle Ages and its idealized values.

Most of these groups would eventually find traces of the Middle Ages of their dreams, a composite period made up of preconceived notions from literature, painting and spectacle. For nearly all but devout Catholics, however, this would not take place in the far-off medieval villages of rural France.

Ironically, a much more popular and secular version of the Middle Ages thrived in fin-de-siècle Paris as groups dedicated to 'resurrecting' the medieval past 'recreated' it and put it on display. Here, the popular and commercial qualities of the Middle Ages were celebrated as resoundingly authentic, as in the ancestral medieval fairs that brought farmers, peasants, artisans and public together in times of celebration. Ultimately, the most successful pilgrimages of fin-de-siècle France did not lead to a Catholic Middle Ages of contemplation, solitude and prayer, but rather to a joyous secular Middle Ages of laughter, crowds and pleasure that strikingly resembled the fair-like atmosphere of Lourdes described by Zola.

# Feasts, fools and festivals: the popular Middle Ages

*The Court of Miracles*! It is, in fact, the representation of the entire Middle Ages, set so well, with the breadth of a poem, in Victor Hugo's *Notre-Dame de Paris*. Truants and wenches, suits of armor and gypsy girls, among whom the undying figures of Esmeralda, Quasimodo, Claude Frollo, and Gaston Phébus stand out, there was certainly enough there to tempt the talent and imagination of M. Colibert. In fact, the architect had much more than the brilliant fancy of the author of *Notre-Dame de Paris* to guide him. He had his perfect knowledge of the Middle Ages, his understanding of old Paris, its customs and its morals.

Paul Combes in Les Merveilles de l'Exposition: Paris en 1400[685]

The Exposition Universelle of 1900 was the spectacle of the decade, ending the century on a triumphant note of display, drama and consumerism.[686] Among the most alluring of the abundant international exhibits and pavilions enticing the viewer to experience the thrills of far-off lands and exotic entertainment were two medieval French villages replete with shops, taverns, entertainment and costumed inhabitants.[687] *Paris en 1400: Reconstitution de la Cour des Miracles* consisted of a crenelated castle opened along l'Avenue de Suffren, while *Le Vieux Paris* recreated a Paris composed largely of monuments that no longer existed.

Both exhibits, which proved enormously popular, reveal the extent to which the French of the fin de siècle idealized the Middle Ages and longed to return to it. This chapter explores the paradox involved in such 'recon-stitutions' of the Middle Ages: while people admired the medieval period, they generally did so on their own terms, adding contemporary values to what they knew of the past. 'Recreating' the Middle Ages thus meant different things to different groups, who were often inspired by literary and artistic representations of the Middle Ages. Some longed for the popular and boisterous fifteenth century celebrated by Victor Hugo, while others were drawn to the royal entries and jousting described by twelfth and thirteenth century romances. Some wanted to emulate the festive and drunken schoolboy antics glorified by François Villon, while others turned to medieval documents to create as 'authentic' a version of the Middle Ages as possible or to provide instruction for visitors. In each case, modern fantasies and conceptions of the medieval period were combined with study of extant medieval documents and projected on the past to 'recreate' it for others. In turn, such public spectacle tended to transform what each group had previously envisioned as an ideal world, free from individualism and profit, into commercial attractions par excellence, where the Middle Ages were 'consumed' with gusto. It was in these spaces of entertainment and leisure that popular and scholarly appropriations of the Middle Ages were often most deeply entwined.

### Paris en 1400: reconstitution de la Cour des Miracles

*Paris en 1400* (Fig. 7.1) was advertised as a 'historical and archeological reconstitution of the Cour des Miracles,' the brainchild of architect Eugène Colibert, the creator of the 'Old Bastille' exhibit at the 1889 Paris World's Fair and a former student of Viollet-le-Duc.[688] The 'reconstituted fifteenth-century city' occupied 4000 square meters on the Avenue de Suffren, near the Eiffel Tower, and consisted of a large castle and its interior courtyard in which Colibert had 'recreated' a medieval village. Paul Combes, author of an illustrated guidebook to the exhibit, described his first impression as 'being transported back five centuries' and finding himself in a 'picturesque corner of Paris in 1400,' surrounded by old houses with strange forms and bizarrely sculpted cornices, cabarets, and dark little shops.[689]

While a religious edifice – la Chapelle des Filles-Dieu – was prominent, *Paris en 1400* did not represent the 'Age of Faith' so longingly evoked by writers such as Verlaine and Huysmans and by the editors of *Le Pèlerin*. Nor was it the staunch Middle Ages lauded in patriotic discourse and Republican textbooks. Instead, *Paris en 1400* presented the Middle Ages as spectacle: a world of colorful banners, soaring turrets, wandering gypsies, thieves and soldiers. *Paris en 1400* displayed history as consumer fantasy. The exhibit injected life into the streets by introducing commercial goods and entertainment and by presenting even labor as spectacle: the village included a weaver at his loom, a blacksmith's shop, two curiosity shops selling bibelots, antiques and souvenirs, a perfume shop, a porcelain shop, a potter at his wheel, a female manuscript illuminator at her task, a pewtersmith, a silversmith and an artisan making stringed instruments. The village also contained a museum of medieval artifacts and a tavern.[690]

In addition to 'picturesque' and commercial enterprises, the exhibit contained a full complement of entertainment, including what were described as 'wandering thieves,' 'gypsies' and the other 'miscreants' immortalized in the 'Cour des Miracles' of Hugo's novel. Such characters were introduced to give life to the city and to portray 'medieval morals'; the entertainment took place around the visitors strolling through the exhibit. The first play told the story, in pantomime, of 'Le mariage à la Cruche cassée,' the wedding scene of Esmeralda and Gringoire from Victor Hugo's novel.[691] It ended with the procession of the various truants singing and gallivanting through the courtyard. For Combes, this fascinating performance gave him the impression of 'reliving, for several minutes, five centuries later […] tidbits of the lives of our forefathers.'[692] The second major performance of *Paris en 1400* represented

another aspect of medieval 'morals.'[693] Instead of the violent and criminal tendencies of the gypsies, it 'recreated' the elaborate ceremonies accompanying a royal entry of Charles VI and Queen Isabeau of Bavaria. The 'brilliant procession' included banners, trumpet fanfares and elaborate costumes as the royal entourage entered the city. Welcomed by the court, the queen picked a champion and a joust ensued. The tournament finished, the ceremonial procession left the courtyard to the sound of music. A. P. de Lannoy, medieval scholar and author of a guidebook to activities in Paris, was particularly impressed by this spectacle:

7.1   *L'entrée fortifiée, Paris en 1400*

A new sport called the tournament is all the rage there [*Paris en 1400*]. It consists of throwing one's adversary from his horse, in the presence of a king draped in gold and azure, of a princess coiffed in the style of Isabeau de Bavière, and of a fanfare in which the musicians have the mugs of the scoundrels at the Pont-au-Change [...] even if I did not like the Middle Ages, I would have loved them at the Avenue de Suffren.[694]

While picturesque and clearly enjoyable, this Middle Ages is, as Paul Combes's text continually insinuates, based primarily on a literary 'invention' of the Middle Ages: Victor Hugo's *Notre-Dame de Paris*: 'La Cour des Miracles'! It is [...] the representation of the entire Middle Ages [...] of *Notre-Dame de*

*Paris* of Victor Hugo.' By the end of the nineteenth century, the scenes of ribaldry, royal entries and popular celebrations chronicled by Hugo had worked their way into the popular consciousness of what the Middle Ages had really been.[695]

Both Combes and Colibert argue for the historical authenticity of the exhibit by insisting that the 'historical and architectural reconstitution' of *Paris en 1400* goes beyond the 'brilliant fantasy' of Hugo and is, instead, based on Colibert's 'perfect knowledge of the Middle Ages.' Since Colibert had studied with Viollet-le-Duc, contemporaries considered his medieval pedigree beyond reproach: '[he] masters his Middle Ages completely, [he] was better qualified than anyone to reconstitute, with remarkable precision, [medieval] style and customs.'[696] As the nature of the spectacle reveals, however, this alleged 'complete mastery' of the Middle Ages was largely limited to Victor Hugo's novel and to the work of Henri Sauval, the seventeenth-century historian who had informed it. The true inspiration for *Paris en 1400* emerges from the stockholder documents – decorated with an armored knight, an official seal, a crenelated castle and the Eiffel Tower – and published to encourage investment in the venture; the exhibit's ultimate goal was to capitalize on the popularity of the 1889 Bastille exhibit by 'exploit[ing]' the public's interest in the Middle Ages (Fig. 7.2).[697]

Although Colibert purported to be concerned with recreating a Middle Ages based on historical documents, his primary concern was the construction of an amusing dream Middle Ages that would appeal to customers interested in seeing Hugo's novel come to life. He opened it a year before the World's Fair so that people could enjoy 'this resurrection of fifteenth-century Parisian society' before the crowds arrived, and to avoid the competition of other displays.[698] Information distributed to potential stockholders emphasizes the lucrative nature of the shops, restaurants and concert halls contained in the exhibit.[699]

In contrast to the somber Moyen Âge of spirituality or faith sought by Catholic pilgrims or the *Gesamtkunstwerk* appreciated by Symbolist artists, La Cour des Miracles was the joyous ancestor of today's popular medieval-themed amusement parks. As in today's festivals, which also incorporate decidedly Renaissance costumes, concepts and customs, attracting visitors and creating a mood of revelry to encourage them to spend money often supersedes issues of historical accuracy.[700] Such endeavors have since grown into a profitable industry catering to the dream Middle Ages of consumer fantasy. The numerous *fêtes médiévales* held all over France each summer advertise 'Spells and Enchantments' or invite visitors to consort with 'troubadours, fire breathers, sword swallowers, tight-rope walkers, fortune tellers, talking animals […] torturers, minstrels and clowns.'[701] Run by nationwide corporations that send teams of workers dressed in anachronistic peasant skirts and frilly blouses or leather breeches, the *fêtes* offer customers food, drink and trinkets and encourage spending in local shops and restaurants; they have not changed markedly in content since the 1890s (Fig. 7.3).[702] The staff of these amusement parks cater to the same hunger for the

past, the same hope of experiencing the Middle Ages as 'real' that so thrilled people at the end of the nineteenth century.

### The Feast of Fools: *Les escholiers* of Hugo, Villon and Rabelais

The Middle Ages on display at the 1900 World's Fair was the culmination of a vision rather than its starting point. Indeed, since the publication of Victor Hugo's 1831 *Notre-Dame de Paris* – a book whose protagonists were

7.3   Home page
of La Compagnie
des Fer-vêtus

# La Compagnie des Fer-vêtus
Compagnie d'animations médiévales - (Association loi 1901)

Au fil du moyen-âge,
la compagnie des Fer-vêtus
vous propose une épopée fabulese:

- des costumes authentiques
- des reconstitutions de combats
- des campements festifs
- des déambulations de saltimbnques

Et vous fera revivre des scènes historiques qui
marquront votree imaginiare.

Pour tous renseignements, contactez nous :

- Véronique au 01.69.41.82.61 ou
- fervetus@hotmail.com.

Siège de l'association :
31 rue Montesquieu - Le val d'Albian
91400 SACLAY

Evènement du Jour | 22/05/1271 : funérailles nationales de Louis
IX (à Notre Dame de Paris).

(Mise à jour : 19/04/2001)

itinerant writer Pierre Gringoire (a sixteenth-century poet and playwright) and *escholier* Jehan Frollo – tavern life, student high jinks and the criminal ways of the denizens of the Cour des Miracles had been accepted by the French as key elements of the Middle Ages, components of a way of life celebrated in the writings of François Villon and François Rabelais. The opening passages of *Notre-Dame de Paris* abound with local color, as playwright Pierre Gringoire wrestles with the festive and unruly crowd assembled for a Feast of Fools celebration and a royal entry while trying to direct the performance of the new play he has written. Hugo, who was influenced by a variety of modern and medieval sources while writing the book, was also highly familiar with the works of Villon and Rabelais; his novel created a powerful image of the medieval populace as simple, joyous, mischievous folk drawn to entertainment.[703] Jehan Frollo, the schoolboy and younger brother of the archdeacon of Notre-Dame, is the ultimate representative of this tendency: a frequenter of taverns and bars, he does little but sing, make merry and cause trouble. By the end of the nineteenth century, the *escholier* or joyous medieval schoolboy had become a popular literary *topos*, appropriated by writers as varied as Théodore de Banville, Théophile Gautier, Jean Richepin, Albert Robida and Paul Verlaine.[704]

Hugo's lively portrait of the medieval populace and its fondness for street fairs and rebellion appealed to the late nineteenth-century sensibility, but above all to students, who saw in the characters of Jehan Frollo, Pierre Gringoire, François Villon and François Rabelais counter-culture figures that corresponded to their own values. Victor Hugo's characters were a staple for the many student carnivals and parades organized in the late nineteenth century.[705] An excellent example can be seen in a May 1898 street fair sponsored by law students at the Sorbonne. They attempted to recreate, in modern Paris, a medieval Feast of Fools and of the Ass, based on the scene that opens Hugo's novel. While the celebration resembled other student-run festivities such as those held annually for Mardi Gras and mid-Lent,[706] journalists, participants and spectators were all struck by the students' conscientious research, which they labeled 'the recreation,' 'reconstitution,' 'reconstruction' or 'renewal' of the Middle Ages in modern France. 'Do you like the Middle Ages?' asked a journalist for the daily newspaper *Le Temps*. '[Students] put them everywhere […] There was nothing but *basochiens*, schoolboys, male and female gypsies, ribald fellows and wenches.'[707]

Indeed, the 300 costumed participants formed quite a motley crew. The 'provostship' (the 'fifteenth-century trumpeters of the provost […] dressed in the style of the court of Charlemagne,' the provost and twenty-five archers in suits of chain mail) led the parade down the Boulevard Saint-Michel and through the Latin Quarter.[708] This introductory group of officials was followed by 'The Fools,' a group of rogues (the 'loyal friends of Villon'), members of the University (including *escholiers*) and Pierre Gringoire. Following Gringoire was a fourth group – *La Basoche* – composed of various acting troupes and the denizens of the Court of Miracles, including La Esmeralda.[709]

Student organizers intended this parade of characters to draw attention to the events of the two-day celebration: they would lead to the performance space near the Sorbonne where they had recreated a 'medieval Paris,' a kind of street fair replete with stalls featuring artisans of the Middle Ages: glassmakers, booksellers, silver, gold and pewter smiths, bird trainers, surgeons, barbers, parchment makers, instrument makers, public writers, fortune tellers and street criers who would call 'Ohé! les eschollers!' [sic]. They would charge admission to this area as well as to representations of medieval plays: *Le Mystère d'Adam*, *La Farce du Cuvier*, *La Farce du Pâté et de la tarte* and *La Farce de Maître Mimin*. In addition, 'very modern singer-songwriters,' including Jehan Rictus and Théodore Botrel ('Le Barde Breton'), gave performances with a medieval flavor in local taverns during the inter-missions.[710] The students hoped to create as 'picturesque' an effect as possible so as to maximize profits, which would be distributed to the poor.[711] That evening participants danced in the streets until 2 a.m. The festivities began again the following day with the street fair and the theatrical performances. The participants in this modern Feast of Fools were delighted by the 'joyous nature,' 'charm' and 'gaiety' of the celebration.[712]

Despite such praise of the celebration's authenticity, the highly secular festival was hardly faithful to the medieval Feast of Fools, which took place in and around the Church.[713] In fact, the students themselves had little pretension to historical accuracy, preferring to label their celebration 'literary' and 'artistic.' The highly anachronistic mix of characters and time periods from Antiquity to the nineteenth century – Virgil and the Sibyl, archers from the court of Charlemagne, François Villon, Pierre Gringoire and fictional characters from *Notre-Dame de Paris* – reveals the extent to which the students were primarily concerned with the spirit of the event. Their focus on the theatrical aspects of the Feast of Fools – election of a pope of fools, parades, performances, popular participation and drinking and merrymaking – appropriated the secular activities of medieval schoolboys, thus renewing their links to their predecessors, *les escholiers*. Like their medieval counterparts – the law students who participated in medieval theatrical groups like *Le Royaume de la Basoche* – the modern students broke the rules, mocked authority and mixed classical, medieval and modern characters all in the name of good fun.[714]

Indeed, the image of *l'escholier* in the nineteenth century had become inseparably linked to a beer tankard and to camaraderie in taverns (Fig. 7.4). Albert Robida, in a book entitled *Les Escholiers du temps jadis*, described them as 'wandering in the university area, going from cabarets to churches [...] allowing themselves, in the back of chapels, to empty bottles and to roll dice,' while Pierre de Nouvion, in a story about a medieval cabaret, portrayed them as running down the Montagne Sainte-Geneviève from the Sorbonne, making a fracas, looting and pillaging as they made their ways to cabarets, their *haut lieu* or center of operations.[715]

The large majority of the texts found in the souvenir program published by the student organizers of the 1898 Feast of Fools underlined this link to the mischievous, hard-drinking *escholiers* of the past, and it is no coincidence that the modern students made their headquarters in a tavern at the heart of the Latin Quarter. Nearly all of the contributors emphasized the link between *escholier*, drinking, chasing girls and composing poems or songs. The eclecticism of the publication also reflects their dedication to the *coq-à-l'âne* tradition fostered by drinking and writing.[716] Scholarly essays about the origins of The Feast of Fools are surrounded by satirical woodcuts, lithographs, jokes, serious poems and translations of medieval Latin poems, all of which had been contributed by artists, writers, historians and musicians of the time.[717] Homages to François Villon use archaic vocabulary and spellings, as Villon himself had done in his 'Ballade du vieil langage françois,' while some mimic the actual rhyme schemes and vocabulary used in specific poems of Villon's *Testament*.[718] Rabelais and Pierre Gringoire are also honored with a variety of drinking songs.[719] The entire program abounds with references to the Middle Ages, tavern culture, student performers, fools and asses, often with direct quotes from medieval texts.[720] Such attempts to imitate medieval culture belie the commonly accepted idea that nineteenth-century writers used the Middle Ages simply as a theme, without knowledge of medieval literature; in fact, these writers knew Villon and Rabelais well enough to create elaborate pastiches of their form, style and subject matter.[721]

In the Feast of Fools celebration of 1898, students drank, caroused and made noise while wearing unconvincing and poorly-made costumes.[722] What

then in their performance would have caused the overwhelming appreciation of spectators, who enthused about the 'reconstruction,' 'recreation' and 'reconstitution' of medieval times? The joyous good humor of the event, which brought together people from all social classes and political affiliations, was a key element that reminded audiences of the festivities of the Middle Ages. Scholarship of the late nineteenth century often highlighted the alleged links between cooperation among social classes and the medieval spirit. Victor Fournel, whose interest in street culture ranged from the reconstructions of Baron Haussmann to all forms of modern entertainment, had published *Le Vieux Paris: Fêtes, Jeux et Spectacles* in 1887.[723] No form of popular amusement escaped Fournel's pen, from religious parades and royal processions to 'freak shows,' animal tamers, wax figures, wandering minstrels and acrobats. The book opens with a discussion of theatrical representations of the Middle Ages, the liturgical and mystery plays to which Fournel traces all other diversions. For Fournel, what distinguished these representations above all was their *public* nature; like the performances of the modern *escholiers*, medieval plays and processionals unfolded on the street, thriving on the curiosity of the crowd who often followed the acting troupes from locale to locale.[724] Such events brought together people from all social classes, united by their interest in spectacle.

The students' celebration did include people from all walks of life: they relied on professors such as Louis Petit de Julleville for information about medieval theater, translators of medieval plays (A. P. de Lannoy, Gassies des Brulies and the brothers Adenis), actors from Le Théâtre Antoine, L'Odéon and La Comédie Française, police and ministerial personages who marched in the procession, *chansonniers* and the artisans who worked in the 'medieval village,' barkeepers of the Latin Quarter and writers and artists of different political and religious affiliations who contributed works to the souvenir program. The fact that admission was charged did not seem to impact negatively on the spectacle. On the contrary, because the students were raising money for the poor, its commercialization was seen less as capitalizing on the Middle Ages for profit than as an attempt to share the medieval heritage (and its potential profits) with all. During this weekend of festivities, students rubbed elbows with politicians and professors, theatrical professionals and amateurs, artisans and artists, thus leaving established order and hierarchical roles behind as everyone participated in making the celebration a success and in raising money for charity.[725]

In addition to involving many different kinds of people in the planning of their festivities, students claimed a holiday – The Feast of Fools – whose origins could be considered particularly Gallic,[726] and they championed the word-play, comic situations and scatological humor proper to what was then being called *l'esprit gaulois* (Gallic spirit). Indeed, late nineteenth-century France was fascinated with humor – and especially *l'esprit gaulois* – as a national legacy. Hand in hand with recent educational reforms that posited Gaul as the mythic origin of the French nature ('Nos ancêtres les gaulois'),[727] *l'esprit gaulois* identified a particularly French brand of humor. Although very loosely defined, the student antics and joyous activities of the Feast of Fools incarnated nearly every aspect of this type of humor, which Joseph Bédier defined as a simple and optimistic national sentiment linking *les escholiers* from the Middle Ages to Villon, Rabelais, Molière and nineteenth-century *chansonniers*.[728]

Much as fin-de-siècle France returned to medieval stories and heroes following the Franco-Prussian war in order to take heart after the depressing defeat, leading scholars recommended returning to the wholesome laughter of the Middle Ages evident in the Feast of Fools celebration – *l'esprit gaulois* – as good medicine. According to Louis Morin, the French nation had been depressed since the defeat of the Franco-Prussian war: 'we have cried over ourselves long enough, now let's live a little.'[729] Indeed, it was renewing the spirit of the past that enthused the spectators of this celebration. Jules Claretie, director of the Comédie Française and a columnist for *Le Temps*, commented on the 'healthiness' of the students' laughter and their revival of the spirit of Rabelais in a passage that echoes Rabelais's message to the reader in *Gargantua:* 'better to laugh than to write tears […] laughter is unique to man.'[730] He thanks the students for conjuring up 'these farces of our good ancestors, accomplices and companions of sincere cheerfulness, who consoled themselves for unavoidable sorrows with the joyful *enfants sans souci.*' Louis Morin, too, congratulated the students and encouraged them to keep close to heart the words of the traditional students' drinking song 'Gaudeamus igitur' ('Let us be merry').[731] Such responses reacted to the 'carnivalesque' qualities of student merrymaking, what Bakhtin would later call the 'regenerative power of laughter,' 'temporary liberation from the prevailing truth and from the established order,' to convey to the public a more positive state of mind.[732]

Scholarly appreciation of this 'medieval revival' thus focused less on the direct comparison with medieval practices than on the reproduction of the spirit latent in medieval texts. By repeating the words of their medieval counterparts, the 'joyous schoolboys,' 'carefree children' (*enfants sans souci*) and mischievous rogues celebrated by Villon, Gringoire and Rabelais, and by pronouncing the words of little-known medieval plays, which were praised as the 'truly original attraction of this renewed holiday,' the students 'awakened the dead.' As Helen Solterer has shown, repeating the words of one's ancestors revives their spirit; it has the effect of bringing them back to life.[733] While the celebration was hardly an accurate representation of the medieval world, the students raised public morale and inspired pride in the nation's literary heritage by echoing the words of their ancestors. The celebration itself and its links to medieval origins thus played into the rising sense of pride in French traditions that followed the national identity crisis provoked by the Franco-Prussian war. *L'esprit gaulois* admired by the audience in the 1898 spectacle was not only a particularly licentious type of merry-making; it was also inherently French.

### *Rire est le propre de l'homme*: Rabelais, *l'esprit gaulois* and the tavern

Joyous camaraderie that brought together people from diverse social classes and political affiliations was also evident in the numerous taverns – the centers of *l'esprit gaulois* – opened in the late nineteenth century. Latin quarter taverns had long been the *haut lieu* of *les escholiers*, but in the late nineteenth century new ones flourished in Montmartre; they grew into rich cultural centers of literary, artistic and musical production.[734] As we saw in Chapter 5, many such taverns were billed as 'Gothic cabarets' and fitted with Gothic or Renaissance decor, while others simply publicized themselves as 'medieval' even if – like the student celebration of the Feast of Fools – their medieval atmosphere was conferred only by the mood of popular revelry found inside them.[735] La Taverne du Moyen Age was such a place, convivial, yet lacking in any period decoration (and criticized by contemporaries for the false advertising of its name).[736]

Like the student organizers of 1898, some tavern owners resolutely embraced the spirit of the Middle Ages as the ideal of a patriotic and simple time of equality and fraternity, a way of combating post-war pessimism. Phillip Dennis Cate identifies the Bon Bock dinners held after the Franco-Prussian war at Krauteimer, an Alsatian restaurant in Montmartre, as among the first to celebrate l'esprit gaulois in the fin de siècle.[737] Beginning in 1875, Emile Bellot (described by friends as 'a Rabelaisian, a jolly wine sniffer') organized lunches and dinners at the restaurant in honor of the lost provinces of Alsace and Lorraine.[738] These became the celebrated monthly 'Bon Bock dinners' at which writers, artists, musicians and politicians came together to drink and perform under a Republican banner declaring equality and fraternity. Bellot collected contributions from participants which he published as *Album du Bon Bock*, whose stated mantra invoked gaiety, intelligence, conviviality and 'our immortal grand master, Rabelais.'[739]

As a result of the success of these dinners, a number of artistic taverns grew up in Montmartre.[740] Nearly all explicitly identified Rabelais as the master of ceremonies. L'Abbaye de Thélème, one of the most notable, was even named after the celebrated abbey of Rabelais's *Gargantua*, whose motto is 'Do what you will.' Rabelais and his writings had become extremely popular at the end of the century, not least because of two popular illustrated editions of his works, those of Gustave Doré (1873) and Albert Robida (1885–1886), which introduced Rabelais's works to a new generation of readers.[741] Although today Rabelais is considered a resolutely Renaissance author, the late nineteenth century saw him as much more of a transitional figure. For the fin de siècle, Rabelais's use of medieval folk culture, the Gargantua legend and especially his reputed authorship of the 1532 *Grandes et inestimables chroniques du grand et énorme géant Gargantua*, all linked him to the idealized image of a pleasure-loving Middle Ages that celebrated l'esprit gaulois.[742] Accordingly, people like Mermeix, the author of a 30 May 1886 article for *Le Courrier Français* entitled 'Les Chroniques de l'Abbaye de Thélème,' contrasted Rabelais's 'simple wisdom' and propensity for pleasure to the artifice of the fin de siècle and wondered what the writer would make of his descendants.[743] The cover of this publication portrayed Rabelais stepping out of a painting to join the residents of the fictional city of Thélème in a toast (Fig. 7.5).

All of Paris welcomed Rabelais, especially at l'Abbaye de Thélème, where the raucous and irreverent sensibility of the late medieval period was believed to have been resurrected. Inebriated customers ordered from waiters dressed as monks, surrounded by a décor that resembled the Sainte-Chapelle but with stained-glass windows and panels representing Rabelaisian scenes.[744] As the image of Rabelais gained popularity, the author himself became conflated with his characters. Gargantua's resounding 'A Boire! A boire! A boire!' drowned out the serious philosophical messages conveyed by

7.5   Henri Pille, *Rabelais sort de son cadre pour trinquer avec les Thélémites*, 1886

Rabelais's books. The name Rabelais thus became synonymous with a toastmaster, a figure endlessly celebrated by the crowd. In April of the same year, the *Courrier Français* devoted an entire issue (*Les Chroniques de Thélème*) to Rabelais – featuring Gargantua astride the towers of Notre-Dame – and the homage continued in subsequent issues. When the journal adopted the café as its official meeting place (holding its soirées there every Friday from six till midnight), it did so with an official *fête* devoted to Rabelais.[745] For those who wanted even more Rabelais, Jules Garnier exhibited 160 of his paintings representing 'L'Oeuvre de Rabelais.'[746] All of popular Paris had joined the toast to Rabelais, who had come to epitomize a joyful, hard-drinking vision of the Middle Ages for late nineteenth-century readers.

Rabelais, like his predecessor, François Villon, appealed to young artists not only for his salacious reputation, but also for the quality of his writing. While their popularity in taverns was often associated with concerns about patriotism and camaraderie, their disruptive laughter also served more subversive aesthetic purposes. Both writers' use of word play, rebuses, satire and celebration of wine and tavern culture endeared them to a generation of Montmartre artists rebelling against what they considered the bourgeois values of literary movements like Naturalism. As a result, Rabelais and Villon became alternative literary father figures.[747] Georges Bourdon, one of the organizers of *Les Escholiers*, an avant-garde theater troupe founded in 1888, would credit the vogue for Rabelais and the Middle Ages as an inspiration for the group's name and subject matter.[748] As high school students, he and his friends (including Aurélien Lugné, later known as Lugné-Poë, the founder of the Théâtre de l'Oeuvre), met in l'Abbaye de Thélème to plan their association, which was originally called La Basoche. Their conversations and advertisements were phrased in Rabelaisian tones: 'Adonc, cy venez! Vous, frisques, galliers, joyeulx, plaisancts … '[749] After invoking their debt to their 'master' Villon, and reciting numerous verses of his poetry, the troupe performed at Le Chat Noir cabaret.[750] Throughout the long career of *Les Escholiers*, they remained faithful to their medieval origins, especially in the Gothic imagery used for their programs and invitations, in their repertoire and in their association rules, written in a style that evokes that of Villon and Rabelais.[751]

It is little surprise that the Old French-speaking *Les Escholiers* and their medieval-inspired repertory were welcomed at Rodolphe Salis's Chat Noir[752] and that Salis seems to have been the inspiration for the 1880s vogue for medieval French.[753] Like its sister cabaret, Les Quat'z'Arts (named for the four arts of the Ecole des Beaux Arts), the space was dedicated to fostering relations among the arts.[754] The eccentric Salis, who dubbed himself 'Seigneur de Chatnoirville-en-Vexin,' routinely spoke Old French to his guests and was depicted (especially in *Le Chat Noir*, the cabaret's eponymous publication) as a medieval hosteller, welcoming his guests as 'Lords' and 'Ladies,' and insisting that Villon and Rabelais had frequented his bar (see Fig. 6.4).[755] One of those influenced by Salis was Jean Moréas, author of the 1886 'Symbolist Manifesto,' who often spoke in Old French and sought, in his poetry and in *l'Ecole romane* he founded, 'the communion of the French Middle Ages and the Renaissance, melted and transfigured in the principle […] of the modern Soul.'[756] He performed at Le Chat Noir in the early 1880s. Other 'medievales-que' characters included Paul Verlaine and Aristide Bruant, both of whom were labeled 'the modern Villon' at various points in their careers.[757] In addition to the medieval-accented conversation within it, activities in the artistic cabaret were eclectic and consisted of poetry readings, musical performances, contests, shadow theater and improvisations.[758] Participants included writers, musicians and artists from the entire political and religious spectrum, including Paul Verlaine, Jean Richepin, Emile Zola, Léon Bloy, Claude Debussy, Erik Satie, Henri Rivière, Albert Robida, Willette and Henri Pille.[759]

An example of the eclecticism of Le Chat Noir and its use of medieval subjects can be seen in the phenomenon of the *chanson*, whose popularity Salis attempted to revive. The history of the French *chanson*, as Harold Segel has pointed out, dates back to the Middle Ages. It was in the early 1880s that new singers brought traditional French songs back to the public's attention, focusing on issues of social concern, much as François Villon gave voice to the dispossessed and the poor in his *Testament*.[760] Le Chat Noir became a showplace for *chansonniers* such as Léon Xanrof, Jules Jouy, Maurice MacNab, Jean Richepin and Aristide Bruant, who sang about the Paris streets and the people who inhabited them.[761] These singer-songwriters were often compared to medieval poets or to troubadours, humbly carrying on a noble medieval pursuit in a modern age that did not appreciate them.[762] Yet these and others also celebrated the *coq à l'âne* tradition, singing scatological or nonsensical songs intended to provoke the audience, satirize it or simply to make it laugh. One of the favorite practices of Chat Noir singers, for example, was to juxtapose a sentimental song – like Delmet's well-known 'Femme qui passe' (Passing Woman) – with a parody of it – Vincent Hyspa's 'Le Noyau qui ne passe pas' ('The Stone that will not pass').[763]

To chronicle the activities of the artistic cabaret and to advertise them, Salis began publishing *Le Chat Noir*; it functioned both as a history of creative production and as a vehicle for self-promotion and marketing.[764] The pages of *Le Chat Noir* abounded with off-color stories, tales and fabliaux written in archaic French, often with Gothic lettering and small-scale vignettes of costumed monks, princesses and saints, a veritable showcase for the imaginary Middle Ages of legend. A few examples include 'Comment fust le fieur Jehan Faulcon piteufement debouté par une oifelière qui avoit nom Blanche' and 'D'un Moyne qui défrichoit les pucelaiges pour complaire à la Saincte Escripture, laquelle dist: "Arrachez la maulvaise herbe!".' They were liberally illustrated by *Chat Noir* artists including Adolphe Willette, Henri Rivière, Henri Pille, Théodore Steinlein, Uzès and Oswald Heidbrinck (see Fig. 6.4).[765] *Le Courrier Français*, begun in 1884 by Jules Roques, also focused on Montmartre events and used many of the artists and writers who contributed to *Le Chat Noir*. The two publications shamelessly advertised each other's activities.[766] Both were filled with poems renewing medieval fixed forms of the ballad and the rondeau, often composed in Old French and accompanied by medievalizing illustrations or musical scores. *Le Courrier Français* sponsored annual costume balls and the two publications jointly hosted a 'Fête Villon' in 1885 at which numerous poems were composed in honor of their great 'master.' Victor Marguerrite composed a special poem, 'Ballade à Villon pour être dite en l'hostellerie du Chat-Noir,' for the occasion. The envoi of this poem read: 'Un coup de vin pour le pauvre Villon!'[767]

*L'esprit gaulois* and its affiliations with the Middle Ages were in constant evidence in the text and illustrations of *Le Chat Noir* and *Le Courrier Français*. Town criers, parades, feast days and the ever-ubiquitous crowd elbowed their way into many of the prints decorating numerous issues, accompanied by medievalesque poetry written in Gothic script. Many advertisements featured half-page displays with illustrations from medieval and neo-medieval works including *Les Quatre Fils Aymon* (illustrated by Eugène Grasset), *Le Livre d'heures de Louis Legrand* and *Le Puits sans vin*. Other pages came from the collaboration of the writer Roger-Milès and the illustrator Henri Pille, both dedicated habitués of the Chat Noir. In 1889 they assembled their vision of the past in a volume entitled *Pages d'Autrefois retrouvées par Henri Pille racontées par L. Roger-Milès,* advertised often in the pages of the *Courrier Français.*

Such experimentation reveals the popularity of the Middle Ages among the members of the artistic avant-garde of the fin de siècle and shows their familiarity with medieval page layout and the content of certain types of medieval narrative and stylistics. In general, however, they used medieval subject matter and themes as a springboard for their own aesthetic experiments. Indeed, what appealed to these artists was less the subject matter of Rabelais and Villon than their irreverent attitude, what members of Le Chat Noir called *fumisme* or *l'esprit chatnoiresque*[768] and what André Breton would later label 'black humor.'[769] Phillip Dennis Cate and Mary Shaw have pointed out that we often tend to see the most important avant-garde events of the twentieth century – notably Jarry's productions of *Ubu Roi* and Dada's Cabaret Voltaire – as isolated movements, even though we should be aware of the ways in which they were firmly grounded in the rich and rebellious cabaret culture of the 1880s and 1890s.[770] Similarly, Jarry and Apollinaire should be studied further against the backdrop of the *coq-à-l'âne* tradition of the late Middle Ages and the Renaissance that flourished in cabarets like Le Chat Noir.[771]

As they exploded genres, mocked artistic authority, parodied bourgeois rites and rituals and submitted everything to ironic examination, modern day Rabelaisians evoked the medieval tradition while foreshadowing the nihilism and parodic humor of Jarry, Tzara, Duchamp and the Dada circle. Not only did Rabelais and Villon provide an alternative to the classical and Academic traditions, but they had engaged openly with elements of popular culture, an important strategy that the avant-garde – in particular the Dadaists – would use to develop their art. They would combine references from popular culture with elements of mass culture, forever transforming 'high art.'[772] Symbolist artists like Denis, Bernard and Gauguin had also fixed on medieval works as a way of liberating their own style (albeit in a more reverential vein); their breaking of nineteenth-century aesthetic rules, too, would have a profound effect on the formation of twentieth-century modernism.

## Conserving the past: *Vieux Paris* and the threat of the modern

Although the Chat Noir featured an eclectic mix of modern and medieval, its insistence on the 'medieval nature' of its *esprit chatnoiresque*, specifically through 'Seigneur Salis', linked it, in the fin-de-siècle mind, with *l'esprit gaulois*. If the student organizers of the 1898 Feast of Fools included modern *chansonniers* in their recreation, it is because the performers of the Chat Noir had clearly established themselves as the direct descendants of Villon and Rabelais. Much as leading figures had complimented students on resurrecting the medieval spirit, the early cabarets were congratulated for staving off the dangers of the material world through the healthy laughter and late medieval values contained within their walls. Mermeix, for one, saw such subversive, eruptive laughter as an antidote to the corrupted values of the fin de siècle:

But today, we must protect ourselves against sordid conquest. Gaul struggles against the man of money, who comes to replace the man of iron…It is now more than ever that your [Rabelais's] laughter could help us against the new barbarian, the cowardly and deceitful barbarian who does not fight us, but maligns us, robs us, who does not kill his enemy but instead despoils him.[773]

The enemy, as Mermeix insists, was the greedy spirit of the capitalist rather than the sword-bearing soldier of the past. *L'esprit gaulois* was seen as a last defense against the grim invasion of capitalism, a force that devastated the community and the traditional ties of pre-industrial life. The cabaret, an informal watering hole for artists, provided an escape from the present; inside, one found the joyfully fraternal mood of mutual inebriation and parody chronicled by Villon and Rabelais, an antidote to the class divisions that characterized the political and economic spheres.

In the early 1880s, cabarets were thus seen not only as spaces of amusement and artistic innovation, but also as fortresses against the rising armies of consumerism. Yet even these informal close-knit communities were touched by the 'man of money.' Le Chat Noir, the social outcast that originally seated only thirty people and was seen as the incarnation of *l'esprit gaulois* because artists, musicians and performers gathered voluntarily to amuse each other, 'sold out' by moving to a bigger space in 1885.[774] To heighten the sense of spectacle and to advertise the move, Rodolphe Salis organized an ostentatious torchlight procession that made its way through the streets of Montmartre with people carrying 'relics' from the old venue, costumed guards, a crowd and the Chat Noir banner with its motto 'Montjoye-Montmartre.' Formerly the haunt of impoverished and little-known artists, Le Chat Noir became a highly successful commercial extravaganza; the new space held 300 people and multiplied medieval references in its décor. It developed into one of the most coveted addresses in Paris, written about in all of the papers, advertised by two official guidebooks and visited by such dignitaries as Pasteur, General Boulanger, the Rothschilds, the King of Greece and the Prince of Wales.[775] The artist habitués of the old *Chat Noir*, 'troubadours,' 'bards' and 'poets of the streets' who had formerly volunteered their talents for the pleasure of doing so, now became subjects for the spectacle of the consumer cabaret.

They condemned the change in no uncertain terms, as the stained-glass windows Willette created for the new structure suggest. In these panels, which mix medieval and modern figures, the loss of innocence of the cabaret is attributed to greed, represented as the golden calf, the stock market and a Jew with a box of coins. For Phillip Dennis Cate, the meaning is clear: 'as the Chat Noir cabaret gained popular and financial success, Salis had sold out to greed, and the seemingly original idealistic premise that the cabaret was a haven for artists and poets no longer held true.'[776]

It is important to acknowledge the anti-Semitic flavor of the image, especially since Willette also drew a number of negative caricatures of Jews and ran for legislative election in 1889 as the 'Anti-Semitic candidate.'[777] His campaign poster reprises Gambetta's anticlerical slogan, transforming it into 'Le Judaïsme, voilà l'ennemi!' Headed by a song encouraging French nationalism – 'En avant Gaulois et France' – the poster features a group of contemporary workers clustered behind Willette, who is dressed as a Gaul and standing over a tombstone with 'Le Talmud' engraved on it. Brandishing a Celtic axe and holding up the head of the golden calf, his arm points to the text of his anti-Semitic platform. A bare-breasted Gallic Marianne with a rooster's tail and cap sounds the trumpet to encourage them.

As Parisian haunts increasingly succumbed to the attraction of tourist dollars, such 'selling out' was fiercely criticized by contemporaries from all points of the political, literary and artistic spectrum. The popular French culture embodied by Rabelais and Villon came to be pitted against the mass of different cultures exploding in fin-de-siècle Paris. It should come as no surprise that the defense of medieval splendor and communal spirit against the calf of gold, materialism and foreign influences became a mantra for one of the most reactionary populists of the period, the vicious anti-Semite Edouard Drumont. For him too, the money-wielding Jew – and the spirit of corruption that he represented – had put an end to the communal France of the Middle Ages. Drumont yearned for a hearty Rabelaisian Middle Ages, whose 'laughter would kill the new barbarian' (Mermeix's 'the man of money'). Drumont's views were extremely popular; his rancid 1886 *La France juive* was one of the bestsellers of the period.[778] In 1889 he co-founded *La Ligue nationale antisémitique,* and was well known to readers through his editorship of the rabidly anti-Semitic *La libre parole.* He was hailed in the pages of *Le Courrier Français* by Willette, who depicted him as a kind of avenging medieval knight, red cross on his chest and axe in hand, trampling a febrile horned Moses.[779] Spinning a kind of leftist demagoguery while pining for the good old days, Drumont developed a great following among the disenfranchised working class, student populations and petite bourgeoisie who shared his nostalgia for the past. His 1879 text *Les Fêtes Nationales à Paris* is a paean to Royalist splendor wrapped in a cloak of populist sentiment, chronicling with gusto the pageants and royal entries of kings, queens and Republican regimes.[780] Drumont and his followers and collaborators adopted the figure of the Jew to represent the forces of modernity, the cosmopolitan society that was bent on destroying the communal ties and traditional values of France, like those in evidence in medieval celebrations and artistic cabarets.[781] Throughout his writings, Drumont intertwines his hatred of the corrupted Third Republic (which he portrays as a shameless vehicle for international Jewry) with nostalgia for a glorious and bygone era peopled by simple and naive French souls who thrived on legends and stories like those of Perceval and the Quest for the Holy Grail: 'The Aryan remains the frank creature who swooned with ecstasy in the Middle Ages when hearing the *chansons de geste*, the Adventures of Garain le Loherain [sic], of Olivier de Béthune or of Gilbert le Roussillon [sic].'[782] In this reactionary discourse, the Middle Ages and its 'pure' spirit were claimed in a battle against modernity, a xenophobic movement that proposed the spirit and figures of the past as an alternative to modern corruption, greed, decadence and 'foreign' influence.

The seemingly 'authentic' or 'pure' *esprit gaulois* on display in taverns like Le Chat Noir would have pleased Drumont. Its simple and jolly atmosphere derived from the equality – what Charles Rearick had called 'festive fraternity' – that reigned among drinking artists of different social classes. But as such spaces were increasingly transformed into commercial spectacle, casual improvisation gave way to scripted performances where cabaret owners exploited the unpaid performers for their own profit.[783] The medieval past – and especially *l'esprit gaulois* proposed by medieval and Renaissance-like taverns – began to be less about artistic collaboration and innovation than about fostering the image of Paris as a locus of decadent and never-ending pleasure, an image that would prove essential to the city's economy.[784] As A. P. de Lannoy put it: the penchant for self-indulgence in Paris 'makes us the inn of the world.'[785] What artists had experienced as the spirit of the Middle Ages became, for tourists, a trip back to the rollicking Middle Ages, purchased for the price of a beer. Reveling in rowdy pleasure, contributing to a vivid street life and tavern culture could thus be experienced as an act both modern and rooted in the French medieval past. As the culture and economy of fin-de-siècle Paris came more and more to rely on leisure and entertainment, the Middle Ages were remade in this image. Even the subversive laughter of Rabelais was harnessed to the production of revenue and the guarantee of a 'good time for all,' thus perverting the ideals his laughter had represented for artists in the 1880s.

In Paris, the Middle Ages had become a center for discussions about modernization not only because of increased international tourism, but also as the results of Haussmannization became clear: huge swathes of medieval Paris had been wiped out forever, bulldozed to make way for broad avenues and bland modern buildings that would improve the flow of commerce through the streets.[786] Nostalgia for 'Le Vieux Paris' was reflected in a variety of ways, from poems like Baudelaire's 'Le Cygne' – 'Old Paris is no longer (the shape of a city/Changes, alas, more quickly than a mortal's heart)' – and Eugène Atget's twenty-year project to compile photographs of 'Vieux Paris' to the numerous books dealing with 'Vieux Paris' published in the last decades of the nineteenth century.[787] 'Le Vieux Paris' was a term generally used to refer to the medieval core of the city that had continued expanding until the early nineteenth century; while often implying narrow medieval streets, gabled roofs and two and three-storey buildings, it could also encompass structures from the seventeenth and eighteenth centuries.[788] 'Le Vieux Paris s'en va' became a rallying cry in the fin de siècle.[789]

In response, the conservation movement surged. As we saw in Chapter 3, a number of museums and collections dedicated to medieval art and architecture were established in the last decades of the nineteenth century. The mid-nineteenth century saw the birth of such organizations (for example, La Commission des Monuments Historiques), but this tradition was continued with new vigor in Paris after the results of Haussmannization began to appear. A variety of associations and commissions sprang up to defend 'Le Vieux Paris': a few examples include the Musée Carnavalet (museum of the history of Paris), which opened in 1880, La Société d'Histoire et d'Archéologie 'le Vieux Montmartre,' which began in 1886 (responsible for the collection now displayed at the Musée de Montmartre), La Commission Municipale du Vieux Paris, which began in 1897, and Les Amis du Vieux Montmartre. Such associations often published periodicals dedicated to their work, including *Le Vieux Montmartre* (1886–1905) and *L'ami des monuments et des arts parisiens* (1887–1914). Such illustrated publications described parts of old Paris, while guiding the walker through the streets where vestiges of Le Vieux Paris could be found.

A number of authors adopted this technique of providing itineraries and historical commentaries for the admirer of Old Paris. Edouard Drumont was one of the first to turn his attention to the disappearing glories of the past in the highly popular book *Mon vieux Paris: hommes et choses*, published in 1878 and reprinted with additions in 1897. This work provides a nostalgic walk through the small, dark, winding streets of medieval Paris; his narrative was accompanied by illustrations.[790] Lamenting the decline of the apprentice system, Drumont repeatedly contrasts the cold-hearted products of the machine age to those of a guild system requiring pride in labor and religious spirit. Such nostalgia for the disappearing past was echoed by writers such as J.-K. Huysmans, whose *Les Vieux Quartiers de Paris, La Bièvre* (1890, 1898) and *Trois Eglises et Trois Primitifs* (1905, 1908) also guided the reader through the old streets of Paris while expressing sorrow for disappeared or damaged monuments. By the turn of the century, this technique was also adopted by more mainstream guidebooks – Joanne, Baedeker, Touring Guide, Guide Bleu.[791]

Albert Robida, who contributed to many of the publications related to the conservation movement, was in high demand for his drawing skill; he illustrated guidebooks, souvenir postcards and posters.[792] His *Vieille France* series, which took the reader through different areas of France, sparked the imagination of armchair tourists who dreamed about travel, while parents used them to edify their children.[793] He published a similar series of books for Parisians: *Paris de siècle en siècle, Coeur de Paris, Paris à travers l'histoire* (Librairie illustrée, 1898: uniting *Paris de siècle en siècle* and *Coeur de Paris*) and *L'île de Lutèce*. In these works, he displays his drawings of Paris as it might have been, while commenting on the mutability of a city which, like an organism, constantly expands. For Robida, text and image worked in tandem to convey his message. Unlike earlier 'travel writers,' who made luxurious large-format illustrations and watercolors that could be removed from the album and sold individually, Robida preferred small sketches that he could incorporate in the text.[794] Like medieval manuscripts, in which text and image gloss one another, his drawings represent 'Old France' and its monuments as an integral part of the story he tells about the French nation: medieval structures are peopled by costumed figures who animate the scenes and transform the monuments into functional spaces (Fig. 7.6). By giving form to memories of disappeared monuments and ways of life, he reanimated the Paris of the past and linked it inseparably to the Paris in which he lived. Indeed, the title of his book – *Paris from Century to Century* – insists that one must connect each age to the next in order to understand French history.[795]

For Robida, however, 'old France' was primarily medieval and Renaissance France. He was much less interested in monuments from the seventeenth and eighteenth centuries and did not devote much space to them in his books.[796] His primary goal was to draw attention to medieval and Renaissance buildings, edifices that, until Victor Hugo in the first part of the nineteenth century, had largely been dismissed by contemporaries as 'misshapen,' 'inept' or 'monstrous'.[797] Robida echoes Hugo's concerns about medieval monuments: *la vieille France* is rapidly disappearing as modern industry and Haussmannization razes it to make room for new developments: factories, train tracks, roads, buildings. Robida makes this point clear in nearly all of his books. He dedicates *Paris de siècle en siècle*, for example, to Charles Normand, whom he calls a 'Parisian of Paris, Secretary General of the Friends of Parisian Monuments,' and opens the book with a dedication page that underlines the importance of fighting to conserve monuments: 'Always hard at work defending the always endangered artistic interests of Paris.'[798]

Much of the book tells the story of structures that no longer exist or that have been significantly modified since their construction. One of his favorite examples is the church of Saint-Julien-des-Ménétriers, a fourteenth-century church built by a brotherhood of medieval jongleurs (see Fig. 5.7). Robida cites at length a sixteenth-century source (*Le Théâtre des antiquités de Paris*) describing the construction of the church (a hospital and chapel for injured minstrels) and details about its statues of Saint Genest, patron saint of jongleurs, and Saint Julien l'Hospitalier. His picturesque details about the medieval musicians, their comradeship and the performances they put on in front of the church, made the medieval area around the rue Saint-Martin and Les Halles – split up in Haussmann's creation of the Boulevard de Sébastopol – come back to life. Robida nearly always based such information on a variety of medieval and modern sources including Guillot's thirteenth-century *Le dit des rues de Paris*, the Bourgeois de Paris, Christine de Pisan, Philippe de Commines, and Maurice de Sully. Modern sources include Hippolyte Cocheris, Léon Vaudoyer, Edouard Fournier, and François de Guilhermy. Though an amateur, Robida made good use of the abundant studies of

7.6 Albert
Robida, 'A
travers la ville
escholière,' 1895

LE CLOITRE DES CARMES DE LA PLACE MAUBERT

## CHAPITRE VI

### A TRAVERS LA VILLE ESCHOLIÈRE

#### I

DÉBRIS DU COLLÈGE SAINT-MICHEL
RUE DE BIÈVRE

A grande Université de Paris. — Fondation de Mᵉ Robert de Sorbon. — Les quatre nations de la faculté des Arts. — La rue du Fouarre. — Les écoles de médecine. — Le collège des Haricots et son maître fouetteur. — Les pauvres Capettes de Montaigu. — Etudiants vagabonds. — Tavernes et mauvais lieux. — Désordres et bagarres. — Les cinquante collèges. — Immunités et privilèges de l'Université. — La procession du Landit. — Les écoles de droit au Clos Bruneau. — Robert Estienne.

« Les rois de France s'accoutumèrent à porter dans leurs armes la fleur de lys peinte par trois feuilles afin qu'elles disent à tout le monde : « Foi, « Sapience et Chevalerie sont par la provision et « la grâce de Dieu plus abondamment en notre « royaume qu'en les autres. Les deux feuilles de « la fleur de lys qui sont ailées signifient *sens* et « *chevalerie* qui gardent et défendent la tierce « feuille au milieu, par laquelle *Foi* est entendue

medieval art, literature, and architecture published in the last quarter of the nineteenth century, including works by Louis Courajod, Gaston Paris, Léon Gautier, Emile Mâle, and Camille Enlart.

Robida's writings about the history of Paris would culminate in the project that brought Old Paris to the world stage. Increasingly fascinated by the vanished monuments of French history, he proposed to the organizers of the 1900 Paris World's Fair the recreation of an entire city made up of destroyed

7.7  *Le Vieux Paris*

Parisian monuments, for which l'église Saint-Julien-des-Ménétriers would be the centerpiece (see Fig. 5.7). His project was so convincing that the organizers allowed him a huge tract of space – 6000 square meters – running along the Seine from the Alma Bridge to Trocadéro; he and Léon Benouville, head architect of Les Monuments Historiques, built a platform over the water on which to construct it (Fig. 7.7).[799] While Haussmann's bulldozers had destroyed sections of medieval Paris only 40 years earlier, a new 'old Paris' was now painstakingly reconstructed.

The city was comprised of three neighborhoods, separated by winding streets full of shops, taverns and theaters: the Quartier des Ecoles was the fifteenth-century section, by far the largest part of the city; a middle section represented the Central Market of the eighteenth century; and a third section was dedicated to the seventeenth and eighteenth centuries, interspersed with medieval architecture.[800] To accompany the city he had built, Robida published an illustrated guidebook – *Guide historique, pittoresque et anecdotique* – that led visitors through the attraction and explained the historical or aesthetic significance of each structure.[801] The guide provided them with a map of the layout and historical background about the old city walls, fortresses and structures. After paying admission, one entered *Vieux Paris* through the Porte St Michel, which Robida and his family had decorated as if for a royal entry, with banners, escutcheons and tribunes.[802] There one found Le Pré aux clercs, an adaptation of the central arcade of the Couvent des Chartreux (the end of the Luxembourg garden) from the fifteenth century. On the left, one could see the tower of the old Louvre, forty meters high, modeled on that from the reigns of Philippe-Auguste and Charles V. On the left of the tower was the Maison aux Piliers, the first Parisian Town Hall, bought by the city in 1357.

Continuing down the rue des Vieilles Ecoles, one could visit a number of houses representative of medieval Parisian architecture, most of which dated from the fifteenth century. Each of these houses had a sign carrying its name, and each displayed a product. The house of Nicolas Flamel, a building that still existed in 1900 (modified beyond recognition), served as 'Les Trois Ecritoires' and sold paper, illuminated manuscripts, engravings, postcards and photos as well as *La Nef de Lutèce*, the medieval manuscript Robida had composed for the occasion. His first pages featured the medieval scribe (or 'painter-monk') so popular at the time (Fig. 7.8). Next door was 'Au Grand Coq,' another fifteenth-century house that had served as the birthplace of the French press (1631) when Théophraste Renaudot founded *La Gazette de France*. In it, the passerby could buy copies of *La Gazette du Vieux Paris*, a series of carefully wrought illuminated manuscripts dedicated to different periods of French history and written and illustrated by leading literary figures of the time including Jules Claretie, Pierre Loti, Anatole France, François Coppée, Jules Lemaître and Maurice Barrès.[803] These papers also featured advertising (in Gothic lettering, also in the form of a medieval manuscript, for the medieval issues) and announcements about events taking place in the city.

Next to this was a tower with stone steps, like many in the Latin quarter. According to Robida's reasoning, students would naturally have congregated around areas containing books and bars. Robida did not forget François Villon in his plans. He thus recreated A la Pomme de Pin, La Taverne du Pré aux Clercs and Au Grenier des poètes, taverns where (as he put it) 'Villon would have felt at home' and where artists and poets drank while reading or performing ballads, medieval songs, bellringing demonstrations and satirical sketches (many of these performers came from Le Chat Noir).[804]

For Robida, as for the organizers of *Paris en 1400* and the Feast of Fools, it was not enough to rebuild a medieval city; they were above all preoccupied by the *spirit* that had inhabited the monuments. Like Huysmans and Mâle, who directed attention to both the cathedral's 'body' and its 'soul,' Robida wanted to remind his contemporaries that the Middle Ages was not simply composed of buildings; it had been inhabited by a lively people that took an active interest in street culture:

It was never a question, of course, of being purely and severely archeological, of sacrificing everything for a momentary exactness […]; buildings, like living organisms, change and transform across the ages. It was necessary above all to be living, to make choices and to take, here and there, the most curious bits of vanished monuments, of homes of particular interest or famous for historical reasons, and to make an amalgam, a single work that would be picturesque for the eye, teeming with enough life and movement to represent truthfully curious and characteristic aspects of life in the past […][805]

7.8  Albert Robida, *La nef de Lutèce*, 1900

Accordingly, Robida did not simply rebuild a city; he also populated it with actors, musicians, salesmen, shopkeepers, tavern and restaurant owners and clergymen who sold their wares, cooked or performed in the street (Figs 7.9 and 7.10).[806] Concerts by the singers of Saint-Gervais, performers from the Schola Cantorum and organists were held in the chapel (see Fig. 5.7), while Mérovak ('the man of cathedrals') gave bellringing demonstrations. Over

7.9   *Le Vieux Paris: La Rue des Vieilles Ecoles, 1900*

60 000 visitors attended the events that took place in the chapel.[807] In addition, medieval farces were performed at both the cabaret and the theater. The audience could watch medieval dances or listen to modern *chansonniers* like Bobèche (who sang about Abelard and Heloise), Polin or Eugénie Buffet. In the street, the Prévost des Marchands performed pantomimes, monologues and parodies under the direction of composer Eugène Damaré.[808]

The *esprit gaulois* created by such diversions was one of the exhibit's greatest attractions, labeled *chatnoiresque* by guidebook author André Hallays.[809] For those not fortunate enough to be present at the Exposition, a number of books, like that produced for American audiences by the R. S.

7.10 *Le Vieux Paris: Le Chevet de Saint-Julien*, 1900

Peale Company in 1900, brought the thrills of the fair home through photos and text. They enthused about medieval Paris: 'As an object of popular historic interest, nothing can exceed the "old Paris" recreated for this special occasion. It is like stepping into the pages of Froissart and living in the days of Joan of Arc to enter the somber portals of Porte St Michel in this little Paris of ancient times.'[810] Such texts bring to life the busy streets and 'authentic' displays of Old Paris:

Here are seen the quaint steep-roofed, half-timbered houses which still linger in some of the remote corners of France; the richly-wrought, antique weather vanes forming an attractive picture from the river; a castle with its donjon and moat just as it might have stood 'in the brave days of old'; tidy little shops filled with the deft creations of peasant fingers, with peasants themselves and townspeople, living as nearly as possible, in costume and occupation, the old fifteenth century days again.[811]

In fact, like the artistic taverns and cabarets of the fin de siècle, the *Vieux Paris* exhibit appealed to contemporaries' nostalgia for a time of popular merriment and laughter when people roamed the streets in search of camaraderie and amusement. Advertisements for Le Cabaret de la Pomme de Pin at *Le Vieux Paris* drew those who admired the *esprit gaulois* of Villon, Rabelais, cabarets and the student Feast of Fools of 1898: 'Love, sing, laugh, and drink!' read one poster for it.[812]

Guidebooks about *Le Vieux Paris* compared its picturesque and joyous life-filled streets to the boring and sedate corners of modern Paris:

In our era of banal holidays, we have no idea of the magnificence displayed by the Middle Ages in these circumstances, of the extraordinary spectacle of long triumphant marches through the city, brightened by all sorts of diversions and interludes in which the city strove at all costs, nobles, clerics, monks, bourgeois donating their time and energy, powerful and prosperous corporations, each neighborhood trying hard to outdo the others.[813]

The comparison between the sterile, razed streets of Haussmann's late nineteenth-century Paris and the teeming life of the streets of 'old Paris' are made vividly clear by images such as the one serving as the frontispiece to the first issue of *Le Livre et l'Image* (Fig. 7.11). While the modern sector at the top left of the page has nary a living soul inhabiting its right-angled boulevards, its medieval predecessor was crowded with dogs, cats, children and other characters – most prominently a pretty and seemingly virtuous damsel – crammed along its picturesque streets.[814]

Robida had tried to recreate the vibrant medieval dream world of his book illustrations (and succeeded, by all visitors' accounts), but like *Paris en 1400*, the commercialism of the crowds flocking to the exhibit permeated the recreation. *Le Vieux Paris* was, in fact, the third top-grossing exhibit of the fair and many of the leading hotels and restaurants were also contained within its walls.[815] Both *Paris en 1400* and *Le Vieux Paris* were thus highly secular and commercialized. All of the wares on display in the various houses were for sale, one could send postcards of the exhibit and purchase illuminated manuscripts, silverware, champagne and religious trinkets.[816]

7.11    Emile Rondeau, *Le décor de la vie (Autrefois, Aujourd'hui),* 1893

As a character in G. De Wailly's fictional account put it, 'in the disparate series of items on display from the simple bibelot to the *objet d'art*, the modern and old-fashioned, the real or imitation, fraternize most eclectically on the shelves without ruining the tone of the décor.'[817] In spite of what would appear to be the corruption of Robida's medieval dream world by flocks of consumers, the fictional framework of the display, as De Wailly noted, seemed to support the commercialism. Perhaps this was because, as Robida pointed out in his guidebook, this was the first time at a World's Fair that a reconstructed city had included more than façades; his buildings could be fully inhabited.[818] As a result, the crowds did not simply watch a spectacle unfold before them; they felt as though they were a part of the recreation. They participated in the fair and bought products as their ancestors might have done on a fifteenth-century feast day.

### Modern as medieval: the living museum and the search for French origins

From raucous taverns to wandering circus performers, Parisians of the fin-de-siècle period were fascinated by street life, an attraction that had its roots in the narrative of guidebooks and in the eighteenth-century mania to study and document 'folk culture.'[819] Public spectacles of all sorts – jugglers, acrobats, charlatans, fairs, festivals, *fêtes foraines*, *foires*, wax museums, panoramas and masked balls – testified to the turn-of-the-century fascination with new and accessible forms of entertainment.[820] In fact, as many fin-de-siècle scholars pointed out, the perspective of the pleasure-seeking visitor to *Paris en 1400* or *Le Vieux Paris* was not so different from that of their medieval ancestors; both sought spectacle, the injection of life into the streets through consumer goods and entertainment (Fig. 7.12). The exploding street life of the fin de siècle was both compared to and contrasted with ancestral forms of popular culture.

   In *Le Vieux Paris: Fêtes, Jeux et Spectacles*, Victor Fournel implied that the modern spectacles of circus, café-concerts and music hall were a return to an ancient French tradition:

As far and wide as we search our intimate history, we find magicians. The troubadours and minstrels of the Middle Ages blended their poems and songs with entertainment that could charm the crowd or the nobility, particularly with sleight of hand [...] Everything that our jugglers do today in public places, the learned jugglers of the Middle Ages did too, during the intermissions between their more noble activities [...][821]

Other contemporaries, such as Denys Amiel and Germain Bapst, drew links between the modern songs of cabarets and music halls and medieval entertainment.[822] Even the most spectacular and technologically advanced of all modern displays, the Expositions Universelles, were described by scholars like Fournel and Drumont as having a medieval counterpart, an 'embryo,' in old Parisian feasts and fairs.

The study of our old Parisian *foires* offers great interest from very diverse points of view; one could say that they were the embryo of the World's Fairs – with notable differences certainly, but also with certain analogies, such as the division by branches of industry and the classing of objects by country of origin – because visitors came there from all parts of Europe and sometimes the world.[823]

Nine years before Fournel, who must surely have read him, Edouard Drumont offered the same comparison between the World's Fairs and the medieval markets and fairs, which he too referred to as 'embryos of our World's Fairs' for their mixture of classification, didacticism and entertainment.[824] Insisting on the similarities between modern and medieval entertainment and

252    **PARIS EXPOSITION**

performing in the streets. There is a printing-office whence issues the "Gazette of Old Paris," which retails in quaint type the news and scandals of the fourteenth century. The architectural studies for this reconstruction were made by Albert Robida, the architect whose magic pencil

MEDIAEVAL JOKERS

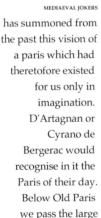

has summoned from the past this vision of a paris which had theretofore existed for us only in imagination. D'Artagnan or Cyrano de Bergerac would recognise in it the Paris of their day. Below Old Paris we pass the large

"THERE WERE GIANTS IN THOSE DAYS"

classification, as did Fournel and Drumont, provided a way of understanding seemingly 'degenerate' modern men as reflections of their allegedly morally superior medieval brethren. Like the sculptures and stained-glass windows of a Gothic cathedral or the didactic current of medieval passion and morality plays, both medieval and modern creations attempted to instruct the people while entertaining them.

Fournel, Drumont and Bapst all rightly focused on the mixture of entertainment and education prevalent in both medieval and modern fairs. An instructive undercurrent was certainly on display in the four events we have studied in this chapter: *Paris en 1400*, the 1898 Feast of Fools, the *esprit gaulois* of artistic cabarets and *Le Vieux Paris*. Like museums, whose values are based on the authenticity of the items they conserve, these four displays actively marketed themselves as presenting the 'real' Middle Ages. In each case, one sees a concerted attempt to go beyond mere nostalgia for the past by establishing credibility, by inscribing the re-enactment within a legitimate historical context. *Paris en 1400*, despite its Hugo-esque depiction of the Middle Ages, included a medieval museum, replete with labels describing the costumes, armor, weapons and furniture on display. It billed itself as providing 'a faithful painting of life and the customs of old, placed in an irreproachably exact setting.'[825] Similarly, the student organizers of *La Fête des Fous* obtained new translations of little-known medieval plays and arranged for musical accompaniment while complementing their celebration with a number of essays about the historical origins of the holiday, written by leading experts in the field.[826] Even cabarets, whose joyous attitude to the Middle Ages was seemingly less educational, performed or imitated the works of medieval and Renaissance poets while taking pains to identify their medieval furniture and stained-glass windows in guidebooks (even if they were spoofs). All of these exhibits functioned, to varying degrees, at the intersection between popular entertainment and nineteenth-century scholarship.

Albert Robida's *Le Vieux Paris* was, of course, the most overtly didactic of the events; it had a clear conservational message to impart as it relied on scholarly research to resurrect the buildings of dreams, structures that had long existed only in the imagination:

The past, days gone by, vanished objects, all of this always conveys a certain spiritual charm. It is pleasurable to dream of this past, so near, but ever fleeting, ever plunging into a thickening fog, ending too quickly in total darkness, and it is then a particularly gripping sensation to try to complete at the least the decor of this dream [...] seeking the framework of life in olden days, destroyed pieces of Paris rediscovered for a little while, buildings or fragments of vanished buildings, the old houses of our Parisian ancestors [...] all of this must temporarily live again once one has crossed the threshold [of *Le Vieux Paris*].[827]

Robida's reconstructed village would provide his contemporaries with a subtle warning about their destruction of the past by reminding them of the beauties and the great achievements that had already vanished.

But why would these various exhibits, which clearly made entertainment their highest priority, try so doggedly to market themselves as 'real,' 'authentic' or 'accurate' reflections of the past? They could simply have marketed the attraction as medieval, as did La Taverne du Moyen Age, without incorporating any real elements from the past. But instead, they made a concerted effort to gather artifacts and documents for their displays. Why bother? Was the attraction of the Middle Ages itself not enough to draw consumers? Although it is easy to dismiss this fin-de-siècle explosion of popular interest in medieval street and tavern culture as a facile attraction to a dream Middle Ages, the organizers' attention to underlining the 'authenticity' of the attraction indicates the public's shifting and increasingly complex relationship to the medieval past. Unlike earlier revivals of interest in the Middle Ages, in which the medieval trappings – costumes, proper names or legends – sufficed to draw spectators, by the turn of the century the public held a much deeper understanding of the Middle Ages and its relationship to the modern French nation.[828]

First of all, by 1900 the French were familiar with medieval literature and history. As we saw in Chapter 1, after the Franco-Prussian war, scholars had forcefully advocated the philological study of the Middle Ages as a way of rebuilding national pride and patriotism. Between 1871 and 1900, scholars took such suggestions to heart; they actively courted the masses, publishing their essays about medieval literature and history in popular magazines and campaigning to make medieval literature an accepted part of the secondary school curriculum.[829] Publications such as Le Pèlerin only accentuated such knowledge of medieval French history. As a result, new generations had first-hand knowledge of the words and spirit of their ancestors. The public no longer wanted only 'fairy tales' about the French past; it was now educated enough to request the 'truth' about the period, historical narratives based on existing documents from the Middle Ages. This was not just patriotism, but 'scientific' curiosity about the medieval period, as Charles Morice described it in 1914.[830]

The emphasis on 'authenticity' prevalent in the marketing of Paris en 1400, The Feast of Fools, medievalizing cabarets and Le Vieux Paris seems to respond to the public's demand for information about the 'real' Middle Ages. To a certain extent, they echo the advertising of the numerous museums established at the time, enormously successful ventures that brought in crowds by publicizing their new acquisitions in newspapers and magazines.[831] As we saw in Chapter 3, museum display had only begun to shift from the idiosyncratic bric-à-brac display of collector Alexandre du Sommerard to a more narrative-driven focus on labeling and organizing artifacts to construct a coherent story about the object's relationship to the past (Courajod's display for the medieval and Renaissance wing at the Louvre, for example). The displays of Paris en 1400 and Le Vieux Paris were not perhaps so different from those of Le Musée de Cluny or Le Musée Carnavalet. Popular interest in the 'real' Middle Ages drew people to medieval museums as it did to neo-medieval recreations, which can be considered 'living museums.'[832]

Yet however much Paris en 1400, the Feast of Fools, 'medieval' cabarets and Le Vieux Paris made a complex historical past more accessible to a public curious about its history, we should be wary of accepting the public's claim to have truly stepped back in time. Such displays reduced the Middle Ages to easily digestible morsels by 'offer[ing] the visitor the illusion of a knowable, self-enclosed world which can be taken in at a glance, revealed to a tourist's gaze in the course of a morning stroll.'[833] Much as museums attempt to educate by presenting rooms of organized material from various centuries, styles or schools, all of medieval history (like all of the Orient or Africa as represented in the colonial exhibitions) was compressed in the space of a few blocks or a few rooms in the four major displays evoked in this chapter. Such miniaturization assured both mastery and full visibility of the period. In addition, the 'taking in' of the past with the purchase of admission was a form of consuming no less commercial than the tourist curios, the craft trinkets and refreshments disguised as 'genuine historical articles' that the visitors were encouraged to purchase.[834]

Moreover, even though museums and events advertised the authenticity of their inspiration, as Dean MacCannell has pointed out, claims of 'recreation,' 'revival' or 'restitution' are often problematic:

Modern museums and parks are anti-historical and unnatural. They are not, of course, anti-historical and unnatural in the sense of their destroying the past or nature, because to the contrary, they preserve them, but as they preserve they automatically separate modernity from its past and from nature and elevate it above them. Nature and the past are made a part of the present, not in the form of an unreflected inner spirit, a mysterious soul, but rather as revealed objects, as tourist attractions.[835]

MacCannell clearly points out the paradox of recreations. Although tourists feel that they are 'reliving' the past in the present, they are only further marginalizing it. Indeed, it is the choices made in selecting, organizing and displaying elements from the past that cause the artificiality of such displays and separate the past from the present. Unlike the medieval streets of Paris that continue to exist as they once were, or unlike cathedrals, whose 'use value' confers on them an aura of 'authenticity' not evident in museums, expositions and 'reconstitutions' of the past are calculated and artificial displays. The 'recreations' of medieval Paris in the late nineteenth century established modern links to the Middle Ages by drawing attention to the past, putting it on display. Housing it in closed contexts, however, separated it from modern life, thereby marginalizing the past.

Each of these exhibits resulted from different kinds of nostalgia for the past, for a Middle Ages represented in books and stage sets. Yet, whether 'un-natural' or not, the events we have studied in this chapter have a popular appeal that extends beyond the permanent display cases of museums; all of these were ephemeral productions resulting from celebrations. In contrast to the other instances of medievalism we have examined, in the popular spaces discussed in this chapter the relationship between the Middle Ages and commercialism was openly embraced. Many other engagements with the medieval heritage attempted to rarefy the Middle Ages, to appropriate it for specific aesthetic or political purposes. They thus tended to deny commercial affiliation and to turn the period into a 'private' or 'inaccessible' Middle Ages defined by their own specific parameters. The events and locales we document in this chapter, however, overtly encouraged the consumption of medieval history. Rather than proposing the period as an idyllic and escapist elsewhere, the Parisian spaces of popular culture embraced a democratic version of the Middle Ages, which was open to all. They were created with the ideal of drawing participants into a festive realm.

As Victor Turner has noted, the word *celebration* comes from the Latin *celeber*: '"numerous, much frequented", and relates to the vivacity – akin to what the great French sociologist Durkheim called "effervescence" – generated by a crowd of people with shared purposes and common values.'[836] Unlike a museum display, in which visitors are generally passive observers, the four events that we have studied in this chapter follow this celebratory model: they were designed to foster audience participation through the consumption of featured products and amusements. The role of the festival visitor is not far from that of a worshiper in a cathedral or that of a pilgrim, figures who, as we saw in Chapter 6, have a more complex relationship with the spectacle when they contribute to it. Because of the involvement of the public in the four events discussed in this chapter, they did retain the 'inner spirit' that MacCannell finds missing in 'revealed objects.' What is more, the active involvement of the public in these activities provides important clues about their hopes and fears about what it meant to be French in a modern society fraught with change.

In a study of the historical pageants that took place in the French countryside in the mid-nineteenth century, Stéphane Gerson has pointed out that festivals are extremely rich in opportunities for reformulating social and national identity:

> A festive genre entails set conventions, frames a space that is saturated with meaning, awakens expectations and invites particular patterns of behavior. At once utopian and disciplinary, the historical pageant thus also provided new opportunities for cultural and political expression. It helped contemporaries think a world in flux and articulate social and territorial identities [...] This festive realm was also a laboratory in which provincial actors sought, with varying success, to define self and community, identity and citizenship.[837]

Although Gerson directs his attention to regional celebrations from 1825 to 1865, the same can be said for the fin-de-siècle historical re-enactments of the Middle Ages we have studied in this chapter. Visitors came to the closed spaces of *Paris en 1400*, the Latin Quarter, cabarets and *Le Vieux Paris* expecting to encounter the Middle Ages that had been marketed to them: an authentic experience of a joyous communal past when *l'esprit gaulois* of feast days turned villages into united groups in which all people worked for the common good. The focus in all of these exhibits on performing poetry, songs and plays from the Middle Ages showed that the *esprit gaulois* of the past was still valid in modern France. In addition, the focus on ancestors like François Villon, who, they thought, was able to drown his sorrows during times of festival, even as he faced prison, war, famine and sickness, provided a strong model for a time in which many worried about social insecurity. Although these events were planned largely for amusement, their representation of a past that valued festivals as restorative helped Parisians define how they wanted to cope with their own problems; they assisted in shaping a new identity for a nation in the midst of modifying all of its old traditions.

It is no coincidence that in each of the events studied in this chapter, the recurring motif was a secular pride in *l'esprit gaulois*, in the national sense of humor and festivity that united the French in brotherhood and allowed them to recover from difficult periods of history. The recognition and dissemination of the concept of a 'gay Paris,' even in the midst of some of the most fierce social battles known to the French nation, confirms France's collective vision of itself as an inherently simple and joyous nation, dedicated to getting along. Everyone, regardless of political or religious affiliation, was invited to participate in events like *Paris en 1400*, the Feast of Fools of 1898, artistic cabarets and *Le Vieux Paris*. Records show that Catholics, Jews, Protestants, Republicans, anarchists and foreigners actively participated in these events.[838] Consuming the past – by paying admission – granted everyone equal access to French heritage.

It is important to remark, however, that although *Paris en 1400*, the Feast of Fools, cabaret performances and *Le Vieux Paris* all created events that praised social harmony, religion is noticeably absent. Each of them was resolutely secular, representing religion as an accessory to common life, not as a core element of French identity. Religion, which had, in the fin de siècle, become a source of friction, seems to have been subsumed, especially in these events, into more unifying secular activities. Accordingly, the Feast of Fools and of the Ass, originally a Church holiday, was adopted not for its religious associations – the arrival of the Magi and the Flight from Egypt – but for its possibilities for social regeneration. Similarly, churches at *Paris en 1400* and *Le Vieux Paris* served as concert halls and not as houses of worship; concerts replaced high mass as people of all beliefs came together to appreciate medieval French music. While pilgrimages also drew upon a unifying communal experience, participation was limited to practicing Catholics. In contrast, the events highlighted in this chapter held a far broader appeal, for much more diverse groups.

The celebratory medieval events of the fin de siècle also reshaped contemporary attitudes toward artistic identity. Although the period was racked by worries about the value of artisanal products in a world increasingly dominated by machine-made and reproduced works of art, the festive medieval recreations reaffirmed the nation's commitment to and appreciation of handmade products. Turner evokes the importance of celebration in the recognition of cultural values by putting artists on display.[839] The medieval artisans so prominently featured in *Paris en 1400* and *Le Vieux Paris* reaffirmed the accomplishments of French ancestors, even if they did work next door to stores selling cheap machine-made reproductions of medieval art. Much as Stuart Merrill had praised the artistic community of Haute-Claire as 'reclaim[ing] the artistic traditions of the [French] race' and as 'renew[ing] the traditions of the industries of art,' throughout the 1900 World's Fair medieval artistic production and its modern practitioners – stained-glass artisans, musicians, manuscript illuminators, sculptors, architects – were posited as continuing the core values of the French nation. And seen in the context of the world that had produced them – medieval objects placed once again among Gothic houses, villagers and churches – these works of art pleased art critics and public alike.

Moreover, the public was invited to enjoy and consume such modern recreations without guilt and judgment. Such machine-made works were elevated in the context of these fairs and events, basking in the reflected glory of their more authentic counterparts. The rift between mass-produced items and artistic legacy could seem – illusorily – to have been bridged.

Yet these displays also functioned to deny the real changes that had occurred since the Middle Ages. Within the constricted space of the fair or festival, major transformations – the shift from artisanal craft to industrialized, mass-produced commodities, for example – were masked by placing the two types of product side by side. In medievalized settings, machine-produced items paraded as authentically-inspired crafts from an age of innocence and communal labor. Further blurring the distinction between medieval and modern, organizers invited nineteenth-century performers to contribute medieval-inspired songs, dances, concerts and poetry. While these performances often took inspiration from medieval works, they produced entirely modern results. The ephemeral works created in artistic cabarets acknowledged medieval French traditions while building on them to create modern art, a practice that brought out the 'modernity' of medieval poets much as painters had revealed the 'modernity' of medieval *Primitifs*.[840] Comparing modern to medieval artworks increased both their historical and their economic value; the 'authentic' flavor of such objects perpetuated the illusion that the medieval past could truly be revived, imbibed or experienced.

If visitors emerged from the displays of the 1900 World's Fair with great enthusiasm for the artistic and social accomplishments of medieval France, it was because, in spite of their anachronisms, *Paris en 1400* and *Le Vieux Paris* were successful in putting France's early achievements on display not only for Paris but for the entire world. Joseph B. Campbell, an American visitor to the Fair, was obviously impressed by *Le Vieux Paris*, which he described in glowing terms: 'National love and pride, combined with rare artistic gifts, have made this reproduction of the old French capital a thing of real beauty and delight.'[841] The 1900 World's Fair, whose goal was to show the world how much the nation had recovered since the Franco-Prussian war, publicized on a worldwide level the stability, fraternity and technological and artistic hegemony of the modern French nation. Nationalism and art came together in the World's Fair and led to the kind of overblown rhetoric of the early years of the twentieth century that proclaimed French Gothic cathedrals superior to all others in the world and announced the 'hegemony' of medieval French *Primitifs*.[842] Not surprisingly, as Françoise Choay has pointed out, this was also the period that began to 'consecrate' historical monuments by developing 'an official cult of historical patrimony.' With the separation of Church and State in 1905, France finally passed laws designed to protect and to make known the superior value of its monuments.[843]

As this chapter has shown, the popular Middle Ages took the form of performance, from street acrobats to music hall to parading students. The past could be construed as a series of vignettes, a spectacle, but also as a participatory event that asked French citizens to reassess their relationship to past and future and to commit to rebuilding the social fabric of a nation torn apart by political, religious and civil war and education. The 'recreated' Middle Ages on display in *Paris en 1400*, the 1898 Feast of Fools celebration, the collections of artistic cabarets and the recreated *Vieux Paris* were not just escapist individual visions of the past; these representations of a medieval France united in pleasure and national pride mixed real and imaginary history while inviting people to examine vestiges of the past in order to reassess what it meant to be French at the turn of the century.

The popular events explored in this chapter performed a complex and important ideological task: they brought attention to the literature, art and history of the medieval period, they reconciled past and present and they legitimated and ennobled the values of the modern world by projecting them onto the Middle Ages. If some of the distinctly 'modern' values were less than noble – the avaricious need to acquire objects, the desire to consume bibelots of all sort, the longing to revel in 'low' amusements rather than the sanctified traditions of established French arts – celebrants rationalized them by rooting them in the Middle Ages. By participating actively in such events, spectators told themselves that their tastes, desires and attitudes were no different from those of their French forebears, even if this was not truly the case.[844] Real differences between the two periods collapsed as visitors and revelers sang medieval songs, downed 'old-style' libations and saw the world (literally) through the stained-glass windows or crenelated towers of medieval structures.

The medieval revival in fin-de-siècle France opened the door to the past, finding in it models, lessons and a spiritual guide for how to live in the present. At the same time, the desires of the nineteenth century led to recreations of the Middle Ages that took the form of festivals, fairs and living museums. These modern values occupied – even haunted – the spaces, as did the top-hatted gentlemen and elegantly robed Parisiennes who roamed their streets, attended their performances and, in their own way, brought the Middle Ages back to life.

# Conclusion

Léon Gautier, a specialist in medieval epics and a well-known translator of *La Chanson de Roland*, insisted, in 1892, on the importance of what could be called 'marketing the Middle Ages,' of bringing knowledge about medieval culture to every level of French society in order to encourage people to familiarize themselves with their national heritage:

> One must not scorn the general public at the risk of being abandoned by it, and it is particularly important not to transform science into some kind of obscure temple where only priests have the right to enter […] Everything, everything must be arranged to assure the decisive triumph of our national epic [*The Song of Roland*]: everything, including *La Bibliothèque bleue* books for children and *images d'Epinal* for countryfolk and the uneducated; everything including tales and alphabets for children […] Let us thus reach out to all ages as to all classes.[845]

Above all, Gautier advocated reading medieval classics out loud and with passion – 'with vibrating voice and shivering heart' – to the public. He wanted to 'take advantage of such a reading to say to young Frenchmen: "Look, children, how impressive France already was then and how much she was loved eight centuries ago".'[846] La Société des Anciens Textes Français was founded by Gaston Paris and Paul Meyer in 1872 with a similar goal: they intended it as a 'national work' that would make medieval France better known by returning to archival sources. Like Gautier, they strove to bring words to life, 'to make the simple language, the heroic dreams, the joyous laughter and the ancient customs of our fathers come alive again.'[847]

In the 1870s, these goals seemed wildly ambitious: in the passage with which we began this book, Charles Morice noted that few but specialists knew much about the Middle Ages and those who did tended to popularize the period as 'charming,' 'sublime' or 'primitive'; they focused less on understanding it than on presenting it as an 'accessory,' an exotic and curious vestige of the past that served their own needs.[848] While specialists like Didron, Louis Vitet, Viollet-le-Duc and Francisque Michel worked tirelessly throughout the nineteenth century to study and classify documents from the medieval past, it was not until the last quarter of the century that their works became widely available to the public at large. Indeed, by 1900, medieval scholars had finally begun to see the fruits of their labor: the Middle Ages could be found everywhere: in political speeches and celebrations, in artists' salons and exhibits, in museums and bourgeois living rooms, in churches and cabarets, in popular journals, books and plays, in pilgrimages, street fairs and festivals. It was so ubiquitous, claimed writers like Adolphe Retté, that the whole period seemed a dizzying and cacophonous tribute to the Middle Ages.[849]

But what were the relationships between philologists like Gaston Paris, who studied medieval documents in order to 'understand the Middle Ages and make them understood,' and more popular consumers of medieval art and history? Although it might seem that a great divide separated high culture attitudes to the Middle Ages from more popular ones, both – as we have seen throughout this study – engaged one another, complementing and fueling each other and bringing more attention to the period itself. Far from scorning the public, scholars as varied as Viollet-le-Duc, Joseph Bédier and Gaston Paris understood the power of a mass market and reached out to it through their publications: 'One must not scorn the general public at the risk of being abandoned by it,' said Léon Gautier.

Like the industrious art historians and curators who mounted important exhibits of medieval art to educate the public, scholars like Gautier, Paris and Meyer realized that bringing medieval literature and history to the French masses was a national mission that would bolster pride in the homeland. And like the Assumptionist Fathers who encouraged the study of medieval saints' lives as therapeutic, their marketing campaign succeeded. Yet the scholars, too, may seem to have fallen victim to their own success: the movement that worked to publicize 'real' medieval culture was indirectly responsible for turning the Middle Ages into a consumer fantasy, spawning Roland and Joan of Arc dolls, card games, clip-out images, dinner plates, lives of the saints postcards and slides, industrially manufactured stained-glass windows and tapestries.[850] They succeeded in revealing the medieval period's artistic accomplishments and love of the French nation, yet their original purpose could seem to have been betrayed as revered medieval legends were used to peddle everything from beer and wine to cheese, chocolate and toothpaste. In the opinion of numerous critics, affiliation with pedestrian consumer goods cheapened the legends' historical or mythical significance.

Well-meaning scholarly initiatives to drum up national pride could thus be seen as contributing to the 'bastardization' of the Middle Ages so deplored by art historians like Léon Ottin and Edouard Didron.[851] But the same can be said for nearly all of the phenomena explored in this book: from artists and art historians, museum curators and priests, entertainers and festival organizers, the attempts of different groups to showcase treasured and unique elements from the past resulted in their reproduction and consumption by the masses, thus leading to complaints that treasured medieval objects had been 'besmirched' by the public eye. For people like Ottin, Didron and Huysmans, the only true way to maintain the 'purity' and 'exclusivity' characteristic of medieval art would be to keep it private and out of sight. As Françoise Choay has argued, it is the process of bringing attention to the national patrimony that can create such a dilemma: '[Monuments are] works that convey knowledge and pleasure, placed at the disposition of all; but also cultural products, made, wrapped up and distributed with an eye to consumption.'[852] Drawing people to literature, museums and historical monuments to educate them about the past often coincides with attracting additional visitors whose admission fees will sustain the museum or monument and whose attention will protect it.

Such debates about the role of the patrimony in the commercial sphere notwithstanding, it has been our objective in this study to reveal the fallacy of the widely expressed fin-de-siècle fear that popular consumption of the past would lead to its destruction. In fact, the popular embrace of the Middle Ages was indispensable for scholars to continue protecting, classifying and interpreting medieval art and literature. The public's interest in the past and demands for accurate information about it led directly to scholars' enhanced abilities to secure and conserve scattered works of art. As such activities were increasingly recognized as making crucial contributions to the French heritage, they garnered even more public and governmental support. Even the Third Republic began to recognize the public's enthusiasm for the popular *animus* of medieval culture, which conformed to its own popularizing goals. Accordingly, the government created new positions for medieval scholars in universities, museums and conservation groups, thus beginning what Michel Espagne has called an 'institutional consecration' of medieval studies.[853]

Popular demand for the Middle Ages lies at the heart of our study and is, as we contend, the element that makes the fin de siècle's relationship to them so different from that of other periods. Much late nineteenth-century fascination with the medieval rests precisely on the relationship between popular marketing and consumption and scholarly publications. While this was somewhat true in the Romantic period (Hugo's use of medieval sources in writing the hugely popular and eminently fictional *Notre-Dame de Paris* is a case in point), it became even more so at the end of the century as an increasingly literate and affluent society demanded what Gaston Paris and Léon Gautier termed 'understanding' of the Middle Ages and what Charles Morice called 'the truth': 'we are tired of the picturesque lie [...] the men of the second half of the last century were overcome by an immense need for truth.'[854]

Although there were plenty of imaginary representations of 'dream' Middle Ages in the fin de siècle, they tended – more and more – to be inspired by authentic medieval art or archival sources. The Symbolists, for example, may have created their own versions of cathedrals or woodcuts, yet they often based them not only on their imagination, but on medieval objects they had seen: the vaulted windows of Notre-Dame de Chartres, medieval manuscripts or manuscript illuminations. Even the most fanciful of interpretations – like *Paris en 1400*, 'medieval' taverns or the Feast of Fools – called attention to their sources, attempting to rationalize the 'truth' of their representations. This focus on source material and on judging representations of the Middle Ages by the 'accuracy' of their reliance on original documents marked a new benchmark in medieval studies: to be considered 'authentic' became a value in itself. It was no longer enough to discuss or display medieval art, literature or history. One also needed to signal its origins and justify its authenticity.

Indeed, scholarly debates about the function medieval art should play in fin-de-siècle society marked a turning point in attitudes toward the collection, consumption and conservation of works from the Middle Ages. As we saw in Chapter 3, until the French Revolution, collecting in France had been associated primarily with the aristocracy. Prestige was predicated on a system of supply and demand: the more exclusive, expensive and inaccessible an object, the more it was desired and the more it conferred distinction.[855] But by the beginning of the twentieth century, new technology had made the reproduction of medieval artworks accessible to everyone, public education had exposed the lower classes to their marvels and disposable income had allowed bourgeois and lower-class patrons to acquire medieval artifacts or their reproductions.[856] Such activities or products thus encouraged the public to emulate the prestigious collectors of the past, while their interest partially negated the exclusivity that the intellectual elite had previously seen in the collection of medieval art.

Nonetheless, an aristocratic perfume clung to medieval art, thus prompting many fin-de-siècle consumers to yearn for reproductions which, they imagined, would confer upon them the distinction of the original owners of the works. For those seeking to legitimate their taste through period style and 'authentic' reproductions, the Middle Ages were perfect. The artists, writers and politicians who filled their houses with medieval artifacts did so not only because they liked them, but also because such acquisitions linked them to the feudal world. Zola, for example, wanted to create the atmosphere of a castle in furnishing his home in Médan; he bolstered his sense of importance by sitting on his Gothic throne.[857] Indeed, even today the Middle Ages symbolize the world of king and court. As catalogs for the American company Design Toscano and European retailers Past Times and Tanjadis (a phonetic spelling of 'temps jadis' or 'old times') insist, the 'aristocratic' pedigree of the objects they sell plays no small role in their appeal (Fig. 8.1).[858] Such works are presented as 'exclusive,' 'exquisite,' 'timeless,' 'elaborate,' 'handcrafted' or 'regal' and tie into questions of stability and family legacy much as they did for the collectors discussed in Chapter 3.[859]

Desire to gain distinction by association with events from the past was one of the major elements responsible for the excellent profits made by *Paris en 1400*, La Fête des fous and *Vieux Paris*, which recreated medieval villages and featured 'medieval' artisans and their wares. The exclusivity of the events themselves, coupled with the attraction and exoticism of the Middle Ages (which appealed to the consumer's sense of fancy, good taste and interest in history and religion), led visitors to associate themselves with such activities. Today, we are jaded by such commercialism; the medieval fair is less attractive, less exclusive, when one can attend it any day, as one can the 'medieval' dinner performances offered at the 'Medieval Times' chain. By contrast, nineteenth-century France was still what Janell Watson

8.1   'Gothic Gallery,' *Design Toscano* catalog, Autumn 2000

has called a 'proto-consumer society.' Because shoppers had not completely accepted the concept of the disposability of goods, acquisitions involved difficult choices. Decisions about selecting one object over another did tend to convey important messages about a person's taste.

As such popular ideas about the Middle Ages flourished, however, those who formerly embraced the appreciation and collection of medieval objects as a mark of distinction began to establish new parameters to distinguish their skills from those of the masses. Indeed, it is critics' insistence on 'truth,' 'authenticity' and 'integrity' that reveals this shift, much more so than their protests against the mass market. From Huysmans's tendency to mock Zola's inability to distinguish 'real' *Primitif* painting from 'fakes,' to Didron's outcries against the 'bastardized' stained glass in taverns, we see a growing aesthetic based less on class or economics (as in pre-Revolutionary France) than on knowledge and education. For Didron and Huysmans, knowing the 'truth' about medieval stained glass or painting became more important than simply having the means to collect it. Increasingly, scholars and academics thus proposed a new definition of the 'connaisseur' that argued that ownership of an object was less important for conveying distinction than being able to develop a coherent and accurate narrative about it. Understanding the Middle Ages became more important than admiring it.

In fact, when considering the often conflicting claims made about the Middle Ages at the end of the nineteenth century (that continue to this day), one is tempted to ask whether Gaston Paris and his colleagues, who so wanted to discover the 'truth' about the Middle Ages, would have been horrified by the ways in which they had brought the period to the attention of the mass market. Léon Gautier, for one, would have answered 'No.' By interesting his contemporaries in all aspects of the Middle Ages and in all of its stereotypes (true and false), he was able to draw more of them to seek further information about the period: in reproduced manuscripts and schoolbooks, museums and library archives. They, in turn, would better understand the period and champion it.

Indeed, it is this shift from what Arthur Johnston has called the 'imputed values' of the Romantic medieval revival to what we could call the 'factual values' that fascinated the fin de siècle. The blend of scholarly and popular combined in an overt interest in discovering the 'truth' about the Middle Ages (even while people continued to create new imaginary values for the Middle Ages) is what distinguishes this period of medievalism from preceding ones. This movement can be seen as a natural offshoot of the positivist nineteenth-century literary studies of Sainte-Beuve and Taine, which emphasized history and biography, but it also developed from the tendency in fin-de-siècle France to use philological methods to study authentic documents. Alongside these 'scientific' developments, however, were other, often religious or aesthetic factors. Religious groups sought to understand medieval history in order to reaffirm the Catholic Church's traditional standing in French society, while artists like J.-K. Huysmans and Remy de Gourmont sought to expose the workings of medieval Catholic symbolism and mysticism.[860] Such curiosity about the Middle Ages and the resultant publications about them increased access to information and enhanced the public's desire to discover the 'real' Middle Ages, to 'resurrect,' 'resuscitate' or 'reconstruct' them.

While it is easy to dismiss popular enthusiasm for the Middle Ages as superficial, it is often curiosity about a topic that leads to greater and more serious consideration of it. Yvette Guilbert, the world-famous 'diseuse' and Montmartre cabaret performer, provides an excellent example. Although she was a member of the working class, she became familiar with medieval poets and songs through the pseudo-medieval atmosphere of Le Chat Noir and other Montmartre cabarets. Despite what can be considered the superficiality of these formative experiences, she went on to make medieval studies her second career. In fact, not only did she classify medieval manuscripts at the Bibliothèque Nationale, but her collection of some 80 000 songs rivaled that of medievalist Joseph Bédier.[861] She published a number of volumes devoted to medieval song and traveled the lecture circuit. In the early twentieth century she was highly in demand – at Columbia and Harvard Universities among others – as a speaker and performer of poetry and medieval songs. The former cabaret singer was even elected to the Société des Anciens Textes Français where she was welcomed by Bédier himself![862] Yvette Guilbert praised Gaston Paris for his work and marveled that the lectures he had given during and after the Franco-Prussian war had inspired so many to love the French Middle Ages: 'As far away as America I found disciples of the great Gaston Paris.'[863] Leading Symbolist writers of fin-de-siècle France owned his complete works or those of La Société des Anciens Textes Français, while others had taken classes at l'Ecole des Chartes.[864] Young artists like Apollinaire and Jarry, who frequented the Chat Noir cabaret, also spent days poring over manuscripts at the Bibliothèque Nationale, basing subsequent literary works on medieval models.[865]

At the beginning of the twentieth century, readers and spectators knew much more about life in the twelfth to fifteenth centuries than had earlier periods, precisely because of the accessibility of texts (in modern and medieval French) and extant art work. As the Middle Ages became more popular and its 'pure' pre-industrial aura more celebrated, the period was used in the service of other causes. Nineteenth-century artists, for example, adopted a monastic identity and praised anonymity, while encouraging critics and dealers to label them *Primitifs* and to send visitors to their artistic communities. Likewise, museum directors granted long interviews to members of the press and allowed reproductions of their new acquisitions to be photographed for inclusion in illustrated periodicals, knowing that this would increase the number of visitors, thus shoring up the financial foundations of their establishment. Each of these cases involved a calculated understanding of supply and demand, sharpened through publicity. Like the Assumptionist Fathers who knew that they would draw people to the Catholic Church by introducing the masses to the medieval world of *Le Pèlerin* and its modern pilgrimages, the intellectual elite appealed to the bourgeoisie and working class in order to encourage them to learn about medieval art, literature and history.

Even scholars used such techniques. Serious medievalists Léon Gautier, Joseph Bédier and Gaston Paris made a conscious decision to popularize medieval works of literature after the Franco-Prussian war and to emphasize their French origin. As Per Nykrog and Howard Bloch have argued, one of Bédier's motivations in writing his modern adaptation of the Tristan legend was to wrench it from its association with Wagner's popular German opera and to reveal its purely French origins. Similarly, Bédier went against all prevailing scholarship to show that the Oxford manuscript of *La Chanson de Roland* dated from after 1100, thus proving its unadulterated French nature.[866] Fustel de Coulanges, too, had chosen to publish his influential essays about the Germanic invasions in a mainstream publication – *La Revue des Deux Mondes* – which was read by thousands of readers.

Such popularization, far from destroying the Middle Ages, as Didron or Huysmans expected it would, created a variety of narratives that fostered a productive social engagement with the French past. Even Gaston Paris found the medievalism of the end of the century much richer than that of previous eras.[867] In fact, it was thanks to the generations of scholars that followed Paris, Meyer and Gautier in literature (including Bédier, Alfred Jeanroy, Mario Roques, Edmond Faral, Gustave Cohen and Jean Frappier) that the field of medieval studies as we know it today was formed; they used the philological methods advocated by the scholars of the fin de siècle and the publications they had established (*Romania*, La Société des Anciens Textes Français) as a foundation from which to bring even more medieval works to the public attention.[868]

Although one could argue that it was the increased efforts of high culture (scholars, museum curators, musicians and Church fathers) to 'sell' the Middle Ages to the public that served as the catalyst for its broader dissemination, the relationship between the two is far more complex. We have tried to show that there is a symbiotic relationship between high and low culture, between popular and academic manifestations of the medieval; they go hand in hand, one complementing the other. Had the public not already been persuaded to take an interest in the Middle Ages and been willing to accept such messages, it would not have done so. Each movement influenced the other in subtle ways, and far from diminishing interest in the Middle Ages, such attention exponentially increased their popularity. As philologists linked medieval literature to nationalism and published easily accessible translations of early French texts, the school system adopted them. As students read these works, they began to demand more detailed information about the period. As educators asked for better teaching material, the government established more public institutions dedicated to the Middle Ages: specialized schools, books, critical texts for teachers and reproduced texts and images.[869] Through increased demand, the public contributed to the rising supply of medieval material: scholars displayed and reproduced documents formerly hidden in archives. But such demand also produced imitations that exploited the popularity of the Middle Ages: pseudo-medieval celebrations, cabarets honoring medieval poets and recreated medieval towns. These events, in turn, fostered a demand for more museums and scientific study of the Middle Ages. Rigorous interest in details about the Middle Ages thus began to exist side by side with persisting myths about the innocent painter-monk and the pure and pious 'Age of Faith.' The medievalism of the fin de siècle made room for both. Such complex relationships between high and low culture developed a rich web of narrative invention about the Middle Ages that brought it to the public attention as a valuable part of the national heritage.

A vogue for the Middle Ages is sweeping France today, leading us to question the phenomenon once more.[870] Why is there a resurgence of medieval fairs, medieval books and movies in twenty-first-century France? Is it because of the publications of the 'new medievalism' and a tendency to employ cultural studies rather than more 'formal' philological approaches?[871] Is it thanks to the works of scholars like Régine Pernoud, Georges Duby and Michel Zink, who worked tirelessly for decades to publish both scholarly and popular texts about the Middle Ages and medieval figures? Zink, himself the author of medievalizing fiction (*Le Tiers d'amours* and *Déodat ou le chevalier de la transparence*), has singlehandedly renewed secondary-school study of medieval literature by supporting the *Lettres Gothiques* editions of medieval texts, which provide access to Old French and side-by-side translations into modern French. Or is it the revival of popular films and spectacles devoted to the Middle Ages: *Les Visiteurs* and its two sequels, Disney's *Le Bossu de Notre-Dame*, *Notre-Dame de Paris* the musical, or recent films about Joan of Arc and Charlemagne? Perhaps it is the enormous number of historical novels set in the Middle Ages and on display in bookstores throughout France? Could it be the advent of a new millennium that fosters interest in the past? Or are the Middle Ages cropping up in reaction to worries about the disappearance of the French franc and the role the country should play in a united Europe? The Middle Ages of popular and high culture continue to develop together, one movement fueling the other as they did at the end of the nineteenth century.

Regardless of the catalyst for the most recent wave of interest in the Middle Ages and the strikingly different ways in which this time is invoked, the Middle Ages remain a treasured part of the French heritage; they are still considered the origin of the modern French nation. Throughout this book we have 'resurrected' the popular and scholarly manifestations of interest in the Middle Ages that occurred at the end of the nineteenth century in order to show the extent of the phenomenon and to probe the questions it often raises. Why, at a time of great political, religious and artistic unrest and worry, did the Middle Ages develop into one of the most cherished and celebrated periods of French history? The country formed museums and held exhibitions of medieval art while modern artists and writers imitated medieval works and the government began to appreciate and protect medieval monuments and cathedrals. We have seen many causes for such fascination in this book: a search for national identity, worries about industrialization and artistic production, disillusionment with modern society and attempts to reinstate the religious core of the nation. In the turbulent period known as the fin de siècle, as today, the Middle Ages had something for everyone: gorgeous art and fascinating architecture, literary and musical creations, political and social resilience and liberating laughter all provided a model for what the French nation had been and could be.

*Consuming the Past* has revealed how interest in the Middle Ages cut across all levels of French culture and profoundly influenced the ways in which the French conceived themselves. In contrast to scholars who have argued that the medieval revival in the nineteenth century was nothing more than a self-serving fad, a fleeting escapist interest in castles and legends, we have argued that it did continue to perpetuate nostalgic Romantic myths about cathedrals, Crusades and supernatural tales, but that it also explored real historical figures, events and art by calling attention to medieval documents and artwork. This curiosity about the vestiges of the material culture of the Middle Ages grew enormously after the defeat of the Franco-Prussian war and developed into an appreciation for, among other things, the accomplishments of the French nation.[872] Using the Middle Ages as an anchor for modern French identity created an indispensable story about France that would later help the nation survive the separation of Church and State; it would hold down a country suddenly drifting away from its familiar order.[873]

As France, the 'eldest daughter of the Catholic Church,' cut ties with the Church in 1905, as she had with the monarchy just over one hundred years earlier, the Middle Ages provided a different kind of original 'family' history that included the people (*le peuple*). It is no surprise that so many of the manifestations of interest in the Middle Ages, from the *Primitifs* to medieval fairs, focus on the popular Middle Ages and return over and over to lower-class ancestors, imaging contemporaries side by side with their medieval forebears. Jules Lemaître summarized this sentiment in describing his response to Gaston Paris's *La Poésie du Moyen Age* (1885):

> The Middle Ages are really us […] the men of these ancient times are really our fathers […] Nothing touches me more than knowing what my faraway ancestors were like, what they said, what they wrote, what they thought, what they suffered, how they dreamed the dream of life – and to find their soul in me. It is the past that makes the present worthwhile and that gives the present its form. It is in the past that we must live, if only to be moved by it: in thinking fondly about our ancestors we think fondly about ourselves.[874]

According to Lemaître, the texts and artwork left by these ancestors and published by scholars like Paris so reflected the sentiments of the people living during the fin de siècle that readers felt as though the Middle Ages were truly at the origin of the modern French nation. This sense of belonging rested less on a shared religious heritage – now being fiercely contested – than on national identity. Medievalism – interest in the historical or imaginary Middle Ages – provided a center for the secular nationalism that grew out of this period and through World War I, serving as a new religion that facilitated the development of a stable sense of national identity once King and Church were gone.

The French did not simply conceive of the Middle Ages as a long-vanished period; they sought traces of them in modern life, thus reaffirming their commitment to the values they believed the Middle Ages represented and their dedication to protecting them or to rebuilding them. This often involved finding the Middle Ages in the fin de siècle: singer-songwriters continuing the traditions of troubadours, pilgrims imitating their medieval forebears, artist *Primitifs* and cathedral worshipers. As people searched for a stable identity in a troubled time, the Middle Ages, with its blend of worship, secular celebrations and beautiful art and architecture provided the perfect model for late nineteenth-century consumption. Buying a piece of the Middle

Ages or participating in neo-medieval festivities worked on two levels: it reminded modern consumers of a glorious past, while allowing them to reattach such artifacts to their time, a new period that would recognize the past and equal its artistic and economic glory.

Vestiges of this concept of the Middle Ages as stable national origin linger in modern medievalism, which continues to embrace Gaston Paris's and Léon Gautier's concept of the Middle Ages as 'knowable' or 'understandable.' As Richard Glejzer has pointed out, this tendency to consider the Middle Ages as 'an object of knowledge' unconsciously repeats the nineteenth-century tendency to overlook the subjectivity inherent in modern interpretations of medieval culture:

> [...] We are still left with a medievalism that pursues the Middle Ages as foundational, as a mythic moment of origin, much like a medieval preoccupation with Troy, forever lost, destroyed, wiped out, and irrecoverable. But unlike the medieval preoccupation with Troy, the New Medievalism expects to raise the city from its ashes, to reconstruct the Middle Ages bit by bit so that the Middle Ages can in turn metonymically hold together the methodology on which it has been generated.[875]

In focusing on the dream of resurrecting a vanished world, Glejzer underlines the goal modern medievalists often share with their late nineteenth-century ancestors: they seek to contextualize the abundant vestiges of medieval culture that exist today, thus formulating a coherent and accurate understanding of the medieval period. As long as we focus on 'resurrecting,' 'recreating' or 'resuscitating' the medieval world in order to understand the artists, writers and thinkers it 'produced,' we will continue to follow the impossible fin-de-siècle dream of accurately 'knowing' the Middle Ages. No amount of contextualization can bring us closer to recreating medieval life.[876]

In France, emphasis still tends to lie on 'understanding' the 'real' Middle Ages because, as Anne-Marie Thiesse has pointed out, 'belonging to the nation means inheriting this common and indivisible patrimony, knowing it and treasuring it.'[877] Even if it was only after 1871 that the medieval period became permanently ingrained in the national imagination as a positive period of French history, it is now an inseparable part of the story of France's past, a *lieu de mémoire*. Indeed, the legends consecrated at the end of the nineteenth century tend to reappear at the beginning of the twenty-first century. As France has struggled with issues of immigration, globalization, linguistic degeneration, economic change and shifting social and gender roles over the last 150 years, figures from the Middle Ages – Clovis, Charlemagne, Joan of Arc, the pilgrim, the cathedral – have appeared over and over again to reflect these concerns, but also to evoke the treasured national collective, a common past.[878] Then, as now, there were many Middle Ages, each appealing to individuals for different reasons. Yet in fin-de-siècle France, nearly everyone came to accept the fiction that the period itself had laid the foundation for modern French society.[879] Indeed, of the numerous representations of the Middle Ages that we have explored in *Consuming the Past*, most focused on the period's structure and stability: everything in the

Middle Ages was understood as having a place in a vast and well-balanced system. From chivalric orders, church hierarchies and brotherhoods (of musicians, actors and monks) to minstrels and pilgrimage groups, the Middle Ages were represented as a time when groups worked in unity against the backdrop of great common dangers (sickness, poverty, violence, invasion).

While the Middle Ages contributed to the construction of a stable national identity in France, they held a deep appeal throughout fin-de-siècle Europe. As an embodiment of a pre-industrial, faith-infused way of life, the medieval world seemed to offer an inspiring model for a culture exhausted by change and the shock of modern metropolitan existence. Its particular appeal in France is undoubtedly due, in part, to the fact that mass culture and other elements of modern city life first took recognizable shape and form in Paris, the 'capital of the nineteenth century.'[880] Above all, the medieval world was perceived as belonging to a cohesive social network – comprised of family, society, guild or order – that was seen as vanishing in the fin de siècle. Troubadour, page or monk-artist, all knew their place and were indebted to those in their circle, tied to a wider network on which they depended and which, in turn, depended on them. The longing for the Middle Ages then as now is driven by a desire for prestige or for a closer-knit community with greater unity, by a craving for a more satisfying spiritual experience or by a sheer love of objects made according to a different measure of time and a different notion of labor. In spite of the many changes since the nineteenth century, the Middle Ages still exert their fascination over us, leading us to study them, to idealize them, to reinvent them. The past consumes us as we continue to consume the past.

# Notes

1. Pendant les trois quarts du XIXe siècle, les archéologues furent à peu près seuls à se douter de l'intérêt que l'étude du Moyen Age, de ses monuments et de ses oeuvres d'art réservait aux esprits modernes. Nous avons montré combien fut superficiel, chez les poètes romantiques, le goût du médiéval [...] Peintres et poètes de ce temps-là, quel que fût leur génie, ne virent dans le Moyen Age qu'un magasin d'accessoires point encore défraîchis, ils y puisèrent des éléments de pittoresque plastique et dramatique, belles draperies et beaux gestes, sans contrôle, sans critique, et leur Moyen Age n'est pas vrai.

    On se fatigue du mensonge pittoresque. Le romantisme en mourut. Les hommes de la seconde moitié du dernier siècle furent pris d'un immense besoin de vérité [...] les travaux d'une pléiade d'hommes distingués [...] créèrent la science de notre archéologie nationale, la révélèrent aux artistes et aux savants, la firent pénétrer dans l'enseignement classique, y intéressèrent les gens du monde, initièrent le peuple même à notre passé artistique [...] 'Introduction' to Auguste Rodin's *Les Cathédrales de France* (Paris: Librairie Armand Colin, 1914), pp. 96, 98. Unless otherwise indicated, all translations from the French are ours.

2. See, for example, Norman F. Cantor's *Inventing the Middle Ages: The Lives, Works and Ideas of the Great Medievalists of the Twentieth Century* (New York: William Morrow, 1991) and the annual 'Makers of the Middle Ages' sessions sponsored by *Studies in Medievalism* at the international medieval congresses in Kalamazoo, Michigan and Leeds, England.

3. A cursory list of such works includes Louis Maigron, *Le Romantisme et la mode* (Paris: H. Champion, 1911); Norris J. Lacy, 'The French Romantics and Medieval Literature: A Biographical Essay,' *Studies in Medievalism* vol. 3 no. 1 (Fall 1987), pp. 87–97; Patricia Ward, *The Medievalism of Victor Hugo* (University Park: Pennsylvania State University Press, 1975); Lionel Gossman, *Medievalism and the Ideologies of the Enlightenment* (Baltimore: Johns Hopkins Press, 1968); Michael Glencross, *Reconstructing Camelot: French Romantic Medievalism and the Arthurian Tradition* (Cambridge: D. S. Brewer, 1995); Paul Frankl, *The Gothic* (Princeton, NJ: Princeton University Press, 1960); Kevin L. Morris, *The Image of the Middle Ages in Romantic and Victorian Literature* (Dover, NH: Croom Helm, 1984); and Clare A. Simmons's concise overview of medievalism from the 18th to the 21st century: 'Introduction' to *Medievalism and the Quest for the 'Real' Middle Ages* (London: Frank Cass, 2000), pp. 1–28. For an introduction to the vast and well-chronicled field of British medievalism see Edward Kaufman and Sharon Irish, *Medievalism: An Annotated Bibliography of Recent Research in the Art and Architecture of Britain and North America* (New York: Garland Publishing, 1988); Arthur Johnston, *Enchanted Ground* (London: Athlone Press, 1964); Alice Chandler, *A Dream of Order: The Medieval Ideal in Nineteenth-Century English Literature* (Lincoln: University of Nebraska Press, 1970); Mark Girouard, *The Return to Camelot* (New Haven: Yale University Press, 1981); Paul Atterbury, Clive Wainwright *et al.*, *Pugin: A Gothic Passion* (New Haven: Yale University Press, 1994); Susan P. Casteras, *John Ruskin and the Victorian Eye* (New York: Abrams, 1993).

4. The notable exception is Janine R. Dakyns's wonderful 1973 study of *The Middle Ages in French Literature 1851–1914* (London: Oxford University Press), which catalogues references to the Middle Ages in the period. Yet even this study, with its impressive breadth, concentrates primarily on literature and not on the broader popularity of the Middle Ages. Similarly, Charles Ridoux's indispensable *Evolution des études médiévales en France de 1860 à 1914* (not yet available when our work went to press), focuses primarily on the scholarly medievalism of the period (Paris: Honoré Champion, 2001).

5. Our choice of the period between the Franco-Prussian war and the separation of Church and State does not propose that medievalism in France was limited to this period. On the contary, it was an influential movement that marked society beginning with the French Revolution (see Chapter 1). The years from 1871 to 1905 merely witnessed the greatest popular interest in the medieval period. Recent examples of scholarship in medievalism include publications related to Leslie Workman's *Studies in Medievalism*, the Centre for Medieval Studies at the University of

Sydney's book series *Making the Middle Ages*, Christian Almalvi's *Le Goût du Moyen Age* (Paris: Plon, 1997) and essay collections edited by Clare A. Simmons (*Medievalism and the Quest for the 'Real' Middle Ages* (London: Frank Cass, 2000)) and Howard Bloch and Stephen Nichols (*Medievalism and the Modernist Temper* (Baltimore: The Johns Hopkins Press, 1996)). The three volumes of *Medieval Scholarship: Biographical Studies on the Formation of a Discipline* edited by Helen Damico (New York: Garland Press, 1995–2000) trace the influence of scholars in medieval studies from the sixteenth to the twentieth centuries. Alain Corbellari's biography of Joseph Bédier and Ursula Bähler's study of Gaston Paris (forthcoming with Droz) are critical pieces for understanding the medievalism of this period.

6.  For an excellent and succinct description of these theories and their application to French history, see Robert Gildea, *The Past in French History* (New Haven: Yale University Press, 1994), pp. 10–12, 340. Although his study traces interpretations of the more recent French past, his claim that 'there is no single French collective memory but parallel and competing collective memories, and that the past is constructed not as fact but as myth, to serve the interest of a particular community' (p. 340) summarizes the dynamics at play in late nineteenth-century French attitudes toward the Middle Ages.

7.  Only one recent publication, the collection of conference presentations edited by Anne Ducrey and entitled *Le Moyen Age en 1900*, has attempted to bridge this gap by focusing on manifestations of medievalism over a short period of time (Lille: *Ateliers* 26, Cahiers de la Maison de la Recherche, Université Charles-de-Gaulle, 2000).

8.  In adopting the term *fin de siècle*, we follow Eugèn Weber, who distinguishes the 1880s and 1890s (this period called itself the fin de siècle), from the decade or so preceding World War I. Later, the entire period came to be known as the *Belle Epoque*. See *France, Fin de Siècle* (Cambridge: Belknap Press, 1986), pp. 1–2.

9.  See Dakyns, who separates her study of the Middle Ages in French literature according to 'colorful' political regimes.

10. See Rosalind Williams, *Dream Worlds: Mass Consumption in Late Nineteenth Century France* (Berkeley and Los Angeles: University of California Press, 1982); Whitney Walton, *France at the Crystal Palace: Bourgeois Taste and Artisan Manufacture in the Nineteenth Century* (Berkeley: University of California Press, 1992); Lisa Tiersten, *Marianne in the Market: Envisioning Consumer Culture in Fin-de-siècle France* (Berkeley: University of California Press, 2001).

11. Malcolm Chase and Christopher Shaw have shown the importance of dissatisfaction with the present for creating nostalgia for the past in 'The Dimensions of Nostalgia,' *The Imagined Past: History and Nostalgia* (Manchester: Manchester University Press, 1989), pp. 1–17. They find that a secular and linear sense of time, disillusionment with the present and availability of objects and images from the past are requirements for creating nostalgia, pp. 2–4.

12. As David Lowenthal notes, 'L'héritage n'est pas l'histoire […] c'est une déclaration de foi dans ce passé.' 'La Fabrication d'un héritage' in Dominique Poulot, *Patrimonie et Modernité* (Paris: L'Harmattan, 1998), pp. 110, 118.

13. See Chapter 1 and our discussion of the writings of Victor Hugo and Viollet-le-Duc.

14. See Chapter 1. Throughout the nineteenth century, the Middle Ages were either praised or denigrated; there was no uniform consensus about their importance for French history and culture.

15. Indeed, we believe that culture is not exclusively 'high culture'; 'all forms of cultural production should be studied with regard to others and to social and historical structures.' This is a central point made by Cary Nelson, Paul A. Treichler and Lawrence Grossberg in their 'Introduction' to *Cultural Studies*, p. 4; eds Lawrence Grossberg, Cary Nelson, Paula A. Treichler (New York: Routledge, 1992), pp. 1–22.

16. We discuss this situation in Chapter 4. For more information about the disastrous results of the separation of Church and State, see Jean-Michel Leniaud, *Les Cathédrales au XIXe siècle* (Paris: Economica, 1993), pp. 81–2 and Louis Réau, *Histoire du vandalisme* (Paris: Editions Robert Laffont, 1994), pp. 813–17. Elizabeth Emery has argued that this defense of medieval religious architecture led to a new appreciation of the medieval heritage after 1905; *Romancing the Cathedral: Gothic Architecture in Fin-de-Siècle French Culture* (Albany, NY: State University of New York Press, 2001).

17. The recent catalog for the Art Nouveau exhibit at Washington's National Gallery makes interesting comparisons in this regard, presenting Art Nouveau as a fusion of Gothic and Rococo. *Art Nouveau: 1890–1914*, ed. Paul Greenhalgh (Washington, D.C.: National Gallery of Art, 2000). See also Stephan Tschudi Madsen, *Sources of Art Nouveau*, trans. Ragnar Christophersen (New York: Da Capo Publishing, Inc., 1980).

18. While the new architectural designs for churches, castles and private residences inspired by Viollet's theories constitute a vast and interesting field for medievalism, this topic merits its own book. In fact, many art historians have already explored his crucial importance for modern architecture. Useful references include the *Actes du Colloque international Viollet-le-Duc* (Paris: Nouvelles Editions Latines, 1982); 'Structural Rationalism and the Influence of Viollet-

le-Duc: Gaudí, Horta, Guimard and Berlage 1880–1910' in Kenneth Frampton, *Modern Architecture: A Critical History* (London: Thames and Hudson, 1985), pp. 64–74; Bertrand Lemoine, *Architecture in France, 1800–1900*, trans. Alexandra Bonfante-Warren (New York: Harry N. Abrams, Inc., 1998), pp. 10–25.

19.  See, for example, Jeffrey Cohen's collection of essays entitled *The Postcolonial Middle Ages* (New York: St. Martin's Press, 2000).

20.  John Ganim's on-going research into eighteenth and nineteenth-century European orientalism and medievalism provides a starting point. Some of his work on this topic has been published in 'Native Studies: Orientalism and Medievalism,' a chapter of *The Postcolonial Middle Ages*, pp. 123–34.

21.  A starting point is Michael Camille's 'The *Très Riches Heures*: An Illuminated Manuscript in the Age of Mechanical Reproduction,' *Critical Inquiry* 17 (Autumn 1990), pp. 72–107. The importance of private collectors of medieval works for the history of medievalism in this period remains a fascinating arena of investigation.

22.  *Manuscript Illumination in the Modern Age*, edited by Sandra Hindman, Michael Camille, Nina Rowe and Rowan Watson, provides an extremely valuable look at the reproduction and collection of medieval manuscripts from the eighteenth to the twentieth century (Evanston: Mary and Leigh Block Museum of Art, Northwestern University, 2001).

23.  Ruskin's theories on art, extremely popular in Britain in the 1850s and 1860s, were little appreciated in France until the 1890s. For an exploration of the belated French enthusiasm for Ruskin and the Pre-Raphaelites in France, see Jean Autret, *L'influence de Ruskin sur la vie, les idées et l'œuvre de Marcel Proust* (Geneva: Droz, 1955). There is an enormous amount of literature dedicated to William Morris, beginning with David Latham's *An Annotated Critical Bibliography of William Morris* (New York: St. Martin's Press, 1991). Points of departure for examining Morris's influence in France are Georges Vidalenc, *William Morris* (Paris: F. Alcan, 1920) and Thomas Walton, 'A French Disciple of William Morris: Jean Lahor,' *Revue de littérature comparée* 15:3 (1935), pp. 524–35.

24.  For a study that looks at the revival of other historical paradigms in this period, see Debora Silverman, *Art Nouveau in Fin-de-Siècle France* (Berkeley: University of California Press, 1989). Although she argues that the French rejected the medieval artisan as a model for art nouveau, preferring instead the rococo artisan, we disagree. Both traditions exerted an influence on new developments in national art.

25.  *Le Figaro illustré* published different variations of this advertisement, but each featuring the same time periods. The December 1900 issue, for example, proposed a Louis XI living room, a Louis XV bedroom and an art nouveau dining room.

26.  See Debora Silverman, pp. 126–32. Because Silverman and others have so well explored late nineteenth-century interest in the eighteenth century, rococo revival and Japonism, we will not linger on these aspects in our book.

27.  See, for example, Stéphane Gerson, 'Pays and nation: The Uneasy Formation of an Historical Patrimony in France, 1830–1870' (Ph.D. thesis, University of Chicago, 1997). This study treats an earlier period, but does reveal links between popular celebration, medievalism and national identity in the French provinces.

28.  In our use of the term 'avant-garde,' we follow the definition proposed by Peter Bürger in 'On the Problem of the Autonomy of Art': a position that attacks 'the status of art in a bourgeois society,' demanding the end of art as an institution and questioning the purpose, production and reception of art in society. In Francis Frascina and Jonathan Harris, eds, *Art in Modern Culture* (London: Phaidon, 1992), pp. 51–63.

29.  He introduced the term *lieu de mémoire* in the eponymous seven-volume work he directed from 1984–1992 (*Les Lieux de Mémoire*. Paris: Gallimard). It has now entered major dictionaries such as *Le Grand Robert de la langue française* to refer to people, places, things and events that have been consecrated as part of the national heritage. See Nora's preface to the English edition, in which he defines the term (*Realms of Memory*. New York: Columbia University Press, 1992), pp. xv–xxiv.

30.  Dean MacCannell, *The Tourist: A New Theory of the Leisure Class* (New York: Schoken Books, 1976), p. 82.

31.  'L'hégémonie de la France, aux XIIe et XIIIe siècles, dans les arts comme dans les lettres, n'est plus contestée aujourd'hui. Les érudits d'Allemagne, d'Angleterre, de Scandinavie, d'Italie, ne sont pas les moins ardents à recueillir nos titres de gloire.' Georges Lafenestre, 'Introduction,' *Expositions des Primitifs français au Palais du Louvre (Pavillon de Marsan) et à la Bibliothèque Nationale* (April 1904), p. xii.

32.  The works were grouped in five sections: paintings and drawings, manuscripts and miniatures, tapestries and painted embroideries, enamels and sculptures. By far the largest group was that of painting, including such newly recognized masters as Nicolas Froment, the Master of Moulins, Jean Bourdichon and Jean Clouet.

33. The series of seven tapestries was created for the chapel in the cathedral of Angers. Commissioned by Duke Louis d'Anjou in 1378, the 65½ foot long hangings were based on manuscript illuminations of the *Apocalypse* in the collection of Charles V. For information on these tapestries see Pierre Marie Auza, *et al.*, *Die Apokalypse von Angers: Ein Meisterwerk Mittelalterlicher Teppichwirkerei* (Munich: Hirmer, 1985).

34. The artists, claimed Lafenestre, ' … avaient déja, d'un oeil libre et hardi, embrassé tout le champ des réalités humaines. Ils n'avaient rien à apprendre de personne en fait de sincerité, délicate ou brutale, d'observation grave ou maligne.' *Exposition des Primitifs français au Palais du Louvre (Pavillon de Marsan) et à la Bibliothèque Nationale* (Paris, 1904), p. xviii. 'Ils sont les premiers constructeurs, les premiers modeleurs d'Europe; leurs verriers et leurs orfèvres n'ont rien à emprunter aux autres.' Henri Bouchot, *L'Exposition des Primitifs français: La Peinture en France sous les Valois* (Paris: Librairie Centrale des Beaux-Arts, 1904), p. ii.

35. 'L'Exposition des Primitifs français n'a pas eu pour but de montrer la superiorité des Français sur les peuples voisins, mais, simplement de prouver leur existence parallèle à d'autres, et en certains cas leur priorité […] Certaines personnes ont parlé avec dédain du faux patriotisme, du nationalisme inattendu soupçonné sous le titre de Primitifs français. Il n'y a pas à nier, Primitifs français n'est ni Primitifs belges ni italiens […].' Henri Bouchot, *Les Primitifs français: 1292–1500/ Complément documentaire au catalogue officiel de l'Exposition* (Paris: Librairie de l'art ancien et moderne, 1904), pp. 7, 28.

36. 'Alors que Cimabué et ses contemporains s'ingénient à grandir au carreau les miniatures des moins orientaux, et se condamnent aux redites, les artistes de l'Ile de France, sans direction traditionnelle, s'émancipent et se cherchent des modèles à leur portée.' Bouchot, *L'Exposition des Primitifs*, p. ii.

37. 'Depuis que les Gaulois, nos ancêtres, amis des couleurs vives et des paroles sonores, furent initiés par leur conquérants aux séductions de la culture gréco-romaine, la pratique des arts, plastiques ou littéraires, n'a guère été interrompu dans notre pays.' Lafenestre, p. i.

38. The *Gazette des Beaux-Arts* of 1904 served as a virtual advertisement for the show, including coverage of the event by the leading organizers and articles devoted to research on the 'newly discovered' *Primitifs* and their works. See *Gazette des Beaux-Arts* 31 (January–June 1904).

39. Dakyns, p. 2.

40. 'Chacun se façonne un moyen âge imaginaire […] et chacun se fait sa foi et son credo politique suivant l'erreur à laquelle il a donné sa préférence ou à laquelle son éducation première l'a enchaîné. Autant de façons d'envisager le moyen âge, autant de partis en France: ce sont nos théories historiques qui nous divisent le plus … ' Fustel de Coulanges, 'L'Invasion germanique au cinquième siècle,' *Revue des Deux Mondes* (15 May 1872), pp. 537–8.

41. This notion is reflected in the title of several books and articles devoted to nineteenth-century medievalism. See, for example, Leslie Workman's constant refinement of the term 'medievalism' in his introductions to the journal *Studies in Medievalism*; Norman Cantor's *Inventing the Middle Ages*; and an exhibition catalog from l'Hôtel de Sully entitled *Le 'Gothique' retrouvé avant Viollet-le-Duc* (Paris: Caisse nationale des monuments historiques et des sites, 1979).

42. On the continued interest in the Middle Ages during and after the Renaissance, see Nathan Edelman, *Attitudes of Seventeenth Century France toward the Middle Ages* (New York: King's Crown Press, 1946), Colleen Hays, 'Literary History and Criticism of French Medieval Works in the Nineteenth Century: The Phenomenon of Medievalism' (Ph.D. thesis, University of Oklahoma, 1993) and Barbara Keller, *The Middle Ages Reconsidered: Attitudes in France from the Eighteenth Century through the Romantic Movement* (New York: Peter Lang, 1984). Certain medieval characters, such as Joan of Arc, never went out of vogue. See Pierre Lanéry d'Arc, *Le Livre d'or de Jeanne d'Arc. Catalogue méthodique, descriptif et critique des principales études historiques, littéraires et artistiques, consacrées à la Pucelle d'Orléans depuis le XVe siècle jusqu'à nos jours* (Paris, Techener, 1894); Marcellin Desfourneaux, 'Jeanne d'Arc après cinq siècles,' *Bulletin de l'Institut français en Espagne* 39 (November 1954); Nadia Margolis, *Joan of Arc in History, Literature and Film: a Select, Annotated Bibliography*. Garland Reference Library of the Humanities, vol. 1224 (New York, Garland Publishing, 1990); and Jeroom Vercruysse, 'Jeanne d'Arc au siècle des Lumières,' *Studies on Voltaire and the Eighteenth Century* 90 (1972), pp. 659–729. For a consideration of attitudes to medieval works prior to the nineteenth century in the field of art history, see Tina Waldeier Bizzarro, *Romanesque Architectural Criticism: A Prehistory* (Cambridge: Cambridge University Press, 1992) and Paul Frankl.

43. See especially Gossman's final chapter, entitled 'Medievalism and Enlightenment.'

44. For more information about the 'troubadour style' see François Pupil, *Le Style troubadour: ou la nostalgie du bon vieux temps* (Nancy: Presses Universitaires de Nancy, 1985); Marie-Claude Chaudonneret, *Fleury Richard et Pierre Révoil: la peinture troubadour* (Paris: Athena, 1980); Henri Jacoubet, *Le Genre troubadour et les origines françaises du romantisme* (Paris: Société d'édition 'Les Belles Lettres', 1929); and the 1971 exhibit organized by the city of Bourg-en-Bresse, *Le Style Troubadour* (Le Musée de Bourg-en-Bresse, 1971).

45. Dakyns, p. 4, and Guiomar, *La Nation entre l'histoire et la raison* (Paris: Editions La Découverte, 1990), pp. 36–7.

46. The term 'fureur gothique' comes from Louis Maigron's description of the trend in *Le Romantisme et la mode*. 'Frenzy' is from Luc Steinmetz's 1978 anthology of texts, *La France frénétique de 1830* (Paris: Phébus, 1978), which evokes a similarly wild emotional investment in the Middle Ages. Though dated, Doolittle's 1933 dissertation, 'The Relations Between Literature and Mediaeval Studies in France from 1820 to 1860' (Ph.D. thesis, Bryn Mawr, Pennsylvania, 1933), remains one of the most valuable reference sources for this period. See Norris Lacy for more recent information about this period's interest in the Middle Ages. In *The Medievalism of Victor Hugo*, Patricia Ward gives a succinct overview of the Romantic infatuation with the Middle Ages.

47. For a discussion of the Gothic Revival in Europe see Frankl; Penelope Hunter-Stiebel, *Of Knights and Spires: Gothic Revival in France and Germany* (New York, NY: Rosenberg & Stiebel, 1989); and Megan Aldrich, *Gothic Revival* (London: Phaidon, 1999). See Frederick S. Frank, *Guide to the Gothic: An Annotated Bibliography of Criticism* (Metuchen, NJ: Scarecrow Press, 1984) for a bibliography demonstrating the voluminous writing about the Gothic Revival in England.

48. Maigron describes such fads and publishes images of early nineteenth-century jewelry and furnishings designed to imitate medieval art.

49. Dakyns, pp. 26–8. Writing in 1914, Charles Morice would similarly comment on the 'superficiality' of the Romantic Middle Ages and their appreciation of the Middle Ages as a 'magasin d'accessoires point encore défraîchis,' p. lxxvi. On a more scholarly level, an extremely valuable study by Michael Glencross exposes the more profound historical influence Arthurian legends exerted over the period from 1812–1860.

50. 'C'est vers le Moyen Age énorme et délicat/[...] Haute théologie et solide morale,/Guidé par la folie unique de la Croix/Sur tes ailes de pierre, ô folle Cathédrale!' Paul Verlaine, *Sagesse* x, 14 (1880). *Oeuvres poétiques complètes* (Paris: Editions Gallimard, 1962), p. 249.

51. 'L'âge de la féerie et des enchantements.' *Le Génie du Christianisme* (Paris: Garnier-Flammarion, Chateaubriand, 1966), p. 73, pp. 400–401.

52. In 1906, art historian André Michel traced Chateaubriand's theories in the works of his colleagues. *Histoire de l'art depuis les premiers temps chrétiens jusqu'à nos jours*, vol. 2 (Paris: Librairie Armand Colin, 1906), p. iv. For more about Chateaubriand's influence, see Emery, *Romancing the Cathedral*, pp. 13–15.

53. See Dakyns, pp. 75–77 and Michel Winock, 'Joan of Arc,' trans. Arthur Goldhammer, *Realms of Memory: The Construction of the French Past*, vol 3 (New York: Columbia University Press, 1993), p. 441.

54. See Jean Mallion, *Victor Hugo et l'art architectural* (Paris: Presses Universitaires de France, 1962), pp. 533–52 for a discussion of theories by which Hugo was inspired. Many of his beliefs about the development of the Gothic style and the Crusades were borrowed from the art-historical works of Sulpice Boisserée. For a more detailed description of Hugo's belief in the inherent democracy of Gothic architecture, see Emery, *Romancing the Cathedral*, pp. 15–20.

55. 'La cathédrale elle-même, cet édifice autrefois si dogmatique, envahie désormais par la bourgeoisie, par la commune, par la liberté, échappe au prêtre et tombe au pouvoir de l'artiste. L'artiste la bâtit à sa guise. Adieu le mystère, le mythe, la loi. Voici la fantaisie et le caprice [ ... la cathédrale] est à l'imagination, à la poésie, au peuple.' *Notre-Dame de Paris*, *Oeuvres complètes*, vol. iv, ed. Jean Massin (Paris: Le Club français du livre, 1967), p. 138.

56. Viollet-le-Duc (1814–1879) was a teenager when Hugo's novel was published; the book greatly influenced his understanding of medieval architecture. For the wide-reaching impact of Hugo's architectural theories, see Jean Mallion. In *Romancing the Cathedral*, Emery traces Hugo's legacy regarding architecture and popular conceptions of the Middle Ages.

57. In the *Dictionnaire raisonné de l'architecture française du XIe au XVIe siècle*, vol. VII (Paris: V.A. Morel, 1875), p. 144. We will return to Viollet-le-Duc and the importance of his theories in Chapter 4.

58. For a discussion of the battles between these scholars and the Ecole des Beaux-Arts that took place over the value of Gothic architecture, see Barry Bergdoll, 'The Ideal of the Gothic Cathedral in 1852' in *A. W. N. Pugin: Master of the Gothic Revival* (New Haven: Yale University Press, 1996), pp. 103–35, and Georg Germann, *Gothic Revival in Europe and Britain: Sources, Influences, and Ideas* (Cambridge, MA: MIT Press, 1973).

59. His bias toward logic over religious belief is clear throughout the *Dictionnaire raisonné de l'architecture française du XIe au XVIe siècle*, but most pronounced, perhaps, in his entry for 'Architecture' in volume 1.

60. 'Mediaeval French Literature', *The North American Review* vol. 128: 267 (Februrary 1879), p. 213.

61. 'La révolution a été une guerre, la vraie guerre, telle que le monde la connaît entre peuples étrangers. Depuis plus de treize siècles la France en contenait deux, un peuple vainqueur et un peuple vaincu ... Notre histoire est l'histoire de cette lutte ... ' (Cited in Amalvi, 1988), p. 21.

Since the sixteenth century one of the leading myths of national origin asserted that the common people of France had descended from the conquered Gauls while the aristocracy shared the blood of the conquering Franks. For a lengthy discussion of this theory and its impact on nationalism in nineteenth-century France see Colleen Beth Hays (1993) and Pierre Nora, ed., *Les Lieux de mémoire* (Paris: Gallimard, 1984). For more about the perceived importance of the Gauls in the formation of French identity, see Pierre Pinon, *La Gaule retrouvée* (Paris: Gallimard, 1991) and Suzanne Citron, *Le mythe national: L'histoire de France en question* (Paris: Editions Ouvrières, 1987).

62. Jean Pommier and Laurence Richer propose that Michelet's shift resulted from his dislike of the Second Empire and its attempt to renew the Catholic values of the past in the nineteenth century. See Emery, *Romancing the Cathedral*, p. 23; Jean Pommier, 'Michelet et l'architecture gothique,' *Etudes de lettres* 26 (December 1954), pp. 17–35; Laurence Richer, *La Cathédrale du feu. Le Moyen Age de Michelet, de l'histoire au mythe* (Nîmes: Editions Palaam, 1995).

63. For a discussion of some of these scholars and the works they studied from 1830–1870, see Dakyns (1973), Glencross (1995), Ridoux (2001) and Bloch and Nichols, eds.

64. 'Pendant les trois quarts du XIXe siècle, les archéologues furent à peu près seuls à se douter de l'intérêt que l'étude du Moyen Age, de ses monuments et de ses oeuvres d'art réservait aux esprits modernes. Nous avons montré combien fut superficiel, chez les poètes romantiques, le goût du médiéval [...]' This is the quotation that begins our book.

65. Between 1871 and 1876, for example, *La Revue des Deux Mondes,* the pre-eminent periodical of the time, devoted nearly 25 per cent of its articles about art and history – many of which purported to trace the origins of modern French institutions – to the Middle Ages. In its previous 40 years of publication it had devoted only six per cent of its art and history articles to medieval topics. 22.8 per cent of the art and history articles from 1871–1876 treat medieval topics. Only 5.89 per cent of articles in these categories discussed the Middle Ages from 1831–1870. See Emery, 'The "Truth" About the Middle Ages: *La Revue des Deux Mondes* and Late Nineteenth-Century French Medievalism,' *The Quest for the 'Real' Middle Ages*, ed. Clare A. Simmons (London: Frank Cass, 2001), pp. 99–114.

66. See Barbara Spackman, *Decadent Genealogies: The Rhetoric of Sickness from Baudelaire to D'Annunzio* (Ithaca: Cornell University Press, 1989) for the term 'rhetoric of sickness' and see A. E. Carter, *The Idea of Decadence in French Literature 1830–1900* (Toronto: Toronto University Press, 1958) for an overview of the phenomenon in France.

67. An 18 December 1897 article in *Le Temps* about the project for a school holiday to celebrate Joan of Arc refers to the memory of the war as a still unhealed wound. 'Le souvenir des humiliations passées dit M. Evellin, doit être fécond. C'est lui qui, de nouveau, trempera les âmes et inspirera les héroïques résolutions. Toujours penser à nos malheurs n'est pas possible, pensons-y souvent, et pour y penser souvent, décidons-nous à y penser en commun. Ne remettons pas non plus la décision nécessaire. Plus se prolongera l'attente, plus risquera de se refermer et de guérir la blessure faite à notre honneur de nation; or, il ne faut pas que cette blessure guérisse, si l'on veut que la fête du patriotisme garde toute son efficacité et toute sa vertu.'

68. For discussions of the prevalence of this theory in the national mindset, see Colleen Beth Hays (1993) and Alfred Leroux, *Essai sur les antécédents historiques de la question allemande 843–1493* (Paris: Alphonse Picard et fils, 1892). Emery traces the explosion of interest in medieval history following the war in 'The "Truth".'

69. 'Il semble qu'il [l'événement] ait changé la face du pays et donné à ses destinées une direction qu'elles n'auraient pas eue sans lui. Il est, pour beaucoup d'historiens et pour la foule, la source d'où est venu tout l'ancien régime. Les seigneurs féodaux passent pour être les fils des Germains, et les serfs de la glèbe pour être les fils des Gaulois. Une conquête; c'est-à-dire un acte brutal, se place ainsi comme l'origine unique de l'ancienne société française. Tous les grands faits de notre histoire sont expliqués et jugés au nom de cette iniquité première. La féodalité est présentée comme le règne des conquérants, l'affranchissement des communes comme le réveil des vaincus, et la révolution de 1789 comme leur revanche.' Fustel (1872), p. 241.

70. 'C'est une étrange erreur que d'avoir cru que la Germanie fût: "la fabrique du genre-humain et la matrice d'où sortent les nations".' Fustel (1872), p. 241.

71. See Emery, 'The "Truth"', p. 103.

72. 'Ce vieux passé, qui n'est plus et qui ne saurait renaître, exerce encore sur nous une domination d'un caractère singulier. Il n'est pas un Français, si ignorant qu'il soit, qui ne parle du moyen âge, qui ne croie le connaître, qui ne prétende le juger [...] Or l'idée que nous nous en faisons, vraie ou fausse, a un tel empire sur notre esprit, que presque tout le courant de nos pensées et de nos opinions vient de là. Observez pourquoi deux hommes pensent différemment sur les questions de gouvernement et de politique, c'est presque toujours parce qu'ils ont deux manières différentes de juger l'ancien régime [...] Deux hommes se rencontrent et discutent sur les affaires publiques; vous croyez qu'ils parlent des intérêts présents, – le plus souvent c'est sur l'ancien régime qu'ils se querellent, et parce qu'ils sont en désaccord sur la façon de

comprendre le passé, les voilà dans l'impossibilité d'être d'accord sur le présent [...] Ainsi l'histoire forme nos opinions.' Fustel de Coulanges, 'La Justice dans le monde féodal,' *Revue des Deux Mondes* (August 1871), pp. 536–7.

73. In the preface to the first volume (1854) of his *Dictionnaire raisonné*, Viollet wrote that 'Ce qui constitue les nationalités, c'est le lien qui unit étroitement les différentes périodes de leur existence; il faut plaindre les peuples qui renient leur passé, car il n'y a pas d'avenir pour eux!' I, p. iii.

74. Eric Hobsbawn and Terence Ranger coined the term in their edited volume *The Invention of Tradition* (Cambridge: Cambridge University Press, 1983). Anthony D. Smith is among the most vocal historians to insist on the crucial nature of myth and history in forging a sense of nationhood. *National Identity* (New York: Penguin, 1991). Anne-Marie Thiesse similarly explores the importance of historical narratives, arguing that it is nationalist discourse that creates the nation and not the reverse. *La Création des identités nationales. Europe XVIIIe–XXe siècles* (Paris: Seuil, 1999), pp. 11–12.

75. 'La fausse interprétation du passé est à l'heure où nous sommes le plus dangereux des poisons [...] Donnez-moi des idées justes sur l'histoire de France, répandez-les à profusion, que le pays s'en nourrisse et s'en pénètre [...] Notre histoire bien comprise est la clé de tous nos problèmes, le principe régénérateur de tout ordre et de tout progrès.' Louis Vitet, *La Revue des Deux Mondes* (15 May 1871), p. 441.

76. See Emery, 'The "Truth",' p. 104.

77. See Anne-Marie Thiesse, who convincingly argues that disseminating well-constructed narratives about common memories and traditions is critical for building nationalism. 'La nation naît d'un postulat et d'une invention. Mais elle ne vit que par l'adhésion collective à cette fiction,' p. 14.

78. Amalvi (1988), p. 26.

79. '[...] il pouvait être salutaire d'évoquer, sur la scène française, avec le souvenir des désastres anciens, le spectacle des héroïques efforts tentés par nos aïeux pour les réparer et pour reconstruire la patrie.' François Coppée and Henri d'Artois, *La Guerre de Cent Ans* (Paris: 1878).

80. 'La France n'a pas connu d'époque plus triste: ni les guerres religieuses du XVIe siècle, ni les guerres modernes comme celle de 1870, ne peuvent donner une idée des souffrances du peuple pendant ces cent seize années.' Edgar Zévort, *Cours moyen. Histoire de France depuis 1328 jusqu'à nos jours, précédée d'une révision de l'Histoire de France depuis les Gaulois jusqu'en 1328 ... Ouvrage rédigé en vue du certificat d'études primaires* (Paris: Picard-Bernheim, 1885), p. 24. This period saw an enormous spate of books and plays on the Hundred Years' War. Although it was the English who battled against the French in this war, France's victimization by another nation served as a parallel for her losses during the Franco-Prussian War.

81. 'Nous nous sommes relevés au XIVe siècle; ne désespérons pas; l'histoire montre comment une réforme sage, vigoureuse et persévérante peut tout sauver et tout rétablir.' A. Carel, *La France après le traité de Brétigny* (Caen: F. Le Blanc-Hardell, 1871), p. 38.

82. See Citron (1987) , Amalvi (1988) and André Simon, *Vercingétorix et l'idéologie française* (Paris: Editions Imago, 1989). For a thorough exploration of this issue in art history, see Chapter 4 in Laura Morowitz, 'Consuming the Past: The Nabis and French Medieval Art' (Ph.D. thesis, New York University, 1996).

83. Henri Martin, *Histoire de France depuis le temps les plus reculés jusqu'en 1789* (Paris: Furne, 1859). Nineteenth-century historians portrayed the native populations of Gaul as Celtic clans resisting Roman culture and customs. The simultaneous existence of Celtic tribes in England, Ireland and Spain seems to have escaped their attention (or at least their interest). Writers with a primarily nationalist stance tended to focus on the Gauls (who lived on what would become French soil), while others were more taken with the Celtic roots of France and its spiritual and religious heritage. For a concise analysis of the roles historians gave to Gauls, Celts and Franks in the development of nineteenth-century historical narratives, see Suzanne Citron, *Le Mythe national*.

84. Paraphrasing Martin, Raison du Cleuziou declared Gothic art an 'art national, disons-nous, art laïque, faut-il ajouter, art anti-monastique, extrasacerdotal, dû aux fraternités d'artisans, aux francs-maçons de l'époque.' Henri Raison du Cleuziou, *L'art national* (Paris: A. le Vasseur Editeur, 1883), p. 46.

85. Winock, p. 443. Indeed, as medievalist Léon Gautier would write in the 1892 edition of *Les Epopées françaises*, it was with the 1870 French defeat against the Prussians that *La Chanson de Roland* and other medieval subjects came into their own. Vol. II (Paris: Librairie Universitaire, 1892), pp. 745–6.

86. 'Roland, lui aussi, était un vaincu; mais une telle défaite n'avait fait subir aucun amoindrissement à sa gloire, et Charlemagne, d'ailleurs, l'avait vengé par une éclatante et décisive victoire. En attendant Charlemagne, nous nous consolâmes avec Roland.' *Les Epopées Françaises*, pp. 745–6.

87.  'Roland, c'est la France faite homme.' *La Chanson de Roland* (Tours: Alfred Mame et fils, éditeurs, 1872), p. vii. Gautier referred to *La Chanson de Roland* as 'l'épopée nationale' and as a rival to the *Iliad* in nearly every preface he wrote for *La Chanson de Roland* and the *Epopées Françaises* after the war.

88.  Paul Déroulède and Henri Martin, respectively. Cited in Winock, p. 441.

89.  For a discussion of Roland as moral and patriotic figure after the war see Amalvi (1988), '*La Chanson de Roland* et l'image de Roland dans la littérature scolaire en France de 1815 à 1914.' Harry Redman, Jr. extensively discusses the use of Roland in nineteenth-century literature in *The Roland Legend in Nineteenth-Century French Literature* (Lexington: University of Kentucky Press, 1991). J. J. Duggan's 'Franco-German Conflict and the History of French Scholarship on the Song of Roland' explores how the French used Roland to compete with Germans (*Hermeneutics and Medieval Culture*, Patrick J. Gallacher and Helen Damico, eds, Albany: State University Press of New York, 1989). For Joan of Arc imagery in the post-war period see Michel Winock (1997), Rosemonde Sanson, 'La Fête de Jeanne d'Arc en 1894: Controverse et Célébration' (*Revue d'histoire moderne et contemporaine* 20 [1973], pp. 444–63) or Marina Warner, *Joan of Arc: The Image of Female Heroism* (New York: Knopf, 1981). The sheer volume of entries in Pierre Lanéry d'Arc's 1894 bibliography of Joan, *Le Livre d'or de Jeanne d'Arc*, clearly reveals the overwhelming popularity she enjoyed between 1870 and 1894.

90.  'L'amour invincible de la patrie, plus fort que la mort, que le découragement de la défaite et que toutes les querelles d'Armagnacs et de Bourgignons, voilà ce qu'enseigne l'humble paysanne qui prêcha l'union de tous les Français et donna sa vie pour la France.' *Le Temps* (12 December 1897).

91.  These rulers include Vercingétorix, Clovis, Hugues Capet, Charlemagne, Saint Louis, Philippe le Bel and Etienne Marcel. See for example Victor Canet, *Clovis et les origines de la France chrétienne* (Lille: De Brouwer et Cie, 1888); Auguste Longnon, *La Formation de l'unité francaise: leçons professées au Collège de France en 1889–1890* (Paris: Editions A & J Picard, 1922); Armand d'Herbomez, *Philippe le Bel et les Tournaisiens* (Brussels: F. Hayez, 1893). Christian Amalvi (1988) discusses the various heroic rulers introduced in the school curriculum. Joan of Arc became a figure of predilection for modern manuscript illumination. See Hindman *et al.*, pp. 162–3.

92.  Paris's introductory article to the first issue of *Romania* establishes the opposition between Roman and German literatures. It is clear that many of these projects were in place long before the war, but it was this conflict that placed them on the national stage.

93.  Gaston Paris was elected to the Collège de France in 1872, to the Académie Française in 1896 and to the Académie des Inscriptions et Belles-lettres in 1876. Meyer became a professor at the Collège de France in 1876, director of the Ecole des Chartes in 1882, member of the Académie des Inscriptions et Belles-lettres in 1883. Gautier was given a chair of paleography at L'Ecole des Chartes in 1871. See Michel Espagne, 'A Propos de l'évolution historique des philologies modernes: l'exemple de la philologie romane en Allemagne et en France,' *Philologiques I*, eds Michel Espagne and Michael Werner (Paris: Editions de la Maison des Sciences de l'homme, 1990, 159–83), p. 175.

94.  Sanson, p. 461. See also Eugèn Weber, *France, Fin de Siècle* and *The Nationalist Revival in France, 1905–1914* (Berkeley: University of California Press, 1959).

95.  On the *Ralliement* see Alexander Sedgwick, *The Ralliement in French Politics: 1890–1898* (Cambridge: Harvard University Press, 1965); David Shapiro, 'The Ralliement in the Politics of the 1890s' in David Shapiro, ed. *The Right in France 1890–1919* (London: Chatto and Windus, 1962) and René Rémond, *L'anticléricalisme en France* (Paris: Fayard, 1976).

96.  Cited in Winock, p. 460.

97.  See Charles Rearick, *Pleasures of the Belle Epoque: Entertainment in Turn-of-the-Century France* (New Haven: Yale University Press, 1985), for details about the beginning of official Bastille Day celebrations. In *La Femme pauvre*, Léon Bloy sets a scene on 14 July 1880; his devout Catholic characters soundly insult the rationale behind this holiday and the form it has been given.

98.  In *Edmond Drumont et Cie.*, Michael Winock shows how Joan of Arc appealed to all religions and all parties; even Jews supported her as a patriotic Esther or Judith figure (Paris: Editions du Seuil, 1982), pp. 67–9. Rosemonde Sanson focuses on these issues and others, clearly showing how it was the proposal's appeal to Catholic tradition that shredded the tenuous peace of the *Ralliement*.

99.  'Il s'agit aussi de rappeler, de vivifier le sentiment de la patrie dans l'âme de tous les Français, sur tous les points de la France.' Cited in Sanson, p. 456.

100.  Sanson, p. 455.

101.  Ironically, the school system was able to institute such a festival where the government had failed. A series of December 1897 articles in *Le Temps* reveal the successful application of the patriotic holiday within the schools, whose self-containment avoided 'l'inconvénient' of popular manifestations in favor of one side or the other (12 December 1897). The celebration

itself was proposed to include both patriotic manifestations and religious worship and would involve patriotic readings, a conference on history, or historical scenes represented by students. They would also join in the singing of patriotic songs such as 'Mourir pour la patrie' (18 December 1897).

102.   'Les cloîtres, traditionnels et confinés dans leur conception hiératique de l'idée et de la forme, furent de très bonne heure contre-balancés par l'artisan laïque, issu des communes; celui-ci entraîna les arts dans une voie plus libre, plus personnelle et rompa avec la tradition … ' Bouchot, *L'Exposition des Primitifs*, p. 9.

103.   'Le bon Camelot,' *La Revue Blanche* V (1893). Founded by the Polish-Jewish Natanson brothers, Alexander, Alfred and Thadée, *La Revue Blanche* ran from 1889–1903. Remembered today for its inclusion of avant-garde art, especially by artists within the Symbolist circle, such as the Nabis, the journal also covered politics, literature, the arts and current events. See Bret Waller and Gail Seiberling, *The Artists of La Revue Blanche*. Exhibition catalog (Rochester: Memorial Art Gallery of Rochester, 1984); Fritz Hermann, 'Les Nabis et *La Revue Blanche*' in Claire Frèches-Thory and Ursula Perucchi-Petri, *Nabis: 1888–1900*, exhibition catalog (Zurich: Kunsthaus/ Paris: Grand Palais, 1993), pp. 68–74; Patricia Eckert Boyer, *The Nabis and the Parisian Avant-Garde* (New Brunswick: Rutgers University Press, 1988).

104.   By the late 1880s, many Republicans were anxious to distance themselves from the Socialists and from the radical left. On the threat to the Republic see Eugèn Weber (1986), Theodore Zeldin, *France 1848–1945: Politics and Anger* (Oxford: Clarendon Press, 1979) and Jean-Marie Mayeur, *Les Débuts de la Troisième République 1871–1898* (Paris: Editions du Seuil, 1973). For an 1890 article urging the Republic to accommodate more conservative elements see 'La République et les conservateurs,' *La Revue Blanche* 97 (March).

105.   '[…] qu'y-a-t-il de changé à ces vieux usages municipaux? Ne voit-on pas aujourd'hui dans les voyages officiels des jeunes filles vêtues des trois couleurs […] offrir, au nom de la population, des voeux et des bouquets au chef de l'Etat?' Germain Bapst, 'Les spectacles et les réjouissances des fêtes publiques au Moyen Age,' *La Revue bleue* 48 (July 1891), p. 38.

106.   Born in Lausanne in 1845, Grasset was hailed for his achievements in many media including stained glass, jewelry and furniture design. For more on Grasset, see Anne Murray-Robertson, *Eugène Grasset, pionnier de l'art nouveau* (Lausanne: Editions 24 heures, 1981) and Chapter 2 of our book.

107.   The emblem of the Third Republic and its motto *fluctuat nec mergitur* is discussed by Silverman, p. 45, who links the Republic's use of aristocratic and imperial imagery (it was used by both Louis XIV and Haussmann) to a desire to inscribe this regime within a stable tradition of French history and to reconcile political differences.

108.   'Et de quelle gloire artistique plus pure pourrait enorgueillir la nation française? Quel peuple peut se parer d'une plus riche et plus splendide couronne?' Louis Gonse, *L'art gothique: l'architecture, la peinture, la sculpture, le décor* (Paris: Librairie Imprimerie Réunies, 1890), p. 4.

109.   'Ces quatre règnes jettent les fondements de l'unité française. Les idées de solidarité, d'association, d'unité, prennent naissance et avec elles, ce sentiment désintéressé et d'essence supérieure qui s'appelle le patriotisme […] C'est avec les milices communales et paroissales que le roi gagne ses victoires; ce sont les solides bourgeois de Dreux, de Soissons, de Beauvais … ' Gonse, *L'art gothique*, p. 135.

110.   For more about *Solidarité*, see Judith F. Stone, *The Search for Social Peace: Legislative Reform in France 1890–1914* (New York: State University of New York Press, 1985).

111.   Proust had served as Minister of the Arts under Gambetta from 1880–1881. He was Vice-President of the *Monuments Historiques* and President of the *Union Centrale des Arts Décoratifs*. For more on this figure see Silverman, pp. 118–20.

112.   The Daru staircase was part of the larger *Nouveau Musée Impérial* commissioned by Napoléon III. In August of 1884, a special commission, led by the architect Edmond Guillaume, decided on a decorative program for the staircase. The mosaics, designed by Lenepveu and executed by students of the *École Nationale de Mosaïque*, included 'Antiquity,' 'The Renaissance,' 'The Middle Ages' and various scenes representing 'France,' 'England' etc. The mosaics were poorly received and heavily criticized on stylistic grounds. In 1934 the whole series was destroyed to accommodate a new decorative scheme. On the mosaics see Christiane Aulanier, *Histoire du palais et du musée du Louvre: Le Nouveau Louvre de Napoléon III*. Vol 4 (Paris: Editions des Musées Nationaux, 1953), pp. 35–40.

113.   Alfred de Lostalot, 'L'art gothique,' *Gazette des Beaux-Arts* 67 (1890), p. 522.

114.   ' … l'auteur de la mosaïque dont on vient de décorer l'escalier du Louvre, y eût appris que l'art gothique est un art français et que, par conséquent, on ne saurait, sans manquer à la verité et au patriotisme, le symboliser par une figure de l'Allemagne.' Lostalot, p. 522.

115.   Indeed, after spending much of the nineteenth century collecting funds to rebuild Cologne cathedral because Gothic architecture was 'German to the core,' German architects realized that not only was Cologne not unique (it was similar to Amiens cathedral), but the style was of French origin! See Emery, *Romancing the Cathedral*, pp. 26–7.

116. Laurens, a staunch Republican, was elected president of the Société des Artistes Français in 1889. A history painter, Laurens won many prizes and received many important state commissions. In 1887, he completed a series of illustrations for the *Récits mérovingiens* of Augustin Thierry (Paris: Hachette, 1875–1883). On Laurens see *Le Moyen Age et les peintres français de la fin du XIXe siècle: Jean-Paul Laurens et ses contemporains*, exhibition catalog (Château-Musée de Cagnes-sur-Mer: 1980).

117. 'Retenons aussi que dans ce milieu intellectuel le goût de l'art et des lettres du moyen âge était fort développé. Autour de 1870, c'étaient les Catholiques qui conservaient pieusement le culte de Dante, des Primitifs italiens et des cathédrales gothiques que la dernière vague romantique avait déjà abandonnés.' Maurice Denis, 'Un humaniste chrétien: Henri Cochin,' *La Revue hebdomadaire* 44 (29 Oct 1927), p. 595.

118. On the left, groups such as the Christian Democrats blended socialist ideas with popular and Christian beliefs. For information on this group see Robert Byrnes, 'The French Christian Democrats in the 1890s: Their Appearance and their Failure,' *Catholic Historical Review* 36 (Oct 1950), pp. 286–306.

119. See Chapter 4.

120. ' … cause plus de mal à l'art sacré que les vents d'incroyance et de doute.' Alphonse Germain, 'L'art religieux,' *Le Saint Graal* 6 (May 1892), p. 155. Germain scorned art that had been 'bêtement démocratisé.' For a brief biography of Germain, see Jean-Paul Bouillon.

121. *Le Spectateur catholique* began publication in Antwerp in January 1897, under the directorship of Edmond de Bruijn. Regular contributors to the journal included Alphonse Germain and Adrien Mithouard.

122. 'On ne renaît pas quand il n'y a pas eu mort. Et le Moyen Age n'avait rien de tué et son esprit vivait plus fécond que jamais!' William Witter, 'Entre l'art catholique et les historiens de la Renaissance,' *Le Spectateur catholique* 8 (August 1897).

123. J.-K. Huysmans was one of the leaders in the movement to rejuvenate the aspects of the medieval art and spirituality that continued to flourish in fin-de-siècle France. For a detailed analysis of his relationship to medieval art, see chapter three of Emery's *Romancing*, 'Huysmans and the Medieval Church,' pp. 89–128, and 'J.-K. Huysmans and the Middle Ages,' *Modern Language Studies* 29.3 (2002).

124. Cochin was a philosopher and historian particularly interested in science; he would later become a member of the Académie Française. Considered a liberal Catholic, he was a supporter of Pius IV and the *Ralliement*. For background information on Cochin see Claire Frèches-Thory and Antoine Terrasse, *The Nabis: Bonnard, Vuillard and their Circle* (New York: Harry Abrams, 1991), pp. 134–40.

125. Denis published Henri Cochin's eulogy, 'Un humaniste chrétien,' in the pages of *La Revue Hebdomadaire*.

126. Quoted in Denis, 'Un humaniste chrétien,' p. 594.

127. 'Il y a aussi, il y avait surtout un esprit public en France; esprit généreux, chevaleresque, pas toujours très pratique, mais toujours très aimable […] Que l'on remonte jusqu'au temps des Croisades, que l'on traverse la longue période des luttes nationales et populaires contre les Anglais, que l'on arrive enfin aux guerres glorieuses du commencement de ce siècle, on trouve toujours nos aïeux animés de ce noble esprit que j'essaie de décrire.' Undated speech reprinted in Denys Cochin, *Contre les barbares* (Paris: Calmann Lévy Editeur, 1899), p. 147.

128. Frèches-Thory and Terrasse, p. 80.

129. As cited and translated in Frèches-Thory and Terrasse, p. 134.

130. The seven panels are *The Departure, Unleashing the Dogs, Le Bien-Aller, The Miracle, The Failing, The Wild Pursuit* and *Arrival at the Hermitage*. See Agnès Delannoy and Marianne Barbey, *Maurice Denis: La Légende de Saint Hubert 1896–1897* (Paris: Somogy Editions, 1999).

131. The 'Chasse' tapestries were often based on manuscript illustrations from the manual *Livre de la Chasse* by Gaston III, Comte de Foix (Gaston Phébus), Bibliothèque Nationale (ms fr 616). One can see a good example of a Franco-Flemish 'Chasse' cycle in the six tapestries that compose *Incidents in a Stag Hunt* at the New York Metropolitan Museum of Art (Southern Netherlands, 1495–1515). For information on the 'Chasse' tapestries, see Adolfo Salvatore Cavallo, *Medieval Tapestries in the Metropolitan Museum of Art* (New York: Abrams, 1993), pp. 359–72. Agnès Delannoy and Marianne Barbey see a more recent model for Denis, the eighteenth-century works of Jean-Baptiste Oudry, pp. 16, 33.

132. In 'Chasse' tapestries, seemingly secular subjects or symbols imparted religious meaning to the viewer. In the *Dame à la Licorne* cycle, for example, the female figure is both 'princess' and – in her purity – an undeniable symbol of the Virgin Mary.

133. For a thorough discussion of this issue, see Chapter 5.

134. Cited in Frèches-Thory and Terrasse, p. 134.

135. Frèches-Thory and Terrasse, pp. 139–41.

136. Adrien Mithouard, *Le Tournament de l'unité* (Paris: Mercure de France, 1901).

137. For a brief, but illuminating analysis, see Claude Foucart, 'Adrien Mithouard et le Moyen Age,' in Anne Ducrey, ed., *Le Moyen Age en 1900*, pp. 21–7.

138. See Laura Morowitz, 'Medievalism, Anti-Semitism and the Art of the Fin de Siècle.'

139. 'Elle plane au-dessus des partis, elle n'est prisonnière d'aucune secte, d'aucun groupe, d'aucune école […] Chacun de nous a le même droit et le même devoir de l'admirer et de l'aimer car elle incarne et résume ce qu'il y a de commun dans les sentiments des Français de tous les partis: l'inaltérable dévouement à la patrie et à la passion de l'indépendance nationale.' Cited in Sanson, p. 449. This 1893 speech was delivered during the commemoration of a statue of Joan of Arc in Vaucouleurs, France. Poincaré was then a representative to the Chamber of Deputies from Lorraine and the Minister of Public Instruction and Fine Arts.

140. 'Ils sont les premiers constructeurs, les premiers modeleurs d'Europe; leurs verriers et leurs orfèvres n'ont rien à emprunter aux autres […] Et les sculptures des cathédrales, les vitraux de Chartres, les manuscrits français en sont là bien longtemps avant que Cimabué paraisse dans le monde.' Bouchot, *L'Exposition des Primitifs*, p. ii.

141. 'Le peintre a le visage émacié des ascètes. C'est un ardent, cest un croyant; la foi qu'il porte en lui le consomme […] Ce n'est plus un homme, c'est la prière même, c'est la foi, c'est l'esprit dégagé de la matière et qui aspire à l'infini.' Georges Olmer, *L'Exposition des Beaux-Arts: Salon de 1886* (Paris: Librairie d'Art, 1886).

142. For information on this painting see Aimée Brown Price, *Pierre Puvis de Chavannes* (Amsterdam: Van Gogh Museum; New York: Rizzoli, 1994), pp. 190–91.

143. Late nineteenth-century periodization of the Middle Ages differed from contemporary art-historical scholarship. Nineteenth-century audiences defined 'medieval' as the period between the fall of the Roman Empire and the early sixteenth century. Painters of the fourteenth and fifteenth centuries thus fell well into their purview. In contrast, recent scholarship has tended to push the border of the Renaissance backward, especially in the field of visual art. Jan van Eyck, for example, is now routinely studied as northern Renaissance, while he was cast as solidly medieval, a true *Primitif,* in the 1890s.

144. The term *Primitif* referred to artists of the medieval era, especially the twelfth through fifteenth centuries and was most often used to describe painters of the fourteenth and fifteenth centuries, although it could less often be used for artists working in diverse media. For nineteenth-century viewers, the central quality of the *Primitif* was his naiveté, his innocence and unselfconscious originality, which lent his works their power and charm. For the nineteenth-century understanding of the *Primitifs* see Michael Paul Driskel, *Representing Belief* (University Park: Pennsylvania State University Press, 1992) and Bruno Foucart, *Le Renouveau de la peinture religieuse en France* (Paris: Athena, 1987). Erwin Panofsky's classic essay on periodization, 'Renaissance – Self Definition or Self Deception?' in *Renaissance and Renascences in Western Art* (New York: Harper and Row, 1972), also explores ideas about the *Primitifs.*

145. According to Raymonde Moulin, 'Ayant choisi "ses" artistes, le marchand organise leur "lancement" ou leur "mise en valeur." L'objectif est pour lui de faire, à partir d'un peintre remarqué par un petit nombre d'artistes, de critiques et de connaisseurs et auquel lui-même croit, une signature, qui, à la limite, possède par elle-même une signification monétaire.' *Le marché de la peinture en France* (Paris: Editions de Minuit, 1967), p. 125. Moulin also notes that the 'monopoly' system launched by dealers such as Daniel Henry Kahnweiler, who claimed exclusive rights to a particular artist, encouraged speculation and therefore increased investment in the art market.

146. On the importance of 'anonymity' to the early Symbolist movement, see Laura Morowitz, 'Anonymity, Artistic Brotherhoods and the Art Market in the Fin de Siècle,' *Art Criticism* 11:2 (1996), pp. 71–9.

147. Such idealization continued into the final decades of the twentieth century. Nineteenth-century accounts edited out the importance placed on the hierarchical organization of the medieval workshop as well as the considerable 'fame' achieved by certain pre-Renaissance artists. See Martin Warnke, *The Court Artist: On the Ancestry of the Modern Artist*, trans. David McLintock (Cambridge: Cambridge University Press, 1993) and Walter Cahn, *Masterpieces: Chapters on the History of an Idea* (Princeton: Princeton University Press, 1979).

148. As Denis stated of the *Primitif*: 'Il voit la nature avec des yeux d'enfant, tandis qu'un moderne la voit avec les yeux du peintre […] sa gaucherie est donc le témoignage de sa sincérité.' Denis, 'Le sentiment religieux dans l'art du Moyen Age' (1913), reprinted in *Nouvelles théories sur l'art moderne, sur l'art sacré 1914–1921* (Paris: L. Rouart et Watelin, 1922), p. 155.

149. For an examination of the actual working conditions of the artist, see Andrew Martindale, *The Rise of the Artist in the Middle Ages and Early Renaissance* (New York: McGraw Hill, 1972). For the conditions within the manuscript workshop, see Jonathan J. G. Alexander, *Medieval Illuminators and their Methods of Work* (New Haven: Yale University Press, 1992).

150.  Symbolism is a notoriously difficult movement to define: it is used loosely to categorize a general idealist and anti-materialist mood prevalent in late nineteenth-century European art and more specifically to evoke visual and literary conventions that favor the ideal over the real, suggestion over statement, and attention to the relationship between signifier and signified. To compound the difficulty in our case, the term 'symbolism' was not introduced until Jean Moréas's 1886 'Manifeste du symbolisme' and many artists and writers we now call 'Symbolist' refused the term in their own day. For a good introduction to the breadth, depth and conflicting definitions of Symbolism see Henri Dorra, *Symbolist Art Theories: A Critical Anthology* (Berkeley: University of California Press, 1995) and Pamela Genova, *Symbolist Journals: A Culture of Correspondence* (London: Ashgate Press, 2002), pp. 158–90. For a discussion of the development of the movement, which crossed media and national borders, see the works of Robert Lehmann; Robert Goldwater, *Symbolism* (New York: Harper and Row, 1979), Robert Delevoy, *Symbolists and Symbolism* (Geneva: Skira/Rizzoli, 1982) and Richard Shryock, 'Reaction Within Symbolism: L'Ecole romane,' *The French Review* (71:4), pp. 577–84.

151.  Debora Silverman discusses the importance of the rococo and classical models for nationalist movements in the art of the time.

152.  'Au moment où l'artiste pense à l'argent il perd le sentiment du beau.' Maurice Denis, *Journal* I (Paris: Editions du Vieux Colombier, 1957).

153.  'Il me faut beaucoup d'argent. Vous comprenez que je n'irai pas dépenser mes économies à Florence. A propos, si vous savez un moyen de vendre la peinture très cher, enseignez-le-moi. Je ne sais pas à quel saint me vouer.' Letter to Jan Verkade. Cited in George Mauner, 'The Nabis, their History and their Art' (Ph.D. dissertation, Columbia University, 1978), p. 286.

154.  In fact, the Salons had been labeled as 'markets' or 'bazaars' by politically conservative critics earlier in the nineteenth century. Patricia Mainardi, for example, mentions that the political right consistently condemned the Salons as commercial, vulgar and of poor quality: *The End of the Salon: Art and the State in the Early Third Republic* (Cambridge: Cambridge University Press, 1993). For Symbolist condemnation of the Salons, see Bouillon and Genova. The movement's distaste for the Salons has its origins in the reactionary ideologies of the nineteenth century.

155.  'Introduction' to the second *Exposition des peintres impressionnistes et symbolistes* at the Galerie Le Barc de Boutteville. Reprinted in *Modern Art In Paris: Post-Impressionist Group Exhibits*, ed. Theodore Reff (New York: Garland Press, 1982). See also Aurier's condemnation of the Salons in 'A propos de trois salons de 1891,' *Le Mercure de France* III (1891). Mirbeau described the invasion of bric-à-brac in a newspaper article: 'Le commerce des tableaux languissait […] dans les grands bric-à-brac de l'avenue de Villiers, les peintres affolés déclouaient des murs leur peluches aux reflets de cuivre, leurs tapisseries aux décolorations anciennes, remplaçaient leurs bahuts historiques vendus par le japonisme à treize sous des bazars.' Octave Mirbeau, 'Nos bons artistes,' *Le Figaro* (23 December 1887).

156.  For J.-K. Huysmans's attack on William Bouguereau's *Adoration des Bergers* and Léon Bonnat's *Saint Denis* see J.-K. Huysmans, 'Le Salon de 1885,' *L'Evolution sociale* (May 1885), p. 16.

157.  For Denis's condemnation of the 'journalistic sketches' of Academic artists see Pierre L. Maud (Denis), 'Le Salon du Champ-de-Mars,' in *Théories*, p. 363. For the controversy surrounding the religious painting of the Naturalists, see Driskel.

158.  Emile Bernard, 'Les Primitifs et la Renaissance,' *Mercure de France* (Nov. 1894), p. 230. J.-K. Huysmans lambasted Béraud in his preface to Remy de Gourmont's *Le Latin mystique*, p. ix. Béraud (1849–1935) studied with Léon Bonnat and became one of the most successful Academic artists of his day. He was a founding member, in 1890, of La Société Nationale des Beaux-Arts.

159.  On the French art market in the nineteenth century see Raymonde Moulin, Robert Jensen, Nicolas Green, Cynthia A. and Harrison C. White, *Canvases and Careers* and Pierre Miquel, *Art et Argent: 1800–1900, L'Ecole de Nature* vol. 6 (Maurs-la-Jolie: Editions de la Martinelle, 1987). For a contemporary account of life in the art trade, see Ambroise Vollard, *Recollections of a Picture Dealer*, trans. Violet MacDonald (Dover Reprint, 1968).

160.  See Peter Bürger, *Theory of the Avant-Garde*, and Thomas Crow, 'Modernism and Mass Culture in the Visual Arts' in Francis Frascina, ed., *Pollock and After* (New York: Harper and Row, 1985).

161.  On the links between art galleries and department stores, see Patricia Mainardi, Rosalind Williams and Rémy Saisselin.

162.  See Patricia Mainardi (1993) and Marie Jeanne Aquilino, 'The Decorating Campaigns at the Salon du Champ-de-Mars and the Salon des Champs-Elysées in the 1890s,' *Art Journal* 48:1 (Spring 1989), pp. 78–84 and Shane Adler Davis, '"Fine Cloths on the Altar": The Commodification of Late Nineteenth Century France,' *Art Journal* 48:1 (Spring 1989), pp. 85–9.

163.  Zola based his descriptions of exhibits (like the remarkable 'L'Exposition de blanc') on his notes from real stores including Le Bon Marché, Le Magasin du Louvre and La Place de Clichy. See Henri Mitterand's notes to *Au Bonheur des Dames* in *Les Rougon-Macquart*, vol. III, pp. 1667–1735.

164.  On this see Williams and Miller.

165. Gaston Lesaulx, introduction to the 1890 *Exposition des peintres impressionnistes et symbolistes*, Galerie Le Barc de Boutteville. Reprinted in Theodore Reff, ed., *Modern Art in Paris: 1855–1900* (New York: Garland Press, 1981), p. 8.

166. 'Il faudrait le courage de résister: 1) à notre sensibilité exacerbée; 2) à notre public qui veut des impressions d'art en cinq minutes!; 3) et à nos marchands.' Denis, *Journal* I (6 Feb. 1898).

167. Denis used the term 'petites toiles bourgeoises' in a letter to Sérusier and in his correspondence, while Paul Ranson often referred to the paintings of the Nabis as 'icons.' See Mauner, p. 32. Beginning in October 1888, the Paris-based Nabi artists banded together in formal experimentation, exhibitions and artistic collaborations. The artists who belonged to the loosely-defined Nabi brotherhood included Maurice Denis, Edouard Vuillard, Pierre Bonnard, Paul Sérusier, Paul Ranson, Félix Vallotton, the sculptor Georges Lacombe, Jan Verkade, Mogens Ballin and Joszéf Rippl-Ronai. For background on the Nabis, see Mauner, Claire Frèches-Thory and Ursula Perrucchi-Petri (1993) and Frèches-Thory and Antoine Terrasse (1991). For an investigation of Nabi interest in medieval art, see Morowitz, 'Consuming the Past' (1996).

168. 'A mon peintre, deux mots: L'incontestable – je vous conteste – plus même – je vous nie, vous et les vôtres.' 'L'esthétique nationale des Beaux-Arts,' *L'Artiste* (Nov. 1 1883), p. 373. Leader of the Salons de la Rose+Croix and a well-known novelist, Sar Joséphin Péladan was one of the most eccentric characters of the late nineteenth century. He dressed in dark velvet and wandered the streets of Paris in a flowing white robe covered by a cloak. His Order of the Rose+Croix sought to exhibit 'ideal art' in a quasi-religious medieval setting full of fanfares, prayers, and other traditions. The majority of the Rose+Croix artists professed a strong faith in Catholicism or in occult mysticism. They were drawn to medieval models in their art and envisioned their project as a holy Crusade against artistic decadence. See Robert Pincus-Witten, *Occult Symbolism in France: Joséphin Peladan and the Salons de la Rose-Croix* (New York: Garland Publishing, Inc., 1976) and *The Salons of the Rose+Croix 1892–1897* (London: Picadilly Gallery, 1968); Jean da Silva, *Le Salon de la Rose+Croix (1892–1897)* (Paris: Syros-Alternatives, 1991).

169. On this notion of the symbol, see the writings of Albert Aurier and Joséphin Péladan. For a discussion of the 'materiality' of painting see Françoise Lucbert, 'Le Symbolisme à travers le naturalisme. Zola, Huysmans et la peinture de Moreau,' *Excavatio* XI (1997), pp. 62–72. Pamela Genova provides a particularly clear comparison of Symbolist aesthetics in literature and art in *Symbolist Journals*, pp. 1–30 and 157–90.

170. 'L'artiste devient le disciple des maîtres anciens dans une abdication de sa modernité.' Quoted in André Mellerio, *Le Mouvement idéaliste en peinture* (Paris: H. Floury Editeur, 1986), p. 59.

171. Bloy longed to be a painter and had been apprenticed to a Parisian architect at the age of eighteen. Along with authentic medieval art, Bloy preferred the stained-glass inspired art of his friend Georges Rouault and the consciously 'crude' paintings (often triptych in format) of the Belgian artist Henri de Groux. Bloy considered himself something of a medieval man and his extensive writings proposed complex theories about the medieval world and its importance for history. On Bloy see Emmanuela Polimeni, *Léon Bloy: The Pauper Prophet* (London: D. Dobson, 1947), Pierre Glaudes, ed., *Léon Bloy* (Paris: Editions de l'Herne, 1988) and Pierre Glaudes, ed., *Léon Bloy au tournant du siècle* (Toulouse: Presse universitaire de Mirail-Toulouse, 1992).

172. *La Femme pauvre*, pp. 167–8.

173. Marchenoir is compared to eleventh-century men on p. 153, while his tongue-in-cheek praise of Léopold occurs on p. 169: 'L'occasion peu banale de la première entrevue de Léopold et de Marchenoir avait été, quelques années auparavant, un article de revue où le critique redoutable réclamait, au nom des bourgeois, les supplices les plus rigoureux pour ce Léopold, qui menaçait de ressusciter un art défunt dont les gens d'affaires n'avaient jamais entendu parler. Cet art qu'on devait croire emmailloté dans les cryptes du Moyen Age, allait-il donc vraiment renaître par l'insolente volonté d'un homme étranger aux acquisitions modernes [...]'

174. 'Rien n'entravait l'esprit des hommes, le doute n'était pas né et des millions d'êtres partaient pour délivrer le tombeau du Christ sans avoir songé un instant à ce qu'ils mangeraient en chemin et de quelle étoffe ils se vêtiraient.' Emile Bernard, 'Les Primitifs et la Renaissance', p. 228.

175. 'Etait-ce une compagnie de ces imagiers, de ces confrères de l'oeuvre sainte qui allaient d'un pays à l'autre, adjoints aux maçons, aux ouvriers logeurs du bon Dieu, par les moines? [...] Nul ne le sait. Humblement, anonymement, ils travaillèrent [...] ils ne besognaient que lorsqu'ils étaient en état de grâce. [...] Ce fut une Croisade, telle que jamais on n'en vit.' *La Cathédrale. Le Roman de Durtal*, pp. 841–2.

176. Huysmans, in an introduction to Remy de Gourmont, *Le Latin mystique*, p. x.

177. Dom Willibrord (Jan) Verkade, *Yesterdays of an Artist Monk*, trans. John Stoddard (London: P. J. Kennedy and Sons, 1930), p. 25.

178. The journal appeared in only eight issues, from 1894 to 1896, and mixed antique prints with works of modern artists including those from the Pont-Aven school. For more information about *L'Ymagier*, see Emmanuel Pernoud, 'De l'image à l'ymage, les revues d'Alfred Jarry et

Remy de Gourmont,' *La Revue de l'art*, 115 (1997:1), pp. 59–65. See also Jacquelynn Baas and Richard S. Field, *The Artistic Revival of the Woodcut in France 1850–1900* (Ann Arbor: University of Michigan Museum of Art, 1984). The website of the Spencer Museum of Art owns and generously displays numerous images from the publication: www.cc.ukans.edu/~sma/almanac/lymtxt.htm

179.   'Des images, et rien de plus, religieuses ou légendaires, avec ce qu'il faut de mots pour en dire le sens et convaincre, par une notion, les inattentifs. Des images d'abord taillées dans le bois, cette matière à idoles, matrice de si bonne volonté; [...] Ici donc, nous ferons la leçon du vieil imagier et nous disons, par des traits, la joie de ceux qui pour un sou unique, ornaient leur muraille d'archangéliques confidences – la joie d'un paysan, encore Breton, qui trouve dans la hotte du colporteur les rudes faces taillées par Georgin, et les coeurs symboliques, et poignants, les Christs dont la douleur pacifie nos douleurs, les miraculeuses vierges et aussi les mystérieux cavaliers qui apportent, messagers du Roi, la nouvelle d'une joie, – et aussi les légendaires Genevièves et les puissants saints mitrés, plus grands que les clochers.' *L'Ymagier* vol. 1 (1894), pp. 6–7.

180.   *Images d'Epinal* were popular prints, of either religious or secular nature. On these images see Mireille-Bénédicte Bouvet, *Le grand livre des images d'Epinal* (Paris: Solar, 1996).

181.   Passages from *Le Mystère de la Passion* were published in 1894 while scenes from *Le Miracle de Théophile* and *Aucassin et Nicolette* appeared in 1896 issues.

182.   See, for example, the July and August 1892 issues of the journal, though his imitation wood prints appear elsewhere. We will return to *images d'Epinal* in Chapter 6 in our discussion of the Catholic journal *Le Pèlerin* and its liberal use of them, along with medieval prints, beginning in the 1870s.

183.   Andrew Martindale outlines the working and training conditions of medieval artists.

184.   The notion of anonymity applied to several of the contemporary prints in the journal as well. In fact, if the editors had not identified the works of artists (like Emile Bernard) by placing captions under them, we would not be able to tell who created them (as is the case in a number of questionable images from this publication). See the attempted attributions by the Spencer Museum for examples of this tendency. For more about Robida's works, see Chapter 7.

185.   ' ... avait pourtant conservé dans son coeur la "tendance" du Moyen Age, l'ardent spiritualisme de l'art gothique, la haine du matérialisme et du classique pastichisme de la nouvelle école!' 'Le Livret de L'Imagier', *Le Mercure de France* (Feb. 1892), p. 169.

186.   *La Femme pauvre*, p. 91.

187.   '[...] J'aurais été de ceux qui défendaient avec une ardeur puérile et violente contre l'envahissement du paganisme classique, l'esthétique du Moyen Age. J'aurais été de ces pieux retardataires, fidèles au hiératisme du passé, pour qui les idées nouvelles annonçaient la prompte décadence.' 'Notes sur la peinture religieuse' (1896), reprinted in *Théories*, p. 30. The fiery preacher Savonarola (1452–1498) profoundly influenced many Renaissance artists, including Botticelli. In the following years, Denis would completely revise his opinion on the 'pagan' art of the High Renaissance and would come to celebrate it as an expression of Latin Mediterranean culture, an ancestor of French classicism.

188.   On the reception of Fra Angelico in the nineteenth century, see Foucart and Driskel.

189.   In 1884, Péladan published an article on Angelico, 'Introduction à l'histoire des peintres de toutes les écoles depuis les origines jusqu'à la Renaissance: l'Angelico,' *L'Artiste* (March 1884), which was read by Denis in 1885. Huysmans reprinted his own essays on Fra Angelico and Rogier van der Weyden in journals and in his novel *La Cathédrale*, pp. 780–96.

190.   On Dulac see 'Charles Dulac: the Mystical Landscape' in Taube Greenspan, 'Les Nostalgiques Re-examined: The Idyllic Landscape in France 1890–1905' (Ph.D. dissertation, CUNY, 1981).

191.   '[...] Il chérissait la pauvreté, méprisait la réclame, se nourrissait de même qu'un ermite, se reposait au hasard des couches monastiques, et il peignait à peine pour lui et tout pour Dieu.' J.-K. Huysmans, 'Charles-Marie Dulac' in *Oeuvres complètes* vol. 16 (Geneva: Slatkine Reprints, 1972), p. 133. Durtal, the protagonist of Huysmans's *La Cathédrale*, deeply admired Dulac's paintings and lithographs.

192.   'Il y vivait [in Italy] dans des couvents de son observance, comme ces artistes du Moyen Age qui séjournaient chez des religieux et payaient leur écot en décorant des chapelles; et le fait est que Dulac n'avait rien d'un homme de notre temps [...]' 'Charles-Marie Dulac,' p. 133.

193.   See Robert Baldick, *The Life of J.-K. Huysmans* (Oxford: Clarendon Press, 1955), pp. 273–6.

194.   A long line of artistic-religious brotherhoods can be traced through the nineteenth century, both in and outside of France. In 1809 the Brotherhood of Saint Luke (also known as the German Nazarene movement) established residence in a monastery in Rome, devoting their art to religious subjects.

195.   See *La Plume* 9 (January 1897).

196.   Wladyslawa Jaworska, *Gauguin and the Pont-Aven School*, trans. Patrick Evans (New York: New

York Graphic Society, 1972), p. 59. On Van Gogh's and Gauguin's notion of modern 'spiritual art,' see Debora Silverman, *Van Gogh and Gauguin: The Search for Sacred Art* (New York: Farrar, Straus and Giroux, 2000). For an exploration of Van Gogh's notions of the brotherhood, see Carol Zemel, 'Brotherhoods: The Dealer, The Market, the Commune' in *Van Gogh's Progress: Utopia, Modernity and Late Nineteenth Century Art* (Berkeley: University of California Press, 1997), pp. 171–206.

197.  Bernard wrote to Emile Schuffenecker about this 'Association des Anonymes,' which would produce art and craft. See Henri Dorra, 'Extraits de la correspondance d'Emile Bernard des débuts à la R&C,' *Gazette des Beaux-Arts* 96 (Dec. 1980), p. 238, and Bernard's letter to Emile Schuffenecker (19 January 1891) in Emile Bernard, *Lettres à Paul Gauguin et à E. Schuffenecker* (Paris: Bibliothèque Nationale de France, Department of Manuscripts, n.a. fr. 14277). See also Morowitz, 'Artistic Brotherhoods, the Art Market and Anonymity.'

198.  Unpublished letter from Bernard to Huysmans, 9 Jan. 1899. Paris, Bibliothèque de l'Arsenal, Fonds Lambert. This letter is quoted and discussed by Jean da Silva, p. 97.

199.  '[…] Commencer une colonie d'artistes chrétiens, oblats bénédictins, à l'ombre du vieux cloître qui y existe.' In *A Emile Bernard. Lettres de Vincent Van-Gogh, Gauguin* […] Brussels: Editions de la Nouvelle Revue de Belgique, 1942.

200.  See *L'Oblat* for a detailed discussion of the medieval traditions linked to oblates and the situation's advantages for artists.

201.  Durtal dreams of such a 'règle douce […] un monde de savants et d'écrivains' in *La Cathédrale*, p. 820. Robert Baldick cites many letters in which Huysmans looks forward to retiring from the civil service in order to live in a cloistered retreat where he can write and pray. He constantly evokes the medieval traditions that continue to exist in the modern cloisters he visits. Baldick also traces the steps Huysmans took to form such a community. At various times, the group included Dom Jean-Martial Besse, Abbé Mugnier, Abbé Ferret, Louis Le Cardonnel, Charles-Marie Dulac, Gustave Boucher, Jean de Caldain, Abbé Broussolle and Charles Rivière.

202.  See Baldick, p. 273.

203.  Georges Rouault, cited in Brian Banks, p. 187.

204.  Unfortunately, however, this ideal model was devastated by the 1904 Law of Associations, in which the French government forced religious organizations to disband. The Benedictines of Ligugé fled to Belgium and Huysmans and his friends were forced to return to Paris. See Baldick, Huysmans's correspondence and *L'Oblat* to measure the level of Huysmans's distress at these anti-clerical laws and their effect on him.

205.  'Et alors – oh que ce serait beau – Je lui élèverais en plein Paris profane une somptueuse chapelle, que mes confrères et moi s'ingénieraient à orner de tableaux, de fresques, de tavoles, de prédelles, de lunettes […] Oh! Que ce serait beau. Et chaque année, notre société artistico-religieuse y viendrait entendre la messe avec sa toile sur le bras […] L'exposition se terminerait par une seconde messe dans notre église!' Denis, *Journal* (12 August 1885) (Paris: Editions du Vieux Colombier, 1957).

206.  The commission is discussed in detail and reproduced by Michael Marlais, 'Conservative Style/Conservative Politics: Maurice Denis in *Le Vésinet*,' *Art History* 16 (March 1993), pp. 125–47. Denis's choice of iconography for the chapel of the Virgin and the chapel of the Sacred Heart reflected his conversion to Royalism and reactionary politics after the turn of the century. Despite the medieval and Renaissance sources behind Denis's work, Marlais reports that his Vésinet decorations were seen as extremely aesthetically progressive and that the inauguration of the church was attended by Odilon Redon, Eugène Carrière and André Mellerio, among others.

207.  Caroline Boyle-Turner, 'Paul Sérusier' (Ph.D. dissertation, 1983), pp. 136 ff., reports that Sérusier had begun work on five canvases depicting scenes from the life of Christ to be mounted on the walls of the newly restored baptistry. His three completed scenes were not approved by the church priest and the project was subsequently abandoned until 1912. In that year, Sérusier painted scenes from the Old Testament directly on the walls of the church in tempera. Importantly, Sérusier only became involved in the decoration of churches after 1900, when Symbolism had largely ceased to be accepted as a kind of substitute religion for Catholicism (see Chapter 4).

208.  Sérusier was introduced to the Beuron method by Verkade and translated Lenz's treatise into French (Didier Lenz, *L'Esthétique de Beuron*, trans. Paul Sérusier, 1905). The history of the Beuron convent and the artistic theory developed by Lenz have been thoroughly explored by Boyle-Turner, *op. cit.*, and Charles Chassé, *The Nabis and their Epoque*, trans. Michael Bullock (New York: Praeger Publishing, 1969). Denis would later criticize Lenz's method for failing to privilege the French Gothic tradition. 'Esthétique de Beuron', *L'Occident* 35 (Oct. 1904).

209.  On Ballins and Verkade see Verkade, *Yesterdays*, and Caroline Boyle-Turner, *Jan Verkade: Disciple hollandais de Gauguin* (Quimper: Musée des Beaux-Arts, 1990).

210.  Boyle-Turner (1983), reports that he was almost persuaded to join during his extended trip to the monastery in 1896.

211. On the Nabis and Symbolist theater see Robert Goldwater, 'Symbolist Art and Theater: Vuillard, Bonnard, Maurice Denis,' *Magazine of Art* 39 (Dec 1946), pp. 266–70; Geneviève Aitken, 'Les Nabis: un foyer au théatre,' in *Les Nabis*, pp. 399–425.

212. 'Cela aurait été le devoir de ceux que je nommais … les Nabis. Mais la recherche de la personnalité, l'invention du journaliste, a dispersé toute cette belle force.' Letter quoted in Caroline Boyle-Turner, *Jan Verkade*, p. 38.

213. See, for example, Laurens, *Le Pape et l'Inquisiteur* (Salon of 1883*); Le Grand Inquisiteur et les rois catholiques* (Salon of 1886); Maignan, *Hommage à Clovis II* (Salon of 1883).

214. At the 1898 Salon, viewers saw Alphonse Moutte's *A Notre-Dame de la Garde*, as well as G. Bouys's *Intérieur d'Eglise.*

215. For other works at the Salon in decidedly medieval style see Paul Delance, *S. Joseph au travail* (1898) and Albert Aublet, *Ecce Homo* (1899). Jean-Paul Laurens, too, exhibited a tempera painting, *La Muraille*, at the Salon of 1895.

216. See, for example, the writings of Maurice Denis or Emile Bernard cited below.

217. For Nabi links to poster advertising see Patricia Eckert Boyer, ed., *The Nabis and the Parisian Avant-Garde.*

218. 'Un art qui est fait de sacrifices, dont la sensualité est exclue, qui préfère l'expression par la forme à l'expression par la couleur, un tel art tient dans l'Esthétique la place du Cartésianisme dans la Philosophie […] et s'accorde avec la magnifique et sévère ordonnance du dogme catholique.' Maurice Denis, 'Les arts à Rome ou la méthode classique' (1896), reprinted in Denis, *Théories*, 55.

219. 'Où est la grandeur du sacrifice? Qu'est ce que la couleur? Une séduction des sens: édifiez-vous un art avec cela?' Letter of Emile Bernard to Emile Schuffenecker, 1 April 1889. Bernard, *Lettres*.

220. See Chapter 5 for the influence of medieval stained glass and tapestries in avant-garde milieus.

221. Vojtech Jirat-Wasiutynski and H. Travers Newton, Jr, *Technique and Meaning in the Paintings of Paul Gauguin* (Cambridge/New York: Cambridge University Press, 2000). See especially Chapter 9, 'Decoration and the Cultural Meaning of Gauguin's Primitivizing Techniques.'

222. See William Morris, *The Art and Craft of Printing* (New Rochelle, NY: Elston Press, 1902), *William Morris and Kelmscott* (London: The Design Council, 1981), H. Halliday Sparling, *The Kelmscott Press and William Morris, Master-craftsman* (London: Macmillan and Co., 1924) and Margaret Bingham Stillwell, *The Influence of William Morris and the Kelmscott Press* (Providence: Press of E.A. Johnson and Co., 1912).

223. 'Je rêve d'anciens missels aux encadrements rythmiques, des lettres fastueuses de graduels, des premières gravures sur bois – qui correspondent en somme à notre complexité littéraire par des préciosités et des délicatesses.' Maurice Denis, 'Définition du néo-traditionnisme' in *Théories*, p. 110. While praising medieval manuscripts, Denis also expressed his desire for book decoration that would 'correspond' to the text, rather than illustrate it.

224. For an interesting article touching on related issues see Michael Camille (1990).

225. This paradox would be taken to an even further degree in the popular and widely disseminated manuscripts of artists like Albert Robida, who imitated medieval manuscripts in his mass-produced illustrated works. For a fuller discussion of his production, see Chapter 7.

226. Denis's first designs for *Sagesse*, a series of woodcuts influenced by the crude hatching and compressed space of Gothic woodcuts (to be followed by 48 lithographs) were not acceptable to Verlaine. Although Denis exhibited them in 1891, the prints were not published until after Verlaine's death in 1896. A new series of color wood engravings, based on Denis's original designs, were finally published by Vollard in 1911. See Jacques Guignard, 'Les livres illustrés de Maurice Denis,' *Le Portique* 4 (1946), pp. 49–71.

227. Denis, 'Le symbolisme et l'art religieux moderne,' in Maurice Denis, *Nouvelles théories sur l'art moderne, sur l'art sacré 1914–1921* (Paris: Rouart et Watelin, 1922), p. 168.

228. Frédéric Destremau compared the arabesques that appear in the painted landscapes of Denis to those found in medieval manuscripts. 'Le Chemin dans les arbres de Maurice Denis, 1891–92,' *Gazette des Beaux-Arts* (Oct. 1988), pp. 155–62.

229. 'Au point de vue de la technique beaucoup sont excellents; à contempler tels encadrements, tels culs-de-lampe, on se reporte irrésistiblement à certains missels du moyen-age, chefs-d'oeuvre d'imagiers inconnus.' Adolphe Retté, 'Maurice Denis', *La Plume* (Sept. 1891), p. 301.

230. For the way in which medieval images functioned in their context, see David Freedberg, *The Power of Images: Studies in the History and Theory of Response* (Chicago: Chicago University Press, 1989).

231. As Leslie Workman has remarked in his various definitions of medievalism, the present is an inextricable component of interpretations of the past. Even art historians are not immune to reading the past through the lens of the present. See for example Gert Schiff's essay on Max Dvorjak in *German Essays on Art History* (New York: Continuum, 1988) and Michael Camille,

'How New York Stole the Idea of Romanesque Art; Medieval, Modern and Post-Modern in Meyer Schapiro,' *Oxford Art Journal* 17 (1994).

232. From the seventeenth century onward, French Academic theory excluded the aesthetic of stained glass and other medieval media from consideration as 'high art.' On this see Harris, pp. 90–93.

233. Armand Point, 'Les Primitifs et les symbolistes,' *L'Ermitage* (July 1895), pp. 11–19.

234. See for example Gustave Ollendorf, 'L'exposition nationale de 1893,' in *La Revue des Deux Mondes* (November 1893). On Puvis's reception see Richard Wattenmaker, *Puvis de Chavannes and the Modern Tradition* (Toronto: Art Gallery of Ontario, 1975).

235. 'Si l'on accotait un Puvis aux *Vendanges* de Gozzoli, on découvrirait non seulement leur parenté, mais que c'est Puvis, qui des deux, semble le Primitif. Ce qu'il peint n'a ni lieu ni date; c'est de partout et de toujours, une abstraction de Primitif, un rêve poétique d'esprit, une ode de l'éternel humain … ' Joséphin Péladan, 'L'Esthétique au Salon de 1883', *L'Artiste* (May 1883).

236. Indeed, Puvis seemed intent on denying such mystical and explicitly Christian 'inspiration' in his own art. Commenting on his *Inspiration Chrétienne*, he wrote: 'Now, if one really wants to take the trouble to look at my *Christian Inspiration*, will one find the glorification of ecstasy and mortification? Not at all, here is what I have done. A religious painter, some Fra Angelico, is busy finishing a mural decoration. Far from being overwhelmed by the infinite, he seems seized with a fever for work […] I would very much like to know if there is anything else in all that than evidence of human activity […] That's my own philosophy and not the contemplative spirit of the Middle Ages.' Cited and translated in Brown Price, p. 106.

237. Camille Mauclair, 'Le Salon de 1894,' *Le Mercure de France* 11 (June 1894), p. 157. Roger Marx praised the 'naïveté forte et la gaucherie savoureuse' of Denis, see Roger Marx, 'Salons de 1895', *Gazette des Beaux-Arts* 14 (1895), p. 24. For Denis's stylistic emulation of Fra Angelico, see Michael Marlais, 'Conservative Style/Conservative Politics.'

238. 'Il était resté fidèle à la tradition médiévale moins savante, plus humaine. Ses peintures murales de l'église de Châteauneuf malheureusement détériorées, ont une évidente parenté avec les fresques françaises du XIIIe et du XIVe siècles, très peu avec les fresques italiennes.' Maurice Denis, introduction to *ABC de la peinture. Suivi d'une étude sur la vie et l'oeuvre de Paul Sérusier par Maurice Denis* (Paris: H. Floury, 1942), p. 117. Rodolphe Rapetti has published a series of interesting studies by René Piot, an early participant at the Nabi gatherings. During his visit to Italy in 1895, Piot made copies after the Trecento frescoes of Andrea Bonaiuti in the Spanish chapel of Santa Maria Novella. In addition, he executed careful copies after paintings by artists such as Taddeo Gaddi and Domenico Ghirlandaio. See Rodolphe Rapetti, *René Piot: 1866–1934*, exhibition catalog (Paris: Réunion des musées nationaux, 1991). Photographs of these copies, painted in tempera, may be found in the dossier on Piot in the Centre de Documentation, Musée d'Orsay, Paris.

239. André (or Andhré) des Gachons (1871–1909) published with his brother Jacques the short-lived medievalizing journal, *L'Album des légendes* (1894–1895). He regularly exhibited with the Salons de la Rose+Croix.

240. Thiebault Sisson, 'L'exposition Grasset,' *La Plume* 122 (May 1894), p. 196.

241. Henri Raison du Cleuziou, 'L'oeuvre d'Eugène Grasset,' *La Plume* pp. 122, 197.

242. ' … un artiste des époques de la prière et de la foi élucidant à travers les terrestres images l'approche des paradis, exprimant les recours en Dieu au bout de toutes les actions humaines.' Camille Lemonnier, *La Plume*, p. 194.

243. ' … ils mènent une curieuse phalange d'artistes et de poètes qui se sont voués à cet art délicieux de faire revivre notre passé, de faire refleurir la légende, de continuer les néo-Primitifs.' Félix Malterre, *La Revue encyclopédique* (1 Feb. 1895).

244. See, for example, J.-K. Huysmans's article 'Noëls du Louvre' in *Oeuvres complètes* vol. 16 (Geneva: Slatkine Reprints, 1972).

245. See Robert Baldick, who argues that one of the reasons for the commercial success of Huysmans's *La Cathédrale* was that a newspaper story, 'Huysmans intime,' stated that he was leaving the world to become a monk at Solesmes. Huysmans was, of course, infuriated by this account and complained of having his soul treated like a 'public urinal.' He was, however, happy to reap the benefits of the publicity. Cited in Baldick, p. 260.

246. 'Duez ne sera jamais un mystique et c'est en vain qu'il cherche à devenir le Fra Angelico de son époque […] Soyez, avec votre solide talent d'une si large envergure, le peintre de choses puissantes et saines de notre époque. Renoncez à cette singulière idée de vouloir faire revivre devant nos yeux, aujourd'hui, si pleine de lumière et si avides de sujets empruntés à l'histoire de l'humanité ou à la vie de nature, ces scènes d'hystérie et de catalepsie hallucinés et malades.' Armand Dayot, *L'exposition des Beaux-Arts – Salon de 1884* (Paris: Librairie d'art, 1884), p. 50.

247. Cited in Vollard, *Recollections of a Picture Dealer*, p. 202.

248. 'Je vois qu'on trouve encore à Hambourg à des prix bien moindres que ceux de Paris, des Primitifs! – Ici, ils sont à des prix fous, absolument inabordables. Il est vrai qu'il y en a pas mal de faux – c'est Zola qui achète ceux-là – et à un prix aussi fort. Par contre, il y a des bibelots d'Eglises, parfois possible. J'en ai acheté des masses, vieux St. Sacrement, encensoirs, chappes – une liquidation d'un couvent où j'ai raflé de ce que j'ai pu – Et des reliques!!' Huysmans letter to Arij Prins (Paris 4 May 1892). Letter 16, p. 238.

249. 'L'Exposition des Primitifs français n'a point été imaginée pour seulement faire la fortune de certains marchands d'antiquité; son but avait une portée plus haute et plus morale.' Bouchot, *Les Primitifs français*, p. 12.

250. The private collecting of medieval works in the nineteenth century is a fascinating subject worthy of much further exploration. For an excellent introduction to this topic, see Michael Camille (1990). As Camille notes, the collection of extant and treasured medieval works of artistic pedigree 'legitimized' the status of such aristocratic collectors. The disenfranchised aristocracy, stripped of power in the political realm, sought compensation in the fields of art and leisure, claiming their heritage via art collecting. See also Hindman *et al*.

251. ' … tout en vivant fort librement et chacun à sa guise.' Jacques Daurelle, *Exposition des oeuvres d'Armand Point et de Haute-Claire*, Galerie Georges Petit (Paris, 1903), p. 1.

252. For primary information on Haute-Claire, see *Armand Point et son oeuvre – par MM. Paul Fort, Paul et Victor Margueritte …* (Paris, 1901).

253. 'C'est au Moyen-Age français que M. Armand Point tente de renouer avec la tradition des industries d'art sans qu'il néglige toutefois ce que la Renaissance italienne nous offre de grâce, de finesse, et d'élégance.' Stuart Merrill, *Armand Point et Haute Claire*, 1–22 Avril 1899: Exposition de tableaux de Armand Point (Paris: Galerie Georges Petit), p. 8.

254. The decoration and marketing of the gallery is discussed by Mainardi, pp. 137 ff.

255. See Mainardi, p. 137. On the Bon Marché see Michael Miller, *The Bon Marché: Bourgeois Culture and the Department Store 1869–1920* (Princeton: Princeton University Press, 1984).

256. 'J'ai bien senti la pensée profonde de M. Huysmans. C'est dans l'alliance de l'art et de la vie monastique qu'il cherche l'avenir fécond de l'Eglise […] Il voudrait réaliser le couvent d'Art, la maison de luxe pour Dieu […] Mais dans l'histoire du Moyen Age nous ne rencontrons rien de pareil […] Tandis que Durtal signe ses livres, et dans l'art il voit un présent de luxe, et à sa maison bénédictine il promet un succès prodigieux. Grave contradiction, dont ce livre porte la marque, et qui gâtera son action comme son unité […]' 'Sur l'Oblat,' in *Huysmans*, Pierre Brunel and André Guyaux, eds (Paris: Editions de l'Herne, 1985), p. 261.

257. Watson, among others, refers to the fin de siècle as a 'proto-consumer culture,' distinguishing it from our own.

258. 'C'est en vertu de cet esprit d'imitation fatale que nos intérieurs, où la lumière est nécessaire à cause du travail, sont obscuris par l'abus des vitraux colorés; que nos petits foyers s'encombrent de grands landiers en fer forgé, faits pour le vaste manteau des cheminées féodales; que nos sièges, au lieu de s'accommoder par leurs courbes aux grâces souples de la femme contemporaine, à ses vêtements aux plis leger, affectent les formes rigides des hautes cathédrales du Moyen Âge, et font d'une Parisienne de cette fin de siècle une Blanche de Castille malgré elle, une châtelaine en pénitence.' 'La Maison moderne – Etudes de décoration et d'ameublement,' *Revue illustrée* 1:8 (April 1886), p. 283.

259. See Emery, 'Bricabracomania: Zola's Romantic Instinct,' *Excavatio* 12 (1999), pp. 107–15.

260. For an overview of the social, political and technological developments that made the last twenty years of the nineteenth century so fertile for illustrated publications, see the introduction to Jean Watelet's *La Presse illustrée en France* (Ph.D. thesis, Université Panthéon-Assas, published by Les Presses Universitaires du Septentrion, 1998), pp. 56–130. A shorter version is published as 'La presse illustrée' in Claude Bellanger ed., *Histoire Générale de la presse française. Tome III: De 1871 à 1940* (Presses Universitaires de France: Paris, 1970), pp. 369–82. See also Ségolène Le Men, *La Cathédrale illustrée* (Paris: CNRS Editions, 1998), for the public's fascination with book illustration.

261. One gains an idea of the completely different aesthetic concerns of these authors by glancing at Jules Huret's 1891 *Enquête sur l'évolution littéraire* (Vanves: Les Editions Thot, 1984). All of these writers but Loti agreed to be interviewed and the journalist classified them by conflicting 'schools.' He grouped Huysmans and Zola with 'Naturalists,' Jean Moréas with 'Symbolists and decadents' and Anatole France with 'Psychologists'. Many of his interviews begin with descriptions of an author's taste in home furnishing, which he links to literary proclivities.

262. One of the forerunners of this vogue was Dornac, whose 1889 series, 'Nos contemporains chez eux,' included leading celebrities from Pierre Loti to Pasteur, Sarah Bernhardt to President Carnot, as well as writers Paul Verlaine, Emile Zola, Edmond de Goncourt and Stéphane Mallarmé. Before this approach, people were generally photographed in studios. For more about 'At Home' photography in England and France, see Alison Gernsheim, *A Concise History of Photography* (New York: Grosset & Dunlap, 1965), pp. 129–39.

263.  'Dans le cabinet de travail [...] il y a là des bois sculptés du moyen âge, des statuettes, des vieux cuivres, des fragments de bas-reliefs bibliques; dans un cadre un curieux morceau de sculpture, le baptême de saint Jean-Baptiste, avec des détails ingénus [...] puis des gravures de Dürer et de Rembrandt et deux anges habillés de plis extraordinaires.' 1891 interview with Jules Huret, later published in *L'Enquête sur l'évolution littéraire.*

264.  Emile Blavet's April 1888 article about the party, written on the trip from Rochefort to Paris, provides the best description of Loti's house, in which each room reproduced a different age, but whose 'gem,' according to Blavet, was the Gothic dining room. 'Mais le bijou de ce logis cosmopolite, c'est la salle à manger, où il n'y a pas une pierre, pas une boiserie, pas un détail d'architecture, d'ameublement ou d'ornementation qui ne soit du plus pur XVe siècle. Dès le seuil, on se sent rajeuni – vieilli serait peut-être plus juste – de cinq cents ans.' His article, republished in *La Vie Parisienne* (Paris: Paul Ollendorff, 1889), describes the event, the people in attendance, the luxury of their costumes and their activities in great detail. He even goes so far as to quote passages from the invitation and menu, pp. 121–34.

265.  ' [...] chez M. Jean Moréas, au pied de la Montagne Sainte-Geneviève, dans une maison à vitraux et à poutrelles, à plafonds écarlates, à escalier de chêne.' O. Malivert, in an article published in *La Vie moderne* (20 November 1886). Quoted in Robert A. Jouanny, *Jean Moréas, écrivain français* (Paris: Lettres Modernes, 1969), p. 78. The description of France's study is published in *Anatole France Himself, A Boswellian Record* by Jean-Jacques Brousson, trans. John Pollock (Philadelphia: J.B. Lippincott, 1925), p. 48. Other writers, including Maurice Maeterlinck and Saint-Pol-Roux created their own Gothic homes, 'Orlamonde' ('Out of the world') and 'Manoir de Cécilian,' respectively. See Dakyns, p. 242.

266.  Zola himself referred to 'cloistering' himself at Médan (see, for example, a recently auctioned *carte de visite* to E. and Michelis de Rienzi). Maupassant's 1882 articles for *Le Gaulois*, Maurice Guillemot's 1887 *Villégiatures d'artistes* and Goncourt's *Journal* all expressed surprise at the extent of Zola's medieval holdings. The lists of objects auctioned after Zola's death confirm both the eclecticism of his collection and the abundance of medieval objects it contained. They are published at the end of *Le Dictionnaire d'Emile Zola*, eds Colette Becker, Gina Gourdin-Servenière and Véronique Lavielle (Paris: Robert Laffont, 1993). For more details about Zola's house at Médan and the medievalism of his Paris apartments, see Emery, 'Bricabracomania.'

267.  *Literature and Material Culture* (Cambridge: Cambridge University Press, 1999), pp. 1–29, 47–50.

268.  For a thorough discussion of the approaches and histories of European collecting see Chapter 1, 'Collecting Practices,' in Susan Pearce, *On Collecting: An Investigation into Collecting in the European Tradition* (London/New York: Routledge, 1995). As Pearce notes, by the late sixteenth century the tradition of the pleasure cabinet – also known as the *Wunderkammer, Kunstkammer,* or *Galleria* – included objects of art, as well as natural history and other esoterica. See also Stephen Bann, *The Clothing of Clio* (Cambridge: Cambridge University Press, 1984).

269.  Clive Wainwright, *The Romantic Interior: The British Collector at Home, 1750–1850* (New Haven: Yale University Press, 1989).

270.  Beckford was also an enthusiastic collector of medieval manuscripts. See the abundant literature on the Gothic revival, including John Wilton-Ely, 'The Genesis and Evolution of Fonthill Abbey,' *Architectural History* 23 (1980), pp. 40–51.

271.  For a brief discussion of the troubadour style see Chapter 1. See also Louis Maigron, *Le Romantisme et la Mode*, for descriptions of costumes, jewelry and furniture modeled on medieval works.

272.  See Dominique Poulot, *Musée, Nation, Patrimoine* (Paris: Gallimard, 1997) and 'Surveiller et s'instruire: La Révolution française et l'intelligence de l'héritage historique,' *Studies on Voltaire and the Eighteenth Century* 344 (1996), pp. 31–143.

273.  See Hindman *et al.*, pp. 49–50.

274.  For thorough analyses of the Musée des Monuments Français see Francis Haskell, *History and its Images*; Stephen Bann, 'The Poetics of the Museum: Lenoir and du Sommerard' in *The Clothing of Clio*, and Dominique Poulot, 'Alexandre Lenoir et les musées des monuments français' in *Les Lieux de mémoire* II: 2 (1992), Paris: Gallimard, pp. 497–527.

275.  'Le musée est une succession de salles, consacrées chacune à un siècle, du XIIIe au XVIIe.' Quoted in Poulot (1992), p. 504.

276.  See Poulot (1992), pp. 502 and 504–9.

277.  Pearce (1995), p. 24.

278.  The museum was so popular that painters Léon-Mathieu Cochereau (1793–1817) and Charles-Marie Bouton (1781–1853) dedicated works to the various rooms of Lenoir's museum; their canvases can be seen today in the section of Le Musée Carnavalet dedicated to vandalism and conservation (Salle 111).

279.  For specific quotes from nineteenth-century historians, see Poulot (1992), pp. 520–21, and Haskell.

280.   Alexandre du Sommerard (1779–1842) was of aristocratic descent. In 1832 he moved into a Gothic hôtel that had been occupied by the Abbots of Cluny in the thirteenth century, located on the Boulevards Saint Germain and Saint Michel. Flanking the hôtel were the remains of the Palais des Thermes, a Roman bath house. In 1834, du Sommerard decided to combine the buildings into a museum for the display of medieval art. For his goals, see his book, *Les Arts du Moyen Age*, 5 vols (Paris: Techener, 1838–1846). The last volume was written by his son. After his death, the property was bought by the State and inaugurated on 16 March 1844. *Musée de Cluny: Guide* (Paris: Editions de la Réunion, 1986). See Stephen Bann for an analysis of the ways in which the two collections were fused.

281.   'Faire revivre le passé *more majorum*.' Quoted in Poulot (1992), p. 521.

282.   *Musée des Thermes et de l'hôtel de Cluny: Catalogue et description des objets d'art de l'antiquité du Moyen Age et de la Renaissance* (Paris, 1883). For an excellent analysis of du Sommerard's conception and organization of the museum see Bann.

283.   From *La Renommée, revue politique, parlementaire, littéraire*, pp. 8–12. Cited in Poulot (1992), p. 522.

284.   The term comes from Susan Pearce, *Museums, Objects and Collections: A Cultural Study* (Leicester/London: Leicester University Press, 1992).

285.   For a thorough discussion of *Vieux Paris*, see Chapter 7.

286.   The series was acquired from the Château de Boussac. The first five pieces are commonly interpreted as depicting allegories of the five senses and the last scene to relate to the idea of the *Liberum Arbitrium*. See Geneviève Souchal, *Chefs-d'oeuvre de la tapisserie du XIVe au XVI siècle*, exhibition catalog (Paris: Grand Palais/ Editions des Musées Nationaux, 1976).

287.   By the late nineteenth century, the museum housed many notable works including the 1502 Saint Etienne tapestries acquired from the Hôtel Dieu d'Auxerre and ten fifteenth-century Flemish tapestries depicting the History of David and Bathsheba, as well as numerous fragments of stained glass from the Sainte-Chapelle.

288.   *Musée des Thermes et de l'Hôtel de Cluny* (1883), p. xx.

289.   Quoted in Daniel Sherman, *Worthy Monuments: Art Museums and the Politics of Culture in Nineteenth Century France* (Cambridge: Harvard University Press, 1989), p. 131.

290.   In the inaugural issue of *Les Annales archéologiques* (May 1844), Didron presents the publication as an alternative to both the official *Bulletin archéologique* and the politically-oriented *L'Univers*, the only other outlet for publishing information about archeology at the time. Though he wants his publication to be less 'official' than government-sponsored publications, it nonetheless singles out a learned readership.

291.   Moïse Schwabe, 'La Collection Strauss au Musée de Cluny,' *Gazette des Beaux-Arts* 5 (1 March 1891), pp. 237–45.

292.   See Chapter 5 for a more detailed analysis of this issue. See also Morowitz (1997).

293.   'Le catalogue de la Collection Spitzer,' *Gazette des Beaux-Arts* 3 (1890).

294.   See Hindman *et al.*, p. 66.

295.   See Watson (1999), Bann (1984), Sherman (1989), Bennett (1995), and Susan Pearce, ed. *Museums and the Appropriation of Culture* (London: Athlone Press, 1994).

296.   This was true, for example, at the 1904 Exposition des Primitifs français, discussed in detail in Chapter 1.

297.   See Hindman *et al.*, for a discussion of the earlier museum politics of nineteenth-century rulers, pp. 143–4.

298.   Bennett, p. 28.

299.   The term comes from Pearce, *Museums, Objects, Collections*.

300.   Louis Courajod and Paul Frantz Marcou, *Musée de sculpture comparée (Moulages) – Palais du Trocadéro. Catalogue Raisonné publié sous les auspices de la Commission des Monuments Historiques* (Paris: Imprimerie Nationale, 1892); Camille Enlart and Jules Roussel, *Catalogue général du Musée de sculpture comparée au Palais du Trocadéro* (Paris: Henri Laurens, 1929). For the influence of molding makers, see Poulot (1992), p. 525.

301.   ' … pour détruire l'idée d'une prétendue infériorité du second … ' Enlart and Roussel, *Catalogue général du Musée de sculpture comparée au Palais du Trocadéro (Moulages)*, p. 5.

302.   For an analysis of the scholarship devoted to differentiating the Romanesque from other medieval periods see Bizzarro. Creating educational museums was a critical step in improving knowledge of medieval art because, as Françoise Choay and Jean Mallion have pointed out, architects and art historians of the time were stunningly ignorant about medieval structures. Because their training had focused primarily on classical architecture, they were unable to recognize valuable medieval architecture, let alone understand how it had been constructed or

how it could be repaired. Choay, *L'Allégorie du patrimoine* (Paris: Seuil, 1999), pp. 111–12 and Mallion, pp. 27–32.

303.   In 1916, Henri Chaine, the chief architect of *Les Monuments historiques*, wrote a preface for the publication of these courses, in which he called them a complement to Viollet's work. A. de Baudot, *L'Architecture. Le passé. Le présent* (Paris: Henri Laurens, 1916), p. v. Baudot begins his treatment of medieval architecture with the following phrase: 'Nous arrivons maintenant à cette grand époque du moyen âge dont l'immense effort, dû au génie de la France, a jeté un si vif et si nouveau jour dans le domaine de l'architecture.' p. 50.

304.   For biographical information on Courajod see André Michel, introduction to Louis Courajod, *Leçons professées à l'Ecole du Louvre (1886–1896)* (Paris: 1899); Haskell, pp. 442–4.

305.   For a more thorough exploration of Courajod's politics, see Morowitz (1996) and 'Louis Courajod, the Louvre, and the Barbaric Middle Ages,' *Studies in Medievalism*, forthcoming 2003.

306.   These were published posthumously in 1899.

307.   For an exploration of French Celtic culture as a challenge to latinized France see Morowitz (1996). See also Marc Antliff, *Inventing Bergson: Cultural Politics and the Parisian Avant-Garde* (Princeton: Princeton University Press, 1993).

308.   'Il [Roman art] était resté partout le produit d'une importation violente, d'une intrusion militaire.' Courajod, 'Les Origines,' p. 47.

309.   'Les masses populaires, restèrent profondément étrangères à l'art romain, aussi étrangères sans doute qu'elles le sont aujourd'hui à certains de nos arts cultivés en serre chaude dans certains milieux mondains ou académiques.' Courajod, 'L'élément celtique ou Gaulois,' *Leçons* (17 and 24 December 1890), p. 76.

310.   Louis Courajod, *Histoire du département de la sculpture moderne au Musée du Louvre* (Paris: Ernst Leroux, 1894).

311.   'La formation d'un musée de sculpture du moyen âge et de la Renaissance exige de revendications qui, pour n'être pas toutes couronnées de succès n'en doivent pas moins se continuer avec persévérance, parce qu'elles seront approuvées quand on verra, par l'ensemble de la nouvelle collection ce qu'elles ont produit.' Letter of 29 October 1850 from Léon de Laborde to the director of the Louvre, quoted in Courajod (1899), p. 189. Laborde himself was no stranger to the amassing of medieval objects for personal pleasure. Haskell describes him as 'an aristocrat whose fine art collection served to shield him from the modern world,' p. 441. Laborde had been named to his position in 1847.

312.   'Le goût du jour et la mode semblaient ne vouloir encore accepter, du moyen âge et de la Renaissance, que la bimbeloterie. Nous ne pouvons nous empêcher de remarquer le subit abaissement du sentiment public.' Courajod (1899), p. 239.

313.   ' … l'organisation complète et chronologique de l'histoire de l'art pendant la période du moyen âge et de la Renaissance.' Letter of 27 November 1850 from the director to the Minister. Quoted in Courajod (1899), p. 201.

314.   ' … un judicieux esprit de classification scientifique.' Courajod (1899), p. 239.

315.   The pieces already there by the 1850s included the tomb of Philippe de Commines and a thirteenth-century statue of a King of Juda (Childebert) from Saint Germain-des-Près. Well familiar with the works of Lenoir, Courajod had published a monograph about him: *Alexandre Lenoir et le Musée des monuments français* (1878–1887).

316.   André Michel et Gaston Migeon, *Le Musée du Louvre: sculptures et objets d'art du Moyen Age, de la Renaissance et des temps modernes* (Paris: Librairie Renouard, 1912).

317.   Paul Vitry, *The Museum of the Louvre: A Concise Guide to the Various Collections*, trans. Charles H. Hauff (New York: Gaston Braun, 1912).

318.   See especially an obituary article in *Le Temps*, in which T. de Wyzewa praised his taste and proclaimed him 'un des ces esprits clairs et vraiment français qui ont à la fois le don de bien voir et de bien comprendre'. 12 December 1896.

319.   Works from the seventeenth century and after were placed on the other side of the court, along the side of the Pont du Carrousel and La Rue de Rivoli.

320.   See, for example, *En Route* or Huysmans's article 'Noëls du Louvre' in *Oeuvres complètes* vol. 16 (Geneva: Slatkine Reprints, 1972).

321.   For a discussion of *Vieux Paris*, see Chapter 7.

322.   As both Shane Adler Davis and Rémy Saisselin have argued, the Expositions Universelles can be seen as 'temporary' versions of the new bourgeois department store. In both arenas, the middle-class consumer was dazzled by the sheer volume and opulent display of the latest technological and decorative products. For the ways in which consumerism was reconciled with Republican values, see part two of Tiersten, 'Civilizing Consumption,' in her *Marianne in the Market*.

323. See Walton and Silverman.

324. Proust was assisted by Alfred Darcel, the administrator of the Musée de Cluny. For information about the 1889 Exposition see Louis Gonse and Alfred de Lostalot, eds, *Exposition Universelle de 1889: Les beaux-arts et les arts décoratifs – L'art français rétrospectif au Trocadéro* (Paris: Journal *Le Temps*, 1890); *L'art décoratif à l'Exposition Universelle de 1889* (Paris: A. Calvas Editeur, 1890); Emile Molinier, 'Exposition rétrospective de l'art français au Trocadéro: I. Le Moyen Age,' *Gazette des Beaux-Arts* 2 (August 1889).

325. Among the private collectors who lent works to the show were M. Picard, M. Wasset, M. Nodet, M. Mohl, M. Shiff and M. Le Breton. Molinier, 'Exposition rétrospective,' *La Gazette des Beaux-Arts* 65 (1 August 1889), pp. 145–66.

326. 'A l'entrée voici les trésors les plus anciens de nos églises et de nos abbayes. Le monastère est notre premier atelier ... ' Edmond Bonnafée, 'Exposition rétrospective de l'art français au Trocadéro,' in Gonse and Lostalot, p. 511.

327. ' ... une des grandes oeuvres d'éducation artistique accomplie depuis dix ans.' Molinier, p. 146.

328. 'Pour nous qui vivons parmi les morts, travaillant sans relâche à reconstituer leur chronologie, leur nationalité, leur famille, le Trocadéro sera une mine abondante de révélations. Jamais les trésors de nos églises ne s'étaient présentés avec un tel ensemble; jamais on ne les avait réunis côte à côte, ni rapprochés des spécimens similaires de nos cabinets parisiens. Parmi les monuments tirés des collections privées ou des musées de province, un grand nombre figurent ici pour la première fois et n'avaient encore passé par aucune Exposition.' Edmond Bonnafée, 'Exposition Universelle de 1889: Au Trocadéro,' *Gazette des Beaux-Arts* 65 (1 July 1889), p. 9.

329. 'C'est encore, si vous voulez, un incomparable cabinet d'amateur; car l'amateur s'appelle la France et tout, ou presque tout ce qu'il expose est son oeuvre et porte sa signature. Dans ce salon de bonne compagnie, chacun parle la même langue et s'entend à demi-mot.' Bonnafée, p. 5.

330. In *Art Nouveau*, Gabriele Fahr-Becker traces the impact of Viollet-le-Duc's theories about innovation with iron and glass and about the Gothic style. Such ideas inspired innovation in buildings, metro signs and interior decoration (Cologne: Könemann Verlagsgesellschaft mbH, 1997): 75–84, 136–47, 195–7. We discuss the impact of Viollet's theories further in Chapter 4.

331. On the exhibit see Emile Molinier, Roger Marx and Paul Frantz Marcou, *Exposition Universelle de 1900; L'Art Français des origines à la fin du XIXe siècle* (Paris: 1901) and the *Catalogue officiel illustré de l'Exposition rétrospective* from the fair.

332. Tapestries included the famous 'Apocalypse' tapestries from the Cathedral of Angers (for more on them see below), as well as 'Chasse' tapestries from Notre-Dame de Nantilly.

333. This shift is paralleled by the private marketing of medieval manuscripts. By the mid-nineteenth century, dealers had begun to cut out individual leaves and cuttings from manuscripts, promoting their reception as independent works of art, aesthetic 'fragments.' For a discussion of this issue, see Hindman *et al.*

334. See, for example, Didron's suggestion that artists use Viollet's models as inspiration for new designs instead of copying them. Cited in Pierre Auzas, *Viollet-le-Duc* (Paris: Caisse nationale des monuments historiques et des sites, 1979), p. 132.

335. For the best account of the reproduction of medieval works throughout the nineteenth century, see Hindman *et al.* The section entitled 'Reproductions' is particularly informative.

336. Camille (1990), p. 72.

337. The more specialized *La Gazette des Beaux-Arts* is full of images and articles, but even an extremely mainstream publication like *l'Illustration* published elaborate illustrated articles about museums and their acquisitions. In the first few months of 1898, for example, there are articles about the Louvre (5 March), the Musée Condé at Chantilly (16 and 23 April) and the Musée Carnavalet (21 May). *Le Figaro illustré* dedicated elaborate coverage to the World's Fair retrospective of medieval art (May 1900), and other issues, notably that dedicated to *Les Grands Musées de France* in 1900, depicted museums (Fontainebleau, Carnavalet, Versailles, Chantilly, Luxembourg, Gobelins, Compiègne) and their collections. Even daily newspapers like *Le Temps* regularly carried articles dedicated to new acquisitions. See for example 'Une nouvelle salle au Musée de Cluny,' *Le Temps* (30 May 1888); 'La sculpture du moyen age et de la Renaissance au Louvre,' *Le Temps* (25 July 1889).

338. Alfred Darcel, the director of the Musée de Cluny, highly praised the works of the Odiot collection in an 1889 article, 'La Collection de M. Ernest Odiot.' *Gazette des Beaux-Arts*, 64 (1 March 1889), pp. 247–58.

339. For the reputation of the Duc de Berry, see Camille (1990).

340. For a review of both of these books see Bernard Prost, 'Les arts à la cour du duc de Berry: d'après les récentes publications de MM. Jules Guiffrey, Alfred de Champeaux et Paul Gauchéry,' *Gazette des Beaux-Arts* (1 September 1895), p. 254. The article included four reproductions from manuscripts in the Bibliothèque Nationale.

341. As noted, for more on Germain, see Bouillon.

342. Alphonse Germain, *Notre Art de France* (Paris: E. Girard, 1894).

343. 'A tous les artistes que laissent indifférents les vains succès d'exposition, – il y en a, Dieu merci! – et qui s'efforcent de faire dire quelque chose à leur oeuvre, et rêvent pour elle une destination; à ceux-là de méditer sur ce thème: l'art décoratif intime, d'en chercher la mise en pratique. Et s'ils tiennent à empreindre cet art d'originalité indigène, à le baser sur des principes appropriés, oh! qu'ils s'inspirent alors des ancêtres du xiiie siècle.' Germain (1894), pp. 47–8. Interior decoration was hugely in fashion in the second half of the nineteenth century and decorating guides flourished. For more about this fad, see Watson, pp. 47–56.

344. For the centrality of the decorative arts to French nationalism, see Silverman.

345. For a discussion of the do-it-yourself manuscript publications, see Hindman *et al.*, p. 149.

346. See Huysmans, 'Le Musée des arts décoratifs et l'architecture cuite,' *L'art moderne/Certains* (Paris: Union Générale des Editions [10/18], 1975), p. 338.

347. The Vitraux Français poster is by Eugène Ogé and can be consulted at the Bibliothèque Fourney (#214016). The Musée de la Publicité and the Bibliothèque Fourney in Paris own a great variety of such posters. See, for example, an 1895 *Harper's* poster featuring Joan (Musée de la publicité #10348), an 1892 poster of 'La Lorraine, bière française' (Musée de la publicité #199855), a non-dated poster for wines of Bordeaux featuring Saint George killing the dragon (Musée de la publicité #2000.54), or an 1897 Comte de Champagne poster featuring a crusader being served by his lady (Musée de la publicité #15109).

348. The purchase of extant medieval works, as well as contemporary works in medieval style, is part of the far larger interest in emulating the feudal nobility, a practice exhibited by both the bourgeoisie and the aristocracy of the nineteenth century. This complex phenomenon requires a separate study, one that can only be hinted at here and falls outside the scope of the current project. For a starting point see Pierre Bourdieu, *Distinction: A Social Critique of the Judgement of Taste*, trans. Richard Nice (Cambridge: Harvard University Press, 1984) and the works of Rosalind Williams and Janell Watson.

349. Walton, p. 32.

350. 'Ce n'est donc pas assez que le premier venu puisse copier à la grosse les meubles du Musée de Cluny! Je sais bien que l'on n'est pas obligé de les acheter, mais il faut bien les voir puisqu'ils emplissent des boulevards entiers et des rues!' 'Le Musée des arts décoratifs et l'architecture cuite,' p. 338.

351. Walter Benjamin explores many of these issues in 'The Work of Art in the Age of Mechanical Reproduction,' *Illuminations*, trans. Harry Zohn, ed. Hannah Arendt (New York, 1969).

352. This is the point that Huysmans makes in his article: because the state will confuse authentic objects with the thousands of fakes in circulation, real medieval art will vanish forever, pp. 337–8.

353. '[...] des tryptiques de Primitifs, des hommes d'armes en panoplies, de vieilles étoffes, des vitraux, [...] le cabinet de travail est, ainsi que la maison entière, encombré de toute une bricabracomanie qui étonne; et ce n'est pas qu'Emile Zola soit amateur; lorsqu'on le questionne là-dessus, il ne s'attarde pas, on ne le sent pas, comme un Goncourt ou un Anatole France, jouir du bibelot rare qu'on caresse des doigts, qu'on tourne et retourne, qu'on pelote, non, il a accumulé tout cela pour se faire un décor à son existence, son romantisme d'instinct aiguillé sur les choses d'église du Moyen Age [...] on perd pied au milieu de tout cela.' *Villégiatures d'artistes* (Paris: Ernest Flammarion, Editeur, n.d.), pp. 94–5. Guillemot's interview, probably from 1891, is too early to be a reflection of the backlash against Zola for his role in the Dreyfus Affair.

354. See Emery, 'Bricabracomania.'

355. Zola's frenzied excursions to buy old objects must have been like the shopping frenzies of his semi-autobiographical character, Pierre Sandoz, in *L'Oeuvre*: 'Ils couraient ensemble les brocanteurs, ils avaient une rage joyeuse d'acheter ... ' *Les Rougon-Macquart* vol. 4 (Paris: Editions Fasquelle et Gallimard [Edition de la Pleiade], 1966), p. 323.

356. Huysmans's correspondence with Arij Prins, notably letter 116, mocks Zola's tendency to be taken in by overpriced fakes attributed to the *Primitifs*.

357. '[...] Zola n'est point collectionneur. Il semble acheter, un peu pêle-mêle, au hasard de sa fantaisie excitée, suivant les caprices de son oeil, la séduction des formes et de la couleur, sans s'inquiéter comme Goncourt des origines authentiques et de la valeur incontestable.' 'Emile Zola,' *Le Gaulois* (14 January 1882).

358. Larousse stresses the shifting nature of the term 'collector' in his *Grand dictionnaire encyclopédique* by distinguishing the 'good collector' (a person who uses logic and reason to put together a complete set of objects) from the bad (a person who passionately acquires objects for the pleasure of doing so, without regard to the over-arching nature of the group of objects).

359. Pierre Larousse echoes this sentiment in his definition of 'collectionneur.' He argues that contemporaries should adopt a new definition of the collector, one that justifies seemingly whimsical purchases by their scientific and – by extension – social utility. For him, the museum – one of the nineteenth century's greatest achievements – should be the ultimate repository of private collections; a public showcase and laboratory that will educate the public.

360. '[…] la plupart des objets précieux classés au musée de Cluny, et échappés par miracle à l'immonde sauvagerie des sans-culottes, proviennent des anciennes abbayes de France; de même que l'Eglise a préservé de la Barbarie, au moyen âge, la philosophie, l'histoire et les lettres, de même elle a sauvé l'art plastique, amené jusqu'à nos jours ces merveilleux modèles de tissus, de joailleries que les fabricants de choses saintes gâtent le plus qu'ils peuvent, sans en pouvoir toutefois altérer la forme initiale, exquise. Il n'y avait dès lors rien de surprenant à ce qu'il eût pourchassé ces antiques bibelots, qu'il eût, avec nombre de collectionneurs, retiré ces reliques de chez les antiquaires de Paris, de chez les brocanteurs de la campagne.' A Rebours (Paris: Gallimard, 1977), p. 174.

361. Watson, p. 23. Indeed, Huysmans meant des Esseintes as a pastiche of contemporaries like Robert de Montesquiou, whose home was understood by many contemporaries to have served as the model for the eclectic fictional recluse. See Edgar Munhall, Whistler and Montesquiou: The Butterfly and the Bat (New York: Frick Collection, 1995).

362. 'Car à voir combien de députés, quand ils ont fini de voter des lois anticléricales, partent faire un tour aux cathédrales d'Angleterre, de France ou d'Italie, rapportent une vieille chasuble à leur femme pour en faire un manteau ou une portière, élaborent dans leur cabinet des projets de laïcisation devant la reproduction photographique d'une Mise au tombeau, marchandent à un brocanteur le volet d'un retable, vont pour leur antichambre chercher jusqu'en province des fragments de stalles d'église qui y serviront de porte-parapluie et le vendredi saint à la "Schola Cantorum", sinon même à l'église Saint-Gervais, écoutent "religieusement", comme on dit, la messe du pape Marcel, on peut penser que le jour où nous aurions persuadé tous les gens de goût de l'obligation que c'est pour le gouvernement de subventionner les cérémonies du culte, nous aurions trouvé comme alliés et soulevé contre le projet Briand bon nombre de députés anticléricaux.' From his 16 August 1904 article for Le Figaro entitled 'La Mort des cathédrales.' Reprinted in Contre Sainte-Beuve (Paris: Gallimard, 1971), pp. 782–3.

363. See Maurice Larkin, Church and State after the Dreyfus Affair: The Separation Issue in France (New York: Barnes and Noble, 1974) for tables showing the division of property among these groups, pp. 153, 155.

364. See Réau for shocking examples of the vandalism that followed the separation of Church and State, pp. 813–17. His examples are often reactionary, but do evoke the climate of the time.

365. A particularly good fictional example of this tendency occurs in Anatole France's 1897 L'Orme du Mail, in which the wife of Jewish prefect Worms-Clavelin collects Christian objects (her collection is compared to 'un trésor de cathédrale'), while her husband negotiates conflicts between Republican and Catholic politicians. Thanks to Bill Calin for bringing attention to this example.

366. Although Choay uses this expression to refer to a mentality that prevented nineteenth-century city planners from preserving a monument surrounded by the neighborhoods in which it once stood, the term can be applied with similar effect to those who would isolate a single object – a stained-glass window, for example – from the rest of the cathedral that surrounded it. L'Allégorie du patrimoine, p. 103. See Chapter 5 for much more analysis of the ways in which people tended to take individual works of medieval art such as stained glass and tapestries out of their religious context for use in private homes, offices, or entertainment venues.

367. 'La plus haute et la plus originale expression du génie de la France.' 'La Mort,' pp. 142 and 144.

368. This does not pretend to be an exhaustive summary of Riegl's theories; we introduce only those terms most important for our own discussion of the monument. For a fuller discussion of Riegl's theories, see Le culte moderne des monuments, trans. Daniel Wieczorek (Paris: Editions du Seuil, 1984), Margaret Olin, Forms of Representation in Riegel's Theory of Art (State College, PA: Pennsylvania State Press, 1992) and Margaret Iversen, Alois Riegl (Cambridge, MA: The MIT Press, 1993).

369. In focusing on the uniqueness that tradition bestows on the cathedral, Proust also anticipates the arguments of Walter Benjamin, who wrote, in 'The Work of Art in the Age of Mechanical Reproduction,' that the unique value of the 'authentic' work of art lies in ritual, its original use value. Yet while Proust mourns the passing of these vanished traditions, Benjamin sees their disappearance as a necessary step in the transition to the modern age and its forms of mass culture.

370. See Pierre Clarac's notes to the Pléiade edition of 'La Mort des cathédrales' for a description of its publication history, pp. 770–72. Proust and Barrès met in 1892. After both La Bible d'Amiens and 'La Mort des cathédrales,' Barrès wrote Proust congratulatory letters. The title, 'La Mort des cathédrales,' echoes that of Barrès's La Mort de Venise, published in 1902. Proust responded by encouraging Barrès to write something like La Mort de Venise in praise of the cathedral of Vézelay (20 August 1904, letter 122: IV, 220). Barrès would evoke Proust's title in 1914 when he

published *La Grande pitié des églises de France*, speeches he had given earlier while defending churches from the secular backlash that followed the 1905 separation of Church and State.

371. Auguste Rodin used all of these terms to describe the cathedral, borrowing from Viollet-le-Duc, who had first called it 'le Parthénon français,' and from Proust, who evoked it as 'le génie de la France.'

372. For a brief history of ideas about Gothic style see Louis Réau, 'Le mépris pour l'art du Moyen Age,' in *L'Histoire du vandalisme*, pp. 136–8. The term Gothic was first widely applied by Giorgio Vasari, who associated the style with the Barbarians in his 1550 *Vite*. The derogatory term spread throughout Europe and was applied indiscriminately to all nonclassical architecture from the sixth to the fifteenth centuries. Tina Waldeier Bizzarro traces the primarily negative French attitudes toward Romanesque and Gothic architecture from the sixteenth to the nineteenth centuries in *Romanesque Architectural Criticism: A Prehistory*, pp. 1–2, 7–8. Paul Frankl traces the reception of Gothic architecture through eight centuries of writing.

373. See Françoise Choay, *L'Allégorie du patrimoine*, pp. 57–8.

374. On guidebooks see Jean Mallion, pp. 23–4; Choay discusses the beautification projects of French kings on pp. 12–13.

375. 'La Bande noire' was published in 1824 in *La Muse française*, then republished in *Odes et Ballades*. He printed a passage against vandalism in *La Revue de Paris* in July–August 1829 and his essays against demolition appeared in *Le Nouveau Keepsake français, La France littéraire* and *La Revue des Deux Mondes* from 1831–1832. See Jean Mallion, pp. 425–44.

376. Montalembert's 1 March 1833 'Lettre à M. Victor Hugo' praises Hugo for being 'le premier [à déployer] un drapeau qui pût rallier toutes les âmes jalouses de sauver les monuments de l'ancienne France.' Quoted in Mallion, p. 444. Mallion discusses contemporary reactions to *Notre-Dame de Paris* and remarks on reviewers Paul Lacroix, Sainte-Beuve and Théophile Gautier and their enthusiasm for the great erudition and love of the cathedral evident in the book, p. 61. See Emery, *Romancing the Cathedral*, for a more extensive analysis of Hugo's impact on the nineteenth-century conception of Gothic architecture.

377. 'Inspirons, s'il est possible, à la nation l'amour de l'architecture nationale. C'est là, l'auteur le déclare, un des buts principaux de ce livre; c'est là un des buts principaux de sa vie.' Jean Mallion reprints Hugo's interventions in the Comité and provides examples of his commitment to preserving monuments throughout Europe, even until a few months before his death, pp. 481–512. *Les Cathédrales de France au XIXe siècle*, Jean-Michel Leniaud's magisterial work on the functioning and financing of restoration projects in nineteenth-century France, also provides an overview of the administrative details pertaining to the Comité (Paris: Economica, 1993).

378. On Didron fils, see Chapter 5. The first issue of *Les Annales archéologiques* dates from May 1844: 'le moyen âge, qui n'est pas le plus connu, malgré son puissant intérêt, sera étudié avec une prédilection particulière,' p. 2.

379. Huysmans, in his 1898 novel *La Cathédrale*, often does acknowledge the value of Didron's contributions to Gothic art and wishes that he had gone even further. For a discussion of Mâle's debt to Didron, see Catherine Brisac and Jean-Michel Leniaud, 'Adolphe-Napoléon Didron ou les média au service de l'art chrétien,' *Revue de l'art* 77 (1987): pp. 33–42.

380. This theme crops up throughout his works, but for a clear example see his 'Histoire de la peinture sur verre en Europe,' *Annales archéologiques* 23 (January–February 1853), p. 45.

381. For a comprehensive list of restoration projects as well as detailed biographies of the architects and functionaries involved in the nineteenth-century restoration movement, see Leniaud's *Les Cathédrales au XIXe siècle*.

382. See Bergdoll, 'The Ideal of the Gothic Cathedral in 1852,' pp. 110–20 (note 58).

383. Sir John Summerson explores Viollet's 'disgust' for institutions as a result of his fierce independence in 'Viollet-le-Duc and the Rational Point of View,' *Eugène-Emmanuel Viollet-le-Duc. 1814–1879* (London: Architectural Design and Academy Editions, 1980), pp. 7–13. For more about Viollet's conflicts with the Academy and responses to critics as well as extracts from his letters to them, see Geneviève Viollet-le-Duc, *Esthétique appliquée à l'histoire de l'art/Viollet-le-Duc et l'Ecole des Beaux-Arts: la bataille de 1863–64* (Paris: Ecole nationale supérieure des Beaux-Arts, 1994).

384. See the introduction to Barry Bergdoll's *The Foundations of Architecture: Selections from the Dictionnaire Raisonné of Viollet-le-Duc* (New York: Braziller, 1990).

385. Although Boileau and Vaudroyer responded to and interpreted Viollet's theories in their works, Viollet himself violently criticized them, proclaiming them 'parodies' of his theories. Regardless of the result, it was his writings that had prompted such experimentation. See Barry Bergdoll's numerous writings about Viollet and his impact on contemporaries, specifically 'The Ideal of the Cathedral' and *Léon Vaudoyer: Historicism in the Age of Industry* (New York: Architectural History Foundation and MIT, 1994).

386. Bertrand Lemoine, *Architecture in France, 1800–1900*, trans. Alexandra Bonfante-Warren (New York: Harry N. Abrams, Inc., 1998), pp. 10–25.

387. See Stephan Tschudi Madsen, *Sources of Art Nouveau*, trans. Ragnar Christophersen (New York: Da Capo Publishing, Inc., 1980) and Gabriele Fahr-Becker, *Art Nouveau* (Cologne: Könemann Verlagsgesellschaft mbH, 1997).

388. The *Actes du Colloque international Viollet-le-Duc* held in Paris in 1980 provides a glimpse of the staggering number of architects around the world who have been profoundly influenced by Viollet's theories (Paris: Nouvelles Editions Latines, 1982).

389. Pierre Auzas outlines the reception of Viollet-le-Duc's various publications in *Viollet-le-Duc* (Paris: Caisse nationale des monuments historiques et des sites, 1979).

390. See Emery, *Romancing the Cathedral*, for more about late nineteenth-century attitudes toward the Gothic cathedral.

391. Today, the use of taped religious music in medieval French churches provides an interesting illustration of this concept. Tourists are significantly more respectful of holy sites and remain silent when background music is played; it reminds them of the cathedral's religious function as the architecture alone does not.

392. See the chapter of Elaine Brody's *Paris: A Musical Kaleidoscope* entitled 'Wagner in France and France in Wagner' for a discussion of the love/hate relationship between the French and Wagner, pp. 21–59. Gerald D. Turbow provides very good descriptions of some of these battles in 'Art and Politics: Wagnerism in France,' *Wagnerism in European Culture and Politics*, ed. David Large and William Weber (Ithaca: Cornell University Press, 1984), pp. 134–66.

393. The concept of a total work of art was by no means new, but Wagner packaged it with an appealing new name and striking visual and auditory examples that appealed to the younger generation.

394. See Turbow, pp. 151–3. As he points out, Zola's novel *L'Oeuvre* gives a good idea of the influence of Wagner on artists and intellectuals of the time.

395. See Elaine Brody, pp. 51–2.

396. For more about the history of the Bayreuth festival, see Frederic Spotts, *Bayreuth: A History of the Wagner Festival* (New Haven: Yale University Press, 1994).

397. See Robert Pincus-Witten, *The Salons of the Rose+Croix 1892–1897* (London: Piccadilly Gallery, 1968), pp. 68–9.

398. See Martine Kahane and Nicole Wild, *Wagner et la France* (Paris: Herscher, 1983), pp. 35–6.

399. In *History through the Opera Glass*, George Jellinek traces the nineteenth-century passion for historical operas (White Plains, NY: Pro/Am Music Resources, Inc., 1994). Many featured characters from medieval epic and romance (Charlemagne, Le Cid, Lohengrin, Parsifal, Tristan, King Arthur) or the Crusades.

400. See, for example, the numerous editions of *Le Manuel pour les Visiteurs de Bayreuth* by Frédéric Wild (1897) and *Souvenir de Bayreuth, Fantaisie en forme de quadrille sur les thèmes favoris de 'l'Anneau du Nibelung' de Richard Wagner* by André Messager. Gabriel Faure, too, published 'souvenir' music related to his Bayreuth experiences.

401. In fact, as Richard Sieburth has noted, Dujardin was publishing *La Revue wagnérienne* and the Symbolist *Revue indépendante* at the same time, using many of the same authors for both publications. See 'The Music of the Future' in *A New History of French Literature*, ed. Denis Hollier (Cambridge, MA: Harvard University Press, 1989), pp. 789–98, 794.

402. He used this expression – 'la vie considérée à travers un vitrail' – in the 1890 preface to an unpublished collection of religious poems, *Chorus mysticus*, to describe his motivation for writing a collection devoted to 'liturgical poetry.' *Paul Valéry–Gustave Fourment: Correspondance 1887–1933*, ed. Octave Nodal (Paris: Gallimard, 1957), pp. 218–19.

403. See Sieburth, pp. 792, 797. A. G. Lehmann has succinctly summarized the three ways in which Wagner's art was 'total' for the Symbolists: in its combination of different media – art, music, poetry, costumes – working together; in its use of myth to create characters who represent all of humanity; and in its use of epic to provide a total meaning of life. *The Symbolist Aesthetic in France* (Oxford: Basil Blackwell, 1968), pp. 229–30.

404. 'Richard Wagner et Tannhäuser à Paris,' *Oeuvres complètes* (Paris: Robert Laffont, 1980), pp. 849–72, 852.

405. Lehmann shows the ways in which Baudelaire adapts Wagner's theory to fit his own aesthetic beliefs, which are based heavily on Platonic and Romantic ideals, pp. 104–14.

406. 'Richard Wagner et Tannhäuser,' p. 853. The emphasis is Baudelaire's.

407. See Brody, pp. 53–4, Sieburth and Lehmann, pp. 194–207, for a detailed comparison of the theories of Baudelaire and Wagner and of their incompatibility.

408.   *Le Roman de Durtal*, p. 738. Huysmans establishes a parallel between Saint Augustine and Mallarmé's definitions of Symbolism, though grossly misrepresenting Mallarmé in the process.

409.   This was, in fact, one of the goals of Jean Moréas, author of the 'Symbolist Manifesto' and leader of *L'Ecole romane*, which purported to revive medieval language. See Richard Shryock, 'Reaction Within Symbolism: L'Ecole romane,' *The French Review* 71:4, pp. 577–84, and Robert A. Jouanny.

410.   'Ils ont préféré dans leurs oeuvres l'expression par le décor, par l'harmonie des formes et des couleurs, par la matière employée, à l'expression par le sujet. Ils ont cru qu'il existait à toute émotion, à toute pensée humaine, un équivalent plastique, décoratif, une beauté correspondante. Et c'est probablement à des idées comme celles-là que nous devons, entre autres choses, les Primitifs, le chant grégorien et les cathédrales gothiques.' 'Préface de la IXe exposition des peintres impressionistes et symbolistes,' *Théories*, p. 27. In 'Notes sur la peinture religieuse' (1896), he noted: '[…] le symbolisme est une théorie chrétienne,' *Théories*, p. 42.

411.   Symons coined this phrase in 'J.-K. Huysmans,' an article that appeared in the *Fortnightly Review*, March 1892. Valéry is quoted in Robert Baldick, p. 87. Antoine Adam proposes that *A Rebours* was the primary catalyst that brought the forgotten Verlaine back into the literary limelight: *The Art of Paul Verlaine* (New York: New York University Press, 1963), p. 118.

412.   *A Rebours*, p. 328.

413.   '[…] Le salut viendra aux hommes par l'Art, qui expliquera la vérité, chassera des âmes le funeste aveuglement […] l'Art est mauvais s'il reste seulement un Art; l'Art est sacré, s'il est un moyen à nous faire chercher notre bonheur,' p. 250: 'La Religion de Richard Wagner et la Religion du Comte Léon Tolstoï,' *Revue wagnérienne* 8–9 (8 October 1885), pp. 237–56. Much of this article summarizes beliefs that Wagner expressed in his 1880 essay entitled 'Religion und Kunst.' For the intersection of art and aesthetics in Huysmans's writings, see the works of Robert Ziegler, especially 'From Prostitution to Prayer: The Writer and his Public in J.-K. Huysmans,' *The French Review* 67:1 (Oct. 1993), pp. 37–46.

414.   'Toute la liturgie catholique avec ses décors et ses accessoires, dont chacun est une invention de génie, suffit à ceux que tourmente obscurément un conflit d'idéal et de sensualité.' Cited in Dakyns, p. 265. Elskamp wrote about medieval religious art in *Le Bulletin de l'Académie royale de langue et de littérature françaises* xxxvi (1958), p. 46 while Rodenbach is quoted from *La Vocation* (Paris: Ollendorff, 1895), p. 47.

415.   See Chapter 3.

416.   'L'idéal de toutes ces oeuvres est le même et, par des moyens différents, atteint.' *En Route* (*Le Roman de Durtal*), p. 314.

417.   'Ah! La vraie preuve du catholicisme, c'était cet art qu'il avait fondé, cet art que nul n'a surpassé encore! C'était, en peinture et en sculpture les Primitifs; les mystiques dans les poésies et dans les proses; en musique, c'était le plain-chant; en architecture, c'était le roman et le gothique. Et tout cela se tenait, flambait en une seule gerbe, sur le même autel; tout cela se conciliait en une touffe de pensées unique: révérer, adorer, servir le Dispensateur, en lui montrant, réverbéré dans l'âme de sa créature, ainsi qu'en un fidèle miroir, le prêt encore immaculé de ses dons.' *En Route*, p. 313.

418.   In his preface to Remy de Gourmont's *Le Latin mystique*, p. vii.

419.   'Combien de fois des Esseintes n'avait-il pas été saisi et courbé par un irrésistible souffle, alors que le "Christus factus est" du chant grégorien s'élevait dans la nef dont les piliers tremblaient parmi les mobiles nuées des encensoirs, ou que le faux-bourdon du "De profundis" gémissait, lugubre de même qu'un sanglot contenu, poignant ainsi qu'un appel désespéré de l'humanité pleurant sa destinée mortelle, implorant la miséricorde attendrie de son Sauveur!' *A Rebours*, pp. 324–5.

420.   The official title of the Schola Cantorum was 'La Société de propagande pour des Chefs d'Oeuvres religieux.' Dom Pothier published a seminal work for Gregorian chant – *Les mélodies grégoriennes* – in 1880 (reprinted in 1980 by Stock), while Dom Guéranger worked nearly singlehandedly to restore the Benedictine order and to reintroduce plain chant into church services in France. See Dom Louis Soltner, *Solesmes and Dom Guéranger 1805–1875*, trans. Joseph O'Connor (Orleans, MA: Paraclete Press, 1995) for more about the early influence of Chateaubriand on Dom Guéranger. See Katherine Bergeron, *Decadent Enchantments: The Revival of Gregorian Chant at Solesmes* (Berkeley: The University of California Press, 1998), for more about the development of plain chant within the monastery setting. Elaine Brody discusses the nationalist goals of the Schola Cantorum, p. 232. The first issue of la revue *La Tribune de St-Gervais* (1895), the monthly bulletin of La Schola, makes the dedication to plain chant (and to new music based on it) extremely clear. Charles Bordes would publish a number of works, including an *Anthologie des maîtres religieux primitifs* (1892) and he was responsible for creating Les Chanteurs de Saint-Gervais.

421.   See Andrew Thomson, *Vincent d'Indy and his World* (New York: Oxford University Press, 1996), for descriptions of the goals of the Schola Cantorum, its association with Dom Guéranger and Pothier and for a description of the concerts performed by the groups affiliated with the school,

pp. 80–81, 117–18, 125–6. For more about medieval music in late nineteenth-century Paris, see Harry Haskell, *The Early Music Revival: A History* (Mineola, NY: Dover Publications, Inc., 1996), pp. 44–72.

422.  Article in *Le Temps*, 11 April 1899.

423.  See Robert Pincus-Witten, pp. 63, 215.

424.  *The Symbolist Aesthetic in France*, p. 40.

425.  For more about Mérovak's adventures, see Maurice Hamel's 'Mérovak: l'homme des cathédrales,' *La Gazette des Beaux-Arts* (January 1962), pp. 53–60; Léon Riotor's 'L'homme des cathédrales,' *La Plume* (September 1898), pp. 527; and Felix Hautfort, 'L'Homme des cathedrales, Mérovak évoquera l'âme gothique,' *La Plume* (15 May, 1899), pp. 328–35.

426.  'Ces petites églises où les esprits s'échauffent, ces enceintes où le ton monte, où les valeurs s'exagèrent, ce sont de véritables laboratoires pour les lettres.' Cited in *Bibliographie des Revues et Journaux Littéraires* by Jean-Michel Place and André Vasseur (Paris: Editions de la Chronique des lettres françaises, 1973), pp. 7–8. Valéry made this analogy in a speech for l'Académie Française.

427.  For more about *Le Rêve*, which was published in *La Revue illustrée* with illustrations by Jeanniot, see Emery, *Romancing the Cathedral* and '"A l'ombre d'une vieille cathédrale romanesque": The Medievalism of Gautier and Zola' (*The French Review*. 73:2. December 1999), pp. 290–300 and Morowitz, 'Zola's *Le Rêve*: Naturalism, Symbolism and Medievalism in the Fin-de-siècle,' (*Excavatio* 9. 1997), pp. 92–102. Jean Lorrain wrote 'Le bal mystique' for *Le Courrier Français* (25 January 1891), p. 4. The pages of this periodical are full of neo-medieval artwork and odes to the cathedral.

428.  Among the most powerful of these is 'Vers pour Miss Lilian,' in which Tailhade compares the whiteness and purity of medieval virgins with the perverted 'lilies' of modern France. The poem was published with an illustration by Henri Rivière in *Le Chat Noir* (24 Jan 1885), p. 421. Tailhade's poem was included in *Vitraux* (*Oeuvres de Laurent Tailhade*. Paris: Mercure de France, 1923), pp. 186–7. See also Carlos Schwabe's painting *La Vierge aux lys* (1899).

429.  Germain Nouveau, 'Les Cathédrales' in *La Doctrine de l'Amour* (1904), Léon Bloy, *Le Désespéré* (1886) et *La Femme pauvre* (1897), Adolphe Retté, *Cloches en la nuit* (1889), Anatole France, 'Le Jongleur de Notre Dame' (1906), Jules Laforgue, *Les Complaintes* (1885), Huysmans, *Là-Bas*, *En Route*, *La Cathédrale*, *L'Oblat*, and Proust, *A la recherche du temps perdu* (especially *Du côté de chez Swann*). 'Le mouvement symboliste a été surtout un retour vers le Moyen-Age.' In G. Le Cardonnel and Ch. Vellay, 'La Littérature contemporaine,' *Mercure de France* (1905) p. 284. Cited in Dakyns, p. 206.

430.  'Le mouvement que des pions de l'Ecole Normale et que des feuilles ont annoncé est donc, en somme, nul. Il se trouvera peut-être de vagues dilettantes, quelques sceptiques qui rôderont, en littérature, autour des choses pieuses et les saliront en y touchant […] il en sera de même pour les autres arts; on découvrira, comme à l'exposition des Rose-Croix, des peintres qui choisiront l'article religieux, s'il est en vogue, et dessineront des personnages frustes qu'ils cercleront avec du fil de fer […] Ce seront de froides singeries, de faux décalques des Primitifs […]' p. xi.

431.  See Richard Griffiths, *The Reactionary Revolution: The Catholic Revival in French Literature 1870–1914* (London: Constable, 1966), p. 108.

432.  'Mais gloire aux cathédrales!/Pleines d'ombre et de feux, de silence et de râles/Avec leur forêt d'énormes piliers/Et leur peuple de saints, moines et chevaliers,/Ce sont des cités au-dessus des villes,/Que gardent seulement les sons irréguliers/De l'aumône, au fond des sébiles,/Sous leurs porches hospitaliers.' 'Les Cathédrales' (vv 1–8) in *Oeuvres complètes* (Paris: Gallimard [Bibliothèque de la Pléiade], 1970), pp. 510–14.

433.  *The Reactionary Revolution*, p. 108.

434.  For more about Verlaine's relationship to younger poets and their embrace of him as 'medieval' and as 'master' of the Decadent movement see Antoine Adam, pp. 117–19, 131.

435.  Morice, 'Introduction', p. lxxxiii. For more about the Catholic revival of literature that occurred in the nineteenth century, see Richard Griffiths (1966) and Gugelot, *La Conversion des intellectuels au catholicisme* (Paris: CNRS Editions, 1988). Verlaine's *Sagesse* was read by nearly all new artist converts. See Chapter 2 for Verlaine's reluctance to accept Denis's illustrations.

436.  See Chapter 1 and note 50 for more about this citation.

437.  Despite clear evidence to the contrary, many scholars still refuse to accept the legitimacy of Huysmans's conversion, preferring to see his Durtal novels as an extension of des Esseintes's 'dilettante' fascination with medieval art. See Baldick, pp. 203–5 and 223–39 and Michael Issacharoff, *J.-K. Huysmans devant les critiques en France* (Paris: Editions Klincksieck, 1970), for biographical details about the conversion and articles in the press that debated whether his conversion was real. Richard Griffiths gives a persuasive reading about the legitimacy of Huysmans's conversion, while Gugelot's study of the converts of 1885–1935 returns again and again to the importance young Catholics attached to Huysmans as mentor and role model.

438.  For a lengthy analysis of Huysmans's contributions to scholarly medievalism, see Elizabeth Emery, 'J.-K. Huysmans and the Middle Ages.'

439.  See Gugelot, pp. 56–61.

440.  *La Conversion*, p. 21. Like Gugelot, we use the term 'conversion' in its largest sense to include not only those who change religions, but also those who return to a religion they had previously abandoned. See Emery, *Romancing the Cathedral*, for a discussion of Huysmans's Durtal cycle as a 'conversion narrative.'

441.  See Gugelot, pp. 19, 27, 115–16 and especially the chapter entitled 'Les Fils prodiges.'

442.  'Je commençais alors à écrire et il me semblait que dans les cérémonies catholiques, considérées avec un dilettantisme supérieur, je trouverais un excitant approprié et la matière de quelques exercices décadents. [...] Puis, n'ayant rien de mieux à faire, je revins aux vêpres. Les enfants de la maîtrise en robes blanches et les élèves du petit séminaire de Saint-Nicolas-du-Chardonnet qui les assistaient, étaient en train de chanter ce que je sus plus tard être le *Magnificat*. [...] Et c'est alors que se produisit l'événement qui domine toute ma vie. En un instant mon coeur fut touché et *je crus*.' 'Ma conversion' in *Oeuvres en prose* (Paris: Gallimard [Bibliothèque de la Pléiade], 1965), pp. 1009–10, 1113.

443.  'Les musées sont des cimetières plus ou moins fastueux, où les oeuvres, détournées de leur destination initiale, perdent le meilleur de leur sens et de leur splendeur. Elles avaient été composées pour embellir et pour signifier une place publique, une église, un palais de justice, une salle de réception, ou de méditation: aux prix de quels efforts, dans le froid tohu-bohu d'un musée, parvient-on à rejoindre la réelle pensée de l'artiste! Le peuple ne va guère dans les musées. Les merveilles qu'il y voit entassées sont pour lui des objets inertes, froids, muets, incompréhensibles. [...] La cause de ce malheur est dans cet individualisme forcené qui dispersa les éléments du monde moderne et que nous avons vu poindre avec la Renaissance … . D'où ce désir, plus ou moins raisonné, mais universel, de réunion, d'unité que nous notions plus haut.' pp. lxxxviii–lxxxix.

444.  *Contre Sainte-Beuve*, p. 777.

445.  See our discussion of the artificiality of museum display in Chapter 3.

446.  *Le Roman de Durtal*, pp. 711–14.

447.  While Huysmans argued that the Church was to blame for this, Maurice Denis disagreed: he felt that lackluster modern religious art was not a product of the Church's teaching. 'Le Symbolisme et l'art religieux moderne' (1918), in *Nouvelles Théories*.

448.  '[...] Ils appartenaient à toutes les classes de la société [...] mais l'amour divin fut si fort qu'il supprima les distances et abolit les castes [...] quand je songe au Sacré-Coeur de Paris, à cette morne et pesante bâtisse édifiée par des gens qui ont inscrit leur nom en rouge sur chaque pierre!' *La Cathédrale*, pp. 842–6.

449.  8 March 1896, letter 143 to Arij Prins, p. 282. This project also harks back to Romantic historiography as it echoes Michelet's enthusiasm for reanimating the past through books. See Emery, *Romancing the Cathedral*, for a more lengthy discussion of his didactic goals.

450.  June 1897 letter to Cécile Bruyère. Cited in Baldick, p. 249. Letter of 22 February 1897 to l'abbé Ferret. *Lettres inédites à l'abbé Ferret (Une étape de la vie de Joris-Karl Huysmans)*, ed. Elisabeth Bourget-Besnier (Paris: A. G. Nizet, 1973), p. 111.

451.  See Emery, *Romancing the Cathedral*, for more details about visitors to Chartres and their reliance on Huysmans as a scholarly source, pp. 111–13.

452.  *Religious Art in France: The Thirteenth Century. A Study of Medieval Iconography and its Sources*, ed. Harry Bober, trans. Marthiel Mathew (Princeton: Princeton University Press, 1984), p. vii.

453.  *Religious Art*, p. 397.

454.  *Religious Art*, p. 396.

455.  When Mâle's *L'Art religieux* was published, Huysmans was invited to review it. Huysmans praised Mâle for addressing both 'body' and 'soul' of the cathedral. He retracts his previous complaint about the lack of works devoted to medieval symbolism: 'now this work exists, at least for the thirteenth century.' Article reproduced in *Huysmans* (ed. Pierre Brunel and André Guyaux Paris: Editions de l'Herne), pp. 347–8. Huysmans's last article about symbolism, 'La Symbolique de Notre-Dame,' also acknowledges Mâle's fine work. *Oeuvres complètes*, vol. xi, p. 173. Denis had a personal correspondence with Mâle, parts of which are preserved in the Denis archive at the Musée Départmental Maurice Denis, Saint Germain-en-Laye.

456.  *Religious Art*, p. 401.

457.  Proust had borrowed his friend Robert de Billy's copy, and when he returned it, some four years later, Billy described its dilapidated condition: ' … il n'avait ni couverture ni page de garde et portait les marques de toutes les disgrâces qui peuvent assaillir un livre, lu au lit, dans le voisinage des remèdes.' (*Marcel Proust: Lettres et conversations*. Paris: Editions des Portiques, 1930), p. 111. Proust was a friend of Mâle and turned to him for guidance about cathedrals. He

is also one of the models for the painter Elstir in *A la recherche du temps perdu*. See Elizabeth Emery, *Romancing the Cathedral*.

458.  'La Mort,' p. 144. Proust's knowledge of both Mâle's work and of Gothic architecture in general can be gauged by the humorous pastiches of Gothic stained glass and sculpture that he sent to his friends. See his *Lettres à Reynaldo Hahn*, ed. Philippe Kolb (Paris: Gallimard, 1956) and Philippe Sollers, *L'oeil de Proust: Les dessins de Marcel Proust* (Paris: Stock, 1999). As Sollers argues in the section about Proust's 'medieval' drawings, many of these sketches were traced directly from Mâle's book, p. 83.

459.  'La Peinture sur verre en France' in André Michel, ed., *Histoire de l'Art*, vol. 1 (Paris: Librairie Armand Colin, 1906), pp. 372–96. Cited in Harris, p. 103.

460.  Barrès. *Mes Cahiers*. Vol 9, 1911–1912 (Paris, Plon, 1929–1957), p. 411.

461.  'Le passé nous est cher et nous le voulons présent. Si de cette piété il fallait une preuve, on la trouverait dans le succès des livres de M. Lenôtre et de M. Georges Can qui disputent aux romanciers les plus populaires, l'étalage et la renommée. Jamais les vieux logis et les résidences princières n'ont eu pèlerins plus fervents. Aussi, que Barrès annonce son intention de demander au gouvernement ce qu'il entend faire "pour protéger la physionomie architecturale," ce ne sont pas seulement les catholiques, dont la piété est intéressée à la conservation des églises, – ni les élites sociales qui sollicitent avec lui cette explication, – ni des croyants esthéticiens, comme M. Péladan, – ni un Henri de Regnier, poète de *La Cité des Eaux*, qui se plaît aux grandes scènes d'autrefois, – ni un Albert Flamant, – ni un André Hallays, ni des lettrés affranchis du dogme, comme M. Lucien Descaves; c'est le coeur de toute la France qui bat avec le sien.' *Pour l'art contre les vandales* (Paris: Jouve & Cie, Editeurs: 1910), p. 95.

462.  *Les Cathédrales*, p. 214.

463.  *Les Cathédrales*, pp. 63–4.

464.  See Chapter 6 of his *Theories of the Leisure Class* (New York: A. M. Kelley, 1965).

465.  *A la recherche du temps perdu* I, 60–61.

466.  'Si le vitrail est resté en honneur dans nos églises, s'il occupe un nombre assez considérable d'artistes et d'artisans, son introduction dans la décoration des fenêtres de quelques édifices publics de l'ordre civil, des habitations les plus confortables et de certains lieux de réunion, tels que les restaurants et les brasseries, a procuré beaucoup plus de travail encore, en ces dernières années, à nos ateliers spéciaux. Le bon marché, fils de la mode, a vulgarisé le vitrail que l'on voit partout maintenant. Gothique bâtard et Renaissance avachie hurlent d'être accouplés aux vitrines vieillotes des cabarets et de quelques boutiques, en cette fin de XIXe siècle.' *Le Vitrail: conférence faite à la société de l'Union Centrale des arts décoratifs* (Paris: Librairie des arts décoratifs, 1898), p. 9.

467.  'Au centre, dans l'axe de la porte d'honneur, une large galerie allait de bout en bout, flanquée à droite et à gauche de deux galeries plus étroites, la galerie Monsigny et la galerie Michodière. On avait vitré les cours, transformées en halls; et des escaliers de fer s'élevaient du rez-de-chaussée, des ponts de fer étaient jetés d'un bout à l'autre, aux deux étages. L'architecte […] ne s'était servi de la pierre que pour les sous-sols et les piles d'angle, puis avait monté toute l'ossature en fer, des colonnes supportant l'assemblage des poutres et des solives. Les voûtins des planchers, les cloisons des distributions intérieures, étaient en briques. Partout on avait gagné de l'espace, l'air et la lumière entraient librement, le public circulait à l'aise, sous le jet hardi des fermes à longue portée. C'était la cathédrale du commerce moderne solide et légère, faite pour un peuple de clientes.' *Les Rougon-Macquart*, vol. 3, pp. 611–12. These vaulted windows can still be seen in the stores today. They are beautifully reproduced in Lemoine's *Architecture in France 1800–1900*.

468.  In referring to the 'commodification of culture', we follow the arguments of cultural historians such as T. J. Clark, Francis Frascina and Michael Miller. The term refers to the spread of capital into new territories – including leisure, entertainment and the art market – in the late nineteenth century. Gothic works, remnants of a pre-industrial (and pre-capitalist) cultural system that were (paradoxically) heavily marketed in the fin de siècle, evoked (referenced) and exorcized (disavowed) the 'specter of the commodity' (the term is from Marx). For an early but still important analysis of the commodification of culture, see Guy Debord, *La Société du spectacle* (Paris: Editions Champ Libre, 1967).

469.  The phrase 'ancien et moderne à la fois' comes from Charles Saunier, 'Vitraux pour Jeanne d'Arc,' *La Plume* (November 1893), p. 456.

470.  See the quotation that begins Chapter 4.

471.  The list of items auctioned after his death shows that Zola owned 43 stained-glass windows. The huge fifteenth-century window in his study at Médan came from the chapel of Malestrat and told the story of Mary-Magdalene. Zola designed two of the windows for his house at Médan, one of which is still on display in the Maison Emile Zola. One represented popular actor Dailly in the role of Mes-Bottes (from the novel *L'Assommoir*), while the other displayed scenes from Zola's books, notably the mythical garden of *La Faute de l'abbé Mouret*. Zola's

correspondence reveals that he met often to discuss these projects with the artist in charge of them, Henri Baboneau. For images of Zola's medieval decor in Médan and Paris, see *Zola, Photographer*, ed. François Emile-Zola and Massin, trans. Liliane Emery Tuck (New York: Henry Holt and Company, 1988), pp. 30–31, 108; Jean and Hélène Adhémar, eds, *Zola* (Paris: Hachette, 1969).

472.   See Chapter 4. Jerrold Seigel explores the mirroring of bourgeois culture in bohemian spaces in *Bohemian Paris: Culture, Politics, and the Boundaries of Bourgeois Life* (New York: Viking Press, 1986).

473.   John Grand-Carteret, *Raphaël et Gambrinus ou l'art dans la brasserie* (Paris: L. Westhausser, 1886), p. 43. See also André Warnod, 'La Grande Pinte,' *Bals, Cafés et Cabarets* (Paris: Eugène Figuière et Cie, 1913).

474.   'At that time, medieval and Renaissance, or Louis XIII cabarets were just beginning to be opened. The '"Grand" Pinte' [sic] was typical of them. But the painters met there without any fanfare, just as they might have done on the boulevard. Salis, on the other hand, dreamt of reintroducing the hubbub, the antic madness, and the ironplated chanson into our watered-down customs. Moreover, understanding well that all the arts are brothers, he asks himself why literary people do not join together with painters in order to lend them a few fleeting syllables, perhaps adorned with sonorous rhymes.' *Dix ans de Bohème*, pp. 252–3. Cited in Harold B. Segel, *Turn-of-the-Century Cabaret* (New York: Columbia University Press, 1987), p. 20 (Segel's translation).

475.   For details about the Chat Noir and its unusual decor and activities, see Michael L. J. Wilson, 'Portrait of the Artist as a Louis XIII Chair' in Gabriel P. Weisberg, *Montmartre and the Making of Mass Culture* (New Brunswick: Rutgers University Press, 2001), pp. 180–203. The collection of essays in this book situate such cabarets and Montmartre itself in the context of fin-de-siècle Paris.

476.   These objects belonged to the second Chat Noir, which had moved to a larger space in 1885. Although the *Chat Noir-Guide* lists all of these objects, it was famous for its mockery of bourgeois attitudes and often invented stories that it presented as true. Descriptions in the guide should thus be taken with a grain of salt, as the 'relics' of poet Villon would suggest. For a description of the first Chat Noir, see Georges Montorgueil's preface to *Collection du Chat Noir 'Rodolphe Salis'* (Paris 1898), pp. vii–xiii.

477.   The *Veau d'or* tapestries were described as '[…] digne des grands maîtres vitrailleurs du moyen âge,' while *La Vierge au chat* was allegedly deeply desired by Louis II of Bavaria. *Chat Noir-Guide* (Paris: Charles Blot, n.d.), pp. 13, 31. For more on the Chat Noir's collections and these windows, see Mariel Oberthür, *Le Chat Noir: 1881–1897* (Paris: Editions de la Réunion des Musées nationaux, 1992) and Armond Fields, *Le Chat Noir: A Montmartre Cabaret and its Artists in Turn-of-the-Century Paris* (Santa Barbara, CA: Santa Barbara Museum of Art, 1993). Anne Murray-Robertson discusses Grasset's contributions to the cabaret on pages 37 and 52 of her book.

478.   Many of the articles and announcements made by the cabaret, such as this one, from a 10 July 1886 issue of *Le Chat Noir*, described it as medieval: 'En ce fantaisiste logis du Chat Noir, où courent des souvenirs du moyen âge, et où l'Extrême-Orient mêle sa robe violette et d'or au manteau de Villon et aux cottes des anciennes ribauldes … '

479.   *La Vie à Paris, 1884* (Paris: Victor Havard, 1885), p. 219.

480.   'Le moyen âge, on le sait, possédait au plus haut degré le sens de l'ornementation intérieure; donc rien d'extraordinaire à ce que les murs des cabarets ne fussent pas entièrement nus. Toutefois, l'on se tromperait fort si l'on assignait à cette décoration le sens actuel; il ne s'agissait pas de tableaux ou de fresques, mais bien de murs et de plafonds peints avec des ornements quelconques […] Mais l'ornementation devait, avant tout, son caractère aux vitres plombés, aux ferrures, aux hautes cheminées, aux boiseries, aux tables et aux sièges.' Grand-Carteret, p. 2.

481.   Grand-Carteret, pp. 46–8.

482.   W. C. Morrow and Edouard Cucuel, *Bohemian Paris of Today* (Philadelphia: J. B. Lippincott Company, 1900), pp. 295–303.

483.   Professional *chansonniers*, like Marcel Legay, also performed songs like 'Les Cloches': 'Les cloches Catholiques,/du haut de leur bellfroi,/ Voyaient avec effroi/ La résurrection des Grandes Republiques./ Les cloches rêvaient,/en quatre-vingt onze,/ Les cloches de bronze/ Rêvaient.' Quoted in Morrow and Cucuel, p. 300.

484.   On the eclectic variety of cabarets, see John Grand-Carteret (1886) and Charles Rearick (especially the chapter entitled 'Bohemian Gaiety and the New Show Business').

485.   'Ces aménagements artistiques de salles à boire, ces restitutions historiques, plus ou moins fidèles, plus ou moins heureuses, sont encore un nouveau triomphe à enregistrer à l'actif du dieu Bibelot, ce dieu tout-puissant de notre modernité tourmentée, qui a soif de style et de couleur, peut-être parce qu'elle ne possède ni style ni couleur. C'est en effet, le bibelot et le

tableautin, venant de partout, et revêtant toutes les formes, qui se sont introduits maîtres dans la brasserie.' Grand-Carteret, p. 43.

486.  See the quotation that begins this chapter.

487.  Léon Ottin, *Le Vitrail: son histoire, ses manifestations diverses à travers les âges et les peuples* (Paris: H. Laurens, 1896).

488.  'Au lieu de s'élever en décorant nos édifices publics et nos palais elle s'est diminuée dans l'estime du public en se gaspillant en menue monnaie dans les brasseries, et les casinos, à l'Eden Théâtre, au Comptoir d'Escompte, au Casino de Paris, au Moulin Rouge … ' Ottin, p. 100.

489.  'Depuis quelques années, le public prend un vif intérêt aux manifestations des arts appliqués à la décoration et l'art si particulièrement du vitrail semble jouir, en ce moment, d'une faveur spéciale. Réservé autrefois presque exclusivement aux édifices religieux, il pénètre aujourd'hui non seulement dans les hôtels princiers, mais dans nos modestes habitations, et il envahit, à notre grand regret parfois, jusqu'aux établissements publics.' Delalande, 'Les Vitraux aux Salons de 1894,' *La Plume* (June 1894), p. 290.

490.  'M. de Tocqueville a dit que "dans les démocraties les arts industriels tendent à créer, en grand nombre et à bas prix, des produits imparfaits, et à donner à ces produits des apparences brillantes, l'hypocrisie du luxe étant un des caractères des moeurs démocratiques".' Didron (1898), p. 9. Didron was not alone in this complaint. As Tiersten notes, 'Middle class elites and their critics alike had thus feared that the entrenchment of a bourgeois public in 1877 had put France's aesthetic patrimony in jeopardy by launching the presumably tasteless bourgeoisie into a position of political power from which it threatened to squander that inheritance,' p. 3. See also pp. 64–8.

491.  'Le goût public se porta de préférence vers les styles anciens, et sans avoir conscience de l'erreur qu'ils commettaient, les artistes et les artisans donnèrent satisfaction à ce goût en reproduisant, souvent par des moyens économiques et imparfaits, les ouvrages des styles en faveur.' *Exposition Universelle de 1900*, p. 5.

492.  For discussion of bibelots see Chapter 3.

493.  See the definition of bibelot proposed by Janell Watson, pp. 1–29, 47–50.

494.  By the late nineteenth century, the term *décoratif* had become loaded; it referred to art that aimed for a monumental, site-specific and pleasing surface design. Rather than mere decoration, however, *le décoratif* evoked important works such as Renaissance murals or Assyrian reliefs. Puvis de Chavannes was celebrated as a leading master of the *décoratif* for his mural designs. For more on the *décoratif*, see Gloria Groom (1993) and Marie Jeanne Aquilino, 'The Decorating Campaigns at the Salon du Champ-de-Mars and the Salon des Champs-Elysées in the 1890s,' *Art Journal* (Spring 1989), pp. 78–84.

495.  'C'est l'étude des vitraux anciens qui reste la meilleure école, non pas que nous pensions que les peintres-verriers doivent se proposer de les reproduire, de les copier dans leurs formules étroites; mais nous pouvons, de cette étude, dégager les principes toujours vrais.' *Exposition Universelle Internationale de 1900 à Paris: Rapports du Jury International – Classe 67* (Paris: Imprimerie Nationale, 1901), p. 8.

496.  See Harris, pp. 87–110. She analyzes Didron's disappointment with the display and with the minor role accorded to stained glass in these fairs.

497.  'Rétrospective remontant à l'origine même du vitrail et présentant des spécimens de toutes les époques.' Class 67 of the display consisted of these stained-glass works, most of which came from the collection of the Service des Monuments Historiques. See Daumont-Tournel.

498.  Silverman focused much attention on this association, linking many prominent members to interest in the rococo revival.

499.  For an account of the museum see Lucien Magne, 'Le Musée du Vitrail,' *Gazette des Beaux-Arts* 34 (Oct. 1886), pp. 297–311. Magne reported that most of the glass pieces were taken from windows that had undergone restoration. Many hailed originally from the Abbey of Gercy, after which they had been placed in the church of Varennes at Seine-et-Oise.

500.  For discussion of the museum and its display practices, see Chapter 3.

501.  'Dès le présent, les époques anciennnes de l'art sont représentées dans le Musée du vitrail par des oeuvres de premier ordre, dont l'étude fournira pour l'art moderne un enseignement permanent.' Magne (1886), p. 299.

502.  See Pierre Le Vieil, *L'Art de la peinture sur verre et de la vitrerie; Traité historique et pratique de la peinture sur verre* (Paris: Académie Royale des Sciences, 1774).

503.  A few examples include Olivier Merson, *Les Vitraux* (Paris: Ancienne Maison Quantin/ Librairies Imprimeries réunies, 1895); Fernand de Mély, *Etudes iconographiques sur les vitraux du treizième siècle de la cathédrale de Chartres* (Bruges: 1888) and Joseph Denais, *Les Vitraux, statues et tableaux de l'église Notre-Dame de Beaufort* (Beaufort: Bassy, 1890). For an excellent analysis of the

perception of stained glass in France, see Anne F. Harris, 'The Spectacle of Stained Glass in Modern France and Medieval Chartres: A History of Practices and Perceptions' (Ph.D. thesis, The University of Chicago, 1999). The first chapter treats the seventeenth and eighteenth centuries, while the second traces such discourse through the middle of the nineteenth century.

504. 'La peinture du moyen-age est tout entière dans ces décorations translucides qui perpétuaient les traditions et les exemples destinés à l'éducation religieuse et morale du peuple.' Lucien Magne, *L'oeuvre des peintres-verriers*, p. 1.

505. 'Cependant, si la technique des vitraux était chose profane il est certain que l'iconographie adoptée par les artistes qui les dessinaient sur une table enduite de craie, demeura fixée jusqu'au milieu du XIIIe siècle par des traditions d'Eglise.' These comments come from Bertaux's review of Emile Mâle's *L'Art religieux au XIIIe siècle* (1898) in *La Revue des Deux Mondes* (May 1899), pp. 177–204.

506. 'Ils se préoccupèrent de faire étalage de leur science et de leur habileté, beaucoup plus que de procurer l'édification des fidèles et la gloire de Dieu. [...] Mais d'autres causes devaient ruiner encore plus à l'art, parmi eux la soi-disante Réformation qui détruisit en France vingt mille églises!' Noël Lavergne, p. 17.

507. See Harris, Chapter 1.

508. 'La décadence du vitrail date de l'introduction dans cet art des méthodes applicables à des tableaux de chevalet, et qui sont en désaccord absolu avec la décoration d'une surface. [...] Dès la fin du XVe, on peut dire que l'art du vitrail cesse d'exister.' *Exposition Universelle*, p. 3.

509. 'Aveuglés par les déclamations contre le gothique, à la mode à la fin du XVIIIe siècle, les chapitres de nos belles cathédrales rivalisaient d'ardeur pour détruire les vitraux peints, les dinanderies, les jubés, les autels, et tout le reste.' Louis de Farcy, 'Un atelier pour la reproduction des anciennes tapisseries,' *La Revue de l'art chrétien* (July 1904), p. 1.

510. ' ... sous le régime de la Terreur, sous le gouvernement du Directoire et de la République, on ne s'occupe plus des vitraux que pour les briser.' Lavergne, p. 19.

511. 'La plupart des tapisseries offertes jadis par des pieuses aux paroisses de Paris, ont disparu sous la Révolution.' Jules Guiffrey, 'Les tapisseries des eglises de Paris,' *La Revue de l'art chrétien* (1889), p. 1. See also Charles Simon, 'Les Origines de nos tapisseries,' *La Revue des revues* (July 1889), pp. 82–91.

512. 'Des efforts ont été faits avec succès: mais ces efforts seraient stériles, si les artistes restaient isolés les uns des autres.' Magne (1885), p. xxxiv.

513. Emile Delalande claimed that 'C'est en effet presque en vedette que sont placés cette année les vitraux aux Champs-Elysées,' p. 291.

514. On Grasset see Chapter 2.

515. As Didron noted: 'Ces règles, Mesdames et Messieurs, sont celles du Moyen Age; respectées à peu près par la Renaissance, elles doivent être celles de notre temps.' Didron (1898), p. 7.

516. See Harris, pp. 72–86.

517. 'Et les vitraux alors étaient décoratifs, surtout décoratifs, en même temps que symboliques. Ceux que l'Abbé Suger fit faire pour St. Denis, ceux de ce temps qui subsistent encore dans les cathédrales de Chartres, de Bourges, etc. en font foi. Le but est la décoration, l'embellissement de l'église ... ' Lavergne, p. 10.

518. 'La décoration des surfaces par la peinture, la mosaïque, le vitrail ou le tissu, était nécessairement soumise à des lois analogues. On n'eût pas compris alors le tableau isolé destiné à produire l'illusion d'une figure, d'un paysage ou d'une scène. C'eût été pour les artistes du XIIIe siècle une application secondaire, inférieure à la décoration monumentale dont ils comprenaient la grandeur ... ' Magne (1885), p. iii.

519. See Chapter 2.

520. For an analysis of decorative painting see Aquilino (note 494).

521. Copies of Robida's cartoons for the stained glass are published in *Le vieux Paris, études et dessins* and include minstrels singing to the Virgin Mary, Saint Cecilia and her musicians, and the story of the chapel's foundation as a hospice for injured minstrels. He collaborated with a Monsieur Richard to have the windows made. For more about Saint-Julien-des-Ménétriers and its role in *Le Vieux Paris*, see Chapter 7.

522. ' ... contre-sens de composer en 1883 une verrière neuve dans la forme et à l'imitation d'une verrière du XIIIe siècle.' Magne (1885), p. xxxii. Daumont-Tournel expressed the same sentiment: 'L'architecture des édifices religieux, faite en imitation des monuments anciens invitait d'ailleurs les peintres-verriers à faire des pastiches ... ' p. 8.

523. See Saunier's ideas about 'ancien et moderne à la fois,' note 469.

524. Stalled by the anti-clerical Republic, the project was resumed in the receptive climate of the Ralliement. See Edouard Didron, 'Le Concours des vitraux de Jeanne d'Arc pour la cathédrale

d'Orléans,' *Revue des arts décoratifs XIV* (1893–1894). Also see 'Les verrières de Jeanne d'Arc à la cathédrale d'Orléans,' *Société archéologique et historique de l'Orléanais* XI:161 (1897).

525. Some of the other participants in the contest included Henri Carot (who would later execute stained glass designs by Denis), Victor Prouvé, Joseph Anglade, Emil Hirsch, Ludovic Latteux-Bazin and Joseph Vantillard.

526. Didron (1893–1894), p. 198.

527. Félix Gaudin, 'A propos du concours des vitraux de Jeanne d'Arc,' *La Plume* 113 (1894), p. 69.

528. In her monograph on the artist, Anne Murray-Robertson divides Grasset's stained glass production into 'sacred' and 'profane' works. *Grasset: pionnier de l'art nouveau*, p. 62.

529. 'Dans son sens générique, ce terme sert à désigner toute sorte d'objets vieux, tels que bahuts, armures, bronzes, tableaux, etc. Le goût prononcé du public pour ces sortes d'objets a donné lieu à une industrie nouvelle, la *fabrication du vieux neuf*, exécutée plus ou moins habilement. Il faut souvent un oeil très exercé pour distinguer un vieil objet de curiosité authentique d'avec un objet faux. En général, le mot bric-à-brac est employé comme terme de mépris; on l'applique dans la langue usuelle à des objets de peu de valeur.' Ernest Bosc, *Dictionnaire de l'art, de la curiosité et du bibelot* (Paris: Firmin-Didot, 1883), p. 133. The emphasis is Bosc's. Cited in Watson, p. 33.

530. 'Soustraire encore la tapisserie du dix-neuvième siècle à la domination franche et inavouée du passé, pour lui assigner un caractère, une date, en l'obligeant à refléter la ressemblance de notre temps, à enfermer dans ses travaux l'idéal moderne.' Marx, cited in Pierre Vaisse, 'La querelle de la tapisserie au début de la Troisième République,' *Revue de l'Art* 22 (1973), pp. 66–86. Vaisse's article remains the best account to date of the late nineteenth-century tapestry revival in France.

531. See for example Jules Guiffrey, *Les tapisseries des églises de Paris* (1889). Other important publications of the period include Bernard-Maillard, *La Tapisserie ancienne et moderne* (1886); Simon, 'Les origines de nos tapisseries,' *Revue des revues* xiii (1896); Paul Blanche, *Notes sur quelques tissus du haut moyen age* (1897). Guiffrey was lauded for discovering important documents on the 'Apocalypse' tapestries of Angers in the Archives Nationales.

532. Louis Gonse was an extremely important critic of medieval, Japanese and contemporary art. For biographical detail and an examination of Gonse's ideas see Chapter 1. See also Morowitz, 'Consuming the Past,' Chapter 3.

533. 'Il n'y a pas longtemps encore les anciennes tapisseries étaient dans le plus complet discrédit. [...] Si la superiorité des tapisseries françaises depuis la création des Gobelins est un fait unanimement reconnu, le rôle des artisans de notre passé aux époques plus reculées n'avait pas été présenté jusqu'ici sous son véritable jour.' Louis Gonse, 'La tapisserie, son histoire depuis le moyen âge jusqu'à nos jours par Jules M. Guiffrey', *Gazette des Beaux-Arts* 33 (1 Jan. 1886), pp. 82–5.

534. Vaisse, p. 70.

535. ' ... tout objet gothique était condamné d'avance; ce mot même était presque une injure ... ' Louis de Farcy, 'Histoires et description des tapisseries de l'église Cathédrale d'Angers,' *Revue de l'Anjou* 24 (May/June 1897), p. 357.

536. The six-piece 'Quest of the Grail' series, designed by Edward Burne-Jones and woven at Merton Abbey in 1892, was shown in the English pavilion of the 1900 fair to great critical acclaim. On the threat of Morris's work to the French tapestry industry see Jules Guiffrey (1900), pp. 222–36 and Alfred Darcel, 'Union Centrale des Beaux-Arts appliqués à l'industrie: Exposition de l'histoire de la tapisserie,' *La Gazette des Beaux-Arts* 2 (1876).

537. Henry Havard attributed medieval tapestries to Queen Mathilda and Judith of Bavaria. Although counter-arguments were put forward in the second half of the nineteenth century, many scholars persisted in ascribing the Bayeux tapestry (technically an embroidery) to La Reine Mathilde. See Shirley Ann Brown, *The Bayeux Tapestry: History and Bibliography* (London: Boydell Press, 1988), pp. 25–6.

538. 'Avant de connaître la ville, le seul nom de Bayeux me disait surtout la fameuse tapisserie ou plutôt le grand album de broderie sur lequel la femme du duc Guillaume illustra de son aiguille très artiste en sa naïveté, l'histoire de la conquête du royaume d'Angleterre; ce nom évoquait les figures de ces Normands coiffés de casques coniques à nasal, se précipitant en mille navires à la bataille et à la curée, les archers, les cavaliers, les évêques, les moines de Guillaume, guerroyant contre les Saxons d'outre-Manche, tous emportés, comme leur duc, par l'âpre désir de *gainger*.' Robida, *La Normandie* (Paris: La Librairie Illustrée, 1890), p. 159.

539. 'L'une et l'autre perdirent ce caractère quand elles se séparèrent de l'architecture pour prendre une vie propre. La peinture textile, conduite alors à sa perfection arrivait à temps pour prendre la place de la peinture sur verre et de la sculpture dans le rôle élevé qu'elles désertaient [...]' Charles Loriquet, *Les tapisseries de Notre-Dame de Paris* (Paris: Librairie de l'Académie, 1876), p. iv.

540. On this see Vaisse. See also Jeroen Stumpel, 'The Grande Jatte, that Patient Tapestry,' *Simiolus* 14:316 (1984), pp. 209–24.

541. ' … comme la nécessité évidente aujourd'hui de simplifier les modèles, d'étendre les lumières, d'accuser les vigueurs, de cerner dans certains cas les contours, de réduire enfin les couleurs au plus petit nombre d'éléments.' Guiffrey (1900), p. 230.

542. 'Plus on s'éloigne du Moyen Age, plus on perd les traditions de l'art véritable de la tapisserie, en sacrifiant l'effet général aux détails, les sujets principaux aux accessoires.' Louis de Farcy (1897), p. 359.

543. On this issue see Madeleine Caviness, 'Broadening the Definitions of Art: The Reception of Medieval Works in the Context of Post-Impressionist Movements' in *Hermeneutics and Medieval Culture*, ed. Patrick J. Gallacher and Helen Damico (Albany: State University of New York Press, 1988).

544. 'La conception la plus logique, la plus rationnelle du vitrail a été celle des premières époques, une verrière était considérée comme une mosaïque, un tapis lumineux, le décor d'une surface plane. Jusqu'au milieu du XVIe siècle, dans les vitraux légendaires et dans les compositions ornementales des arbres de Jessé, ce principe fut appliqué. Nous pouvons le retenir en laissant de côté les caractéristiques de style et chercher à l'accorder avec les tendances d'art de notre temps.' p. 8. The Tree of Jesse, a theme often found in Gothic art, depicts the lineage of Christ.

545. ' […] Une surface plane recouverte de couleurs dans un certain ordre assemblé.' *Théories*, pp. 1–13.

546. 'La remise en faveur de l'ancien art gothique (le vitrail) arrive à son heure […] cette recherche de naïveté et d'archaïsme qui est un des signes de l'évolution contemporaine […] telle oeuvre de MM. Gauguin, Anquetin, Denis qui s'accommoderait fort, sauf les indispensables retouches d'appropriation, d'être traduite par le vitrail.' p. 586.

547. 'Pour retrouver dans une oeuvre d'art aussi réelle que chez Gauguin, la présence du soleil, il faut remonter jusqu'à l'art du vitrail gothique, jusqu'aux tapis d'Orient.' Maurice Denis, *L'Ermitage* 2 (15 Dec. 1906), p. 325.

548. Yvanhoé Rambosson stated that the works of the Nabi Jan Verkade ' … tiennent au vitrail'. 'Quatrième Exposition du Barc de Boutteville', *Mercure de France* VII (April 1893). In his monograph on Bonnard, Antoine Terrasse observed that ' … there is in the blue and mauve landscapes of Bonnard, at the end, a light that recalls the stained glass of Chartres.' *Bonnard* (Paris: Gallimard, 1988), p. 7. For Gustave Coquiot, Bonnard's *La jeune fille au lapin* inevitably evoked stained glass with its integration of figure and surface. Gustave Coquiot, *Pierre Bonnard* (Paris: 1922), p. 58.

549. Aristide Maillol, linked in the 1890s with the Nabi group, also drew inspiration from the tapestries displayed at the Musée de Cluny. He established a tapestry workshop in his hometown of Banyuls-sur-Mer in 1893, with the explicit aim of 'resurrecting the beautiful ancient tapestry tradition' that the Gobelins factory had destroyed. Works such as *Music for a Bored Princess* (1897) or *The Concert of Women* (1896–1897) refer directly to heraldic and courtly tapestries. The highlighted folds of the women's dresses, the floral border and the tilted, flattened perspective point to Gothic inspiration. Maillol exhibited his tapestries at the Salon de la Société Nationale in 1893, 1895, 1896, 1897 and 1899. See Wendy Slatkin, *Aristide Maillol in the 1890s*, Ph.D. dissertation (Pennsylvania State University Press, 1982).

550. While drawing inspiration from the medieval tapestries on display at the Musée de Cluny, the Nabis produced works that responded directly to the new tapestry reforms recommended by administrators and critics in the field. From 1890–1898, Paul Ranson created numerous tapestry designs embroidered in wool by his wife, France Ranson. For examples of the medievalizing tapestries of the Nabis, such as Joszéf Rippl-Ronai's *Dame en Robe Rouge*, see Frèches-Thory and Terrasse.

551. See Christiaan Vogelaar, 'Emile Bernard and the Decorative Arts,' in Stevens *et al.*, *Emile Bernard 1868–1914: a Pioneer of Modern Art*, exhibition catalog (Mannheim: Städtische Kunsthalle/Amsterdam: Van Gogh Museum, Waander Publishers, 1990).

552. As a teenager, Bernard had done the same to the windows of his parents' bedroom. Vogelaar, p. 335.

553. Letter from Theo (27 Sept 1890) quoted in Vogelaar, p. 337.

554. For Bernard's interest in the *décoratif* strategies of the medieval artist, see Vogelaar (1990) and Jirat Wasiutynski, 'Emile Bernard and Paul Gauguin: The Avant-Garde and Tradition' in Stevens *et al.*, pp. 48–63.

555. Edouard Dujardin, 'Aux XX et aux Indépendants: le Cloisonnisme,' *La Revue Indépendante* 3 (March 1888), pp. 487–92.

556. Critics as astute as Félix Fénéon made this observation: 'Les larges traits dont M. Bernard cerne les accidents de terrain et des êtres sont le réseau de plomb d'un vitrail.' Félix Fénéon, 'Autre Groupe Impressionniste,' *La Cravache* (6 July 1889), p. 1.

557. See Vogelaar, p. 336.

558. In *Le Rêve*, Zola repeatedly refers to his protagonist, Angélique, as 'une petite vierge de vitrail.' The book's primary intertext is *The Golden Legend* and the saints' lives recounted in it. Paris referred to Joseph Bédier's 1900 adaptation of the *Roman de Tristan et Iseut* as 'resuscitating' the medieval characters and their ways, presenting them as 'personnages d'un vieux vitrail.' 'Préface' to *Le Roman de Tristan et Iseut* by Joseph Bédier (Paris: Union générale d'édition [10/ 18], 1981), p. 14. See Dakyns, pp. 244–7 on the Symbolist use of such legends.

559. See Naomi Morgan, 'La Légende de saint Julien l'hospitalier ou la vision à travers la vitre,' *Image [&] Narrative: Online Magazine of the Visual Narrative* 3: special issue on *Illustrations*. Many authors admired Flaubert's idea, but others, like Huysmans, criticized him for not going far enough (*En Route*). If one opens the pages of *La Plume*, *Le Chat Noir*, *Le Courrier Français*, or *Le Mercure de France* during the 1880s and 1890s one nearly always finds stained glass inspired poems, one of Laurent Tailhade's *Vitraux*, Catulle Mendès's *La Verrière*, Stuart Merill's *Fastes* or Jean Moréas's *Cantilènes*. Paul Claudel's *L'Oeil écouté*, though much later, also belongs to this tradition. A few examples from *Le Chat Noir* include 'Vitrail' by Alphonse Allais (26 September 1885) and 'Vitraux' by Alred Massebieau (9 April 1887), while *La Plume* published 'Vitrail,' a poem dedicated to Verlaine by Paul Redonnel (15 February 1891).

560. 'Visite hier à Cluny. Les tapisseries et les enluminures de missel. Calendriers. Dans les tapisseries je ne pense qu'à un agrandissement purement et simplement. Mon petit panneau – cela ferait le sujet d'une décoration. Expression d'un sentiment intime sur une grande surface, voilà tout! La même chose qu'un Chardin, par exemple. Différence d'avec l'Italien. Voilà des tapisseries aussi importantes, savantes qu'un Véronèse. Pourquoi sont-ils si inconnus? Petit morceau très ancien, en teintes plates grossières d'un charme de couleur très puissant couleurs tranchées sur fond clair. Cela me fait penser à certaines de mes machines.' Edouard Vuillard, Journal entry (16 July 1894). Journal MS 5396 Carnet 2, p. 44 V. Cited in Gloria Groom, p. 220. Here, Vuillard's use of the term 'machine' refers to large-scale finished pieces, but the term is loaded and resonates with the distinctly anti-industrial connotations of the pre-modern tapestry.

561. Both Roseline Bacou, 'Décors d'appartement au temps des Nabis,' *Art de France* (IV 1964), pp. 190–205 and James Dugdale, 'Vuillard the Decorator,' *Apollo* (Feb. 1965), have drawn attention to Vuillard's interest in mille-fleur tapestries, particularly those on display at the Musée de Cluny. The panels were displayed in Vaquez's library at 27 rue du Général Foy. The series consisted of *The Piano, Reading*, *The Library* and *The Drawing Room*. See Groom, pp. 90–97.

562. See Louis de Farcy (1897) and Louis Gonse (1886), p. 84.

563. 'C'est aux sujets profanes du Musée d'Angers ou la Licorne à Cluny qu'il pensait lorsqu'il évoquait les princesses de légende, à la fois monastiques et rustiques, aux visages secrets, telles enfin que les chantaient les poètes symbolistes de notre jeunesse. Il les groupait dans les compositions sans sujet défini, mais non sans mystère. Il leur donnait des costumes du temps de la Reine Anne [...] Images d'un passé fabuleux, figures de grâce hiératique qui font penser à des cantilènes grégoriennes, à la mélancolie des chansons populaires ou aux airs de danse qu'on entend encore dans les coins reculés de la Bretagne.' Maurice Denis, Introduction to *ABC de la peinture*.

564. 'Sérusier estimait que la tapisserie représente l'art national de la France [...] Son goût pour la tapisserie lui venait sans doute du sens profond qu'il avait de la décoration murale [...] Peut-être sa nostalgie du Moyen Age lui venait-elle en partie du regret d'une époque où l'idée du décor coloré s'associait si facilement à celle de l'espace mural.' *Rétrospective de Paul Sérusier*. Mai 1947. Musée Galleria, 1947.

565. For the mythic associations of Brittany and the Symbolist avant-garde see Gill Perry, 'The Going Away: A Prelude to the Modern,' in Charles Harrison *et al.*, *Primitivism, Cubism, Abstraction: The Early Twentieth Century* (New Haven: Yale University Press, 1993); Griselda Pollock and Fred Orton, 'Les Données Bretonnantes: La Prairie de Représentation,' *Art History* (Sept. 1980). For discussion of this issue in relation to the Nabis see Morowitz, 'Consuming the Past,' Chapter 4.

566. Bing has received a great deal of recent scholarly attention. For information on Bing and his Galerie de l'Art Nouveau and Maison de l'Art Nouveau see Silverman, Gabriel S. Weisberg, *Art Nouveau Bing: Paris 1900* (New York: Abrams, 1986) and Nancy Troy, *Modernism and the Decorative Arts in France: Art Nouveau to Le Corbusier* (New Haven: Yale University Press, 1991).

567. For information on this commission see Frèches-Thory and Terrasse, pp. 182–7; Weisberg (1986), pp. 52–3.

568. The subjects were as follows: Paul Ranson, *Moisson Fleurie*; Ker-Xavier Roussel, *Le Jardin*; Pierre Bonnard, *Maternité*, Henri Ibels, *Eté*; Edouard Vuillard, *Marroniers*; Maurice Denis, *Paysage*; Félix Vallotton, *Parisiennes*; Henri Toulouse-Lautrec, *Papa Chrysanthème*, Albert Besnard, *La Cascade*, P. A. Isaac, *Iris et Roseaux*. The titles of Sérusier's sketches, which do not survive, have not been determined.

569. For a reproduction of Vallotton's *Parisiennes*, see Frèches-Thory and Perucchi-Petri, p. 390, cat. no. 214.

570. See *La Revue Franco-Américaine* 1 (1895) and Jacques-Emile Blanche, 'Les objets d'art I: Au Salon du Champs de Mars,' *La Revue Blanche* 15 (May 1895).

571. 'Un caractère hasardeux.' Victor Champier, 'Les arts décoratifs au Salon de 1895: Le Champ de Mars,' *Revue des arts décoratifs* 15 (1895), p. 420.

572. 'Le point de départ des vitraux américains, y est-il dit, c'est le retour à la mosaïque de verres de couleurs, employés dans les belles verrières gothiques du XIIIe siècle sans l'application de couleurs vitrifiables par laquelle, dès le XIVe siècle, on a terni l'éclat natural du verre. La raison en était que, dans les églises on se laissait aller trop exclusivement à la préoccupation du sujet, le souci de la couleur ne venait qu'en seconde ligne. Les Américains, au contraire, veulent avant tout la couleur.' Champier, p. 420.

573. 'On me dispensera de faire ressortir en détail la médiocre science archéologique dont témoigne ce début solennel. L'époque où le vitrail du moyen âge a réalisé le plus nettement l'idéal d'une large mosaïque translucide c'est le XIIe siècle. Or le zèle du sujet n'y a nui de nulle sorte à la splendeur des colorations.' Champier, p. 20.

574. For the anti-nationalist criticism directed at Bing see Silverman, pp. 278–83, and Troy. Both discuss Bing's attempts to redress this situation through his use of rococo motifs at the 1900 Exposition Universelle.

575. 'L'amateur invinciblement attiré vers le verre, le juif n'ayant d'yeux que pour le plomb, c'est-a-dire que l'argent – car il s'empressait de procéder à la transmutation immédiate au cours du jour.' Ottin, p. 361.

576. This was, of course, patently false, as most members of the art-historical community were quick to acknowledge. As we saw in Chapter 3, the Strauss and Rothschild families were among the most discerning collectors of medieval art of their day.

577. 'Il n'y a qu'un moyen de sortir du bourbier où nous nous enlisons, c'est de revenir à l'esprit ancien aux modes anciennes, c'est d'être comme autrefois des gens qui croient à quelque chose, qui mêlent Dieu à leurs fêtes comme à leurs tristesses nationales, et que la croyance à l'éternité, la préoccupation d'accomplir ici-bas leur mission grandissent, transforment et rendent capables de donner à l'histoire des siècles comme ceux de Charlemagne et de saint Louis.' Le Clerc (a pseudonym used by Father Vincent de Paul Bailly) on the front page of *La Croix*, 3 May 1889.

578. Among the most notable of these were public prayer in atonement for the loss of the Franco-Prussian War, organized in the National Assembly, the national subscription responsible for the construction of the Sacré-Coeur basilica in Paris and the development of Lourdes as a major international pilgrimage center. For a detailed history of the marketing and political maneuvering used to construct the basilica as a 'work of national reparation,' see Raymond Jonas, *France and the Cult of the Sacred Heart* (Berkeley: University of California Press, 2000).

579. See the end of Chapter 5.

580. Thomas Kselman describes the shock of the defeat and ensuing waves of French miracles in *Miracles and Prophecies in Nineteenth-Century France* (New Brunswick, NJ: Rutgers University Press, 1983), pp. 113–19, while Joseph Grenier analyzes reactions to the situation in Catholic newspapers of the time, 'To Reach the People: La Croix, 1883–1890' (Ph.D. thesis, Fordham University, 1976), pp. 16–17, 214–16, 342–4.

581. 'C'est une démarche pieuse faite par manière de procession publique vers quelque sanctuaire privilégié, pour s'y trouver en communication plus intime avec Dieu [...] nous allons en pèlerinage pour faire comme ont fait nos pères *sicut fecerunt patres nostri*; car les pèlerinages ont toujours été dans les moeurs de l'humanité, aussi bien que dans la tradition de l'église.' *Manuel du pèlerinage Lorrain à Notre-Dame de Lourdes*. 12th ed. (Saint-Dié: Imp. Humbert, 1899), pp. 92, 95.

582. This quote comes from the first issue of *Le Pèlerin*: 'Grâce aux pèlerinages nationaux, il sera prouvé qu'il y a une France catholique qui proteste contre les insolents blasphèmes de la France sceptique et athée, qu'il y a une France qui adore le Dieu de nos pères … Cette France, c'est la France nouvelle, la France qui se souvient de ses traditions, dont le bon sens, le sens honnête et religieux, se révèle devant les théories grossières de l'athéisme révolutionnaire, c'est la France de Charlemagne et de saint Louis qui relève la croix, marche vers Dieu en qui est son espoir et de qui seul lui viendra le salut.' (12 July 1873), p. 8.

583. See Sandra Zimdar-Swartz, *Encountering Mary from La Salette to Medjugorje* (Princeton: Princeton University Press, 1991) for more about Marian apparitions of the nineteenth century. For a history of belief in the Immaculate Conception and its resurgence in the nineteenth century see Edwin O'Connor, *The Dogma of the Immaculate Conception: Its History and Significance* (South Bend: University of Notre-Dame Press, 1958).

584. Monsignor Fournier, the bishop of Nantes, provides a remarkable example of this tendency. He proclaimed the defeat a result of the nation's 'guilt' – 'Sin has attracted the terrible blows of divine justice' – and proposed religious repentance as a way of making up for these sins. 'Allocutions de Mgr Fournier,' *La Semaine religieuse du diocèse de Nantes*, 10 September 1870, p. 441. Cited in Jonas, p. 149. Jonas's book traces the impact of such ideas, which prompted

religious affirmations all over France and led to the construction of the Sacré-Coeur basilica in Paris as a 'voeu national,' a reparation for French sins. See also his account of pilgrimages to Montmartre, 'Sacred Tourism and Secular Pilgrimage: Montmartre and the Basilica of the Sacré-Coeur,' in Weisberg, ed. (2001), pp. 94–119.

585.    The comprehensive maps, summaries and descriptions of nineteenth-century pilgrimage sites in Jean-Emmanuel Drochon's *Histoire illustrée des pèlerinages* provides an excellent perspective on the popularity of pilgrimages in the fin de siècle (Paris: Plon, 1890).

586.    See the inaugural issue of *Le Pèlerin* for a discussion of the Conseil's objectives (12 July 1873), pp. 2, 10–11. See also Paul Castel, *Le P. François Picard et le P. Vincent de Paul Bailly dans les luttes de presse* (Rome: Maison Généralice, 1962), p. 38 and Grenier, pp. 411–12.

587.    See the first issue of *Le Pèlerin*, which discusses the desire to increase local pilgrimages by running them on the national level (12 July 1873), p. 3. See also Michael R. Marrus, 'Cultures on the Move: Pilgrims and Pilgrimages in Nineteenth-Century France,' *Stanford French Review* 1 (1977), pp. 205–20.

588.    Joseph Grenier's dissertation about the newspaper *La Croix* and Paul Castel's discussion of Fathers Picard and Bailly provide excellent background on the development of the Assumptionist order. See also Rémi Kokel, *Vincent de Paul Bailly, un pionnier de la presse catholique* (Paris: Editions B. P., 1957); Lucien Guissard, *Les Assomptionistes d'hier à aujourd'hui* (Paris: Bayard, 1999) and *Emmanuel d'Alzon dans la société et l'Eglise au XIXe siècle*, ed. René Rémond and Emile Poulat (Paris: Le Centurion, 1982).

589.    According to Grenier, Castel and Kokel, it was the war that gave the Assumptionists their new mission. In an 1871 meeting, Father d'Alzon and his priests decided that they would 'contribuer au relèvement moral et spirituel de la patrie malheureuse' by creating a 'ligue catholique, destinée à la défense de l'Eglise, et de ressusciter la *Revue de l'enseignement chrétien* qui bataillera pour conquérir la liberté de l'enseignement supérieur … ' Quoted in Castel, p. 29.

590.    See Castel, p. 38.

591.    'La France assiste depuis un an à un spectacle des plus consolants pour les âmes chrétiennes. Il s'est trouvé qu'après les plus grands désastres dont notre pays ait jamais été éprouvé, une même pensée est sortie tout à coup du sein de la nation. La France catholique, ramenée à la pénitence par le malheur, s'est tournée spontanément vers Celle que les chrétiens invoquent sous le nom de la *Mère de miséricorde* et de *Refuge des pécheurs* […] Jamais, depuis le temps des croisades et de Jeanne d'Arc, on ne vit une telle manifestation, et une manifestation aussi éclatante, aussi courageuse de la foi chrétienne. […]' Article by Father A. Tilloy in the inaugural issue of *Le Pèlerin* (12 July 1873), pp. 3–8.

592.    Issues from 6 September 1873 and 20 January 1877. These are fairly representative of the kinds of publicity found in most issues.

593.    See 'A Nos Amis' (*Le Pèlerin*, 1 January 1877), pp. 1–2 and Grenier, pp. 125–6. The Assumptionists were not alone; in fact, a number of Catholics reached out to the working class at this time, notably Albert de Mun (Les Cercles Catholiques, 1871 and l'Association catholique de la jeunesse française, 1886) and Marc Sangier (Le Sillon, 1884).

594.    According to Watelet, none of the major weeklies appearing from 1843 to 1870 could be considered particularly religious, pp. 376–80. Grenier also discusses earlier Catholic publications on pp. 119–24. R. Howard Bloch's delightful *God's Plagiarist: Being an Account of the Fabulous Industry and Irregular Commerce of the Abbé Migne* (Chicago: The University of Chicago Press, 1995) paints the portrait of an earlier model of a priest, l'abbé Migne (1800–1875), who used new developments in printing and paper technology to disseminate popular editions of religious works. Migne's *Ateliers Catholiques* churned out the hundreds of volumes of *La Bibliothèque universelle du clergé* as part of a similarly apostolic initiative to rebuild the Church. Yet even inexpensive books were luxurious in comparison to periodicals, whose costs could be subsidized by advertisements.

595.    See Hindman *et al.*, pp. 132–6. Curmer (1801–1870) produced an amazing variety of deluxe editions with an impressive critical apparatus and varied the editions so that they could be used for study, prayer or as gifts. Because of their deluxe nature, however, the books of hours had only 500 to 850 subscribers, beginning with the imperial family.

596.    These statistics vary widely according to region and decade. According to studies done by Antoine Prost, Michel Fleury and Pierre Valmary on wedding registers throughout the century, we know that, on average, 95 per cent of brides and grooms could sign their own names by the 1890s. Antoine Prost, *Histoire de l'enseignement en France 1800–1967* (Paris: Librairie Armand Colin, 1968), p. 96 and Michel Fleury and Pierre Valmary, 'Le Progrès de l'instruction élémentaire de Louis XIV à Napoléon III d'après l'enquête de Louis Maggiolo (1877–1879),' *Population* 12:1 (1957), p. 79. Cited in Grenier, pp. 47–8. For another view of literacy rates in the last half of the century, see Roger Price, *A Social History of Nineteenth-Century France* (New York: Holmes & Meier Publishers, 1987), pp. 330–38.

597.    For an excellent overview of the illustrated press and the social, political and technological developments that made the last twenty years of the nineteenth century so fertile for

publishing, see the introduction to Watelet, pp. 369–82. Hindman *et al.*, p. 154, describe the advantages of heliogravure, which combined photography with printing. The technique dated from the 1850s.

598.  For descriptions of religious imagery in nineteenth-century France, their audience and their expense, see Catherine Rosenbaum-Dondaine, *L'Image de piété en France, 1814–1914* (Paris: Musée-Galerie de la SEITA, 1984) and 'Un siècle et demi de petite imagerie de piété,' *Revue de la Bibliothèque Nationale* 6 (1982). Huysmans maligns the *images sulpiciennes* throughout his oeuvre, notably in *La Cathédrale* and *L'Oblat*, in which he discusses the appalling state of Catholic art in the fin de siècle.

599.  As Richard Griffiths has shown, this was a widespread phenomenon from within the Church: they attempted to provide followers with an alternative to the increasing materialism of society. Louis Roussel began *La France illustrée*, a Catholic publication, in 1874, in order to offer an alternative to more secular periodicals: 'Gravures scandaleuses, romans immoraux, propos ignobles, rien n'est épargné pour corrompre l'âme et dévoyer l'intelligence des masses […] Le journal illustré catholique doit se dresser comme un rempart devant l'invasion du journal illustré sectaire et pornographique: oeuvre difficile et que nous poursuivons sans relâche, sûrs d'un succès prochain, grâce au dévouement des amis qui nous soutiendront dans nos luttes hebdomadaires.' This is the text of an 1894 article from *La France libre illustrée*, a supplement to *La France illustrée*. Cited in Watelet, p. 474.

600.  '[…] Il ne sait qu'une seule politique: connaître, aimer, servir Dieu, et par ce moyen obtenir la vie éternelle.' 'A nos amis' (*Le Pèlerin*, 1 January 1877), p. 2.

601.  Notre-Dame de Salut would be a recurring motif in *Le Pèlerin*; later articles carry the story of her miraculous powers (see, for example, the issue from 14 April 1877), pp. 223–6.

602.  This extremely long article by Father Vincent de Paul Bailly traces each detail in illustrator M. E. Mathieu's work. The article appeared in the 3 March 1877 issue to accompany the new cover. 'La ville infernale, le cloaque impur, le cratère qui vomit sa lave révolutionnaire sur la province.' 'On le dépose donc comme un de ces pauvres malades de Lourdes aux pieds de Marie; Celle qui apporte le salut à la France, le regarde avec compassion.' pp. 121–2.

603.  These goals were not unlike those of other religious groups who attempted to help the working class. The social vision promoted by *Le Pèlerin* found an echo in political movements that targeted the Christian working class. See Robert Byrnes (1950).

604.  On anti-clericalism during this period, see René Rémond, *L'anticléricalisme en France de 1815 à nos jours* (Paris: Fayard, 1976). Gambetta repeated this aphorism as 'Le cléricalisme, c'est l'ennemi' in *La République française* in 1880. Cited in Castel, p. 93.

605.  See Castel, pp. 61–2 for quotes from the correspondence of the Assumptionist Fathers in 1878. They described the situation as 'des persécutions de plus en plus ardentes' and as 'à la veille de la bataille.'

606.  'Un journal de propagande précieux.' 'A Nos Amis' (*Le Pèlerin*, 1 January 1877), p. 1.

607.  'Il n'y avait pas, au moyen âge, un pan de muraille dans les églises qui ne fût utilisé à ce langage d'une éloquence spéciale, et d'ailleurs le culte lui-même est un magnifique tableau qui vient, en frappant les yeux, orner les grandes paroles qui sont proférées. Les livres saints, les missels et les heures étaient splendides d'enluminures, dont la richesse, comme la pieuse naïveté, désespère les imitateurs. Chaque page s'habillait d'un cadre, chaque lettre voulait devenir une vignette […] Nos vieilles vies de saints, celles où nous puisons souvent, dans le *Pèlerin*, ont été, un peu plus tard, ornées de gravures en taille-douce qui exigeaient alors un immense labeur; nos pères, cependant, ne marchandaient pas la dépense pour ces illustrations difficiles. Telle ancienne Bible possède des centaines de ces gravures, et aucun éditeur de notre siècle de photographes, n'a produit, dans les éditions illustrées, un travail qui approche de ceux-là. L'imagerie, autrefois si répandue, détruite par l'austérité janséniste, fut tout à fait chassée du sanctuaire; aucun prêtre respectable n'eût voulu s'en occuper, on l'abandonna avec mépris aux seuls marchands, et, faute de tout conseil, elle est tombée dans le ridicule. […] Mais le *Pèlerin*, vieux routier qui a vu maints sanctuaires, qui a souvent gratté le badigeon pour retrouver les fresque naïves et pieuses d'autrefois; lui qui a visité de riches églises d'Espagne et surtout d'Italie, qui a admiré sur les bords du Rhin et jusqu'au fond de l'Allemagne, les poèmes en pierre des cathédrales, réclame des images vraies. Il attache les images sur son manteau, parce que regarder la figure d'un saint est une prière, il se plaît, au spectacle des belles actions, comme aux beautés de la nature.' *Le Pèlerin* (3 March 1877), pp. 121–2.

608.  One of the clearest examples of this complaint is evident in a pamphlet entitled 'Pourquoi nous vous délaissons,' written by Claude-Anthime Corbon, a member of the working class who rose to the position of senator in 1875. In this publication, he proposed a number of reasons for the common people's abandonment of the Church, including, above all, its attachment to monarchist politics and its resulting refusal to acknowledge the inherent equality of all men. He begins his essay by comparing the modern church to its medieval counterpart, arguing that, at the beginning of the Middle Ages, many priests came from the lower classes and remained faithful to their origins. In the Middle Ages, he argues, the Catholic Church recognized that all humans were equal in the eyes of God. He uses thirteenth-century cathedrals as the perfect

example of the medieval spirit, insisting that returning to the use of images and to the equal treatment of working class and bourgeoisie will bring the masses back to the Church. 'Pourquoi nous vous délaissons. Lettre de l'ouvrier-sénateur Corbon à M. Le sénateur-évêque Dupanloup' (Paris: Imprimerie nouvelle, 1877).

609. As Hindman *et al.*, have shown, there were a number of ventures to reproduce or imitate manuscripts throughout the century in France. Though this was largely an elitist pursuit from 1840 to 1870, the last quarter of the century witnessed an increase in publications directed to a wider market. Father Bailly was probably familiar with Paul Lacroix's popularizing series of chromolithographies about the Middle Ages published in the 1870s. He directed these primarily toward children, hoping that the combination of text and image would engage their imagination. See pp. 136–8. Interestingly, modern reproductions tended to cost significantly more than originals, pp. 131, 137.

610. *The Power of Images: Studies in the History and Theory of Response* (Chicago: The University of Chicago Press, 1989), pp. 79–80, p. 65.

611. The publication abounded with sketches of works by Fra Angelico and Fra Lippi (see, for example, 25 Feb. 1882, 24 Feb. 1883, 21 April 1884 or 29 June 1885) or Giotto (8 Dec. 1884 and 19 Jan. 1885) and scenes from Books of Hours (25 Nov. 1882).

612. Unifying text and image was one of the goals of the publication and, it would seem, one of the most difficult editorial tasks. When they did not have enough money to hire illustrators, they had to make the rounds of bookshops to buy inexpensive prints around which they could build a story. See Castel, p. 53, for Father Bailly's description of such activities.

613. 'Son blason porte un coeur, symbole de charité, accosté des ailes de la contemplation, et marqué du *Tau*, signe de la souffrance (une des figures de la croix). Au-dessus brille le Soleil de Justice, figure du Christ; au-dessous le croissant renversé de la lune, symbole de ce bas monde, changeant comme la lune. Tout autour des étoiles, symboles des Saints au milieu desquels le pèlerins aime à vivre.' *Le Pèlerin* 22 Feb. 1879, p. 117.

614. Until 1896 (the 1000th issue), the periodical was published only in black and white. See Watelet, pp. 394–5, for a brief history of its evolution.

615. Other periods are also represented in *Le Pèlerin*, but because of the paper's focus on early Christian saints linked to the French nation, even the artwork from subsequent periods tends to represent medieval stories or Biblical tales.

616. The editorials included in nearly every issue often underline this dedication to bringing back a 'Universal Church' in which Church and State were closely united. This message occurred over and over in other publications of the Assumptionists, including *La Croix*, begun in 1883 with a more overtly political agenda. As Grenier has argued, 'The union of Church and state as it existed in medieval Christendom was an ideal to which *La Croix* harked back with nostalgia […].' The thirteenth century was that most often mentioned. See Grenier, pp. 196–219.

617. 'Pour le *Pèlerin* […] son succès est dû à la forme adoptée, il fait pénétrer bien des idées justes et il pénètre lui-même dans des milieux où ne sont pas admises des revues religieuses.' Father Picard to Father Emmanuel d'Alzon. Cited in Castel, p. 54.

618. Cited in Watelet, p. 394. Kokel also traces the readership of the periodical across the period. In order to gauge the success of *Le Pèlerin*, one can compare it to *La Revue des Deux Mondes*, considered the most successful periodical of the time. It had 18 000 subscribers in 1874. See Claude Bellanger, *Histoire Générale de la presse française. Tome III: De 1871 à 1940* (Presses Universitaires de France: Paris, 1970), p. 391.

619. Best known of these is *La Croix*, begun in 1883 as a daily complement to *Le Pèlerin* with a more politicized component. Both *Le Pèlerin* and *La Croix* are still published today. According to Watelet, La Maison de la Bonne Presse had the best presses in Paris, capable of printing 7000 copies an hour in six colors (p. 397). The publishing house was also among the first to encourage the employment of women (Les Oblates de l'Assomption and their helpers), partly as a way of saving money and partly to include them in this apostolic work. For more about the 'family' environment of La Bonne Presse, see Castel, pp. 151–3.

620. According to Watelet, there were 10 000 such committees in 1903 and 50 000 'zélateurs' committed to distributing the paper, p. 394. See Grenier, pp. 157–61 for detailed descriptions of variants of such creative techniques used to sell *Le Pèlerin* and *La Croix*.

621. See Watelet, p. 397 and Castel, p. 312. Many issues of *Le Pèlerin* advertised this series, which proved enormously successful (56 000 sold in 1886 with some issues reprinted up to three times), to the point that many people read the paper just for *La Vie des saints*. See Castel, p. 57 for more about this. On the first page of the first issue of 1880, the series is advertised for its bulk (12 months constitute 400 pages), for its popularity and for its moral value. Its distribution is highly encouraged: 'Les petites vies illustrées des Saints que nous allons mettre au jour ne seront donc pas pour les seuls lecteurs du *Pèlerin*; elles sont destinées à être distribuées en grand nombre comme des tracts et comme les excellentes *Petites Lectures* de St Vincent de Paul, avec qui elles ne feront pas double emploi.'

622. This is the case of the volume in the collection of Elizabeth Emery, which belonged to the priest of Saint-Pol-de-Mons. Each newsprint issue was carefully organized by saint's day and contains bookmarks to selected pages. Small religious images of devotions flourished throughout the century and were given as gifts, but this saint's lives series was different in its focus on both text and image. For more about the proliferation of detachable religious images, see Rosenbaum-Dondaine.

623. Hindman *et al.* describe many of the luxury manuscripts available on the nineteenth-century market. See the chapter entitled 'Reproductions.' As they note, however, most of these were prohibitively expensive; as such, only the wealthiest members of society would have been able to own them or to give them as gifts. As mass printing became increasingly inexpensive, a variety of publications, including illustrated missals of Lourdes or La Salette based on medieval manuscript illumination (many of them advertised in the pages of *Le Pèlerin*), became available to the lower classes. Nonetheless, one can gauge the stark poverty of the working-class families to whom *Le Pèlerin* was donated by reading Zola's *Germinal*. The Maheu family's only wall decoration consists of 'violent illuminations' of the emperor and his wife, soldiers and saints, given to them by the mining company. *Les Rougon-Macquart*, vol. 3, p. 1149.

624. 'Défendre les faibles était la grande affaire des chevaliers d'autrefois. Les faibles de nos jours ce sont les malheureux qu'on trompe, qu'on séduit, qu'on corrompt par la mauvaise presse. C'est à vous de les défendre en leur apportant le bon journal. Voilà l'oeuvre capitale à laquelle vous devez travailler sans relâche et sans vous rebuter jamais.' Cited in Castel, p. 407.

625. As we saw in Chapter 4, a number of Symbolist journals embraced similar (though secular) goals. Publications such as *Le Saint-Graal*, *Durendal*, *La Trève-Dieu* created organizations of 'chevaliers' dedicated to protecting the artistic values disseminated by their publications. See Dakyns, pp. 212–14.

626. 13 December 1896, p. 11.

627. Henriot was the pseudonym of Henry Maigrot (1857–1933), who also published in a number of widely read periodicals, notably *L'Illustration*. Uzès was the pseudonym of Achille Lemot (1847–1909).

628. Kokel tells the story of Father Bailly's meeting with Uzès in Le Chat Noir and his near rejection of the heavy-drinking illustrator. But the artist, who was near starvation, convinced the priest of his skills and talent won out over moral considerations. Bailly often visited Le Chat Noir to collect Uzès's work for *Le Pèlerin*, p. 89.

629. For examples of the variety of types of publications including references to pilgrimages, see for example *La Plume*, which published a number of poems or essays about pilgrimages including 'Pèlerinage' by Maurice Desombiaux (15 June 1891, pp. 200–201), 'Les Pèlerins' by Léon Denis (1 December 1892, p. 501), or 'Les Pèlerins bretons' by Louis Tiercelin (1 December 1891, pp. 424–5). *Le Courrier Français* published extracts from *Les Rêves pèlerins* by Georges Bidache (1 May and 25 December 1898), while *Le Chat Noir* included 'La Ballade du pèlerin' by F. Loviot (19 September 1891) and 'La légende du temps nouveau. Pèlerinage par J. Delaquys' (14 September 1895). Even *Le Figaro illustré* and *La Revue des Deux Mondes* printed stories about pilgrimages: 'L'Eternel Pèlerin' by Narcisse Quellian (August 1898, p. 157) and 'Le Pèlerinage du Père Jacques' by George Duruy (1 December 1886, pp. 626–61), respectively.

630. *Mercure de France* 12 (1899), pp. 666–71. He would later publish this poem in the collection *Petites légendes* (1900).

631. See, for example, the highlights of the yearly Salons published in *Illustration*. From 1898 to 1900 the journal reproduces at least one if not several paintings depicting pilgrimages, including 'L'offrande à la Vierge; XIVe siècle' by Mademoiselle Sonrel (30 April 1898, p. 320) and 'Procession de Notre-Dame des Flots' by Emile Hirschfeld (7 April 1900, p. 209). Pierre Larousse provides a long list of nineteenth-century painters who featured pilgrims in their Salon paintings. 'Pèlerin,' *Grand dictionnaire encyclopédique du XIXe siècle* (Geneva: Slatkine Reprints, 1982).

632. Although much of this information was often diluted for entertainment purposes, other articles were excerpted from recently published histories of the Church or the Crusades or from art-historical works.

633. As we saw in Chapter 2, publications like *L'Ymagier* were crucial for bringing avant-garde attention to *images d'Epinal* and to wood block prints, but this publication did not begin until 1894.

634. Ruth Harris has called *Lourdes* 'perhaps the greatest bestseller of the nineteenth century.' She has determined that, by 1900, Lasserre's work had been translated into at least eighty languages and had sold over a million copies. *Lourdes: Body and Spirit in the Secular Age* (New York: Viking, 1999), p. 180. She reproduces a page of Lasserre's manuscript in this book.

635. A good example of this can be seen in the discourse of the 'promoter' of the Mont Saint-Michel pilgrimage. After enumerating the famous kings and queens who 'rushed' there in the past, he encourages modern pilgrims to visit: 'A l'oeuvre donc! A l'exemple de nos aïeux, préparons-

nous à nous rendre, de toutes parts, à la Montagne Sainte d'où nous viendra le salut!' *Le Pèlerin* (2 August 1873), p. 62.

636.   'C'est bien en effet la foi chrétienne qui prend possession des chemins rapides du plaisir et du négoce, c'est le peuple chrétien qui s'empare des inventions modernes, les met à son usage, et fait à sa piété des routes plus nombreuses et plus promptes.' *Le Pèlerin* (12 July 1873), p. 3. For more about the 'medieval' marketing of pilgrimages and notably Lourdes, see Elizabeth Emery, 'The Nineteenth-Century Struggle for the Soul of Lourdes.'

637.   See Suzanne Kaufman, 'Miracles, Medicine and the Spectacle of Lourdes: Popular Religion and Modernity in Fin-de-Siècle France' (Ph.D. dissertation, Rutgers, The State University of New Jersey, 1996), pp. 99–104, for the history of the development of the national pilgrimage to Lourdes.

638.   'Ce signe est une petite croix de laine rouge que Pie IX avait distribuée à ses défenseurs dans Rome, et que portaient sur leur poitrine les zouaves pontificaux quand ils sont venus verser leur sang pour la France; elle est doublée de blanc et porte au revers la devise: *Domino Christo servire.*' *Le Pèlerin* (19 July 1873), p. 33. An 1899 pilgrimage manual for Lourdes explains that the Pope chose this image to evoke the pilgrims' 'crusade': 'N. T. S. P. le Pape Pie IX daigna donner de sa main aux pèlerins, comme emblême de leur croisade pacifique, la croix de laine rouge avec la devise: *Christo Domino servire*; Servir le Christ, Notre-Seigneur.' *Manuel du pèlerinage Lorrain à Notre-Dame de Lourdes* (12th edition. Saint-Dié: Imprimerie Humbert, 1899), p. 86.

639.   See also Figure 6.6.

640.   The first national pilgrimage was marked by its abundance of banners: four hundred emblems from Marian shrines all over France came together in a giant procession at Lourdes. See Kselman, pp. 118–19. As Alphonse Dupront has noted in his magisterial study of the Crusades and their post-medieval reception, the concept of the Crusades haunted the nineteenth century and the word itself would have invoked medieval pilgrims fighting to free Jerusalem. See *Le Mythe de croisade*, especially volume 2 (Paris: Gallimard, 1997). Such scenes were also prevalent in artistic works. See for example, the numerous nineteenth-century paintings reproduced in Georges Tate's *L'Orient des Croisades* (Paris: Gallimard, 1991). They include Larivière, 'Bataille d'Ascalon' (Musée du Château de Versailles); Victor Schnetz, 'Procession des croisés conduits par Pierre l'Ermite et Godefroy de Bouillon autour de Jérusalem, la veille de l'attaque de la ville' (Musée du Château de Versailles); and Signol, 'Prise de Jérusalem' (Musée du Château de Versailles) in which red and white crosses and banners abound. The government clearly understood the military symbolism of the crosses; they labeled them as subversive: ' … exterior signs designed to bring about hostile protests … ' Letter from the Minister of the Interior describing problems with pilgrims in the North (AD Hautes-Pyrénées 1m232). Cited in Kaufman, p. 45.

641.   'Notre croisade pacifique pour la délivrance du Saint-Père et le salut de la France.' These ceremonies as well as their wording are described in an entry from the second issue of *Le Pèlerin* (19 July 1873), p. 35.

642.   *Manuel* (1899), p. 7. As Régine Pernoud points out in her introduction to the reprint of a 1496 pilgrimage manual, medieval and modern versions of such manuals follow roughly the same format of giving the pilgrim historical and geographical information as well as doctrinal guidance. *Un Guide du pèlerin de terre sainte au xve siècle*, Vol. 1 (Mantes: Imprimerie du petit mantais, 1940), pp. 18–19.

643.   See, for example, an account of 26 July 1873 printed in *Le Pèlerin*, in which people burst into tears during the ceremony, p. 40. For more descriptions of the late nineteenth-century pilgrimage experience, one has only to open any page of *Le Pèlerin* (especially from 1873–1876). The newspaper is full of personal accounts pertaining to all aspects of the pilgrimage experience. There were also a great number of contemporary books written by pilgrims in memory of their trip as well as souvenir booklets and postcards sold to pilgrims. For a fictional account of the experience, see the first chapters of Emile Zola's *Lourdes*, which evokes in detail the travel conditions and spiritual state of the pilgrims.

644.   This is, of course, a mythologized vision of the Middle Ages, fostered by Chateaubriand and the Romantic Middle Ages and furthered by artists and poets. The process of creating this new and powerful image of communal worship results, in large part, from the nature of the periodical and the ways in which its messages were taken up and repeated by priests and readers. As David Freedberg has argued, the reproduction and repetition of images associated with pilgrimages often 'engenders a new and compelling aura of its own,' p. 126.

645.   Although a sleepy little Pyrenees town, by 1900 Lourdes was welcoming more than half a million visitors per year. In the 1860s, as more and more people came to worship at Bernadette's grotto, the missionaries of Notre-Dame de Garaison (the 'Grotto Fathers') bought land, negotiated with government officials to build a complex, changed the course of a river and subsidized railroad lines and highways to provide easy access to the far-away city. They constructed an elaborate complex that would eventually grow to include three churches, a processional staircase, bathing pools, the miraculous cave itself, stations of the cross and a

park. Today the Domain comprises nearly 125 acres and welcomes six million visitors a year. See Stéphane Baumont, *Histoire de Lourdes* (Toulouse: Editions Privat, 1993), pp. 85–96.

646.    *A Lourdes; le pèlerinage belge du 30 août au 12 septembre 1906. Notes d'un pèlerin liégois* (Liège: Imprimerie Demarteau, 1906), p. 19.

647.    '[…] c'est la concurrence effrénée, le raccrochage sur le pas des boutiques dans toute la ville; et l'on va, l'on vient, l'on vire, au milieu de ce brouhaha, mais toujours pour aboutir par un chemin ou un autre, à la grotte.' *Les Foules de Lourdes* (Grenoble: J. Millon, 1993), p. 80.

648.    'Il évoquait les vieilles cathédrales où frissonnait cette foi des peuples, il revoyait les anciens objets du culte, l'imagerie, l'orfèvrerie, les saints de pierre et de bois, d'une force, d'une beauté d'expression admirables. C'etait qu'en ces temps lointains, les ouvriers croyaient, donnaient leur chair, donnaient leur âme, dans toute la naïveté de leur émotion […] Et, aujourd'hui, les architectes bâtissaient les églises avec la science tranquille qu'ils mettaient à bâtir les maisons à cinq étages, de même que les objets religieux, les chapelets, les médailles, les statuettes, étaient fabriqués à la grosse, dans les quartiers populeux de Paris, par des ouvriers noceurs […] *Tout cela, brutalement, jurait avec la résurrection tentée, avec les légendes, les cérémonies, les processions des âges morts.*' *Lourdes*, p. 345 (our emphasis).

649.    For a fascinating study of the kind of commercialism that went on at Lourdes – the sale of candles, holy water, lozenges, postcards and nearly every product imaginable – and the horrified reactions of both Catholics and Republicans, see Suzanne Kaufman, pp. 102–46.

650.    'L'on tourne, du matin au soir, sur la même piste, ne voyant, où qu'on aille, en sus de visages ressassés, que des statues de vierges en plâtre, les yeux au ciel, vêtues de blanc et ceinturées de bleu; pas une boutique où il n'y ait des médailles, des cierges, des chapelets, des scapulaires, des brochures racontant des miracles; le vieux et le nouveau Lourdes en regorgent; les hôtels même en vendent; et cela s'étend de rues en rues, pendant des kilomètres […] des chromos de Bernadettes, en jupe rouge et tablier bleu, agenouillées, un cierge à la main, devant la Vierge, avec des statuettes de Lilliput et des médailles qui font songer à une monnaie de poupée, frappée à la grosse, dans des rebuts de cuivre; et tous ces objets s'améliorent, enflent, grandissent à mesure que l'on se rapproche de la nouvelle ville; les statues poussent, finissent, tout en demeurant aussi laides, par devenir énormes. Les chromos s'amplifient, déguisent en soubrette la fille de Soubirous; le module des médailles augmente et leur métal change; l'or et l'argent se montrent et lorsqu'on atteint l'avenue de la Grotte, c'est l'explosion de la bimbeloterie de luxe.' *Les Foules de Lourdes*, pp. 79–80.

651.    The materialism of pilgrimages was not, of course, new, but endemic, even in the Middle Ages. In the fourth century Saint Jerome called Jerusalem 'worse than Sodom' – and the commerce of pious objects, traffic in relics and the buying of posthumous pilgrimages was common. See Jean Jacques Antier, *Le Pèlerinage retrouvé* (Paris: Le Centurion, 1979), pp. 34–6. Huysmans considers this fact in *Les Foules de Lourdes*, but it does not improve his impression of the modern pilgrimage site, pp. 259–60.

652.    'Les prêtres devraient y réfléchir et songer aussi combien l'élément juif domine maintenant parmi les débitants d'objets de piété. Convertis ou non, il semble bien qu'en sus de la passion du gain, ces négociants éprouvent l'involontaire besoin de retrahir le Messie, en le vendant sous des aspects soufflés par le démon.' *Les Foules de Lourdes*, p. 127.

653.    'Les Pèlerinages à la Grotte de Lourdes dévieraient de leur but, ils perdraient tout leur mérite si, par notre faute, ils venaient se transformer en simples excursions de touristes […] Un pèlerinage n'est pas un voyage de plaisir, mais d'expiation.' *Manuel* (1899), pp. 8–9.

654.    See Kaufman, pp. 112–13.

655.    In *La Faiblesse de croire*, Michel de Certeau describes the status of priests in the modern world as 'enigmatic', akin to characters from folklore, while Church ceremony is seen as 'exotic' or 'theatrical' (Paris: Editions du Seuil, 1987), pp. 7, 91. This tendency had already begun at the end of the nineteenth century.

656.    Zola's relationship to Catholicism is more complex than is sometimes thought. He had broken away from the Church at a relatively young age, possibly because of his engineer father's rational views, but continued to live with devout Catholics (first his mother, then his wife). See 'Le Jeune Zola et les prêtres' in Pierre Ouvrard, *Zola et le prêtre* (Paris: Beauchesne Editeur, 1986). See also Zola's *Oeuvres complètes* IX, p. 409, pp. 871–93; X, p. 881; and his *Correspondance* I, p. 223–7. The trip to the Pyrenées was intended to please Madame Zola, while distancing her from Paris while his mistress, Jeanne Rozerot, gave birth to their son. The Zolas stayed in Lourdes from 13–17 September 1891. See *Correspondance générale d'Emile Zola*, VII, p. 199, note 1.

657.    '[…] Les milliers de pèlerins du pèlerinage national, en une bousculade […] ruisselaient par les rues, assiégeaient les boutiques. On aurait dit les cris, les coups de coude, les galops brusques d'une foire qui s'achève.' p. 340.

658.    For theories of the crowd in nineteenth-century French literature and society, see Naomi Schor, *Zola's Crowds* (Baltimore: Johns Hopkins University Press, 1978), Susanna Barrows, *Distorting Mirrors: Visions of the Crowd in Late Nineteenth-Century France* (New Haven: Yale University Press, 1981) and Robert A. Nye, 'The Origins of Crowd Psychology: Gustave Le Bon and the

Crisis of Mass Democracy in the Third Republic' (London: Sage Publications, 1975). Zola's focus on visual input is akin to what Robert Rosenblum has called 'spectator Christianity,' the shift in paintings from a subjective experience of religion to a depiction of *others* experiencing religion. In the nineteenth century, for example, images of the Crucifixion give way to images of peasants praying in front of a crucifix; *Nineteenth-Century Art*, ed. Robert Rosenblum and H. W. Janson (New York: Harry Abrams, 1984), p. 423.

659.   Such disappointment, as David Freedberg has pointed out, is endemic in religious imagery as visitors often expect to discover a literal incarnation of the signified in the signifier. See what he calls the shift from 'representation' to 'presentation,' pp. 27–30.

660.   Here he saw 'une petite ville, avec ses rues pavées de caillous, ses maisons noires [...] peuplée de visions d'or et de chairs peintes,' an image that corresponded to his preconceived image of the city, p. 340.

661.   For a history of the panorama, see Bernard Comment, *The Painted Panorama*, trans. Anne-Marie Glasheen (New York: H. N. Abrams, 2000) and Stephan Oettermann, *The Panorama: History of a Mass Medium*, trans. Deborah Lucas (New York: Zone Books, 1997). Medieval panoramas, including scenes from the life of Joan of Arc, were particularly popular. See, for example, posters advertising the 'Grand Panorama' at the Musée patriotique de Jeanne d'Arc (Musée de la publicité 997.82.1) and the Hippodrome panorama featuring the burning of Joan at the stake (Musée de la publicité, 14956).

662.   Kaufman, p. 109.

663.   Michel de Certeau has explored the dangers of scientific analysis of religious language. Increasingly, he argues, the Church and its ceremonies are treated as a cultural 'products,' instead of as part of an elaborate allegorical system to bridge the gap between humans and the divine. See pp. 190–98.

664.   The importance of spectators and spectacle was crucial in the recreation of medieval holidays and celebrations, the topic of Chapter 7.

665.   As Suzanne Kaufman has shown, despite their outward embrace of more pilgrimages and more publicity for the Church, leaders were, in fact, ambivalent about the commercialism of Lourdes, especially as more and more pilgrims complained about the excesses and frauds being perpetuated in the name of the pilgrimage; pp. 112–16.

666.   Freedberg, pp. 110–12.

667.   The priests were obviously aware of such criticism, yet they responded by underlining their apostolic mission. See, for example, an early issue of *Le Pèlerin* in which Father Picard (using the pseudonym Tilloy) defended the multiplying pilgrimages as a way of increasing prayers for the salvation of France (9 August 1873), pp. 90–91. Later, Father Bailly would also defend *La Maison de la Bonne Presse* by insisting that they did not make a profit (though he did not mention that this was probably because he reinvested every extra penny in starting new kinds of periodicals). Cited in Castel, p. 224. This said, however, the Grotto Fathers *were* responsible for approving all commercial enterprises linked to the pilgrimage; they were not as disinterested as they liked to make it seem. See Kaufman pp. 102–46.

668.   Once again, an increasingly secular society tends to devalue the absolutely critical importance of communal prayer for believers. See De Certeau, pp. 7–10.

669.   They repeatedly insisted that they did not want to return to the Middle Ages; they simply wanted to reinstate spirituality and underline the importance of God in modern life. See for example, *Le Pèlerin* (9 August 1873), p. 91.

670.   'On nous dit que nous ne sommes pas plus au XIVe siècle, qu'au XVe et que les moeurs ont changé. Je le sais, mais je prie qu'on note bien ce point: il ne s'agit nullement de retourner sur nos pas! Il s'agit de resaisir par dessus les artifices des derniers siècles écoulés, l'ardente sincérité des anonymes, vénérables et glorieux en qui a palpité notre âme nationale [...] Nous ferons, quant à nous, ce que faisaient les gothiques.' Cited in Samuel Rocheblave, *Louis de Fourcaud et le mouvement artistique en France de 1875–1914* (Paris: Les Belles Lettres, 1926), p. 93.

671.   See pp. 183–226.

672.   This is clear in Zola's and Huysmans's differing reactions to the commercialism in Lourdes. While Zola blames the Grotto Fathers and their greed, Huysmans targets the townspeople, who shamelessly profit from the gullibility of pilgrims. See Elizabeth Emery, 'The Nineteenth-Century Struggle for the Soul of Lourdes.'

673.   To be fair to Zola, one must note that he did realize that others considered the pilgrimage to Lourdes as 'authentic.' The characters in *Lourdes* who came for prayer and healing (notably Pierre's friend, Marie de Guersaint), are oblivious to the commercialism around them; they focus only on the purity of their spiritual quest.

674.   Victor and Edith Turner, *Image and Pilgrimage in Christian Culture* (Oxford: Blackwell, 1978): p. 20. A great number of modern anthropologists have built on the work of the Turners to study the relationships between pilgrimage and tourism, from John Urry and Dean MacCannell to N.

H. H. Graburn. John Urry, *The Tourist Gaze* (London: Sage, 1990), Dean MacCannell, *The Tourist: A New Theory of the Leisure Class* and N. H. H. Graburn, 'Tourism: The Sacred Journey' in V. Smith, ed., *Hosts and Guests: The Anthropology of Tourism* (Oxford: Blackwell, 1978). Freedberg, too, dedicates a chapter to the importance of images for pilgrimages, pp. 99–135.

675.  'Introduction' to *Pilgrimages in Popular Culture*, ed. Ian Reader and Tony Walter (London: The MacMillan Press, 1993).

676.  Larousse understood that the concept of pilgrimage was changing in his time: his article on 'Pèlerinage' presents the activity as reaching its apex in the medieval world only to fall off with the Renaissance. Despite several nineteenth-century periods that toyed with the idea of pilgrimage, it was the years 1872–1873 that began a 'fureur des pèlerinages en France.' Disgusted by the gimmicks and the supernatural aspects of Christian pilgrimage, the resolutely scientific Larousse goes on to explain that the pilgrimage is not exclusively Catholic and is practiced in other cultures. A pilgrim, he remarks, can now simply mean 'traveler.'

677.  The term was employed with great frequency in this period. Emile de Saint-Auban's *Un pèlerinage à Bayreuth* (Paris: A. Savine, 1892) reflects reverence for Wagner; an article about the Musée Condé in *Illustration* (16 April 1898: 266–7) mentions medieval manuscripts as a 'place of pilgrimage'; Henry Bordeaux's *Pèlerinages littéraires* (Paris: Fontemoing & Cie, 1913) provides portraits of famous writers; while Proust encouraged the readers of his translations of Ruskin to embark on Ruskinian pilgrimages (*Contre Sainte-Beuve* pp. 69, 71). A 'Pèlerinage positiviste' took place on June 13, 1886. See Charles Chincholle, *Les Mémoires de Paris* (Paris: Librairie Moderne, 1889), pp. 293–8.

678.  *Les Foules de Lourdes*, pp. 125–30.

679.  *Oeuvres complètes* XIV, 2, 278.

680.  Such scenes occur throughout *En Route*, *La Cathédrale* and *L'Oblat*; he calls this feeling 'the soul of vaults,' an atmosphere that has been contained in churches and monasteries since they were built and reinforced by constant prayer. Frédéric Gugelot describes the favored pilgrimage sites of the numerous artists and writers who converted to Catholicism in the last quarter of the nineteenth century: for them the sites took on particular meaning because of their conversion or family situation. *La Conversion des intellectuels au catholicisme en France* (Paris: CNRS Editions, 1998).

681.  See Octave Uzanne's appreciation in Philippe Brun, *Albert Robida, sa vie, son oeuvre* (Paris: Editions Promodis, 1984), p. 20.

682.  See Chapter 5.

683.  See Janine Dakyns, pp. 221–53, for examples of the ways in which many Symbolist writers attempted to create their own vision of the Middle Ages as a buffer against the outside world.

684.  See Elizabeth Emery, '"A l'ombre".'

685.  'La Cour des Miracles! C'est, en effet, l'évocation de tout le moyen âge, si bien mis en scène, avec l'ampleur d'un poème, dans la *Notre-Dame de Paris*, de Victor Hugo. Truands et ribaudes, hommes d'armes et bohémiennes, parmi lesquels ressortent les figures impérissables d'Esméralda, de Quasimodo, de Claude Frollo, de Gaston Phébus, il y avait là de quoi tenter le talent et l'imagination de M. Colibert. L'architecte avait d'ailleurs, pour guider ses efforts, bien autre chose que la brillante fantaisie de l'auteur de *Notre-Dame de Paris*. Il avait sa science parfaite du moyen âge, sa connaissance du vieux Paris, de ses coutumes, de ses moeurs.' Combes, *Les Merveilles de l'Exposition: Paris en 1400* (Paris: Librairie Illustrée, 1900), p. 2.

686.  See Burton Benedict, *The Anthropology of World's Fairs: The San Francisco Panama Pacific International Exhibit of 1915* (Berkeley: Lowie Museum of Anthropology/Scolar Press, 1983); Meg Armstrong, '"A Jumble of Foreignness": The Sublime Musayums of Nineteenth Century Fairs and Expositions,' *Cultural Critique* 23 (Winter 1992–1993), pp. 199–250; and Rosalind Williams.

687.  There were other displays that evoked aspects of the Middle Ages, including the historical costume display, the Basilica San Marco recreated by the Italian government and displays of medieval art, but the recreation of two medieval French cities for one World's Fair was particularly unusual.

688.  See Bibliothèque Nationale (Arsenal) manuscript RT12713, p. 85. The Bastille exhibit was an enormous commercial success that earned over a million francs in two years. For more about this exhibit, see Rearick, pp. 120–21.

689.  'Franchissez la herse, et brusquement, sans transition, vous voilà reporté à cinq siècles en arrière. Sous vos yeux, apparaît le spectacle pittoresque d'un coin de Paris en 1400. Cette vaste esplanade, c'est la Cour des Miracles. Tout autour semblent s'appuyer les unes contre les autres, pour ne point choir, de vieilles maisons aux formes obsolètes, aux corniches bizarrement sculptées, des cabarets, des boutiques sombres.' p. 3.

690.  Combes, pp. 4–6.

691. In this version (probably because of copyright), the names were changed slightly, as were the actions. Here, a Quasimodo and a Phoebus figure vie for the affections of La Esmeralda; a dramatic aerial chase scene between Quasimodo and an archer ends in the death of both. It is Phoebus who marries Esmeralda and promises to uphold the gypsy code.

692. 'On peut revivre, en quelques minutes, à cinq siècles en arrière, dans un cadre et avec des costumes authentiques, quelques bribes de la vie de nos pères.' p. 7.

693. Other events included musical performances, a 'medieval play' entitled *Damoyselles et Chevaliers*, the enthroning of a truant and songs and dances by street criers. See the documents contained in BN (Arsenal) manuscript RT12713 for more details about and photographs of these performances. One program (fol. 86) announces the following events: 'Après-midi. De 2h à 2h ½. Concert promenade des Gardes du Guet. Vieux airs et danses. De 2h ½ à 3h. Parade de la troupe des Truands. Cérémonies des Gueux. De 3 h à 3h ¾. Mystères dans l'Eglise. Ballades et danses populaires. De 4h à 5h. Tournoi en l'honneur de la visite du Roi et de sa Cour. Combat de deux chevaliers en champ clos. Cortège princier. De 5h à 6h. Grande pantomime tirée de Notre-Dame de Paris, de Victor Hugo. A 5h ½ Enlèvement d'Esmeralda. Chute de Quasimodo. Le Soir. De 8h à minuit. Même spectacle que l'après-midi. (Ce Programme sera varié chaque mois avec des attractions inédites.) Prix d'entrée: 1 fr.; le Vendredi: 2 fr.'

694. 'Un nouveau sport y fait fureur, nommé tournoi. Il consiste à jeter son adversaire à bas de son cheval, en présence d'un roi drapé d'or et d'azur, d'une princesse coiffée à la Isabeau de Bavière, et d'une fanfare dont les musiciens ont la trogne des manants du Pont au Change [...] Si je n'aimais le Moyen Age, je l'aurais aimé avenue de Suffren.' A. P. de Lannoy, *Les Plaisirs et la Vie de Paris: Guide du flaneur* (Paris: Librairie L. Borel, 1900), p. 93.

695. Elizabeth A. R. Brown and Nancy Freeman Regalado provide a rich picture of a real medieval royal entry in '*Universitas et communitas*: The Parade of the Parisians at the Pentecost Feast of 1313' in *Moving Subjects: Processional Performance in the Middle Ages and the Renaissance*, ed. Kathleen Ashley and Wim Hüsen (Amsterdam: Rodopi, 2001), pp. 117–54. For more about the extraordinary popularity of Hugo's novel and the illustrations it spawned, see Ségolène Le Men.

696. 'Or M. Colibert, de l'école de Viollet-le-Duc, et qui, à ce titre, possède à fond son moyen âge, était mieux qualifié que personne pour en reconstituer, avec une précision remarquable, le style et les moeurs.' Combes, p. 1.

697. In order to finance the project, the association offered 50-franc stocks or fifty-franc coupons that would – if all went well – pay off handsomely, as had the 1889 Bastille exhibit. See Bibliothèque Nationale (Arsenal) manuscript RT12713, p. 85. This was a common practice for such exhibits, but profit was clearly the major concern of the *Paris en 1400* organizers.

698. See Combes, p. 8.

699. See the documents conserved at the Bibliothèque Nationale (Arsenal), RT12713, pp. 85–7.

700. The Foire Saint-Germain, which presented a 2001 exposition entitled 'Paris en 1400: Au Temps de Charles V,' provides an example of this. Historical accuracy is often secondary (Charles V having died in 1380); piquing consumer interest and catering to visitors' whims are the overriding values.

701. From a brochure for the 'Charmes et sortilèges' medieval fair at Eze, France (summer 2001) and the 'Fête médiévale' of Provins, France (9–10 June 2001). Troubadours, cracheurs de feu, avaleurs de sabre, équilibristes, diseuses de bonne aventure, animaux savants [...] tortures, ménéstrels, saltimbanques [...]. 'Troubadours et baladins, templiers et croisés, lépreux et mendiants, riches marchands et nobles dames feront revivre toute la société du Moyen-âge pendant 48 heures.' [www.provins.org/cca/programme_fete_med.htm] The historical ambiguity of these events is even clearer in the US and the UK, where they are often called 'Renaissance Fayres.'

702. Pictures of such events are regularly posted on the Internet at sites such as [www.geocities.com/steenisbernard/html/med1.html] or [www.multimania.com/medievales/docu/20artisan_fichiers/artisan/_00.html]. The latter portrays nearly all of the medieval artisanal practices also included in the *Paris en 1400* and *Vieux Paris* exhibits.

703. Jean Mallion cites Pierre Matthieu, Philippe de Commines and Jean de Roye as sources for the 'moral' aspects of Hugo's medieval Paris. He also relied on *Le Théâtre des Antiquités de Paris* by Jacques du Breul and *Histoire et recherches des antiquités de la ville de Paris* by Sauval. *Victor Hugo et l'art architectural*, p. 63.

704. See Banville's play *Gringoire* (1866) or his *Trente-six ballades joyeuses*, which imitate Villon's poetry (1873). Théophile Gautier dedicated a chapter of *Les Grotesques* to Villon (1856); Jean Richepin's *La Chanson des gueux* (1876) contains several homages to Villon and *escholiers*; and Albert Robida's *Les Escholiers du temps jadis* is inspired by Villon (1907). See also Nathan Edelman, 'La Vogue de Villon en France 1828–1873,' *Revue d'Histoire littéraire de la France* (43).

705. In the 1890s, students renewed the tradition of sponsoring mid-Lent parades replete with costumes, processions and floats. The Middle Ages were often a popular subject, as one can see

in image archives at the Mairie de Paris and at the Bibliothèque Nationale (Estampes). An 1890 celebration, for example, featured floats of Abélard lecturing students and Saint Genevieve seated on the walls of Paris. See Louis Morin, *Les Carnavals Parisiens* (Paris: Montgredien et Cie, 1897) for drawings of such floats. A notable reinterpretation of Hugo's novel took place in the 1897 Bal des Quat'z'arts when the Atelier Merson created 'Notre-Dame et Quasimodo sur sa cloche, qu'entouraient de si gentes damoiselles, en hennins compliqués, les épaules saillantes hors des longs corsages fourrés d'hermine, et que suivait la Cour des Miracles, dans le plus étrange, le plus impressionnant grouillement de culs-de-jatte, de sabouleux, de malingreux, de capons, de francs-mitous, de cagoux, de narquois et de rifodés, – tous les argotiers du royaume de Thunes.' Morin, pp. 38–9.

706. There was a long Parisian tradition of parades led by butchers (Le Boeuf Gras) and by laundrywomen (Mi-Carême); students often joined in the festivities and designed floats for the occasion. At the end of the century, artists, under the rubric of 'La Vache enragée,' also attempted to compete with such public spectacles. See Louis Morin.

707. 'Ce n'étaient que basochiens, escholiers, bohémiens et bohémiennes, ribaudes et ribauds.' *Le Temps* (30 May 1898).

708. Ibid.

709. Ibid.

710. Article from *Le Temps*. For information about Rictus see Théophile Briant, *Jehan Rictus* (Paris: Seghers, 1973) and about Botrel see Eric Rondel, *Théodore Botrel: Vie et Chansons du Barde Breton* (Fréhel: Editions Club 35, 1996).

711. Raising money for charity was all the vogue at this time, as was creating 'theme' amusements to do so. Le Bazar de la charité, run by wealthy women who played at being shopkeepers in order to earn money for the poor, was perhaps the best example of this. It had existed since 1885, but was remodeled in 1897 by Chaperon, the set designer of l'Opéra, as a medieval street with 22 shops, inns, hotels and a Gothic church. These cardboard and paper medieval decorations fueled the fire that tragically killed 120 upper-class Parisians on 4 May 1897. See Paul Morand's harrowing story based on the event, 'Le Bazar de la charité,' *Nouvelles complètes* II (Paris: Gallimard [Bibliothèque de la Pléiade], 1992), pp. 734–61. It is no surprise that the students chose to hold their performances outdoors given the tragic circumstances of the preceding year.

712. Article by Jules Claretie for *Le Temps* (31 May 1898). Even the *New York Times* reported on the spectacle in detail, calling it 'distinctly interesting' and remarking on the crowds of spectators and their general merriment. They did, however, comment that the modern students were not as rowdy as their medieval predecessors. 12 June 1898, p. 19 column 7.

713. For more about the history of the Feast of Fools celebration, see E. K. Chambers, *The Mediaeval Stage* (Mineola, NY: 1996), vol. 1, pp. 276–335 and Jacques Heers, *Fêtes des fous et carnavals* (Paris: Librairie Arthème Fayard, 1983). First of all, the students held the celebration at Pentecost, in May, instead of during the traditional New Year holidays. Second, they decided to expunge all religious references from the celebration. Given the social tensions of 1898, the year in which the Dreyfus Affair exploded, this precaution seems warranted. It does, however, break with the medieval Feast of Fools and Feast of the Ass, which took place in and around the Church.

714. For more about *Le Royaume de la Basoche*, see E. K. Chambers, *The Mediaeval Stage* and Howard Graham Harvey, *The Theatre of the Basoche: Contribution of the Law Societies to French Mediaeval Comedy* (Cambridge: Harvard University Press, 1941). The group became so legendary in the fin de siècle that a modern opera, *La Basoche*, was performed in 1890, written by Albert Carré with music by André Messager.

715. 'Errant ainsi dans la ville universitaire, allant des cabarets aux églises … se permettaient au fond des chapelles de vider des flacons et de faire rouler les dés … ' Robida, *Les Escholiers du temps jadis* (Paris: Armand Colin, 1917), p. 62. Pierre de Nouvion, 'Un Cabaret au Moyen-Age,' *La Fête des Fous et de l'âne* (Paris: Bertin & Cie, 1898), p. 12.

716. The program, entitled *La Fête des Fous et de l'âne* (1898) can be consulted at the Bibliothèque Nationale Tolbiac and Arsenal or at Pennsylvania State University. The *coq-à-l'âne* tradition of jumping from one topic to another with seeming incoherence, gave rise to many late nineteenth-century literary and artistic movement, notably *Les Incohérents*. See Olga Anna Dull, 'From Rabelais to the Avant-Garde: Wordplays and Parody in the Wall-Journal *Le Mur*' (Cate and Shaw, eds), pp. 199–241.

717. *La Fête des Fous et de l'âne* (Paris: Bertin & Cie, 1898). Serious essays include 'Quelques mots d'historique sur la Fêtes des fous' by Dr Cabanès, p. 15 and 'La Fête des Fous' by Frédéric Loliée, p. 30, while humorous stories invoke people and places linked to the festival: 'Un Cabaret au Moyen Age' by Pierre de Nouvion, pp. 12–13 and 'Saint-Yves à la Fête des fous' by Narcisse Quellien, p. 22.

718. See, for example, Georges Milandry's 'Ballade des dames du mois passé,' which closely follows the form (*huitains*) and the subject matter of Villon's 'Ballade des Dames du temps jadis' and its

well-known refrain ('Mais où sont les neiges d'antan?') while transforming his poem to refer to prostitutes, p. 8. Berard's 'Ballade de mauvais conseil: Aux Amoureux Transis (A la manière de Maitre Villon)' is similar, yet his form is less successful. He borrows the character of Margot from 'La Ballade de la Grosse Margot' while creating the refrain 'Le vin est bon, la ribaude est jolie,' p. 24.

719. 'Rabelais aux étudiants' by Paul Cantonnet, p. 22 and 'Un Cabaret au Moyen-Age' by Pierre de Nouvion, p. 12. 'La Basoche' by Edmond Haraucourt, p. 2, 'Ballade des peu joyeuses commères des tavernes escollières' by D. Caldine, p. 11 and 'Prologue pour une comédie gauloise' by Emmanuel des Essarts, p. 11.

720. Milandy's poem borrows a refrain from Villon, as does Pierre de Nouvion's story about 'Un Cabaret au Moyen-Age,' which he calls La Pomme de Pin (tavern celebrated by Villon) with a sign quoting lines from *Le Testament*: 'Retournez-y quand vous serez en ruyt,/En ce bourdel où tenons notre estat,' p. 12. Jacques Normand's poem 'La Prose de l'Ane' evokes the voice of the revelers speaking to the ass; 'Hez va, sire Asne, hez va! ... *Pulcher ... Fortissimus*,' p. 2.

721. See, for example, Dakyns, who proposes that Symbolist writers had very little knowledge of medieval literature, pp. 270–71. This argument is quickly presented, without looking closely enough at the times when poems were directly inspired from medieval texts. The serious influence of medieval texts on writers and poets is a topic that merits further study.

722. *New York Times* (12 June 1898), p. 19 column 7.

723. Victor Fournel, *Le Vieux Paris: Fêtes, Jeux et Spectacles* (Tours: Alfred Mame et Fils, 1887). For additional writings on street life see Victor Fournel, *Ce qu'on voit dans les rues de Paris* (Paris: A. Delehays, 1858).

724. Fournel was certainly influenced by the writings of Louis de Petit de Julleville, a professor at the Sorbonne, whose *Histoire du théâtre en France* was published from 1880 to 1886. A revival of interest in medieval theater occurred in the 1890s, probably thanks in part to Petit de Julleville's work. The Bibliothèque Nationale contains a great number of medieval plays (generally mysteries and farces) reprinted and performed at the time (even the Chat Noir cabaret put on a shadow-theater production of *Le Mystère de Sainte-Geneviève*). A few years later, cabaret performer Yvette Guilbert would collaborate with medievalists Jospeh Bédier and Gustave Cohen to found two theaters: *Le Théâtre religieux du Moyen Age* and the *Théâtre de la vieille France*. See Knapp and Chipman, *That was Yvette: The Biography of Yvette Guilbert, The Great Diseuse* (New York: Holt, Rinehart and Winston, 1964), pp. 295–6.

725. This fraternal gratefulness to all can be seen in the souvenir program's effusive thanks to all those who collaborated in order to 'faire du bien': 'Merci, hommes d'Etat, politiciens, riches, littérateurs, dessinateurs, et merci à toi aussi lecteur qui en nous achetant donnes ton obole au pauvre,' p. 1.

726. As E. K. Chambers would point out a few years later in *The Mediaeval Stage* (1903), a popular theory attributed the origin of the Feast of Fools to the Gauls, pp. 321, 329.

727. See Suzanne Citron's discussion of Third Republic educational reforms and the attempt to posit Gaul as the starting point for modern France.

728. Alain Corbellari has convincingly argued that Hippolyte Taine was the first to single out *l'esprit gaulois* as a particularly national trait. As he remarks, the concept of *esprit gaulois* dates from the sixteenth century, probably as a mixture of the adjective *gaulois* with the verb *galer* (to have fun). Taine introduced the term in his introduction to *La Fontaine et ses fables*. Although the Gallo-Roman period is clearly not the same as the fifteenth and sixteenth centuries with which *esprit gaulois* came to be associated, the name stuck. See David Trotter, 'L'Esprit Gaulois: Humour and National Mythology' (Europa 2:1 [1996]). Bédier proposed an influential definition of *l'esprit gaulois* in his 1893 work, *Les Fabliaux*, categorizing it above all as 'good humor.' 'Il est la malice, le bon sens joyeux, l'ironie un peu grosse, précise pourtant, et juste. Il ne cherche pas les éléments du comique dans la fantastique exagération des choses, dans le grotesque; mais dans la vision railleuse, légèrement outrée, du réel. Il ne va pas sans vulgarité; il est terre à terre et sans portée [...]' 'Les Fabliaux et l'esprit gaulois,' *Les Fabliaux* (Paris: Librairie Honoré Champion, 1969, pp. 313–19). As Charles Rearick has pointed out, the link between Gallic spirit and nationalism was rampant in the period, pp. 39–43.

729. 'Nous avons pleuré sur nous-mêmes pendant assez longtemps, laissez-nous vivre un petit peu [...]' *Les Carnavals parisiens* (Paris: Montgredien et Cie., c. 1897), p. ix. The students themselves insist on their attempts at helping society. In each of the commemorative programs published to accompany the street fairs, students insisted on the fact that they wanted to amuse the public and show it that the new generation was not 'degenerate' (1894, p. 3) or depressed (1895, p. 3).

730. 'Voyant le deuil qui vous mine et consomme:/Mieulx est de ris que de larmes escripre,/Pour ce que rire est le propre de l'homme.' Claretie, 'La Vie.' The idea of laughter as good medicine was quite popular at the time. See Rearick, pp. 48–50.

731. 'De la gaieté surtout jeunes gens!' Morin, p. 135. 'Gaudeamus igitur/Dum juvenes sumus,/Post jucondam juventutem/Post molestam senectutem/Nos habebit humus.' 'Let us thus be merry/

While we are young/After the joys of youth/After the troubles of age/The earth will possess us.'

732.  Mikhaïl Bakhtin, *Rabelais and his World*, trans. Hélène Iswolsky (Bloomington: Indiana University Press), pp. 45, 10.

733.  In an article on the 1930s theatrical interest in performing medieval plays, she has referred to this process as 'revivalism,' as a way of putting the public into contact with the dead and bringing the past back to life. 'The Waking of Medieval Theatricality. Paris 1935–1995,' *New Literary History* 27 (1996), pp. 357–90. Claretie called the medieval theatrical productions 'l'attraction véritablement originale de cette fête.'

734.  Raymond Casteras evokes the earlier nineteenth-century tradition of writers and artists who used Latin Quarter cafés as meeting places for discussion, writing and performance. He argues that it was Emile Goudeau (founder of Les Hydropathes) who turned these informal settings into more organized centers of artistic creation. *Avant le Chat Noir: Les Hydropathes* (Paris: Editions Albert Messein, 1945). For more about Goudeau and the Hydropathes and their link to Montmartre culture see Daniel Grojnowski, 'Hydropathes and Company,' in *The Spirit of Montmartre: Cabarets, Humor and the Avant-Garde, 1875–1905*, ed. Phillip Denis Cate and Mary Shaw (New Brunswick, NJ: Jane Voorhees Zimmerli Art Museum, 1996), pp. 95–110.

735.  See, for example, an 1884 article for *Le Temps* by Jules Claretie, commenting on the abundance of 'Gothic cabarets' that were flourishing at the time. Reprinted in *La Vie à Paris, 1884* (Paris: Victor Havard, 188), p. 219.

736.  'Que vient faire ici cette enseigne et pourquoi du Moyen-Age? Les vitraux coloriés, les sièges, les tables, le plafond, les femmes, rien ne rappelle cette époque lointaine. Cela n'empêche pas, soyons juste, que le local ne soit d'une certaine richesse. Mais sapristi! Laissons le moyen âge!' 'Les Brasseries, buvettes, et bars servis par des femmes,' *Le Courrier Français* (9 Janvier 1890), p. 4.

737.  The restaurant was situated at 108, Boulevard Rochechouart. Cate provides a marvelous summary of the 'Bon Bock dinners' and has published a number of images from its resulting periodicals. The idea of such dinners grew out of the popular reception at the 1873 Salon of Manet's painting *Le Bon Bock* (The Good Pint), which contemporaries interpreted as a portrait of a good Alsatian patriot (Bellot was one of the models for him), calm in his reflection over political events. As Cate remarks, *l'esprit gaulois* later developed into the philosophy called *fumisme*, pp. 5, 23.

738.  *Les Souvenirs de Galipaux* (Paris: Librairie Plon, 1937), pp. 115–16. Cited in Cate, p. 4.

739.  'Tous égaux, tous unis, nous nous groupons autour de cette bannière républicaine qui porte pour devise; FRATERNITE! Je peux donc dire sans orgueil que si la Gaîté et l'Intelligence et la sympathie étaient bannies du reste de la terre, c'est au *Bon Bock* qu'on les retrouverait. Sur ce, très chers frères, je prie notre immortel grand maître, Rabelais qu'il vous tienne en bonne santé de corps et joyeuse humeur d'esprit.' In the preface to *L'Album du Bon Bock* (Paris: Ludovic Baschet, 1878). Cited in Cate, p. 4.

740.  These included La Grande Pinte (1879), La Brasserie du Bon Bock (1879) and L'Auberge du Clou (1883). Later Gothic arrivals included Le Café du Conservatoire, L'Abbaye de Thélème and Les Quat'z'Arts. For descriptions of such places, see John Grand-Carteret, *Raphaël et Gambrinus*.

741.  His works were also introduced into primary schools in 1882.

742.  As we have seen in Chapters 2 and 3, periodization was much more fluid at the end of the nineteenth century; it allowed artists working until the early seventeenth century to be classified as 'medieval.' For nineteenth-century beliefs in Rabelais's authorship of *Les grandes et inestimables chroniques* as an early draft of *Gargantua*, see Henry Emile Chevalier, 'Rabelais et ses éditeurs,' *La Revue moderne* (25 Nov. 1868). Although it was clear to such authors that Rabelais parodied medieval culture in his works, they still admired him for his attachment to medieval legends and tended to downplay his criticisms of the Middle Ages. A number of twentieth-century authors have studied Rabelais's tendency to borrow and transform medieval traditions. See Jean Larrat, *Le Moyen Age dans Gargantua* (Paris: Belles Lettres, 1973) and Bakhtin. A more recent article is Paul Burrell's 'Rabelais's Debts to the Medieval World,' *Studies in Medievalism* 3:1 (Fall 1987), pp. 77–82. Gustave Flaubert's youthful 'Etude sur Rabelais' (ca. 1838) clearly reveals his contemporaries' two visions of Rabelais: 'moine ivre et cynique' and 'philosophe pratique.' His great admiration for Rabelais's 'immense sarcasm,' ('sarcasme colossal') is not surprising from the future author of *Le Sottisier*. *Oeuvres complètes*, vol. 12 (Paris: Club de l'Honnête homme, 1974), pp. 11–18.

743.  'Si on avait le temps, ce serait une curieuse étude psychologique et sociale à faire, on écrivait la vie de Rabelais en notre temps. Mettez le dix-neuvième siècle avec toutes ses grandeurs et toutes ses misères et ce grand génie de Rabelais en présence. Que se produirait-il?' Mermeix, 'Les Chroniques de l'Abbaye de Thélème,' *Le Courrier Français* (23 May 1886), p. 2.

744.  *Rabelais à Medon*, *La Kermesse* and *Les joyeux buveurs* and the painting *Gargantua sur les tours de Notre-Dame* by Tanzi. A 14 February 1886 issue of *Le Courrier Français* advertised the opening

of the new bar in enthusiastic terms: 'Voici le premier vestibule d'un style pompéiano-moyen-âge, style éminément fantaisiste [...] Ensuite un grand vestibule, gothique, flamboyant, on se croirait à la Sainte-Chapelle sauf ce detail typique que les sinistres gargouilles à queues de monstres sont ici remplacées par de joyeux cochons de lait [...] et que le buste de Rabelais, oeuvre du maître Zacharie Astruc, présidera à la procession.' Emile Goudeau, 'L'Abbaye de Thélème,' *Le Courrier Français* (14 Feb. 1886), p. 6.

745. The invitation read: 'Monsieur, les Thélemites ont l'honneur de vous inviter à fêter le maître François Rabelais en inaugurant son Abbaye de Thélème, 1 place Pigalle, sous la présidence de leur vénérable Prieur Alexis Bouvier.' F. Dassy, *Le Courrier Français* (23 May 1886), p. 3.

746. One exhibit took place in a gallery at 17 Boulevard de la Madeleine. The paintings included *La Vie Inestimable de Gargantua* and *Les Faitz et ditz du bon Pantagruel*; they were also displayed in *La Splendide Taverne* restaurant, a low-key venue more befitting Rabelais's bawdy reputation. See the poster by Albert Guillaume at the Musée de la Publicité (12460). It announces that the paintings are on display after being seized and condemned to burn in London.

747. For an excellent overview of the attraction of Rabelais (especially his use of word games as 'weapons against intimidation') for artistic cabarets and their publications, see Olga Anna Dull. For a list of publications and events related to Rabelais, see the index to *La Revue des Etudes Rabelaisiennes*. In a preface to this volume, Abel Lefranc remembers the spirit of friendship and camaraderie of the 1890s that led to the formation of La Société des Etudes rabelaisiennes, pp. vi–viii.

748. 'Le moyen âge et Rabelais faisaient fureur alors, et l'on s'en aperçut tout de suite.' *Les Escholiers, livre d'or* (Paris: Imprimerie Kapp, 1922), p. xxxi.

749. Ibid., p. lv.

750. 'Etant les Escholiers, nous nous imaginions que, si nous avions un patron, ce serait le bon maître en scholerie, François Villon.' Ibid., pp. lv–lx. According to Bourdon, the boys convinced Jules Noriac to write them a Villonesque play – *Les Neiges d'Antan* – and performed it in 1888 at Le Chat Noir cabaret to huge popular acclaim (they report that it eventually entered the repertory of the Comédie Française).

751. *Les Escholiers, livre d'or* reprints a great number of these programs and invitations. The collection of Auguste Rondel at La Bibliothèque Nationale (Arsenal RT3488) also conserves many of these. An invitation to an inaugural evening is written in antiquated-style French: 'Si cuydez la vie briève, le monde triste et meshaignant, si aymez à vous esbauldir et rigouller merveilleusement, serez le bien et à propous venu aux "ESCHOLIERS" ... Y treuverez bon feu, maigre chière et grande amytié,' p. 112. Similarly, an invitation to a 28 mai 1888 spectacle 'prays' their spectators to 'venir ouïr leurs faictes et plaisans dictz ... ' p. 113. The 'Dix Commandements' begin with the following verses: 'I. Aux "Escholiers" tu entreras,/Et resteras fort longuement!' p. 114.

752. Although Le Chat Noir was called a cabaret, the word cabaret was used in its archaic sense: as a small room or bistro in which one served libations. As Lisa Appignanesi has pointed out, the cabaret dates from Villon's day, when either drunken guests improvised performances or owners invited wandering entertainers to perform, p. 9. She and Harold Segel have noted that Le Chat Noir, which attempts to capture this spirit, was the original artistic cabaret that spawned all imitators throughout Europe. Today, the word cabaret tends to evoke a paying clientele, much more geared toward large audiences, than it did when Rodolphe Salis adopted it to describe his small venue, an informal meeting place of artists who wished to collaborate privately. For definitions of the shift in the sense of the word cabaret, see Appignanesi *The Cabaret* (London: Studio Vista, 1975), pp. 9–12 and Harold B. Segel, pp. xiv–xxiii. In this study, we will use the word 'artistic cabaret' to distinguish Le Chat Noir from its modern equivalent.

753. Jean Moréas's biographer Robert Jouanny links Moréas's fascination with the Middle Ages to his experiences at Le Chat Noir, p. 527. In addition to Salis and *Le Chat Noir*, even the mainstream *Echo de Paris* commissioned poems in Old French. In 1891 they published a 'conte de jadis' de Catulle Mendès and a 'conte en vieux français' de J. Reibrach (14 and 8 January), while announcing four stories by Jean Moréas, which were presented in what Moréas's biographer Jouanny has labeled a 'jargon pseudo-médiéval,' p. 362. Olga Anna Dull has remarked on the abundance of Villon and Rabelaisian-style French generated in Les Quat'z'Arts cabaret and its journal *Le Mur*. Her article reproduces a page of such text, p. 207. The fascination with writing in old French at the turn of the century is an extremely interesting and valuable topic that exceeds the scope of this book, but that certainly merits further study.

754. For more about Le Cabaret des Quat'z'Arts, which was designed by illustrator Henri Pille, see Olga Anna Dull.

755. See, for example, a 24 November 1883 issue depicting Salis in various roles including 'hostelier' (p. 183) or Steinlen's drawing of Salis as 'seigneur.' *Collection du Chat Noir 'Rodolphe Salis'* (Paris 1898), p. 59. A 27 May 1882 advertisement insisted on the cabaret's historical pedigree and named its illustrious visitors.

756. '[...] la communion du Moyen-Age Français et de la Renaissance Française, fondus et

transfigurés en le principe [...] de l'Ame moderne.' From the preface of *Le Pèlerin passionné* (1891), cited in Jouanny, p. 491. Moréas read medieval poetry in the cafés of Paris, where he spoke Old French, and he claimed the Middle Ages as his own. He was recognized by his peers for this attraction to the Middle Ages. See Dakyns, pp. 271–4 for more about contemporaries' interpretation of him as a medievalist. For the objectives of l'Ecole romane and its relationship to the Symbolist movement, see Richard Shryock, 'Reaction Within Symbolism: L'Ecole romane,' *The French Review* 71:4, pp. 577–84. Moréas published a great number of translations of medieval or medieval-inspired works including a very popular and radically simplified version of *Aucassin et Nicolette* in *La Revue indépendante* (February 1888, vol. 10), inspired by the translations of Hermann Suchier and Gaston Paris. He also wrote a number of adaptations of medieval stories, including the *Lais* of Marie de France, under the title *Contes de la Vieille France* (Paris: Mercure de France, 1904), originally published in *La Gazette de France* from 15 August 1897 to 4 June 1901. For more about Moréas and his medievalism see Jouanny (1969) and Dakyns, pp. 273–4.

757.    See Antoine Adam, p. 131 about Verlaine's 'medieval' reputation and Harold B. Segel for more about Bruant and his satirical vision of Parisian life, pp. 48–69. Paul Valéry formalized the comparison between the two in his 1937 *Villon et Verlaine*.

758.    See Cate, pp. 10–12 and 18–25 and Segel, pp. 19–48 for descriptions and reproductions of many of the activities centered around Le Chat Noir and its sister taverns. For essays focusing on the particularly 'chatnoiresque' humor of the cabaret, see Michael L. J. Wilson, 'Portrait of the Artist as a Louis XIII Chair' and Janet Whitmore, 'Absurdist Humor in Bohemia' in Weisberg, ed. (2001), pp. 180–203 and 104–222, respectively. In discussing 'Les Quatre Fils Pharamond', a spoof of *Les Quatre Fils Aymon* posted on *Le Mur* (Les Quat'z'Arts' 'antijournal'), Olga Anna Dull provides a valuable example of the dark humor and social satire that such events could trigger.

759.    See Mariel Oberthür, *Montmartre en liesse 1880–1900* (Paris: Musée Carnavalet, 1994), for more about the extent to which the artistic cabaret fostered a cordial entente among people who were otherwise hostile to one another in society, pp. 22–8.

760.    Villon often featured characters (like la Belle Heaulmière, celebrated in Le Chat Noir), who spoke in the first person. See Nancy Freeman Regalado, 'Speaking in Script: The Construction of Voice, Presence and Perspective in Villon's Testament' in W. F. H. Nicolaisen, ed., *Oral Tradition in the Middle Ages* (Binghampton, NY: Medieval & Renaissance Texts & Studies, 1995); and William Calin, 'Observations on Point of View and the Poet's Voice in Villon,' *L'Esprit-Createur* 7 (1967), pp. 180–87.

761.    For more about the importance of the *chanson* for the popularity of the Chat Noir in the early 1880s and for descriptions of various singer-songwriters, see Segel, pp. 34–48. Although Claude Debussy did not compose his 'Ballades de François Villon' (1910) at the Chat Noir, his affinity for Villon and his work certainly may have begun there. Erik Satie composed many of his early pieces, including 'Les Quatre Ogives,' Sonneries de la Rose+Croix and 'Danses Gothiques' in conjunction with the activities of his 'medievalist' friends from Le Chat Noir. See Nancy Perloff, *Art and the Everyday: Popular Entertainment and the Circle of Erik Satie* (Oxford: Clarendon Press, 1991).

762.    See Jerrold Seigel, *Bohemian Paris* (New York: Viking Penguin, Inc., 1986), p. 221, for Emile Goudeau's comparison of young poets to troubadours. Yvette Guilbert, too, equated the poets of her youth to medieval artists in a number of instances and devoted lectures to proving their resemblance to François Villon and his poetry. See for example *La Chanson de ma vie*, where she establishes medieval poets as the 'source' of *l'esprit chatnoiresque* (Paris: Bernard Grasset, 1927), p. 195. See also Knapp and Chipman, p. 277. Théodore Botrel, publicized as 'le barde breton,' made his living as a representative of bygone times. In World War I he was labeled 'un troubadour avec l'armée Française,' while his songs evoked a long-ago world of churches, bells and Breton legends. For more about Botrel, his life and his 'medieval' image, see Eric Rondel, *Théodore Botrel: Vie et Chansons du Barde Breton* (Fréhel: Editions Club 35, 1996).

763.    For more about the appeal of Delmet and Hyspa and analysis of other satirical songs performed at the Chat Noir, see Steven Moore Whiting, 'Music on Montmartre' in Cate *et al.*, pp. 158–97.

764.    Cate describes the aggressive marketing used by Salis and shows how this innovative idea developed from the popularity of the albums and invitations put out by the Bon Bock dinners to chronicle performances, pp. 7, 24. The magazine was very successful: it ran from 1882 to 1897 (astonishing for a publication of this genre) and went from 12 000 copies sold in its first year to 20 000 copies seven years later. See Segel, p. 28.

765.    These were later published as *Les Contes du Chat Noir* and *Nouveaux contes du Chat Noir* by Rodolphe Salis, Seigneur de Chatnoirville-en-Vexin in 1888, 1891 and 1930. The influence of the Chat Noir and its publication are evident in the 1896 edition of Jarry's *Ubu Roi*, printed by Charles Renaudie in Perhinderion characters and which begins with: 'Adonc le Père Ubu hofcha la poire, dont fut depuis nommé par les Anglois Shakefpeare, et avez de lui fous ce nom maintes belles tragœdies par efcript.'

766. In fact, *Le Courrier Français* was able to support itself nearly entirely on funds from advertisers. See Watelet, *La Presse illustrée en France* vol. 2, part vii, pp. 47–50.

767. This was published in *Le Chat Noir* 5 September 1885. An Uzès 'Hommage' to Villon from *Le Chat Noir* is reprinted in Janet Whitmore (see note 758), p. 215. Other issues during this period reprinted an alleged 'long-lost' Villon poem that had been rediscovered at the Arsenal library alongside an article claiming that the subscription for a statue for Villon had raised 12 000 francs, while Ronsard had received only 26F50 (1 August 1885). The irreverent humor of the publication makes one doubt everything one reads (many people were taken in, for example, by a hoax announcing Salis's death and inviting readers to a wake at the Le Chat Noir).

768. *L'esprit chatnoiresque* was a popular term at the end of the century, closely allied to medieval and Renaissance spirit and especially to *esprit gaulois*, the anachronistic term used to refer to word-play, comic situations and the scatological humor proper to Villon and Rabelais. It had become so popular a concept that even the Prince of Wales (the future Edward VII) used the term to describe the effect of the cabaret. See Guilbert, *La Chanson de ma vie*, p. 221. Jules Claretie borrowed the term in an article in which he described the medieval flavor of the *Vieux Paris* exhibit at the 1900 World's Fair.

769. Breton's *Anthologie de l'humour noir* defines the term and lists his precursors, including many of those who participated in the ephemeral activities of Le Chat Noir: notably Alphonse Allais, Apollinaire and Jarry.

770. See their introduction to *The Spirit of Montmartre*, pp. 5–6.

771. Dull's article provides a wonderful starting point for such work.

772. John D. Erickson, *Dada: Performance, Poetry and Art* (Boston: Twayne Publishers, 1984). For the relationship between mass and popular culture see Thomas Crow (1985), 'Modernism and mass culture in the visual arts' in Francis Franscina, ed., *Pollock and After* (New York, Harper and Row).

773. 'Mais aujourd'hui, il faut nous défendre contre la conquête sordide. La Gaule lutte contre l'homme d'argent, qui vient pour remplacer l'homme de fer … C'est maintenant plus que jamais que votre rire nous aiderait, contre le nouveau barbare, le barbare lâche, perfide, qui ne se bat pas, qui calomnie, qui vole, qui ne tue pas son ennemi, mais qui le dépouille.' Mermeix, 'Chronique', p. 2.

774. In French, a *chat noir* is an outcast (like a black sheep in English). As in English, the word cat or puss also carried equivocal meanings with which the denizens of the cabarets liberally played.

775. See Cate p. 39, Appignanesi p. 20 and Rearick pp. 58–9.

776. See Cate p. 38 and Rearick p. 71. Mariel Oberthür reproduces the windows and provides a detailed analysis of their symbolism in *Montmartre en liesse 1880–1900* (Paris: Musée Carnavalet, 1994), p. 28.

777. The poster, at the Houghton Library, Harvard University, is reproduced in Wilson (2001), p. 202.

778. Edouard Drumont, *La France juive* (Paris: Trident, 1986 reprint of 1886 original). On Drumont see Robert Byrnes, *Anti-Semitism in Modern France*, vol. 1 (New Brunswick: Rutgers University Press, 1950); Pierre Pierraud, *Juifs et catholiques français* (Paris: Favard, 1970). For a thorough discussion of Drumont, medievalism and anti-Semitism see Laura Morowitz (1997).

779. The print, entitled 'Edouard Drumont, l'auteur de la France Juive' appeared in *Le Courrier Français* (16 May 1886). For other anti-Semitic prints see Norman Kleeblatt, ed. *The Dreyfus Affair: Art, Truth and Justice*, exhibition catalog. The Jewish Museum (Berkeley: University of California Press, 1987).

780. Edouard Drumont, *Les Fêtes Nationales à Paris* (Paris: L. Baschet, 1879). Interestingly, Drumont knew the Middle Ages well; he was the grandnephew of Alexander Buchon, a respected scholar of the French Chronicles and of the Crusades.

781. Pierre Birnbaum, 'Anti-Semitism and Anti-Capitalism in Modern France' in Frances Malino and Bernard Wasserstein (eds) *The Jews in Modern France* (Brandeis University Press, 1985); Stephen Wilson, 'Economic Anti-Semitism' in Stephen Wilson, *Ideology and Experience: Anti-Semitism in France at the Time of the Dreyfus Affair* (Rutherford: Fairleigh Dickinson University Press, 1982).

782. 'L'Aryen est resté l'être candide qui se pâmait au Moyen Age en écoutant les chansons de geste, les aventures de Garain le Loherain, d'Olivier de Béthune ou de Gilbert le Roussillon … ' Edouard Drumont, *La France juive* (Paris: Editions du Trident, 1886), p. 11. Drumont, as his praise for Parsifal and Aryans might suggest, was influenced by Wagner, the subject of his first book. Drumont's ignorance reveals itself, however, as he provides incorrect references: Olivier de Béthune is not a recorded character, while Garin le Lorrain and Girart le Roussillon are incorrectly spelled. Thanks to Bill Calin for remarking this aspect of Drumont's reference to the Middle Ages.

783. For the economic status of the artist contributors to artistic cabarets, see Rearick, pp. 69–71.

784. As Charles Rearick has noted, the concept of a 'gay Paris' devoted entirely to amusement dates

from this period: guidebooks widely advertised the formerly bohemian Montmartre as a pleasure palace and theme park. See especially, pp. 40–47.

785.    'Elle est notre fortune. Elle vous fait l'auberge du monde.' *Les Plaisirs et la vie de Paris: Guide du flâneur* (Paris: Librairie L. Borel, 1900), p. 11.

786.    Many critics saw the changes as an attempt to encourage tourism. This was an argument of the Goncourt brothers and later, of Karl Marx: 'It was still less the vandalism of Haussmann, razing Paris to make place for the Paris of the sightseer.' Cited in David P. Jordan, *Transforming Paris: The Life and Labors of Baron Haussmann* (New York: The Free Press, 1995), p. 345. As Jordan shows, such criticism was widespread enough that Louis-Napoléon was aware of it. See especially pp. 191, 345, 348.

787.    'Le vieux Paris n'est plus (la forme d'une ville/Change plus vite, hélas! Que le coeur d'un mortel).' *Les Fleurs du Mal* (Paris: Editions Robert Laffont , S.A., 1980), p. 63: vii-viii. While lamenting the changing world is an old trope, it emerged with renewed vigor at the end of the nineteenth century. Atget's *Vieux Paris* series, which he compiled for over twenty years (he sold them in 1920), is now housed in the Bibliothèque Nationale (Estampes). Many of these images have been digitized and can be consulted from the library's web site: [www.bnf.fr] There were hundreds of publications dedicated to old Paris, including Jules Cousin's *Les Derniers vestiges du vieux Paris, dessinés et gravés d'après nature, par J. Chauvet et E. Champollion* (Paris, 1876), H. Legrand's *Histoire générale de Paris. Topographie historique du vieux Paris, par feu A. Berty, continuée par H. Legrand* (Paris: Imprimerie nationale, 1885), Edmond Neukomm's *Fêtes et spectacles du vieux Paris* (Paris: E. Dentu, 1886) and Eugène-Alexandre Toulouze's *Mes fouilles dans le sol du vieux Paris, accompagnées de figures dessinées et gravées par l'auteur* with a preface by Frédéric Loliée (Dunkerque: Imprimerie de P. Michel, 1888).

788.    See David P. Jordan, pp. 92–9.

789.    See, for example, the cover of *Le Petit Journal* (17 December 1911) that carries this title and shows men pulling down one of Montmartre's last windmills.

790.    Edouard Drumont, *Mon vieux Paris: hommes et choses*, second edition (Paris: G. Charpentier, 1879).

791.    A characteristic example is Félix de Rochegude's *Guide pratique à travers le vieux Paris: maisons historiques ou curieuses, anciens hôtels pouvant être visités en 33 itinéraires détaillés*. Paris: Hachette, 1903.

792.    He drew for *Le Guide à Paris*, a weekly guide for tourists and for *Le Journal des voyages*, another weekly (from 1900–1913). He also made travel posters as well as a series of postcards portraying the French provinces. Other travel writers also got him to illustrate their works: *A travers la Bretagne*, by P. Eudel (Ollendorff, 1898). *A travers la France monumentale* (an album of images by Robida, Baudelot, 1924), *Au fil des Pyrénées: Carnet de route d'autocar* (by G. Rozet, Baudelot, 1921), *Belles villes gauloises entre Rhin et Moselle* (Illustrations of text by contemporary writers, Baudelot, 1915), *Les Châteaux de la Loire* (Travel guide for a train company, Baudelot, 1914), *Les Pyrénées* (another travel guide for a train company, Baudelot, vers 1924). For a complete list of Robida's publications and illustrations, see Philippe Brun.

793.    See Chapter 6.

794.    The classic model of illustrated travel books is Nodier and Taylor's *Voyages pittoresques et romantiques dans l'ancienne France*, whose publication spanned the century (1820–1878) and assembled texts, drawings and watercolors by a number of writers and artists. Today, one most often finds the illustrations on display, separated from the text that once accompanied them.

795.    The word *monument*, as Françoise Choay has remarked, derives from the Latin *monere* (to point out, to remember). It is thus the affective quality of the monument that is so important: 'tout artefact édifié par une communauté d'individus pour se remémorer ou faire remémorer à d'autres générations des personnnes, des événements, des sacrifices, des rites ou des croyances […] Le monument a pour fin de faire revivre au présent un passé englouti dans le temps.' pp. 14, 21.

796.    Denise Delouche, Introduction to *La Vieille France. Bretagne* (Geneva: Slatkine Editions, 1982), p. vii.

797.    See Chapter 1.

798.    'Secrétaire général des amis des monuments parisiens.' 'Toujours sur la brèche pour la défense des intérêts artistiques de Paris toujours menacés.'

799.    See 'A travers l'Exposition 1900: Le Vieux Paris,' *Revue artistique* (Juillet 1899) and *L'Encyclopédie du siècle. L'Exposition de Paris 1900* (Paris: Montgredien & Cie, 1900).

800.    For the purpose of this study, we will focus primarily on the medieval city presented in the first part of *Le Vieux Paris*. Each section was separated and decorations, costumes and the like followed the styles of the periods represented. For more information about the seventeenth and eighteenth century sections, see the detailed descriptions of them in *Exposition Universelle de 1900 – Le Vieux Paris – Guide historique, pittoresque, et anecdotique* (Paris: Ménard et Chaffour, April 1900). Most visitors commented only on the medieval section. In his *A Travers l'Exposition*

*de 1900*, a kind of serial novel involving characters who visited the major sites of the World's Fair, G. De Wailly sends his characters to *Le Vieux Paris*, where they are greeted by a winsome (and buxom) old-French speaking guide – 'haulte dame de Lutèce' – who shows them the medieval section and explains its history (Paris: Fayard Frères, 1900).

801.   *Exposition Universelle de 1900—Le Vieux Paris – Guide historique, pittoresque, et anecdotique*. The richly illustrated booklet was sold for fifty centimes.

802.   Admission fees were one franc during the day on Monday, Tuesday, Wednesday, Thursday and Saturday (doubled after 7:00 p.m.) and two francs on Friday (doubled in the evening). See James B. Campbell, *Illustrated History of the Paris International Exposition Universelle of 1900* (Chicago: Chicago and Omaha Pub. Co., 1900), p. 59.

803.   It was edited by La Société d'Ecrivains des Annales Politiques et Littéraires and sold at the *Vieux Paris* exhibit. 1. Numéro gallo-romain. 2. Numéro mérovingien. 3. Numéro carolingien. 4. Saint-Louis. 5. XIVe siècle, la Tour de Nesle. 6. Moyen Age (in the form of an illuminated manuscript). 7. Rabelais-François Ier. 8. Henry IV. 9. Théophraste Renaudot. 10. Molière. 11. La Régence. 12. Marie Antoinette. 13. L'Ami du Peuple. 14. Bonaparte.

804.   'Une salle où maître François Villon se serait senti chez lui, et où se diront et se chanteront ballades et chansons joyeuses ou satiriques, au tintement des flacons, naturellement.' All of the details in this paragraph come from Robida's loving descriptions of his creations found in his guidebook to *Le Vieux Paris*, pp. 5–8.

805.   'Le Vieux Paris à l'exposition,' p. 65.

806.   James Campbell, a visitor to the exhibit, was impressed by a number of such sights, which he enumerated: 'repasseuses,' printers using screw-driven antique printing presses, butchers roasting meat over spits, 'gauffre' makers cooking waffles to order, wedding parties, musicians and costumed actors interacting in the streets, p. 59.

807.   See Haskell, p. 47.

808.   A list of such diversions appears on the back of Robida's guide to *Vieux Paris* and appeared in advertisements related to the attraction. See also 'A travers l'Exposition 1900,' *Revue artistique* (1900), p. 40. Charles Bordes, the composer, was in charge of Saint-Julien-des-Ménétriers and organized revolving twenty-minute performances every day from 3:00–6:00. 60 000 people are alleged to have attended these 'spiritual concerts.' See Norman Demuth, *Vincent d'Indy: Champion of Classicism* (Westport, CT: Greenwood Press, Publishers, 1974), pp. 14–15. The songs performed by Bobèche at the event can be consulted at the Bibliothèque Nationale (Arsenal MS RT12,710).

809.   Cited in Rearick, p. 141.

810.   *Paris Exposition Reproduced Through Official Photographs* (New York: The R. S. Peale Company, 1900), p. 1. James B. Campbell used nearly identical language to refer to the exhibit: 'like turning back the pages of history to the days of Joan of Arc and the Troubadours to enter the Porte Saint Michel of this little Paris of ancient times,' p. 59.

811.   Caption under photo of *Old Paris, Paris Exposition Reproduced*.

812.   See, for example, the advertisement that promotes the Cabaret de la Pomme de Pin with the words 'Aimer, chanter, rire et boire! Qui que tu sois, Visiteur de mon Cabaret, Salut! Aime! chante! ris! et bois! pendant notre grande Fête.' Bibliothèque Nationale (Arsenal) MS RT12713, p. 9.

813.   'Nous n'avons à notre epoque de fêtes banales aucune idée des magnificences déployées par le moyen âge en ces circonstances, du spectacle extraordinaire de ces longues marches triomphales à travers la ville égayées par toutes sortes de divertissements et d'intermèdes où la grande ville s'ingéniait de toutes façons, la noblesse, le clergé, les moines, les gros bourgeois donnant de leurs personnes, les corporations si puissantes et si prospères, les quartiers cherchant à l'envie à se distinguer.' Robida, *Guide historique*, p. 22.

814.   Such nostalgic yearning for a more colorful epoch is hardly exclusive to nineteenth-century writers. René Héron de Villefosse's 1980 *Nouvelle Histoire de Paris: Solennités, Fêtes et Réjouissances parisiennes* opens with a miniature from Jean Fouquet's 1460 *Grandes Chroniques de France*, depicting the entry of Charles V into Paris. In his first chapter, devoted to the Middle Ages, de Villefosse contrasts the vivid past with the dull present in a manner worthy of the builders of *Vieux Paris*. The medieval street, filled with life, is held up against '[…] la même voie qui ne peut aujourd'hui échapper aux moteurs, aux affreuses sonorités mécaniques qu'ils engendrent et à leurs gaz toxiques et puants, entraînant par la même la disparition de toutes les nuances de la nature.' *Nouvelle Histoire de Paris: Solennités, Fêtes et Réjouissances parisiennes* (Paris: Hachette, 1980), p. 15.

815.   *Le Vieux Paris* took in 1 036 000 francs in receipts. The two top-grossing attractions, the Swiss Village and the Palais du Costume, which earned 2 169 000 and 1 320 000, respectively, also featured historical, traditional or educational information about the past. Although we do not have the space to discuss this phenomenon here, it is clear that spectators were more interested

by exhibits relating to historical and cultural practices than by the modern technological developments so touted by the organizers. See Rearick, p. 121.

816.    See the end of Robida's guidebook, which lists the various commercial ventures of *Le Vieux Paris*.

817.    'C'est là, parmi la série disparate qui s'élève du simple bibelot à l'objet d'art, que le moderne et l'ancien, vrai ou imité, fraternisent dans les étalages de la façon la plus éclectique, mais sans nuire à la tonalité du décor … ' De Wailly, p. 43.

818.    Old cities had been recreated for the Expositions of Antwerp, Brussels, Prague, Bude, Rouen and Geneva and the 1900 exhibit would follow in this tradition. But as Robida pointed out, his was the first functional city. 'Le Vieux Paris à l'Exposition de 1900' p. 65.

819.    See Anne-Marie Thiesse, 'La construction de la culture populaire comme patrimoine national, XVIII–XXe siècles,' in Dominique Poulot, ed., *Patrimonie et Modernité* (Paris: L'Harmattan, 1998).

820.    See Vanessa Schwartz, *Spectacular Realities: Early Mass Culture in Fin-de-siècle Paris* (Berkeley: University of California Press, 1998), and Rearick.

821.    'Si haut et si long qu'on cherche dans notre histoire intime, on y recontre le faiseur de tours de passe-passe. Les trouvères et ménéstrels du moyen âge mêlaient à leurs récits et à leurs chants tous les amusements qui pouvaient charmer la foule ou les seigneurs, particulièrement les tours d'adresse […] Tout ce que font aujourd'hui nos jongleurs de places publiques, les jongleurs lettrés du moyen âge le faisaient aussi dans les entr'actes de leurs plus nobles exercices […]' Fournel, p. 245.

822.    'Mais une autre source de notre music-hall […] apparaît à mon sens: c'est le mystère. Soutiendrai-je la thèse qu'il y a eu déjà dans l'histoire du spectacle un music-hall complet et catholique dans le sens propre et universel du term?' Denys Amiel, *Les Spectacles à travers les âges* (Paris: Aux Editions du Cygne, 1931), p. 249. 'Serait-ce pour cela qu'aucune *Revue des Folies-Bergères* de notre époque ne saurait se passer d'un tableau religieux? […] Le mystère, c'est déjà tout notre music-hall.' Germain Bapst, *Essai sur l'histoire du théâtre en France* (Paris: Hachette, 1893).

823.    'L'étude de nos vieilles foires parisiennes offre un grand intérêt, à des points de vue très divers; on peut dire qu'elles furent l'embryon des expositions universelles – avec des différences notables sans doute, mais aussi avec certaines analogies, telles que les divisions par branches d'industrie et les classements d'objets par pays de provenance – car on s'y rendait de toutes les parties de l'Europe et quelquefois du monde.' Fournel, p. 65.

824.    *Les Fêtes nationales,* unpaginated.

825.    'Un tableau fidèle de la vie, des moeurs d'autrefois, replacées dans un milieu irréprochablement exact.' 'La Cour des Miracles' by G. Moynet. *Encyclopédie du siècle. L'Exposition de Paris 1900* (Paris: Montgredien & Cie, 1900), I, p. 162.

826.    In the commemorative program, Frédéric Loliée, a historian, provided a detailed description of the Feast of the Ass ceremony and its cathedral setting. His essay incorporates phrases from the fools' 'mass,' and included other details taken from the so-called 'Missal of Fools' manuscript from Sens, two copies of which were housed at the Bibliothèque Nationale. He was later cited by E. K. Chambers in *The Mediaeval Stage*, vol. 1, p. 279. Although Gustave Cohen claimed to be the first modern director to translate and represent *Le Jeu d'Adam* on the Paris stage (in 1935), the law students had done so 40 years earlier. See Gustave Cohen, *Le Jeu d'Adam et Eve* (Paris: Librairie Delagrave, 1936), p. 6. A. P. Lannoy's translation can be consulted in La Bibliothèque Nationale (Arsenal). *Le Mystère d'Adam, suivi du Miracle des Fous. Adaptation d'après les textes du Moyen Age* (Paris: A. Charles libraire-éditeur, 1898). Music was provided by Albert Radoux. A recent translation of *La Farce du Pâté et de la tarte* by Georges Gassies des Brulies was used by students.

827.    'Le passé, les jours écoulés, les choses disparues, tout cela est pour l'esprit d'un charme toujours certain. Il est agréable d'y rêver à ce passé si près, mais qui fuit et s'enfonce en un brouillard de plus en plus épais, s'achevant trop vite en nuit complète, et c'est une sensation particulièrement empoignante d'essayer ensuite de réaliser au moins le décor de ce rêve […] Cadre de la vie d'autrefois recherché en ses particularités typiques, morceaux du Paris détruit et retrouvé pour quelque temps, édifices ou fragments d'édifices disparus, vieilles maisons de nos ancêtres parisiens, logis célèbres, coins de rue fameux par quelque souvenir ou quelque légende […] tout cela doit temporairement revivre une fois la porte passée.' Robida, *Exposition universelle*, p. 5.

828.    See the quote from Charles Morice that opens our book.

829.    For philologists' participation in reaching the public, see Emery 'The "Truth".' For information pertaining to increased incorporation of medieval topics in the secondary school curriculum, see Amalvi (1988).

830.    See Morice, pp. lxxvi–xi.

831. See Chapter 3.

832. For a definition of the 'living museum' see Robert Lumley, *The Museum/Time-Machine: Putting Cultures on Display* (London: Routledge, 1988). As Tony Bennett has suggested, one can see the fair as a competitor for the audience of the newly developing museum: 'the fair also confronted – and affronted – the museum as a still extant embodiment of the "irrational" and "chaotic" disorder that had characterized the museum's predecessors,' p. 1.

833. See Bennett, p. 156.

834. Bennett makes a similar point about 'living museums' such as Richmondtown, Virginia.

835. MacCannell, p. 84. Françoise Choay makes similar points about the 'disaffection from real life' that can occur from transforming historical monuments into concert halls, parks and museums. See the chapter of *L'Allégorie du patrimoine* entitled 'Le Patrimoine à l'âge de l'industrie culturelle,' pp. 152–79.

836. 'Introduction,' *Celebration: Studies in Festivity and Ritual*, p. 16.

837. 'Town, Nation, or Humanity? Festive Delineations of Place and Past in Northern France, ca. 1825–1865,' *The Journal of Modern History* 72 (September 2000), pp. 628–82.

838. The 'founding members' list published in *Le Chat-Noir Guide* is, perhaps, most representative of this tendency – it includes everyone from the Rothschilds and the Strausses to Emile Zola, Léon Bloy and Claude Debussy. The souvenir programs published for the Feast of Fools and the *Gazette des Beaux-Arts* also confirm this tendency as artist and writers from left and right joined ranks to make money for charity. Private journals of leading fin-de-siècle figures reveal that they, too, relished the World's Fair exhibits, to which everyone was invited. The memberships of conservation group such as the Société des Amis des Monuments Parisiens also brought together an eclectic group of people, as a one hundred year anniversary volume pointed out: painters, historians, art collectors, art historians and writers joined to preserve 'Vieux Paris.' See Jean Tiberi's introduction to the exhibit catalog for *Cent ans d'histoire de Paris: L'oeuvre de la Commission du Vieux Paris. 1898–1998* (Paris: Ville de Paris, 1999), pp. 9–13.

839. Turner, p. 16.

840. See Yvette Guilbert, *La Chanson de ma vie*. She refers to the 'modernité étrange de certains poètes du moyen âge,' p. 195.

841. Campbell, p. 59.

842. See Charles Morice and Chapter 1 for nationalist discourse related to the 1904 Exposition des Primitifs français.

843. *L'Allégorie du patrimoine*, pp. 152–7. She traces the development of the word 'culture' as attached to monuments up to the end of the twentieth century;

844. As medieval texts like *Le Journal d'un bourgeois de Paris* tell us, the people of the Middle Ages were as fond of festivity as their nineteenth-century descendants, yet they were also concerned by the serious affairs of home and state that occupied them most of the year. Their nineteenth-century descendants, however, were less interested in these mundane aspects of medieval life. They tended to ignore outbreaks of plague, political unrest and protracted battles in their discussion of them; they chose to highlight only those periods of medieval festival and celebration that appealed to their sensibility.

845. 'Il ne faut pas dédaigner le grand public, sous peine d'être abandonné par lui, et il convient surtout de ne point transformer la science en je ne sais quel temple où les prêtres seuls ont le droit d'entrer […] Tout, tout doit être mis en oeuvre pour assurer le triomphe décisif de notre épopée nationale [*La Chanson de Roland*]: tout, jusqu'à la Bibliothèque bleue et aux images d'Epinal pour les campagnards et les ignorants; tout jusqu'aux Contes et aux Alphabets pour les enfants […] atteignons ainsi tous les âges de la vie comme toutes les classes qu'il nous reste à faire.' Gautier, pp. 749, 779.

846. 'D'une voix vibrante et d'un coeur ému.' 'Ce que nous voulions […] c'est surtout qu'on prît occasion de cette lecture pour dire à ces jeunes Français: "Voyez, mes enfants, combien la France était déjà grande et combien elle était aimée il y a plus de huit siècles".' Gautier, p. 749.

847. Cited in Paul Meyer, 'Notice sur Gaston Paris (1839–1903). Extrait du tome XXXIII de *L'Histoire littéraire de la France*,' (Paris: Imprimerie Nationale, 1906), p. xix. For more about the goals of philologists and the publications and institutions they created, see Charles Ridoux.

848. See, for example, Gaston Paris's introduction to *La Poésie du moyen âge*, in which he compares his methods to those of his father's generation: 'Nous comprenons aujourd'hui un peu différemment l'étude du moyen âge. Nous nous attachons moins à l'apprécier et à le faire apprécier qu'à le comprendre et le faire comprendre. Ce que nous y cherchons avant tout c'est de l'histoire.' In *Mélanges de littérature française du moyen âge* (Paris: Honoré Champion, 1912), p. 219. He calls his father's perspective: 'cet enthousiasme aveugle qui trouve sublime ou charmant, tout ce que nous ont conservé de vieux manuscrits,' p. 217.

849. 'Ce fut un défilé de Beaux-Ténébreux et de Princes Charmants […] un moyen âge poussiéreux, fardé, rance à faire vomir. Dans le moderne, ils mirent en scène des artistes barbouillant des

fresques religieuses, à intentions sadiques, sans être, pour cela, d'aucune religion […] On dirait les tapisseries d'artisans maladifs, occupés à tisser leurs rêves d'un univers impossible, à la clarté de lampes multicolores, dans des cellules dont les fenêtres sont murées …' 'La Jeune Littérature,' *Arabesques* (Paris: Bibliothèque artistique et littéraire, 1899), pp. 19–22.

850.   A quick visit to any large auction site, like www.ebay.com, reveals the abundance of such articles, still circulating in today's antique market.

851.   See Chapter 5.

852.   'Oeuvres dispensatrices de savoir et de plaisir, mises à la disposition de tous; mais aussi produits culturels, fabriqués, emballés et diffusés en vue de leur consommation,' p. 157.

853.   For examples of the kind of support the government bestowed upon medieval studies at this time, such as the creation of chairs in medieval history and literature, support for new periodicals, and the introduction of the Middle Ages in the public school curriculum, see R. Howard Bloch, '842. The First Document and the Birth of Medieval Studies,' *A New History of French Literature*, ed. Denis Hollier (Cambridge: Harvard University Press, 1989), pp. 6–13, and Michel Espagne, 'A Propos de l'évolution historique des philologies modernes: l'exemple de la philologie romane en Allemagne et en France,' *Philologiques I*, Michel Espagne and Michael Werner, eds (Paris: Editions de la maison des sciences de l'homme, 1990), pp. 159–83. See also Charles Ridoux.

854.   See the quotation that begins this book.

855.   Thorstein Veblen examined this tendency, especially with regard to increasing industrialization and 'consumerism.' For Veblen, a growing leisure class coveted rare or unique artifacts, which, they felt, would confer prestige on them by linking them to the nobility of old. See also Pierre Bourdieu's theory of distinction detailed in *La Distinction* (Paris: Editions de Minuit, 1979).

856.   In *La Distinction*, Bourdieu reveals the significant importance of education in acquiring 'cultural capital,' pp. 12–106.

857.   In fact, Denise LeBlond described her father's additions to Médan as an attempt to turn it into a feudal estate: 'Le romancier voulut en orner les chapiteaux des colonnes et donner à la pièce un air seigneurial. D'ailleurs Médan fut meublé comme un château, avec des meubles de style et des tapisseries … ' *Zola raconté par sa fille* (Paris: Fasquelle, 1931), p. 115.

858.   Sales catalogue of Design Toscano, Autumn 2001. The company, founded in 1990 by an American couple who fell in love with the gargoyles of Notre-Dame de Paris, is based in Illinois. Their catalogue can be consulted online: www.designtoscano.com.

859.   Today, such genealogies are often sold in leather-bound books of seeming medieval design. Studies of genealogy flourished in the late nineteenth century, especially through the works of Jacques Moreau de Tours and Cesare Lombroso, who traced links between heredity and psychological make-up. Tracing one's ancestors thus took on new importance at this time.

860.   See, for example, Huysmans's *La Cathédrale* (1898) and Gourmont's *Le Latin mystique* (1892).

861.   Yvette Guilbert, *Chanteries du moyen âge* (Paris: Heugel, 1926). See Knapp and Chipman, pp. 329–30. For her travels and speaking engagements, see pp. 207–45, 270–91.

862.   See Knapp and Chipman, pp. 277–9 and 289.

863.   Cited and translated in Knapp and Chipman, p. 208.

864.   These included Ferdinand Hérold, Gustave Kahn, Ephraïm Mikhaël and Pierre Quillard. Anatole France, too, had completed a degree there. For more about the teaching of old French, see Gabriel Bergounioux, 'Introduction de l'ancien Français dans l'université française (1870–1900),' *Romania*, vol. 112 (1991), pp. 243–58.

865.   See, for example, 'Guillaume Apollinaire: The Medieval Tourist,' a paper given by Tina Isaac of the University of Oklahoma at the Thirty-seventh Congress on Medieval Studies at Kalamazoo, MI (2002), which reveals Apollinaire's debt to the medieval manuscripts he studied at the Bibliothèque Nationale.

866.   Nykrog also categorizes Bédier's four main contributions to medieval scholarship as 'efforts to "exterminate" mainly German scholars (or French scholars who had adopted their ideas too readily).' 'A Warrior Scholar at the Collège de France: Joseph Bédier' in Nichols *et al.*, *Medievalism and the Modernist Temper*, pp. 286–307. See also R. Howard Bloch, '842. The First Document and the Birth of Medieval Studies,' *A New History of French Literature*, ed. Denis Hollier (Cambridge: Harvard University Press, 1989), pp. 6–13 and also Alain Corbellari (1997) *Joseph Bédier, Ecrivain et philologue* (Geneva: Droz).

867.   See his introduction to *La Poésie du moyen âge*.

868.   Helen Damico's three-volume collection of biographies of medieval scholars (*Medieval Scholarship: Biographical Studies on the Formation of a Discipline*) is particularly helpful in establishing such filiations. Gerard Brault's entry for Gaston Paris is enlightening in regard to the hundreds of students in Europe and the United States who were influenced by his work.

869. This was, indeed, the case in the post-war period. As Michel Espagne has put it, this period 'consecrated' the discipline of philology. The numerous positions created for professors, expanded interest in l'Ecole des Chartes and publishing houses dedicated to disseminating medieval texts both reflected interest in the Middle Ages and encouraged it. See Michel Espagne, pp. 159–83.

870. See, for example, R. Howard Bloch and Stephen G. Nichol's introduction to *Medievalism and the Modernist Temper*: 'Word's out. There's something exciting going on in medieval studies […]' p. 1.

871. See Marina S. Brownlee, Kevin Brownlee and Stephen G. Nichols, eds, *The New Medievalism* (Baltimore: Johns Hopkins University Press, 1991).

872. Despite the excellence of Janine Dakyns's *The Middle Ages in French Literature*, her conclusion points out the prevalence of different claims on the Middle Ages without going a step further to show how this near-universal embrace of the Middle Ages would prove critical for twentieth-century French identity.

873. Anne-Marie Thiesse proposes that a nation exists once such fictions are created and widely accepted, pp. 11–15. The emblem of the Third Republic provides an excellent example of such nationalist fiction: by borrowing the insignia of medieval water carriers – a ship holding steady through waves – the secular Republic linked itself to a glorious and steady heritage.

874. 'Le moyen âge, c'est bien nous-mêmes … les hommes de ces temps anciens sont bien réellement nos pères' … 'Rien ne me touche plus que de savoir ce qu'ont été mes pères lointains, ce qu'ils ont dit, ce qu'ils ont écrit, ce qu'ils ont pensé, ce qu'ils ont souffert, comment ils ont songé le songe de la vie – et de retrouver leur âme en moi. C'est le passé qui fait le prix du présent et qui donne au présent sa forme. C'est dans le passé qu'il faut vivre, fût-ce pour en avoir pitié: en nous attendrissant sur nos ancêtres, c'est sur nous-mêmes que nous nous attendrissons.' *Les Contemporains*, vol. iii (Paris: Lecène et Oudin, 1886–1889), p. 235.

875. 'The New Medievalism and the (Im)Possibility of the Middle Ages,' *Studies in Medievalism* X (1998), pp. 104–19.

876. Indeed, Glejzer proposes that knowledge of the medieval context is '(im)possible' and such goals misdirect scholarly emphasis to focus on the causes for the production of medieval works instead of on the works themselves, pp. 115–17.

877. 'Appartenir à la nation, c'est être un des héritiers de ce patrimoine commun et indivisible, le connaître et le révérer,' p. 12. Interestingly enough, though Pierre Nora's *Les Lieux de Mémoire* contains a plethora of entries for characters, works of art and events from the Middle Ages, there is no analysis of the period itself as a *lieu de mémoire*.

878. See, for example, the controversy surrounding Pope John Paul II's visit to Reims for the anniversary of the crowning of Clovis in September 1996. While Catholics rushed to the site to celebrate the conversion of the first Christian king, many Republicans embraced the political nature of Clovis's act. Yet others – socialists, gays, leftists – claimed that France did not really begin until 1789. This event repeats, down to the vocabulary, the debates of the fin de siècle. See the numerous articles about this dispute published in *Le Monde* (4 September 1996); each article traces a different party's claims on Clovis.

879. This was what Fustel de Coulanges had requested in his 1872 articles about the fifth-century Germanic invasions: to re-assess the medieval period and to come to a common understanding of its importance for French history (see Chapter 1).

880. See, for example, Walter Benjamin's 'Paris, Capital of the Nineteenth Century,' which makes this argument, in *Reflections: Essays, Aphorisms, and Autobiographical Writings*, ed. Peter Demetz, trans. Edmund Jephcott (New York: Harcourt Brace Jovanovich, 1978).

# Select bibliography

## Periodicals

*L'Album des Légendes*, Consulted 1894–1895.
*Le Chat Noir*, Consulted 1882–1897.
*Le Courrier Français*, Consulted 1884–1900.
*Le Figaro illustré*, Consulted 1883–1905.
*La Gazette des Beaux-Arts*, Consulted 1885–1905.
*Illustration*, Consulted 1871–1905.
*Le Mercure de France*, Consulted 1890–1905.
*Le Pèlerin*, Consulted 1871–1905.
*La Plume*, Consulted 1889–1905.
*La Revue blanche*, Consulted 1891–1903.
*La Revue des Deux Mondes*, Consulted indexes and selected articles 1831–1900.
*Le Temps*, Consulted indexes and selected texts 1861–1900.
*L'Ymagier: Trimestrial d'art et d'imagerie populaire*, Consulted 1894–1896.

## Primary sources

(1942), *A Emile Bernard. Lettres de Vincent Van-Gogh, Paul Gauguin, Odilon Redon, Paul Cézanne, Elémir Bourges, Léon Bloy, Guillaume Apollinaire, Joris-Karl Huysmans, Henry de Groux*, Brussels: Editions de la Nouvelle Revue de Belgique.
(1900), 'A travers l'Exposition 1900,' *Revue artistique*.
(1890), *L'art décoratif à l'Exposition Universelle de 1889*. Paris: A. Calvas Editeur.
(1890) 'Les Brasseries, buvettes et bars servis par des femmes,' *Le Courrier Français*, 9 January.
(1901), *Paris Exposition Reproduced through Official Photographs*, New York: The R.S. Peale Company.
Aurier, Albert (1891), 'A propos de trois salons de 1891,' *Le Mercure de France* III.
Bapst, Germain (1891), 'Les spectacles et les réjouissances des fêtes publiques au Moyen Age,' *La Revue bleue* (48) July.
Baudelaire, Charles (1861) 'Richard Wagner et Tannhäuser à Paris,' *La Revue européenne*, 1 April. Reprinted in *Oeuvres complètes* (1980), Paris: Editions Robert Laffont, pp. 849–72.
Bazalgette, Léon (1898), *L'esprit nouveau dans la vie artistique, sociale et religieuse*, Paris: Société d'éditions littéraires.
Bernard, Emile, *Lettres à Paul Gauguin et à E. Schuffenecker*, Paris: Bibliothèque Nationale de France, Department of Manuscripts, n.a. fr. 14277.
—— (1894), 'Les Primitifs et la Renaissance,' *Le Mercure de France*, November.

Blanche, Jacques-Emile (1895), 'Les objets d'art I: Au Salon du Champs de Mars,' *La Revue blanche* (15) May.

Bloy, Léon (1924), *La Femme Pauvre*, Paris: G. Crès et Cie.

Bonnafée, Edmond (1889), 'L'Exposition Universelle de 1889: Au Trocadéro,' *La Gazette des Beaux-Arts* (65) 1 July, pp. 5–11.

Bouchot, Henri (1904), *L'Exposition des Primitifs français: La Peinture en France sous les Valois*, Paris: Librairie Centrale des Beaux-Arts.

—— (1904), *Les Primitifs français: 1292–1500/Complément documentaire au catalogue officiel de l'Exposition*, Paris: Librairie de l'art ancien et moderne.

Campbell, James B. (1900), *Illustrated History of the Paris International Exposition Universelle of 1900*, Chicago: Chicago and Omaha Pub. Co.

Chambers, E. K. (1903), *The Mediaeval Stage*, London: Oxford University Press.

Champier, Victor (1895), 'Les arts décoratifs au Salon de 1895: Le Champ de Mars,' *Revue des arts décoratifs* (15).

Claretie, Jules (1898), 'La Fête des Fous,' *Le Temps*, 31 May 1898.

Cochin, Denys (1899), *Contre les barbares*, Paris: Calmann Lévy Éditeur.

Combes, Paul (1900), *Les Merveilles de l'Exposition: Paris en 1400*, Paris: Librairie Illustrée.

Courajod, Louis (1894), *Histoire du département de la sculpture moderne au Musée du Louvre*, Paris: Ernst Leroux.

—— (1899), *Leçons professées à l'Ecole du Louvre (1886–1896)*, Paris: n.p.

—— (1888), *Les Origines de la Renaissance en France au XIVe et au XVe siècle*, Paris: H. Champion.

Courajod, Louis and Paul Frantz Marcou (1892), *Musée de sculpture comparée (Moulages)–Palais du Trocadéro. Catalogue raisonné publié sous les auspices de la Commission des Monuments Historiques*, Paris: Imprimerie Nationale.

Darcel, Alfred (1889), 'La Collection de M. Ernest Odiot,' *La Gazette des Beaux-Arts* (64), 1 March, pp. 247–58.

—— (1876), 'Union Centrale des Beaux-Arts appliqués à l'industrie: Exposition de l'histoire de la tapisserie,' *La Gazette des Beaux-Arts* 2, pp. 414–37.

Daumont-Tournel, Léon (1901), *Exposition Universelle Internationale de 1900 à Paris: Rapports du Jury International – Classe 67*, Paris: Imprimerie Nationale.

Daurelle, Jacques (1901), *Exposition des oeuvres d'Armand Point et son oeuvre – par. MM. Paul Fort, Paul et Victor Margueritte …*, Paris: n.p.

Delalande, Emile (1894), 'Les Vitraux aux Salons de 1894,' *La Plume*, June.

Demarteau, Joseph (1906), *A Lourdes; le pèlerinage belge du 30 août au 12 septembre 1906. Notes d'un pèlerin liégois*, Liège: Imprimerie Demarteau.

Denis, Maurice (1927), 'Un humaniste chrétien: Henri Cochin,' *La revue hebdomadaire* (44), 29 October.

—— (1942), *L'ABC de la peinture. Suivi d'une étude sur la vie et l'oeuvre de Paul Sérusier*, Paris: H. Floury.

—— (1957), *Journal tome 1*, Paris: Editions du Vieux Colombier.

—— (1922), *Nouvelles théories sur l'art moderne, sur l'art sacré 1914–1921*, Paris: L. Rouart et Watelin.

—— (1920), *Théories 1880–1910: Du symbolisme et de Gauguin vers un nouvel ordre classique*, Paris: L. Rouart et Watelin.

Didron, Edouard (1893–1894), 'Le Concours de vitraux de Jeanne d'Arc pour la cathédrale d'Orléans,' *Revue des arts décoratifs* (XIV).

—— (1898), *Le Vitrail: Conférence faite à la société de l'Union Centrale des arts décoratifs*, Paris: Librairie des arts décoratifs.

Drumont, Edouard (1886), *La France juive*, Paris: Editions du Trident. Reprint, 1986.

—— (1879), *Les Fêtes nationales à Paris*, Paris: L. Baschet.

—— (1879), *Mon vieux Paris. Hommes et choses*, 2nd edn, Paris: G. Charpentier.

Enlart, Camille and Jules Roussel (1929), *Catalogue général du Musée de sculpture comparée au Palais du Trocadéro (Moulages)*, Paris: Henri Laurens.

—— (1900), *Exposition Universelle de 1900: Catalogue officiel illustré de l'Exposition Rétrospective de l'art français des origines à 1800*, Paris: L. Baschet.

Farcy, Louis de (1904), 'Un atelier pour la reproduction des anciennes tapisseries,' *La Revue de l'art chrétien*, July.

—— (1897), 'Histoires et description des tapisseries de l'église cathédrale d'Angers,' *Revue de l'Anjou* 24 (May/June).

Fournel, Victor (1887), *Le Vieux Paris: Fêtes, Jeux et Spectacles*, Tours: Alfred Mame et Fils.

Fustel de Coulanges, Numa Denis (1872), 'L'Invasion germanique au cinquième siècle,' *La Revue des Deux Mondes* 99/2 (15 May), pp. 536–57.

—— (1871), 'L'Organisation de la justice dans l'Antiquité et les temps modernes. III. La Justice royale au Moyen Age,' *La Revue des Deux Mondes* 94/2 (1 August).

Gaudin, Félix (1894), 'A propos du concours des vitraux de Jeanne d'Arc,' *La Plume* (113).

Gautier, Léon (1892), *Les Epopées Françaises*, vol. II, Paris: Librairie Universitaire.

Germain, Alphonse (1892), 'L'art religieux,' *Le Saint Graal* (6) May.

—— (1894), *Notre art de France*, Paris: E. Girard.

Goudeau, Emile (1886), 'L'Abbaye de Thélème,' *Le Courrier Français*, 14 February.

Gonse, Louis (1890), *L'art gothique: l'architecture, la peinture, la sculpture, le décor*, Paris: Librairie Imprimerie Réunies.

—— (1886), 'La tapisserie, son histoire depuis le moyen âge jusqu'à nos jours par Jules M. Guiffrey,' *La Gazette des Beaux-Arts* (33) 1 January, pp. 82–5.

Gonse, Louis and Alfred de Lostalot, eds (1890), *Exposition Universelle de 1889: Les beaux-arts et les arts décoratifs – L'art français rétrospectif au Trocadéro*, Paris: Journal *Le Temps*.

Gourmont, Remy de (1892), *Le Latin mystique: les poètes de l'antiphonaire et symbolique au Moyen Age*, Paris: Mercure de France.

Grand-Carteret, John (1886), *Raphaël et Gambrinus ou l'art dans la brasserie*, Paris: L. Westhausser.

Guiffrey, Jules (1900), 'Les tapisseries à l'Exposition rétrospective,' *La Gazette des Beaux-Arts* (87) September, pp. 222–36.

—— (1889), 'Les tapisseries des églises de Paris,' *La revue de l'art chrétien*.

—— (1904), *Les tapisseries des églises de Paris*, Paris: A. Picard.

Guilbert, Yvette (1927), *La Chanson de ma vie*, Paris: Bernard Grasset.

Hugo, Victor (1967), *Notre-Dame de Paris*, *Oeuvres complètes*, vol. iv, Paris: Le Club français du livre.

Huret, Jules (1891), *Enquête sur l'évolution littéraire*, Vanves: Les Editions Thot. Reprint, 1984.

Huysmans, J.-K. (1977), *A Rebours*, Paris: Gallimard.

—— (1975), 'Le Musée des arts décoratifs et l'architecture cuite,' *L'Art Moderne/Certains*, Paris: Union générale des éditions, pp. 337–42.

—— (1972), 'Charles-Marie Dulac,' in vol. 16 of *Oeuvres complètes de J.-K. Huysmans*, Geneva: Slatkine Reprints.

—— (1993), *Les Foules de Lourdes*, Grenoble: J. Millon.

—— (1977), *Lettres inédites à Arij Prins*, Geneva: Librairie Droz.

—— (1972), *Oeuvres complètes de J.-K. Huysmans*, Geneva: Slatkine Reprints.

—— (1895), 'Préface au *Latin mystique*,' Paris: Editions du Mercure de France.

—— (1999), *Le Roman de Durtal*, Paris: Bartillat.

—— (1885), 'Le Salon de 1885,' *L'Evolution sociale*, May.

Lafenestre, Georges (1904), *Exposition des Primitifs français au Palais du Louvre (Pavillon de Marsan) et à la Bibliothèque Nationale*, Paris: n.p.

Lanéry d'Arc, Pierre (1894), *Le Livre d'or de Jeanne d'Arc. Catalogue méthodique, descriptif et critique des principales études historiques, littéraires et artistiques, consacrées à la Pucelle d'Orléans depuis le XVe siècle jusqu'à nos jours*, Paris: Techener.

Lannoy, A. P. de (1900), *Les Plaisirs et la Vie de Paris: Guide du flâneur*, Paris: Librairie L. Borel.

Lavergne, Noël (1891), *L'art des vitraux*, Paris: Imprimerie Dumoulin et Cie.

Lesaulx, Gaston (1890), Introduction to 'Exposition des peintres impressionnistes et symbolistes,' Galerie Le Barc de Boutteville. Reprinted in Theodore Reff, ed. (1981), *Modern Art in Paris: 1885–1900*, New York/London: Garland Press.

Lostalot, Alfred de (1890), 'L'Art gothique,' *La Gazette des Beaux-Arts* (67).

Magne, Lucien (1886), 'Le Musée du Vitrail,' *La Gazette des Beaux-Arts* (34), October, pp. 297–311.

—— (1900), *Musée rétrospectif de la classe 67, vitraux, à l'Exposition Universelle Internationale de 1900 à Paris*, Saint Cloud: Belin frères.

—— (1885), *L'oeuvre des peintres-verriers français*, Paris: Firmin-Didot.

Mâle, Emile (1898), *L'art religieux du XIIIe siècle en France. Étude sur l'iconographie du moyen âge et sur ses sources d'inspiration*, Paris: Armand Colin.

—— (1984), *Religious Art in France: The Thirteenth Century. A Study of Medieval Iconography and its Sources*, ed. Harry Bober, trans. Marthiel Matthew, Princeton: Princeton University Press.

—— (1899), *Manuel du pèlerinage Lorrain à Notre-Dame de Lourdes* 12th edition, Saint-Dié: Imprimerie Humbert.

Marx, Roger (1895), 'Les Salons de 1895,' *La Gazette des Beaux-Arts* (14), 1 May, p. 24.

Mermeix (1886), 'Les Chroniques de l'Abbaye de Thélème,' *Le Courrier Français*, 23 May.

Merrill, Stuart (1899), *Armand Point et Haute Claire*. Exhibition catalogue. 1–22 Avril 1899, Paris: Galerie Georges Petit.

Michel, André (1906), *Histoire de l'art depuis les premiers temps chrétiens jusqu'à nos jours*, vol. 2, Paris: Librairie Armand Colin.

Mirbeau, Octave (1887), 'Nos bons artistes,' *Le Figaro*, 23 December.

Molinier, Emile (1889), 'Exposition rétrospective de l'art français au Trocadéro: I Le Moyen Age,' *La Gazette des Beaux-Arts* (65), 1 August, pp. 145–66.

Molinier, Emile, Roger Marx and Paul Frantz Marcou (1901), *Exposition Universelle de 1900: L'art français des origines à la fin du XIXe siècle*, Paris: L. Danel.

Morice, Charles (1914), 'Introduction' to Auguste Rodin, *Les Cathédrales de France*, Paris: Librairie Armand Colin.

Morin, Louis (1897), *Les Carnavals parisiens*, Paris: Montgredien et Cie.

Morrow, W. C. and Edouard Cucuel (1900), *Bohemian Paris of Today*, Philadelphia: J. P. Lippincott Company.

Musée des Thermes et de l'Hôtel de Cluny (1883), *Catalogue et description des objets d'art de l'antiquité du Moyen Age et de la Renaissance*, Paris: n.p.

Natanson, Thadée (1948), *Peintres à leur tour*, Paris: Albin Michel.

Olmer, Georges (1886), *L'Exposition des Beaux-Arts: Salon de 1886*, Paris: Librairie d'Art.

Ottin, Léon (1896), *Le Vitrail: son histoire, ses manifestations diverses à travers les âges et les peuples*, Paris: H. Laurens.

Paris, Gaston (1912), *La Poésie du moyen âge* in *Mélanges de littérature française du moyen âge*, Paris: Honoré Champion.

Péladan, Joséphin (1884), 'Introduction à l'histoire des peintres de toutes les écoles depuis les origines jusqu'à la Renaissance: l'Angelico,' *L'Artiste*, March.

—— (1883), 'L'Esthétique au Salon de 1883,' *L'Artiste*. May.

*La Plume* (1894), Special issue devoted to Grasset, May.

Point, Armand (1895), 'Les Primitifs et les symbolistes,' *L'Ermitage*, July, pp. 11–19.

Proust, Marcel (1988), *A la recherche du temps perdu*, 4 vols. Paris: Gallimard (Bibliothèque de la Pléiade).

—— (1971), 'La Mort des cathédrales,' *Contre Sainte-Beuve: précédé de Pastiches et melanges et suivi de Essais et articles*, Paris: Gallimard (Bibliothèque de la Pléiade).

Raison du Cleuziou, Henri (1883), *L'Art national*, Paris: A. le Vasseur.

Robida, Albert (1900), *Exposition universelle de 1900. Le vieux Paris, études et dessins originaux*, Paris: Imprimerie de Lemercier.

—— (1900), *Exposition Universelle de 1900 – Le Vieux Paris – Guide historique, pittoresque, et anecdoctique*, Paris: Ménard et Chaffour.

—— (1900), *La Nef de Lutèce*, Paris: Imprimerie Lahure.

—— (1890), *Normandie*, Paris: La Librairie Illustrée.

—— (1895), *Paris de siècle en siècle*, Paris: La Librairie Illustrée.

—— (1901), 'Le Vieux Paris à l'Exposition de 1900,' *L'Encyclopédie du siècle*, 2 vols, Paris: Montgredien & Cie, I, pp. 65–6.

Saunier, Charles (1893), 'Vitraux pour Jeanne d'Arc,' *La Plume*, November.

Schwabe, Moïse (1891), 'La Collection Strauss au Musée de Cluny,' *La Gazette des Beaux-Arts* (5) 1 March, pp. 237–45.

Simon, Charles (1889), 'Les Origines de nos tapisseries,' *La Revue des revues*, July, pp. 82–91. XI (no. 161).

Société archéologique et historique de l'Orléanais (1897), 'Les verrières de Jeanne d'Arc à la cathédrale d'Orléans,' XI (no. 16).

Veblen, Thorstein (1965), *Theories of the Leisure Class*, New York: A. M. Kelley.

Verkade, Jan (Willibrord) (1930), *Yesterdays of an Artist-Monk*, trans. John Stoddard, London: P. J. Kennedy and Sons.

Verlaine, Paul (1962), *Oeuvres poétiques complètes*, Paris: Editions Gallimard (Bibliothèque de la Pléiade).

Viollet-le-Duc, Eugène-Emmanuel (1875), *Dictionnaire raisonné de l'architecture française du XIe au XVIe siècle*, 10 vols, Paris: V. A. Morel.

Vollard, Ambroise (1968), *Recollections of a Picture Dealer*, trans. Violet MacDonald, New York: Dover Reprint.

Wailly, G. de (1900), *A Travers l'Exposition de 1900*, Paris: Fayard Frères.

Witter, William (1897), 'Entre l'art catholique et les historiens de la Renaissance,' *Le Spectateur catholique* (8) August.

Zola, Emile (1978–1995), *Correspondance*. Ed. B. H. Bakker et al. Montreal and Paris: Les Presses de l'Université de Montréal and Editions du Centre National de la Recherche Scientifique.

—— (1968), *Lourdes. Oeuvres complètes*, vol. vii. Paris: Cercle du livre précieux.

—— (1960–1967), *Les Rougon-Macquart*, 5 vols, Paris: Gallimard (Bibliothèque de la Pléiade).

## Secondary sources

Adam, Antoine (1963), *The Art of Paul Verlaine*, New York: New York University Press.

Alexander, Jonathan J. G. (1992), *Medieval Illuminators and their Methods of Work*, New Haven: Yale University Press.

Amalvi, Christian (1988), *De l'art et de la manière d'accommoder les héros de l'histoire de France: essais de mythologie nationale*, Paris: Albin Michel.

—— (1996), *Le Goût du Moyen Age*, Paris: Plon.

Appignanesi, Lisa (1975), *The Cabaret*, London: Studio Vista.

Arden, Heather, ed. (1983), *Medievalism in France, Studies in Medievalism* II.2.

—— (1987), *Medievalism in France 1500–1750, Studies in Medievalism* III.1.

Arminjon, Catherine and Denis Lavalle, eds (2001), *20 siècles en cathédrales*, Paris: Monum, Editions du patrimoine.

Baas, Jacquelynn and Richard S. Field (1984), *The Artistic Revival of the Woodcut in France 1850–1900*, Ann Arbor: University of Michigan Museum of Art.

Bacou, Roseline (1964), 'Décors d'appartement au temps des Nabis,' *Art de France* (IV), pp. 190–205.

Baldick, Robert (1955), *The Life of J.-K. Huysmans*, Oxford: Clarendon Press.

Banks, Brian R. (1990), *The Image of Huysmans*, New York: AMS Press.

Bann, Stephen (1984), *The Clothing of Clio: A Study in the Representation of History in Nineteenth Century Britain and France*, Cambridge: Cambridge University Press.

Barmann, L. and C. J. T. Talar, eds (1999), *Sanctity and Secularity during the Modernist Period: Six Perspectives on Hagiography around 1900*, Brussels: Société des Bollandistes.

Baumgartner, Emmanuèle and Jean-Pierre Leduc-Adine (1990), *Moyen âge et XIXe siècle: le mirage des origines: actes du colloque, Paris III – Sorbonne nouvelle – Paris X-Nanterre. 5 et 6 mai 1988*, Paris: Centre d'Etudes du Moyen Age et de la Renaissance de la Sorbonne nouvelle.

Benjamin, Walter (1969), 'The Work of Art in the Age of Mechanical Reproduction,' *Illuminations*, trans. Harry Zohn, ed. Hannah Arendt, New York: Harcourt, Brace and Wood.

Bennett, Tony (1995), *The Birth of the Museum: History, Theory, Politics*, London and New York: Routledge.

Bizzarro, Tina Waldeier (1992), *Romanesque Architectural Criticism: A Prehistory*, Cambridge: Cambridge University Press.

Bloch, R. Howard and Stephen G. Nichols (1996), 'Introduction,' *Medievalism and the Modernist Temper*, Baltimore: The Johns Hopkins Press, pp. 1–22.

Bouillon, Jean-Paul (1990), *La Promenade du critique influent: anthologie de la critique d'art en France 1850–1900*, Paris: Hazan.

Boyer, Patricia Eckert, ed. (1989), *The Nabis and the Parisian Avant-Garde*. Exhibition catalogue, New Brunswick, NJ: Jane Vorhees Zimmerli Museum of Art/Rutgers University Press.

Boyle-Turner, Caroline (1983), 'Paul Sérusier,' Ph.D. thesis, Columbia University.

—— (1990), *Jan Verkade, Disciple hollandais de Gauguin*, Quimper: Musée des Beaux-Arts.

Brody, Elaine (1987), *Paris: The Musical Kaleidoscope 1870–1925*, New York: George Braziller.

Brun, Philippe (1984), *Albert Robida, sa vie, son oeuvre*, Paris: Editions Promodis.

Bürger, Peter (1984), *Theory of the Avant-Garde*, trans. Michael Shaw, Minneapolis: University of Minnesota Press.

Byrnes, Robert Francis (1950), *Antisemitism in Modern France* vol. 1, New Brunswick, NJ: Rutgers University Press.

—— (1950), 'The French Christian Democrats in the 1890s: Their Appearance and their Failure,' *Catholic Historical Review* 36 (October), pp. 286–306.

Cahm, Eric (1996), *The Dreyfus Affair in French Society and Politics*, New York: Longman Publishing.

Camille, Michael (1994), 'How New York stole the idea of Romanesque Art: Medieval, Modern and Post-Modern in Meyer Schapiro,' *Oxford Art Journal* (17).

—— (1990), '*Les Très Riches Heures du Duc de Berry*: An Illuminated Manuscript in the Age of Mechanical Reproduction,' *Critical Inquiry* (17:1 Autumn).

Cantor, Norman (1991), *Inventing the Middle Ages: The Lives, Works and Ideas of the Great Medievalists of the Twentieth Century*, New York: William Morrow.

Castel, Paul (1962), *Le P. François Picard et le P. Vincent de Paul Bailly dans les luttes de presse*, Rome: Maison Généralice.

Castelnuovo, Enrico (1983), 'La "cathédrale de poche": enluminure et vitrail à la lumière de l'historiographie du 19e siècle,' *Zeitschrift für Schweizerische Archäologie und Kunstgeschichte* (40), pp. 91–3.

Cate, Phillip Dennis and Mary Shaw (1996), *The Spirit of Montmartre: Cabarets, Humor, and the Avant-Garde, 1875–1905*, New Brunswick, NJ: The Jane Vorhees Zimmerli Art Museum.

Caviness, Madeleine (1988), 'Broadening the Definitions of Art: The Reception of Medieval Works in the Context of Post-Impressionist Movements,' in Gallacher, Patrick J. and Helen Damico, eds, *Hermeneutics and Medieval Culture*, Albany: State University of New York Press.

Certeau, Michel de (1987), *La Faiblesse de croire*, Paris: Editions du Seuil.

Chapuis, Julien (1998), 'Early Netherlandish Painting: Shifting Perspectives,' in Maryan Ainsworth, ed., *From Van Eyck to Bruegel: Early Netherlandish Painting in the Metropolitan Museum of Art*, New York: Harry Abrams.

Château Musée de Cagnes sur Mer (1980), *Le Moyen Age et les peintres français de la fin du XIXe siècle: Jean-Paul Laurens et ses contemporains*.

Choay, Françoise (1999), *L'Allégorie du patrimoine*. Paris: Editions du Seuil.

Citron, Suzanne (1987), *Le mythe national: L'histoire de France en question*, Paris: Editions Ouvrières.

Corbellari, Alain (1997), *Joseph Bédier, Ecrivain et philologue*, Geneva: Droz.

Da Silva, Jean (1991), *Le Salon de la Rose+Croix, 1892–1897*, Paris: Syros-Alternatives.

Dakyns, Janine R. (1973), *The Middle Ages in French Literature: 1851–1900*, London: Oxford University Press.

Damico, Helen (1995–2000), *Medieval Scholarship: Biographical Studies on the Formation of a Discipline*, New York: Garland Publishing, Inc.

Davis, Shane Adler (1989), '"Fine Cloths on the Altar": The Commodification of Late-Nineteenth Century France,' *The Art Journal* 48:1 (Spring), pp. 85–9.

Delannoy, Agnès and Marianne Barbey (1999), *Maurice Denis: La Légende de Saint Hubert 1896–1897*, Paris: Somogy Editions.

Doolittle, Dorothy (1933), 'The Relations Between Literature and Mediaeval Studies in France from 1820 to 1860,' Ph.D. thesis, Bryn Mawr.

Driskel, Michael Paul (1992), *Representing Belief: Politics, Religion and Society in Nineteenth Century France*, University Park: Pennsylvania State University Press.

Ducrey, Anne, ed. (2000), *Le Moyen Age en 1900*, Ateliers 26, Lille: Cahiers de la Maison de la Recherche Université Charles-de-Gaulle.

Dugdale, James (1965), 'Vuillard the Decorator,' *Apollo*, February, pp. 94–101.

Duggan, Joseph (1989), 'Franco-German Conflict and the History of French Scholarship on the Song of Roland,' in *Hermeneutics and Medieval Culture*, Patrick J. Gallacher and Helen Damico, eds, Albany: State University Press of New York, pp. 97–106.

Dull, Olga Anna (1991), 'From Rabelais to the Avant-Garde: Wordplays and Parody in the Wall-Journal *Le Mur*,' in Phillip Dennis Cate and Mary Shaw, *The Spirit of Montmartre*, pp. 199–241.

Edelman, Nathan (1946), *Attitudes of Seventeenth Century France toward the Middle Ages*, New York: King's Crown Press.

—— (1936), 'La Vogue de Villon en France 1828–1873,' *Revue d'Histoire littéraire de la France* (April–June, July–September), pp. 211–23, 321–39.

Emery, Elizabeth (1999), '"A l'ombre d'une vieille cathédrale romanesque": The Medievalism of Gautier and Zola,' *The French Review* 73:2 (December), pp. 290–300.

—— (1999), 'Bricabracomania: Zola's Romantic Instinct,' *Excavatio* 12, pp. 107–15.

—— (2002), 'J.-K. Huysmans and the Middle Ages,' *Modern Language Studies* 29.3.

—— (2000), 'The Nineteenth-Century Struggle for the Soul of Lourdes: A Modern Pilgrimage,' *The Year's Work in Medievalism 1999* (2000), pp. 103–14.

—— (2001), *Romancing the Cathedral: Gothic Architecture in Fin-de-Siècle French Culture*, Albany: State University of New York Press.

—— (2001), 'The "Truth" About the Middle Ages: *La Revue des Deux Mondes* and Late Nineteenth-Century French Medievalism,' in *The Quest for the 'Real' Middle Ages*, Clare A. Simmons, ed., London: Frank Cass, pp. 99–114.

Espagne, Michel (1990), 'A Propos de l'évolution historique des philologies modernes: l'exemple de la philologie romane en Allemagne et en France,'

*Philologiques I*, eds Michel Espagne and Michael Werner, Paris: Editions de la Maison des Sciences de l'homme, pp. 159–83.

Foucart, Bruno (1987), *Le renouveau de la peinture religieuse en France: 1800–1860*, Paris: Athena.

Frank, Frederick S. (1984), *Guide to the Gothic: An Annotated Bibliography of Criticism*, Metuchen, NJ: Scarecrow Press.

Frankl, Paul (1960), *The Gothic: Literary Sources and Interpretations through Eight Centuries*, Princeton: Princeton University Press.

Frèches-Thory, Claire and Ursula Perucchi-Petri (1993), *Nabis: 1888–1900*, Exhibition catalogue, Zürich: Kunsthaus/Paris: Musée d'Orsay.

Frèches-Thory, Claire and Antoine Terrasse (1991), *The Nabis: Bonnard, Vuillard and their Circle*, New York: Harry Abrams.

Freedberg, David (1989), *The Power of Images: Studies in the History and Theory of Response*, Chicago: University of Chicago Press.

Genova, Pamela (2002), *Symbolist Journals: A Culture of Correspondence*, London: Ashgate Press.

Glejzer, Richard (1998), 'The New Medievalism and the (Im)Possibility of the Middle Ages,' *Studies in Medievalism* X (1998), pp. 104–19.

Glencross, Michael (1995), *Reconstructing Camelot: French Romantic Medievalism and the Arthurian Tradition*, Cambridge: D. S. Brewer.

Gossman, Lionel (1968), *Medievalism and the Ideologies of the Enlightenment: the World and Work of La Curne de Sainte-Palaye*, Baltimore, Johns Hopkins Press.

(1979), *Le Gothique retrouvé avant Viollet-le-Duc: catalogue de l'exposition de l'Hôtel de Sully*, Paris: Caisse nationale des monuments historiques et des sites.

Green, Nicolas (1987), 'Dealing in Temperaments: Economic Transformations of the Artistic Field in France during the Second Half of the Nineteenth Century,' *Art History*, March.

Grenier, Joseph A. (1976), 'To Reach the People: *La Croix*, 1883–1890,' Ph.D. thesis, Fordham University.

Griffiths, Richard (1966), *The Reactionary Revolution: The Catholic Revival in French Literature 1870–1914*, London: Constable.

Groom, Gloria (1993), *Edouard Vuillard, Painter-Decorator: Patrons and Projects 1892–1912*, New Haven: Yale University Press.

Gugelot, Frédéric (1998), *La Conversion des intellectuels au catholicisme en France 1885–1935*, Paris: CNRS Editions.

Harris, Anne F. (1999), 'The Spectacle of Stained Glass in Modern France and Medieval Chartres: A History of Practices and Perceptions,' Ph.D. thesis, The University of Chicago.

Haskell, Francis (1993), *History and Its Images: Art and the Interpretation of the Past*, New Haven/London: Yale University Press.

Hays, Colleen (1993), 'Literary History and Criticism of French Medieval Works in the Nineteenth Century: The Phenomenon of Medievalism,' Ph.D. thesis, University of Oklahoma.

Hindman, Sandra, Michael Camille, Nina Rowe and Rowan Watson (2001), *Manuscript Illumination in the Modern Age*, Evanston: Mary and Leigh Block Museum of Art, Northwestern University.

Jensen, Robert (1988), 'The Avant-Garde and the Trade in Art,' *Art Journal* (Winter), pp. 360–68.

Jirat-Wasiutynski, Vojtech and H. Travers Newton, Jr (2000), *Technique and Meaning in the Paintings of Paul Gauguin*, Cambridge/New York: Cambridge University Press.

Jonas, Raymond (2000), *France and the Cult of the Sacred Heart: An Epic Tale for Modern Times*, Berkeley: University of California Press.

—— (2001), 'Sacred Tourism and Secular Pilgrimage: Montmartre and the Basilica of the Sacré-Coeur,' in Weisberg, ed., *Montmartre and the Making of Mass Culture*, New Brunswick, NJ: Rutgers University Press, pp. 94–119.

Jordan, David P. (1995), *Transforming Paris: The Life and Labors of Baron Haussmann*, New York: The Free Press.

Jouanny, Robert A. (1969), *Jean Moréas, écrivain français*, Paris: Lettres Modernes.

Kaufman, Suzanne (1996), 'Miracles, Medicine and the Spectacle of Lourdes: Popular Religion and Modernity in Fin-de-Siècle France,' Ph.D. thesis, Rutgers, The State University of New Jersey.

Keller, Barbara (1984), *The Middle Ages Reconsidered: Attitudes in France from the Eighteenth Century through the Romantic Movement*, New York: Peter Lang.

Kleeblatt, Norman, ed. (1987), *The Dreyfus Affair: Art, Truth and Justice.* Exhibition catalogue, The Jewish Museum, Berkeley: University of California Press.

Knapp, Bettina and Myra Chipman (1964), *That was Yvette: The Biography of Yvette Guilbert, The Great Diseuse*, New York: Holt, Rinehart and Winston.

Kokel, Rémi (1957), *Vincent de Paul Bailly, un pionnier de la presse catholique*, Paris: Editions B. P.

Kselman, Thomas A. (1983), *Miracles and Prophecies in Nineteenth-Century France*, New Brunswick, NJ: Rutgers University Press.

Lacy, Norris J. (1987), 'The French Romantics and Medieval Literature: A Biographical Essay,' *Studies in Medievalism* vol. 3 (1), Fall, pp. 87–97.

Le Men, Ségolène (1998), *La Cathédrale illustrée de Hugo à Monet: Regard romantique et modernité*, Paris: CNRS Editions.

Lehmann, A. G. (1968), *The Symbolist Aesthetic in France*, Oxford: Basil Blackwell.

Lemoine, Bertrand (1998), *Architecture in France, 1800–1900*, trans. Alexandra Bonfante-Warren, New York: Harry N. Abrams, Inc.

Leniaud, Jean-Michel (1993), *Les Cathédrales au XIXe siècle*, Paris: Economica.

MacCannell, Dean (1976), *The Tourist: A New Theory of the Leisure Class*, New York: Schoken Books.

Maigron, Louis (1911), *Le Romantisme et la Mode*, Paris: H. Champion.

Mainardi, Patricia (1993), *The End of the Salon: Art and the State in the Early Third Republic*, Cambridge: Cambridge University Press.

Mallion, Jean (1962), *Victor Hugo et l'art architectural*, Paris: Presses Universitaires de France.

Marlais, Michael (1993), 'Conservative Style/Conservative Politics: Maurice Denis in *Le Vésinet*,' *Art History* (16) March, pp. 125–47.

Martindale, Andrew (1972), *The Rise of the Artist in the Middle Ages and Early Renaissance*, New York: McGraw Hill.

Mauner, George (1978), 'The Nabis, their History and their Art,' Ph.D. thesis, Columbia University.

Mayeur, Jean-Marie (1973), *Les Débuts de la Troisième République 1871–1898*, Paris: Editions du Seuil.

Médiathèque Municipale Valéry Larband (1983), *Emile Mâle: Le symbolisme chrétien. 28 Mai–20 Juin 1983.* Exhibition catalogue, Vichy.

Miller, Michael Barry (1984), *The Bon Marché: Bourgeois Culture and the Department Store 1869–1920*, Princeton: Princeton University Press.

Miquel, Pierre (1987), *Art et argent, 1800–1900*, Maurs-la-Jolie: Martinelle.

Morowitz, Laura (1996), 'Anonymity, Artistic Brotherhoods and the Art Market in the Fin de Siècle,' *Art Criticism* vol. 11 (2), pp. 71–9.

—— (1996), 'Consuming the Past: The Nabis and French Medieval Art,' Ph.D. thesis, New York University.

—— (1997), 'Medievalism, Anti-Semitism and the Art of the Fin de Siècle,' *Oxford Art Journal* (20:1), pp. 71–9.

Morowitz, Laura and William Vaughan, eds (2001), *Artistic Brotherhoods in the Nineteenth Century*, London: Ashgate Press.

Morrissey, Robert (1997), *L'empereur à la barbe fleurie*, Paris: Editions Gallimard.

Moulin, Raymonde (1967), *Le marché de la peinture en France*, Paris: Editions de Minuit.

*Le Moyen Age* (1982), two-volume special issue of *La Licorne* 6 (1–2).

Murray-Robertson, Anne (1981), *Eugène Grasset: pionnier de l'art nouveau*, Lausanne: Editions 24 heures.

Nora, Pierre, ed. (1984–1992), *Les Lieux de mémoire*, Paris: Gallimard.

Oberthür, Mariel (1992), *Le Chat Noir: 1881–1897*, Paris: Editions de la Réunion des Musées nationaux.

Pearce, Susan (1992), *Museums, Objects and Collections: A Cultural Study*, Leicester/London: Leicester University Press.

—— (1995), *On Collecting: An Investigation into Collecting in the European Tradition*, London/New York: Routledge.

—— ed. (1994), *Museums and the Appropriation of Culture*, London: Athlone Press.

Polimeni, Emmanuela (1947), *Léon Bloy: The Pauper Prophet 1846–1917*, London: D. Dobson.

Poulot, Dominique (1992), 'Alexandre Lenoir et les musées des monuments français', *Les Lieux de mémoire* II: 2, Paris: Gallimard, pp. 497–527.

—— ed. (1998), *Patrimoine et modernité*, Paris: L'Harmattan.

Price, Aimee Brown (1994), *Pierre Puvis de Chavannes*, Amsterdam: Van Gogh Museum; New York: Rizzoli.

Rearick, Charles (1985), *Pleasures of the Belle Epoque: Entertainment in Turn-of-the-Century France*, New Haven: Yale University Press.

Réau, Louis (1994), *Histoire du vandalisme*, Paris: Editions Robert Laffont.

Redman, Harry, Jr. (1991), *The Roland Legend in Nineteenth-Century French Literature*, Lexington: University of Kentucky Press.

Rémond, René (1976), *L'anticléricalisme en France: de 1815 à nos jours*, Paris: Fayard.

Ridoux, Charles (2001), *Evolution des études médiévales en France de 1860 à 1914*, Geneva: Droz.

Riegel, Aloïs (1984), *Le culte moderne des monuments: son essence et sa genèse*, trans. Daniel Wieczorek, Paris: Editions du Seuil.

Sanson, Rosemonde (1973), 'La Fête de Jeanne d'Arc en 1894: Controverse et Célébration,' *Revue d'histoire moderne et contemporaine* (20), pp. 444–63.

Saisselin, Rémy (1984), *The Bourgeois and the Bibelot*, New Brunswick, NJ: Rutgers University Press.

Sedgwick, Alexander (1965), *The Ralliement in French Politics: 1890–1898*, Cambridge, MA: Harvard University Press.

Segel, Harold B. (1987), *Turn-of-the-Century Cabaret*, New York: Columbia University Press.

Shapiro, David (1962), 'The Ralliement in the Politics of the 1890s,' in David Shapiro, ed., *The Right in France 1890–1919*, London: Chatto and Windus.

Sherman, Daniel (1989), *Worthy Monuments: Art Museums and the Politics of Culture in Nineteenth Century France*, Cambridge, MA: Harvard University Press.

Sieburth, Richard (1989), 'The Music of the Future,' in *A New History of French Literature*, ed. Denis Hollier, Cambridge, MA: Harvard University Press, pp. 789–98.

Silverman, Debora S. (1989), *Art Nouveau in Fin de Siècle France: Politics, Psychology, Style*, Berkeley: University of California Press.

Simmons, Clare A. (2000), 'Introduction' to *Medievalism and the Quest for the 'Real' Middle Ages*, London: Frank Cass, pp. 1–28.

Smith, Anthony D. (1991), *National Identity*, New York: Penguin.

Solterer, Helen (1996), 'The Waking of Medieval Theatricality. Paris 1935–1995,' *New Literary History* 27, pp. 357–90.

—— ed. (1997), *European Medieval Studies Under Fire, 1919–45*, special issue of *The Journal of Medieval and Early Modern Studies* 27.3.

Stevens, Maryanne *et al.* (1990), *Emile Bernard 1868–1914: a Pioneer of Modern Art*, Exhibition catalogue, Mannheim: Städtische Kunsthalle/Amsterdam: Van Gogh Museum, Waander Publishers.

Stumpel, Jeroen (1984), 'The *Grande Jatte*, that Patient Tapestry,' *Simiolus* 14 (no. 316), pp. 209–24.

Thiesse, Anne-Marie (1999), *La Création des identités nationales*, Paris: Editions du Seuil.

Tiersten, Lisa (2001), *Marianne in the Market: Envisioning Consumer Culture in Fin-de-siècle France*, Berkeley: University of California Press.

Troy, Nancy (1991), *Modernism and the decorative arts in France: Art Nouveau to Le Corbusier*, New Haven: Yale University Press.

Turbow, Gerald D. (1984), 'Art and Politics: Wagnerism in France,' *Wagnerism in European Culture and Politics*, eds David Large and William Weber, Ithaca: Cornell University Press, pp. 134–66.

Turner, Victor, ed. (1982), *Celebration, studies in festivity and ritual*, Washington, D.C.: Smithsonian Institution Press.

Vaisse, Pierre (1973), 'La querelle de la tapisserie au début de la Troisième République,' *Revue de l'Art* (22), pp. 66–86.

Vogelaar, Christiaan (1990), 'Emile Bernard and the Decorative Arts,' in Maryanne Stevens *et al.*, *Emile Bernard*.

Walton, Whitney (1992), *France at the Crystal Palace: Bourgeois Taste and Artisan Manufacture in the Nineteenth Century*, Berkeley: California University Press.

Ward, Patricia (1975), *The Medievalism of Victor Hugo*, University Park: Pennsylvania State University Press.

Watelet, Jean (1998), *La Presse illustrée en France 1814–1914*, Ph.D. thesis, Université Panthéon-Assas, published by Les Presses Universitaires du Septentrion.

Watson, Janell (1999), *Literature and Material Culture from Balzac to Proust: The Collection and Consumption of Curiosities*, Cambridge: Cambridge University Press.

Wattenmaker, Richard (1975), *Puvis de Chavannes and the Modern Tradition*, Toronto: Art Gallery of Ontario.

Weber, Eugèn (1986), *France, Fin de Siècle*, Cambridge: Belknap Press.

—— (1959), *The Nationalist Revival in France, 1905–1914*, Berkeley: University of California Press.

Weisberg, Gabriel P. (1986), *Art Nouveau Bing: Paris 1900*, New York: Abrams.

—— ed. (2001), *Montmartre and the Making of Mass Culture*, New Brunswick, NJ: Rutgers University Press.

White, Cynthia A. and Harrison C. (1965), *Canvases and Careers: Institutional Change in the French Painting World*, New York: Wiley.

Williams, Rosalind (1982), *Dream Worlds: Mass Consumption in Late Nineteenth Century France*, Berkeley: University of California Press.

Wilson, Michael L. J. (2001), 'Portrait of the Artist as a Louis XIII Chair,' in Gabriel P. Weisberg, *Montmartre and the Making of Mass Culture*, pp. 180–204.

Winock, Michael (1997), 'Joan of Arc,' trans. Arthur Goldhammer, *Realms of Memory: The Construction of the French Past*, vol. 3. New York: Columbia University Press, pp. 433–82.

Zeldin, Theodore (1979), *France 1848–1945: Politics and Anger*, Oxford: Clarendon Press.

# Index

Numbers in *italic* indicate page numbers for references within image captions; note numbers are given without a page number.